DOCKERS
The impact of industrial change

DAVID F. WILSON

DOCKERS

The impact of industrial change

FONTANA/COLLINS

First published in Fontana 1972

Printed in Great Britain
by Richard Clay (The Chaucer Press), Ltd,
Bungay, Suffolk

To Ann

Contents

	Introduction	9
1	The Nature of Casualism	17
2	The Protagonists	29
3	First Reforms	62
4	The Age of Bevin	72
5	The National Dock Labour Scheme	93
6	Containers and Dockwork	134
7	First Steps towards Modernisation	155
8	The Devlin Inquiry	172
9	Decasualisation at Last	181
10	The TGWU Reforms	192
11	Wasteful Practices	212
12	The Wages Structure	225
13	London Modernisation and the Container Ban	239
14	The National Dock Strike	273
15	Conclusions	278
	Appendices	308
	Notes	321
	Bibliography	326
	Index	331

Abbreviations

AIC	Associated Industrial Consultants
BTDB	British Transport Docks Board
DEP	Department of Employment. Ministry of Labour (MOL) pre-1969, Department of Employment and Productivity (DEP) 1969-70
DWRGLU	Dock, Wharf, Riverside and General Labourers' Union
GMWU	General and Municipal Workers' Union
ILA	International Longshoremen's Association
ILWU	International Longshoremen's and Warehousemen's Union
LMSA	London Master Stevedores' Association
LOTEA	London Ocean Trades Emolyers' Association
LPEA	London Port Employers' Association
MDHB	Mersey Docks and Harbour Board
NAPE	National Association of Port Employers
NASD	National Amalgamated Stevedores and Dockers
NDLB	National Docks Labour Board
NIRC	National Industrial Relations Court
NJC	National Joint Council
NMC	National Modernisation Committee
NTWF	National Transport Workers' Federation
NUDL	National Union of Dock Labourers
OCL–ACT	Overseas Containers Ltd–Associated Container Transportation
PLA	Port of London Authority
STGWU	Scottish Transport and General Workers' Union
TGWU	Transport and General Workers' Union
TUC	Trades Union Congress
TUR	Temporary Unattached Register
WLTBU	Watermen, Lightermen, Tugmen and Bargemen's Union

Introduction

British dockers seldom stay out of the headlines and their reputation as a tightly-knit community, loyal to their mates, overpaid and strike-prone, has survived a decade of intense pressure to reform the ports. When there is trouble on the waterfront, dockers are readily blamed. When exports are delayed and ships held up, dockers are labelled bloody-minded and irresponsible. When the blacking of lorries at Liverpool led to the first major confrontation under the Industrial Relations Act, when worker took worker to the new industrial court and the issue of working with containers dragged on through a spring and a summer, the fact dockers precipitated the crisis evoked more resignation than surprise.

This image, though unbalanced and oversimplified, persists. It ignores many of the reasons why British ports have failed to provide as cheap or reliable a service as ports on the Continent, but it has been sustained to a great extent by the nature of the modernisation programme which was launched in the 1960s with two Government inquiries – under Lord Rochdale and Lord Devlin.

The Rochdale report of 1962 identified labour relations as one area among many in need of change. The system of casual employment had been inherited in its essentials from the nineteenth century; unions and employers were ill-organised and riven by sectional jealousies; and the men felt little compunction to work efficiently for employers who had no compunction about refusing them permanent jobs. But these shortcomings were found to be no more remarkable than the deficiencies of investment, management expertise or central planning of port development.

This report called for reforms to tackle all the problems of the ports, to end their recurring financial crises and the strike record which vied with shipbuilding and the motor industry as the worst in the country. But many of its recommendations fell by the wayside and, with the onset of new transport technology and the election of the Labour

Government, the impetus for reform was to concentrate more and more on labour relations.

The Devlin Inquiry, set up in 1964, examined labour relations alone and, in the second half of the decade, the public was to judge the performance of the ports chiefly on the performance of the docker; modernisation became synonymous with post-Devlin reforms in the field of labour. The docks industry had long recognised the weakness and hidden costs of casualism but it had been incapable of eradicating a system of employment which was deeply-rooted in the institutional structure of the ports. The economic and political climate of the 1960s, however, provided fresh stimuli and modernisation was the industry's reaction to external pressures.

Ship-owners had an obvious interest in the efficient working of the docks. In port, a vessel is not earning and can cost up to £1,000 a day in port charges and crew and maintenance costs. Since conventional cargo ships may spend more than half their life in port, owners must try to reduce this idle time and the need for quick turn-rounds intensified after the Second World War as competition from foreign fleets cut into the traditionally British share of trading routes.

The UK shipping industry owned 44 per cent of world tonnage in 1914 but only 11·5 per cent in 1968 and the contracting share of the market was matched by declining profits. From the halcyon days when Sir Alfred Booth could boast that Cunard had averaged a 20 to 25 per cent annual dividend, profits dropped steadily and reached a nadir in 1962–3, with industry-wide pre-tax profits of £4,100,000, or a 0·6 per cent return on the £732 million capital employed. In no year of the 1960s did pre-tax profits exceed 4·8 per cent of capital employed, compared with an all-company average of nearly 13 per cent.

These returns were inadequate by any yardstick; but the industry was none the less slow to adapt to new forms of technology which offered better margins. In the words of another inquiry, shipping companies here and overseas 'continued to order ships designed to be efficient for the 40 per cent of their time spent at sea, rather than the 60 per cent which they spent in port. Further they continued to invest money even though the existing and prospective profits were minimal.'[1]

In the 1960s, British shipping awoke suddenly to the potential of unitisation and containers, pioneered in the United States on the West Coast and Atlantic seaboards. They switched investment to vessels which maximised earning capacity by needing only one or two days to load and discharge in port and correspondingly fewer dockers to perform the work.

The fruit of initial conservatism and the later bold switch to containers were different chiefly in degree, not in kind for dockers. Dwindling profits on conventional services had demanded savings in cargo-handling, the heaviest item in operating costs. By the same token, investment in specialist ships for roll-on/roll-off, unit-loading or container services could only be justified by complete efficiency of port operations and, for container ships in particular, the financial balance between a successful and unsuccessful service hinged on two issues – load factor and a clockwork turn-round.

But, with a conventional ship where each item of cargo has to be loaded from rail or lorry to quayside shed, then placed under a crane, lifted on board and stowed in the hold – and where discharging was an equally labour-intensive reverse procedure – the turn-round time could be speeded up by putting more men on the job and paying them by tonnage output. If the cargo could be moved in larger units, manning scales might be paired; but so long as each of these steps in conventional handling was retained, there was ample work for dockers.

But, for containers, the labour requirement was drastically reduced. The container is no more than a massive storage box, which has to be packed and unpacked at the start and end of its journey. But its contents do not have to be handled at any point *during* its journey. It is simply sealed on dispatch and placed on lorries, railcars or ships by gantry crane. Thus it passes *through* the port without needing any detailed work by dockers.

Completely new types of labour agreement were needed for handling containers. Manning levels had to be slashed and, with one gang of dockers moving a larger tonnage in far less time than five or six gangs could have managed in the past, piecework was inappropriate as a payment system. The difficulty was that the displacement of jobs was so large that a ship-owner could not set up a service without other port employers reaching protective agreements for the rest of the work force.

Ship-owners, with the container lobby to the fore, played a vital role in shaping the modernisation programme and, although they seldom met the unions face-to-face across the negotiating table, they guided the undertakings which actually employed dockers towards port-wide agreements which could accommodate the new technology of transport.

The pressure of the shipping companies was scarcely less significant than the election of the Labour Government in 1964 and 1966. Harold Wilson and Ray Gunter set up the Devlin Inquiry within two weeks of taking office and, once the report was published, pledged the party to implement its recommendation to decasualise dock labour. This commitment was much more than the acceptance of changes which the industry was already moving towards; it was a chance, after thirteen years in the wilderness, to associate the party with a humanitarian reform and to prove its working-class conscience at a period when economic policies were alienating rank-and-file support.

Gunter, in particular, threw his weight behind decasualisation – even to the point of relegating Labour's promise to nationalise the ports to a poor second place – and the resources of his Ministry were willingly given to assist the negotiations.

This economic and political backcloth explains in large measure why dockland reforms, first advocated in the nineteenth century, took place when they did and why they were pressed through when every previous attempt had failed. Casualism could doubtless have survived in Britain, as it did in Antwerp and Marseilles, but for the impact of technology on a system of labour relations which could not receive it and it was the Devlin Committee's task to find a means of adapting a volatile, conservative industry to the container age.

This book studies the origins of the problems which the Committee faced and the complex negotiations between 1965 and 1970 to implement the Devlin recommendations. I concentrate especially on London which is Britain's largest port and was a pioneer in breaking away from the casual system and the chaotic wage structure it gave rise to. The study is confined to labour relations and the part of the port which handles deep-sea trades and employs two-thirds of the dockers. This is not to deny the importance of the riverside wharves and the lighterage industry, but these are trades unique to London as an entrepôt port and they do not offer parallels with other major ports in the history of modernisation.

The Devlin report had a simple and strongly-argued theme: that casual employment denied men some of the basic securities found in other industries, that it bred casual attitudes and that modernisation would be resisted so long as the casual system remained. It set out a two-stage programme for reform which involved, first, the abolition of casual labour and then the negotiation of productivity bargains which would tighten discipline and end restrictive practices. *The first stage is commonly known as Phase I or Decasualisation and the second as Phase II. I shall use these terms. The key Phase II deal in London applied to the enclosed docks for the deep-sea trades; lesser agreements covered the wharves and lighterage. Henceforth, when I talk of the London agreement I mean only the enclosed docks agreement, unless otherwise stated.*

Decasualisation was achieved throughout the country on 18 September 1967, and port-by-port Phase II agreements began in 1969. But the most important was London's which covered 10,000 dockers along 26 miles of waterfront and virtually bought the rulebook from the unions – something never previously attempted in the docks and seldom in any sector of UK collective bargaining. The modernisation programme proved to be extremely expensive. Labour costs virtually doubled in four years, port charges rose steeply and, even with the removal of restrictive practices, turn-round times in conventional cargo-handling often worsened. London was particularly unfortunate since it suffered three major industrial disputes during this period. An unofficial strike following Decasualisation lasted seven weeks and in 1970 London dockers were instrumental in calling the national dock strike which shut down all ports for nearly three weeks. Moreover, it had to endure a ban on new container work at Tilbury for two and a quarter years, forcing OCL–ACT vessels – the pride of the British container fleet – to be diverted to Rotterdam and Antwerp.

The majority of Phase II deals were not as expensive as London's, but they were considered a success if they merely maintained the pre-Devlin standards of output in spite of large increases to the wages bill.

To anyone unacquainted with the docks, it is perplexing how the purported modernisation of an industry can produce both a vast increase in wages and declining, or at best static, outputs. Productivity bargaining is not a totally inexact science and the port negotiators were aided by Government services and management consultants. Moreover, Phase II was never that erring child of wage restraint, the bogus productivity deal aimed at slipping pay increases past Government vetting machinery; it was a sincere attempt to usher in a brave new world.

It is also perplexing to see the docks thrown into turmoil over the issue of who should work with containers. If the purpose of modernisation was to enable containers to replace traditional dockwork, surely one of the first problems for determination would be job demarcations between dockers and groups with competing claims?

The crisis came early in 1972, when Liverpool shop stewards refused to allow containers into the docks, unless satisfied this would not deprive dockers of work. They picked on companies which stuffed and stripped containers around Liverpool and when three of the victims complained to the National Industrial Relations Court, injunctions were granted to stop the unofficial boycott.

It was one of the first uses of the new Act and, when blacking continued, the Transport and General Workers' Union was fined £55,000 for contempt, but this was reversed on appeal. An unexpected bonus of the court hearings was the public dissection of union organisation. People realised that a union's commitment to fight for its membership ran counter to the imposition of headquarters command on an unwilling rank-and-file.

While lawyers argued the rights and wrongs of union accountability, the shop stewards and the men refused to comply with the court's or the union's instruction. The whole crisis was highly-politicised because the unions had not yet been forced to test the might of the law. But the union movement's obsession with its opposition to the law obscured the original grievance.

To the dockers, there was no question about their proper course. They supported Liverpool's defiance because they all were faced with declining job opportunities in a historical context which virtually excluded them from new forms of work.

Conflicts of working rights and demarcations are seldom simple, but they were particularly intractable in the docks because the restricted definition of dockwork was inseparable from casualism itself. Dockwork was defined in law to protect men from the evils of casual labour and no other manual work is subject to such rigid control. Adapting the functions and area of dockwork was a vital task of modernisation, but it was initially ignored. This omission is the most curious part of the Devlin story and it certainly was not due to any reluctance to examine both the institutions and attitudes of the industry.

The Devlin programme was not solely a wage bargain in which the benefits to the men were set against the benefit to port employers, their clients and notionally the public at large. It was also an attempt to

make good the past of an industry, which was ill-governed and struc-
turally flawed, and to change the basic behavioural determinants of
both sides.

It was an ambitious but unavoidable task, since the docks represent
a far broader social microcosm than most industries and attitudes are
deeply rooted in historical conflict. Docker communities were built
around the place of work, jobs were kept in the family and the inter-
action of social and working life did produce loyalties and protective
practices which were based on casualism and justified by its per-
petuation.

Modernisation tried to change these fundamentals and the very
magnitude of the task perplexed the negotiators and persuaded them
to assume that common interest and team spirit alone could see them
through. In 1967, a London employer told his men: 'We must learn
to work together for our mutual benefit. This will take time – one
cannot wipe out the past overnight – but the benefits can be very great
for you, for us and for the port and the country in general.'[2] In 1970,
Peter Shea, the London docks secretary of the Transport and General
Workers' Union, declared: 'We are all in this together. If we are not
careful there will be more employers than men at the labour exchange.'

The advocates of harmony were also the advocates of a complete
change of the wages structure for Phase II, abandoning piecework in
favour of a consolidated, high basic wage. They did not carry the
industry forward united and, as a result, two distinct types of agreement have emerged, one retaining the incentive element in the pay
packet and the other forsaking it.

The docks now rank high in the debate on work motivation and are
being scrutinised, in the wake of mining and motor manufacture, to
observe the effect on outputs after the removal of incentive payments.
The success of changing casual attitudes and the wages system are
important areas for research and detailed work is already being undertaken at the London School of Economics, Nuffield College, Warwick
University and the National Ports Council. It is early yet to make
meaningful comparisons between conditions before and after modernisation and, at industry level, it is well-nigh impossible, for want of
good statistics and because of the difficulty in isolating the impact of
labour agreements on overall operations. But at company level – for
instance Fred Olsen Lines at Millwall, certain Port of London
Authority operations, Liverpool Maritime Terminals and container

berths at Tilbury, Southampton, Grangemouth and Liverpool – detailed studies have begun.

I hope in this book to provide essential background to such work, with particular insights into how the modernisation agreements were reached. The Devlin programme cannot be understood outside its historical context and I have concentrated much on the early background of the docks to explain the chosen paths of reform.

I am indebted to many people for help and encouragement. My experience of labour relations is that of a journalist and the journalist's freedom to seek out information must be matched by people's willingness to impart it, for the truth to emerge. Many people, especially rank-and-file dockers, have been generous with their time and opinions. But special thanks are due to Mrs Thelma Stevenson, who handles press relations for the London and national port employers and is a credit to a profession commonly derided for withholding rather than disseminating information; to Messrs John Kiernan, David Lloyd, Brian Nicholson and Tim O'Leary for showing me personal papers; and to Joel Fadem of Nuffield College and Tony Lane of the Department of Sociology at Liverpool University for useful criticism.

The assistance of Sir Andrew Crichton, Messrs E. Allen, E. Bainbridge, H. Battie, G. Cattell, G. Cooper, J. Hovey, R. F. Hunt, J. L. Jones, L. Lloyd, J. Morris Gifford, L. Reynolds, T. Roffey, P. Shea, R. J. Shillady, G. Tonge and officers of the Department of Employment has been invaluable. Finally, my thanks to Ann who was not deterred by the tribulations of my research and authorship from becoming my wife.

CHAPTER ONE

The Nature of Casualism

'Labour frequently or constantly underemployed is injurious to the interests of the workers, the ports and the public and it is discreditable to society. It undermines all security and is apt to undermine all self-respect on the workers' part ... If men were merely spare parts in an industrial machine, this callous reckoning might be appropriate. But society will not tolerate much longer the continuance of the employment of human beings on these lines. The system of casualisation must, if possible, be torn up by the roots. It is wrong.' Report of the Shaw Commission, 1920.

The casual employment of dock labour had troubled the British conscience for the past hundred years. It was criticised as a cause of poverty, degradation and inefficiency in Victorian days, it was condemned by Lord Shaw's Commission of Inquiry in 1920, in terms – quoted above – which could hardly give a clearer mandate for reform. It also brought a stigma to the docks which the considerable growth in earnings since the Second World War has not dispelled, and it cast a paralysing shadow over employers and unions alike, blighting successive attempts to introduce a system of employment more in keeping with the practices of other industries.

In the simplest terms, the casual system allowed an employer to engage men by the hour or half-day, to match a widely fluctuating labour requirement. Men would present themselves at the dock-gate, or any other recognised hiring point, and foremen would call on as many as the business of the day demanded; those hired were usually kept to the end of each loading or discharging operation before being paid off, and those who did not find work at the main call could wander round the dock in the hope of finding a job elsewhere or go home until the next hiring.

The system placed minimal obligations on the employer who virtually hired for each job by the piece, paying either for hours worked or tons moved. He took no responsibility for the welfare of men who sought a living from dock labour but were not actually in his employ, and yet he depended on a supply of men in excess of his average needs to cope with business peaks.

The free call was absolutely central to this hiring system. Up to 1912 it allowed anyone to apply for work in the docks and it naturally attracted the unemployed of other industries who swelled the number at the dock-gate in times of depression. After the First World War, entry to the docks was regulated but the free call remained the means of deciding how most men should be chosen for work up till 1967.

To early observers, the manifest results of casualism were the acute poverty and chronic underemployment of dock labour. Poverty had long been associated with the waterfront and John Taylor (1580–1653), the water poet apprenticed to a London lighterman, was one of the first to complain of the privations of his class.

'Our hope is that we shall be reckoned as much as horses, for horses have meat, drink and lodging though they be but seldom ridden and many of them have a warm footcloth when thousands of serviceable men are like to starve through want and nakedness,' he wrote in 1630.[3]

The poverty still shocked the Victorian philanthropists. Mayhew stated in 1851 that his visit to London was a climax of misery and wretchedness; Beatrice Webb, writing a generation later, found terrible irony in the co-existence of rich goods and the destitution of those who handled them – touching everything but possessing none. In a casual industry, it was difficult to quantify the extent of poverty in so far as the proportion of people at the dock-gate who did not find work might not correspond with the number who actually depended on dock labour for a livelihood. But the records of the relief agencies are a source of information and they correspond with Charles Booth's findings that 30·7 per cent of London's population lived in poverty. The Charity Organisation Society believed that roughly half the applicants it dealt with came from casual trades, and figures given to the 1908 Royal Commission on the Poor Law showed that pauperism was three times higher among dock labourers than the national average.

Better statistics are available after the First World War, and the pattern clearly emerges of extreme poverty when trade was depressed but comparative affluence when the ports were busy. In the depression year of 1923, the West Ham guardians reported that 44 per cent

Table 1 Basic rates and earnings 1914–38

	Basic weekly rates			Average weekly earnings				Cost-of-living index July 1914 = 100
	Docks	Engineering	Building	Docks	Engineering	Building	All industries	
1914	36s 6d	22s 10d	26s 5d	NA	NA	NA	NA	100
1920	88s 0d	70s 9d	87s 8d	NA	NA	NA	NA	249
1924	67s 4½d	40s 1d	55s 6d	(73s 11d)	52s 9d	NA	56s 3d	175
1931	67s 4½d	42s 1d	51s 1d	(71s 7d) 42s 6d	51s 8d	56s 5d	NA	147½
1935	66s 3½d	43s 4d	50s 6d	(70s 3d) 52s 0d	67s 7d	61s 2d	64s 6d	143
1938	72s 5d	50s 0d	54s 5d	(70s 0d)	75s 0d	66s 0d	69s 0d	156

Note: Dock figures cover Ministry of Labour's dock, wharf and riverside grouping and subsequently its harbour, docks and waterways grouping. These yielded higher earnings than for the registered dockers alone and more accurate earnings figures, from Liverpool sources, are included for 1931 and 1935. All rates and earnings cover males of 21 and over. The engineering and building tables cover labourers only for basic rates but all workers in the trade for earnings.

NA = Not available.

of men on poor relief were dockers and, in the parish of St Georges in the East, the proportion was 75 per cent. Once the dockers were covered by national employment benefit, a further measure was provided and the records show that the industry drew, on average, three and a half times as much from the fund as it paid in.

The depression of the 1930s was particularly severe on the ports. The tonnage handled in 1913 – 67,000,000 – was matched in the late 1920s but dropped to 52,000,000 in 1931 and was not to exceed the 1913 figure in peace-time years until 1953. Many dockers today remember the poverty of the 1930s, when a frying pan was the status symbol in a dockers' household, and the scars are deep. Dockland earnings in these years were some 15 to 25 per cent lower than in the building trade and the reason was not poor rates of pay but underemployment. In Liverpool, for instance, the rate for a 44-hour week was 67s 4½d in 1931 against 42s 1d in engineering and 51s 1d in building. But in the other trades average earnings were higher than the basic rate while, in the docks, they were a third lower than the minimum payment had a full week been worked. It was not till the years of full employment, following the Second World War, that the docker benefited from his high basic rate and elaborate bonus payments. Once he was able to work, his earnings rose rapidly and have since always been near the top of the earnings league for manual workers.

The extent of unemployment was estimated to vary between 30 and 40 per cent in the days when access to the industry was unrestricted and, between the wars, it varied between 26·5 and 39·8 per cent (see Appendix I). Latterly it has remained much higher than the national average but it never rose to more than 14·8 per cent and, while this affected the men's security of income, it did not drag down their standard of living to an unacceptable level.

The effect of such underemployment and poverty was disastrous for the men, who frequently depended on relief or secondary sources of income. Many families relied on their womenfolk to supplement the household budget and the availability of their labour led to the establishing of many of the more lowly forms of women's work in dockland areas. Dockers liked to have a second trade to fall back on and shoe-making was common in London. It was this trade which provided Ben Tillett with his initial union experience – with the National Union of Boot and Shoe Operatives – while he worked as a tea cooper in dockland warehouses in the late 1880s. For Londoners hop-picking was another favourite occupation, providing both a holiday and supplementary income. The tradition of a second *self-employed* job still survives, in cab-driving, working in pubs or window-cleaning and decorating.

Alternative jobs could help men who did not expect a full-time living from the docks but not the class most depressed by casualism, those who were out-and-out dock labourers and unwilling to jeopardise any position they had secured by looking for outside employment. Their earnings were always liable to great fluctuation and the safest method of household budgeting was to assume an income of the lowest level of earnings. The effect on families was predictable. 'It is very largely the offspring of the underemployed casual labourers who are growing up stunted, undernourished and inadequately clothed,' the minority report of the Poor Law Commission stated. 'In the vast majority of cases the children lack not food and clothes alone, but even a minimum of home care. Needless to say, it is such children in the main, when they grow up, who recruit the ranks of unskilled and largely unskilled labour.'[4]

From this economic plight, there stemmed another product of casualism noted by Victorian reformers – the demoralisation of the labour force. The term was used to explain the puzzling inability of men so wretched to better themselves by the accepted standards of the day – self-help, temperance and thrift. Instead, there was excessive drinking, brawling, gambling and a happy tolerance of each other's vices. The reformers failed to recognise these as evidence of a counter-culture but hypothesised that the entire labour force was dragged down by 'loafers' who had no intention of making a serious living in the docks. The pristine docker was an honest man of muscle, but corrupted by the dregs of society who had gravitated to the docks. He then could not avoid becoming a 'parasite' himself. Mayhew called the dockers a striking instance of brute force and brute appetite. 'This class of labour is as unskilled as the power of the hurricane. Mere muscle is all that is needed, hence every human locomotive is capable of working there.' Beatrice Webb found that the public saw the dock labourer as either an irrecoverable ne'er-do-well or a down-fallen angel and – clearly on the side of the angels herself – thought it perfectly understandable that the professional dock labourer should be demoralised. 'He retires disgusted; why exert himself to rise early and apply regularly if he is to be unofficially dismissed, not for any lack of duty or any special failure of strength, but simply because another has sunk from a higher plane of physical existence and is superior to him in brute force.'⁵ From Liverpool, there is a graphic account of the docker, kicked out of bed by his wife at 6 a.m., going to the dock-gate but refusing to join the call; then going on a tour of the pubs to tune into the grapevine for news of work and returning home, drunk, by mid-morning.

Demoralisation, as a symptom of poverty, is still common today but it was accentuated in the docks by the *process* of casualism, as well as by the effects. The basic hiring procedure of the free call was degrading and the men knew it. Descriptions abound and the picture is always the same, with the men herded like animals, shoving and jostling to get the foreman's attention. From Mayhew onward, in fact, lurid accounts of the call were *de rigueur* for writers on dock affairs. Mayhew set a high standard; he wrote of men streaming through the dock-gate as soon as the hiring foremen made their appearance. 'Then begins the scuffling and scrambling forth of countless hands high in the air to catch the eye of him whose voice may give them work. As the foreman calls from a book of names, some men jump upon the backs of the others so as to lift themselves high above the rest and attract the notice of him who hires them. All are shouting, some cry aloud his surname, some his Christian name, others call out their own name, to remind him that they are there. Now the appeal is made in Irish blarney – now in broken English. Indeed it is a sight to sadden the most callous, to see thousands of men struggling for only one day's hire; the scuffle being made the fiercer by the knowledge that hundreds out of the number there assembled must be left to idle the day out in want. To look in the faces of that hungry crowd is to see a sight that must be ever remembered. Some are smiling to the foreman to coax him into remembrance of them; others, with protruding eyes, eager to snatch at the hoped-for pass.'⁶

Mayhew wrote in the days of sail and the pandemonium got worse with the arrival of the steamship. The age of the leisurely turn-round was past and the demand for labour had spread into wider peaks and troughs. The saying was that dockers dared not have a name of more than four letters lest the foreman refused to write it down. Of the later descriptions, pride of place must go to Ben Tillett – if not for accuracy, certainly for hyperbole.

'In a building that would hold very few in comfort, men were packed tightly unto suffocation, like the black hole of Calcutta, and those struggling men fought desperately and tigerishly, elbowing each other, punching each other, using their last remnants of strength to get work for an hour or half hour for a few pence . . . Coats, flesh, even ears were torn off; men were crushed to death in the struggle. The strong literally threw themselves over the heads of their fellows and battled with the milling crowds to get near the rails of the cage, which held them like rats – human rats who saw food in the ticket.

'A grinning caller-on walked up and down protected by these stout iron bars facing the raging and shouting mass and as he walked, the mass swayed with him. He faced the iron bars and moving from one end to the other, he would pick and choose the slaves with wanton brutality as one throws scraps to hungry wolves, to delight in the exhibition of a savage struggle for existence with the beasts tearing each other to pieces.'[7]

In modern days, the hiring procedure was still crude. The call stands might be in the open air or in primitive buildings and, in Liverpool, the men used to congregate under the overhead railway, which thereby earned its title of the 'dockers' umbrella.' For the most part, they were orderly and outsiders were hard-pressed to follow the rapidity of nods and signs by which the foremen took on his favoured gangs. Occasional calls were pure scrambles and one or two of the London wharves kept the reputation for strife and violence which Tillett would have recognised. But the essential degradation remained. Men were putting themselves up for auction without the security of knowing that they would get work when they wanted it. Sir Jack Scamp, the employers' representative on the Devlin Inquiry, was shocked to see London dockers being called from across a road and making their way to the foreman, past busy traffic. In Liverpool, some calling was still by touch, with the foreman tapping chosen men on the shoulder.

What accounts for the persistence of a hiring system which was condemned as inhuman and known to be an inefficient means of distributing labour, long after it had disappeared from other industries? The answer lies primarily in the fluctuating nature of dockwork and the stubborn belief, among employers and labour leaders, that the free call was the only practical method of matching the supply of labour to demand. In short, casualism was regarded as inevitable.

The long-term cause of fluctuation is the rise and fall of trade, which could take place over several years for individual ports or the nation as a whole. This phenomenon was pronounced in the nineteenth century and in the 1920s, when the value of trade could swing by as much as 50 per cent in one year. In 1913, for example, the value of imports passing through London was £254,000,000. In the boom year of 1920 it was £652,000,000 but in 1921 it dropped to £415,000,000. More recently, the changing economics of transport have inflicted similar drastic changes in port traffic. Bristol and Hull used to have flourishing coastal trades which have now been lost to road haulage, and London has lost most of its short-sea traffic to roll-on/roll-off ferry services operating from East Anglian ports and Tilbury. While the cause is different, the effect on labour is similar to the cyclical depressions of yesteryear – an inflexible labour force is left with a diminishing supply of work, but without the prospect of future expansion.

The seasonal nature of many trades is a further cause of fluctuation, although the peaks and troughs are much smaller nowadays because of improvements in shipping, warehousing, canning and refrigeration. In the nineteenth century, however, the physical limits of cultivation and the freezing over of Baltic and Canadian sea-passages meant commodity trades were more markedly seasonal and caused the competition between ship-owners to bring back the first of the new season's goods like wool, grain and tea.

Bunching puts a heavy demand on labour and even in ports large enough to handle a variety of traffic, and thus to even out the peaks, labour requirement still fluctuates on a seasonal basis. For instance, London used to have peaks between April and November for handling softwoods; July and November for China tea; August and January for Indian tea; February and July for wool; September and April for sugar and grain and between October and December for dried fruit. In Liverpool, the demand for labour was highest between October and March, with overlapping peaks in fruit, cotton and timber. For smaller ports dependent on a few commodity trades, seasonal fluctuation was still a major obstacle to permanent employment in the 1960s and the National Association of Port Employers (NAPE) told Lord Devlin that decasualisation would be impractical in nineteen ports – Aberdeen, Ardrossan, the Ayrshire ports, Barrow and Silloth, Fleetwood, Gloucester, Goole, Grangemouth, Greenock, Grimsby and Immingham, King's Lynn, Methil, Newhaven, Preston, the Tyne and

Wear, Great Yarmouth, West Cornwall, Widnes and Wisbech – because of the small labour forces and the very wide fluctuation of trade.

A third basic cause of fluctuation is the vagaries of wind and tide. In the days of sail, this was probably the most important factor in determining how many dockers would find work each day. An adverse wind could stop all vessels getting to their berths for a week or more; storms could force ships to seek shelter for days on end. This was regarded then as an inescapable governance of port affairs and, on a smaller scale, it still has an influence on operations. A stevedoring employer might indent for six gangs in the expectation of getting a ship to discharge, only to find it delayed by weather or tide; and rain can still bring all shipwork to a halt.

The justification of casualism as a necessary response to trade fluctuation was readily used as an excuse for shying away from reform, even in the last decade. This was one of the main contentions of the Labour party study group when it set out the case for nationalising the ports; it berated the industry for accepting too glibly that work loads were unquantifiable and said that a single port operator would be far better placed to forecast work and distribute labour than the multiplicity of employers – the ship-owners, their agents, stevedoring and lighterage companies – who failed to co-ordinate information between themselves. It was true that, by the time of Devlin, advance information about arrival times of ships and the loads they were carrying made it easier to assess daily labour requirements, but fluctuation was still an undeniably important factor. In Appendix 4 it is shown that the maximum demand for labour in any year since 1953 exceeded the minimum by 50 to 60 per cent, nationally, and in individual ports by up to 300 per cent; thus casualism, with its reserve pool of labour, remained a logical way of meeting the peaks without expensive commitments when business was slack.

In the formative years of the docks industry, there was a second reason for the unquestioning acceptance of casualism; namely, a failure to understand the inevitable consequences of the system. For a long time the poor had been accepted as part of the industrial landscape. The philanthropic response of carefully-supervised charity and moral strictures was enough to ease the Victorian conscience. However, in the 1880s men like W. T. Stead and articles like 'The Bitter Cry of Outcast London' and 'Squalid Liverpool' drove home the enormous extent to which poverty lurked behind the comfortable façade of Victorian prosperity and sparked off both the movement of new unionism and the serious social research of the 1890s and 1900s. In the 25-year period from 1887, there were three Royal Commissions and six major inquiries in which the docks problem loomed large. Beatrice Webb, Charles Booth and Eleanor Rathbone contributed detailed analyses of conditions in London and Liverpool and the first Court of Inquiry into a labour dispute was held: it examined the London dock strike of 1912 and set a telling precedent – the men ignored its findings.

During this period, it became obvious that the genuine concern of the philanthropists for the downtrodden had made no impact and the assumption that the poor could uplift themselves by self-help was naïve. (In her memoirs, Beatrice Webb recalls a telling instance when a woman applied for help through the Charity Organisation Society and was slipped a sixpence under the table by a kindly commissioner while Octavia Hill lectured on her why she should not be given the money and offered the 'soundest advice.' The sequel is also related. The commissioner's misdemeanour was discovered and he was 'melted into tears for his own delinquency.')[8] The fault lay not in the poor but in the social structure. The system of employment in the docks thus came under scrutiny and Beatrice Webb reached the astonishingly perceptive conclusion that the problems of labour were inseparable from the problems of trade. Unfortunately Booth, who brought this research to a far wider audience by incorporating it verbatim in the seventeen volumes of *Life and Labour of the People in London*, failed to capitalise on this theory or on his own detailed information about the living conditions of the labour force. In his eight gradations of living standards, he put the lowest beyond help and urged that the second lowest, who constituted 7·5 per cent of the labour force, should somehow be severed from society before they dragged down their fellows. For the London dock companies, he evolved a scheme for achieving this by grading labour into priority lists, but it ignored the fact that the unions could not accept the crushing out of men from the industry nor that casualism depended on having a large surplus margin.

It was not until William Beveridge published *Unemployment, A Problem for Industry* in 1909 that the full implications of casualism were successfully analysed. Beveridge's contribution to the debate on casual labour was the assertion that the margin of surplus labour was an integral part of the system and the system would not work without it; furthermore, the margin could not be made to disappear of its own accord, as Booth's scheme envisaged, even in circumstances of the most dire poverty. He found that all industry had a degree of casualism through turnover, sickness or idleness and that the problem was chiefly of *underemployment* not unemployment through the 'loss of some work by a large minority rather than chronic idleness of a few. Turning to the docks, he identified three elements in the surplus margin of labour.

First, there was the margin required to meet the volume of trade on the assumption that each stevedoring contractor might need his maximum requirement simultaneously. In theory this could be very high but, as we have seen, in large ports only few trades had over-lapping peaks and by 1920 Ernest Bevin was able to claim that a 10 per cent reserve was sufficient to cover trade fluctuation – a figure which gained currency and was to be quoted again at the Devlin Inquiry.

A further increase in the margin resulted from poor deployment, called by Beveridge the 'friction' of the labour market. In ports the size of London or Liverpool, several hundred employers would call on men simultaneously at their own stands and it was impossible to know where they could best find work. The result was that one sector might find itself with an acute labour shortage while another had an equal surplus. For instance, a group of ten wharves might require a maximum of 100 men each at some point in a year, but collectively their requirement never exceeded 800 on the same day. If these wharves formed a single labour market and hired collectively from one call-stand, 800 men could cover any contingency; with individual calls, however, the necessary pool would have to be 1,000. This was an obvious area for reform by regulation. Booth had estimated in 1891 that the 320 wharves on the Thames had a theoretical maximum requirement of 21,353 men but that 17,994 would have sufficed with a single labour market. Rathbone concluded her survey in Liverpool by stating that the 'present irregularity of employment is much greater than is arithmetically necessary to balance the irregularity of work in the port, taking it as a single labour market.'[9]

Custom and ignorance kept this part of the margin in being but the third element was inherent in the casual system so long as entry to the docks was unrestricted. This was the 'chance' element, the men who looked to the docks for occasional work and could displace regular dockers from their livelihood just by attending the call. They helped to drag others below the poverty line, but it, too, was a problem which would respond to regulation, by restricting entry only to men who sought a full-time living.

After Beveridge, the case for reform was established beyond question. It began three years later with a scheme to eliminate 'friction' in Liverpool and continued during the First World War with the registration of dockers. These were palliative measures which set the pattern for all subsequent reform until the Devlin programme, but they did not touch the real nature of casualism which was the uncertainty whether a man, who wanted to work, would actually be employed.

By the 1960s the most distressing symptoms of early casualism – poverty and underemployment – had been overcome but affluence and comparatively full employment had produced new symptoms which shackled the industry to the traditions of the past. The men were still insecure and still were divided against each other, as well as against the employers, by the struggle for high-earning jobs. The reason, quite simply, was that the structure of the industry had remained casual. The pattern of employment had been defined in the heyday of steam when the employer was free to engage men as he chose at the call and any man was free to seek work. When reform began, the institutional structure was stratified and it resisted change long after the conditions which gave rise to casualism had disappeared. Palliative reform was achieved precisely because it allowed the employing structure and the men's response to survive and the effect of reform, ironically, was to strengthen the *concept* of casualism through the eradication of its obviously evil consequences.

By the 1960s, casualism was as deeply-rooted in the docks as it ever had been and this meant that decasualisation, to be meaningful, required far more than the granting of permanent employment. The casual attitudes of men and management had to go as well and an employment structure based on the free-for-all had to be replaced by a distribution of work and earnings which could be seen to be just. The task of the Devlin programme thus was to change the surviving determinants which had created casualism in the nineteenth century, and to understand how this could be achieved it is necessary to examine the employment structure in the ports and the formal and informal organisation which the docker had developed to counter it.

CHAPTER TWO

The Protagonists

'*The futility of the attempt to separate the labour question from the trade question is becoming every day more apparent.*'   Beatrice Webb, 1887.[10]

The shape of industrial relations in dockland has been determined by the haphazard growth of the ports and the correspondingly haphazard structure of employment and trade unionism.

Raw material for the dock labour force came from two main sources, the Irish navvies who dug out the dock basins in the first half of the nineteenth century and the colourful array of men associated with river work in the days of sail. Mayhew records an awesome variety of men at the call – sailors, Polish refugees, old soldiers, publicans and anyone who had fallen on hard times.

But in London, as in Liverpool or New York, it was the Irish, settled in communities round the docks they had built, who proved to be the most homogeneous group. Separated by their religion and clannishness, they got a reputation for looking after their own which has survived to this day.

At the start of this century more regular groupings were established and the idea that every walk of life was represented at the dock-gate was more a subject for humour than reality. London could usually produce a discarded heir to a baronetcy who had fallen through drink and Jimmy Sexton, the general secretary of the National Union of Dock Labourers (NUDL), recalled the jokes in Liverpool about dockers having to compete with ex-cabinet ministers, jockeys and owners and trainers who had been warned off, broken-down company promoters, unsuccessful tradesmen and out-of-work counter-jumpers – to say nothing of gaolbirds and the scourings of the doss house.'[11]

It is clear, however, that the percentage of agrarian labour in the docks was low, doubtless because men were reluctant to leave the land for an industry more stigmatised than their original calling. In some instances, green labour was imported to counter incipient trade unionism, as at Millwall, and this accounts for the men's continuing antipathy in Liverpool to the 'woolly-backs' and in London to the 'carrot-crunchers' at Tilbury.

The docker, as we know him, emerged with the building of the first enclosed docks – non-tidal basins shut off from the sea or river by lock-gates. They had the advantage over riverside wharves and anchorages of protecting vessels from weather and tide and protecting their cargo from pilferage. The earliest enclosed docks were developed as private ventures, but needed parliamentary sanction to handle dutiable goods which hitherto had passed through a limited number of bonded wharves.

Digging out the basins and operating the docks were large-scale enterprises and the extent of capital investment, coupled with the need to serve local commercial interests, soon attracted money from the municipalities. In Bristol, for example, the corporation built the city's entire dock system but, more frequently, the developments of the mid-nineteenth century were inspired by a drawing together of civic and mercantile interests in public authorities like the Mersey Docks and Harbour Board, set up by Act of Parliament in 1858. Interest-bearing bonds in the authorities were available to the public, but the equity market was served mostly by the railway companies who built docks at their coastal railheads and these ports, like Hull and Southampton, now form the nationalised part of the industry, under the British Transport Docks Board.

Diverse forms of port ownership provided a varied structure for employing dock labour. On the whole, private companies hired their own labour for handling goods on the quay and used contractors for the more fluctuating work of discharging and loading ships. But some public authorities and municipalities avoided day-to-day operations and the Mersey Docks and Harbour Board, for instance, only had a minimal interest in dock labour until the Rochdale report urged it to operate some berths; it now employs nearly a fifth of the port labour force, much the same proportion as the Port of London Authority (PLA) has in London.

In either case it was axiomatic that the port was best served by allowing anyone to operate as an employer and few requirements were made of people's fitness to employ. In Liverpool, again, an application to employ could be validated by two householders' signatures and most authorities had no regulations whatsoever.

Table 2 shows how this structure has been passed down little changed from Victorian times to our own day, with four types of port control and the scattered involvement of the controlling bodies in labour relations.

Table 2 Ownership of sixteen major ports			
Public authorities, trusts, etc.[1]	*Municipal*	*Private*	*Nationalised*
London	Bristol	Felixstowe	Hull
Liverpool[3]	Manchester[2]		Southampton
Glasgow[3]			
Leith/Grangemouth[3]			Cardiff
Newcastle			Newport
Middlesbrough			Swansea
			Immingham

[1] In all ports in this category, except Liverpool, local authorities have automatic minority representation on the Board.

[2] Manchester Corporation supplies 11 of the 21 directors to the Board of the Manchester Ship Canal company.

[3] In these ports, the authority is not a long-established employer of labour. But the Mersey Docks and Harbour Board and the Clyde Port Authority expanded into cargo-handling after the publication of the Rochdale report in 1962.

Source: 1962 Rochdale report and the Docks and Harbour Authorities' Association.

The divorce of owner from port employer was extended by a like separation of port employer and ship-owner. As users of a port, ship-owners were represented on the governing boards to give advice on the kind of berths they needed and such issues as pilotage, conservancy and towage. But the British practice has been to exclude the port employer from any direct financial stake in the ports and to involve the ship-owners only indirectly.

Authorities in England usually leased quay space to the ship-owner and retained ownership of dock installations whose use was then paid for by a variety of charges on ships and goods.

In continental ports like Rotterdam, most port employers, however, were ship-owner controlled from the start and it has been the custom to involve them in the well-being of the port by leasing undeveloped quay space on long tenancy agreements, and letting them provide cranage and shed facilities. This has relieved the authority of heavy capital charges and has committed employers to investments which reduce their freedom to move at will.

The British practice assumed – and aggravated – a fundamental divergence of interest between the port authority and ship-owner. Then as now, port-owners wanted to maximise revenue from port dues, on the tonnage charges on ships, charges on cargo passing over the quays and from warehousing, so long as this was consistent with the vitality of the port. The ship-owner and merchant, however, were interested primarily in getting goods passed through the port as quickly as possible and wanted labour geared to fast turn-round. In theory, the port-owner liked every berth full all the time. The ship-owner wanted his vessels away and sailing.

Fast turn-round was seldom consistent with stable employment of dock labour. Had there been a control structure, which accommodated the conflicting interests of port-owners, the shipping companies and the men, it might have avoided the most vicious forms of nineteenth-century casualism. But it was the needs of ship-owners alone which won the day and, incidentally, killed the chances of the London dock companies surviving as private undertakings.

The Victorian ship-owners were tough-minded individualists who brooked no interference in the way they ran their business. Just as Brunel had resisted Government intervention to impose safety standards on the railways, so the Liverpool Steamship Owners' Association objected to the temerity of Samuel Plimsoll in proposing before Parliament that ships should have a loading-mark painted on the waterline. They would no more be penalised by legislation which did not apply to foreign competitors than they would tolerate organisation of the labour market in the ports, if it deprived them of the freedom to draw on an ample pool of men.

Casual labour suited their interests and the superseding of sail by steam intensified the need for the casual pool. The turn-round of sailing vessels had been governed as much by the routes they traded, the need for frequent repairs and the time taken to revictual as by the period of time needed for actual cargo-handling. The steamship, however, was a higher capital investment and it could spend a far higher proportion of its life at sea, so the pressure on port operations became acute. It was a situation paralleled closely in our day by unit-loading and containerisation and it could have been met, as it was under the Devlin programme, by the banding of employers into bigger and better-equipped units – but the Victorian reaction was quite different. Competition and the natural process of economic selection were paramount.

Rather than mechanise or draw labour from a common source in port, the ship-owner came to rely still more heavily on a casual supply and the use of incentives to ensure high outputs. Ironically, ports like London, Liverpool and New York which relied on unfettered casualism got the reputation for really fast turn-rounds before the First World War, rather than the better equipped and more mechanised ports like Hamburg.

The reliance on casualism multiplied the number of employing companies in the docks. The ship-owner might have to use the labour of the port authority or dock company for some operations but he could also set up his own labour department for shipwork, or put his business out to the numerous stevedoring and portering companies which grew up as labour-only sub-contractors.

This period also threw up a further type of small employer, the middleman contractor who tendered for work from larger master stevedores for a fixed sum and paid his labour by the hour. The 'contractor' was usually from the ranks of labour himself and might switch between employing a gang one week and himself working for hire the next. The jobs he performed were small, the profit margin tight and so the men were squeezed mercilessly, often being forced to work for less than the accepted port rate. (James Larkin, organising for the National Union of Dock Labourers in Glasgow, found contractors' men the most degraded class of labour. Many who unloaded iron and manganese ore from Spanish ships in the Clyde were meths drinkers and they sometimes slept in the holds rather than go home. In 1908, Larkin told the Parliamentary Committee investigating piecework in the docks that the middleman contractor should be abolished; he was cheated by his master and made up the loss by cheating the men. In Belfast he said he could not deal with the contractors until *he* had organised them into an association capable of resisting their bosses. One of the main aims of the great 1889 'dockers tanners' strike in London was to replace contract labour with piecework.)

With the multiplication of small employers, the malpractices of casual hiring worsened. Most involved foremen accepted favours from men who were driven to pay for the privilege of being employed. The favours might mean buying drinks or cigarettes for the foreman, or borrowing money from him at exorbitant interest rates; and the mythology of dockland maintains that men allowed the foreman to sleep with their wives, though Jimmy Sexton, the general secretary of the NUDL, said this was rare even in the worst days of the nineteenth century.

But the practice of hiring agents forcing men into debt was wide-spread in most casual ports. In New York, the system was known as loan-sharking and was still common after the Second World War. In Liverpool, the practice was for the 'gombeen man' (literally, usurer) to exact a rate of interest of 3d on a forced loan of 1s, to be repaid from wages. According to Sexton, the gombeen man 'gets to be a foreman, he may come from Cornwall or Wales and he abuses his position by giving preference to men who will borrow money from him whether they want it or not.'[12] When men were forced to be debtors, he said, the effect of the system was little different from accepting a cut in earnings to get work.

The small employer had no difficulty establishing himself, thanks to the support of ship-owners and to the absence of qualifications to practise his trade. Survival was ensured if he could serve a particular market or keep a handful of regular clients and his presence has been the most important characteristic of the employment structure of the industry.

In 1960, there were still 1,500 registered employers providing work for a labour force of 70,000 men – an average of one employer for every forty-three men. Some were large and well-equipped under-takings; the PLA was the largest public employer with an average daily requirement of more than 4,000 men and Scruttons Ltd in London was the largest private employer with more than 3,000. But the great majority were still no more than labour-only contractors, with negligible administrative and clerical organisations, little capital behind them and without resources to contemplate keeping a labour force on a permanent basis. Of the 400 employers in London alone, the smallest in fact had a single operation a year, requiring six men and, reputedly, operating from a caravan and a telephone kiosk. Another senior employer was not entirely in jest when he said his great-est skill was the ability to read rivals' bills upside down on their desks!

Under the casual system, however, the multiplicity of employers was not a purely one-sided arrangement. To union organisers, the small employer was often more amenable to industrial pressure than the dock companies or large stevedoring undertakings. Because the small employer was dependent on one or two contracts, he did not dare lose custom and the early experience of the London unions was that a small master stevedore was often the first to break the employers' concerted line of defence. The large undertakings could enforce the rulebook – unless ordered not to by clients – but the small company found it easiest to wriggle out of disputes with under-the-counter payments or simple concession of claims.

The large number of employers created a bargaining structure in which they seldom spoke with one voice and their authority was often undermined by the overriding will of ship-owners. This fragmentation of interest has frequently weakened their position at the negotiating table and, in London, this process has been most marked.

Before the 1889 strike there was a possibility that the London dock companies, which were to be incorporated into the PLA by the Act of 1908, could have a determining voice in labour affairs. London had many attributes which favoured stable employment – the port handled a sufficient variety of trades to offset seasonal fluctuation and, in its dock companies, it had employing units which could absorb large numbers of permanent men. They were regarded as a bastion against pure casualism and their failure to provide a labour service satisfactory to the ship-owner enabled the myriad of small employers to develop, and fatally split the quayside labour functions of the port authority from the shipwork undertaken by master stevedores.

The essential flaw in labour relations in Britain's largest port was its piecemeal development along 69 miles of the River Thames, where growth had been determined by the rivalry between dock companies rather than by an overall rationale. London was by no means the first port to develop dock systems. In 1800, it only had the tree-lined Howland dock in Rotherhithe, used to shelter sailing vessels from high winds while cargo was still handled in the river, for 'overside' work into barges, or at the custom wharves. But London's importance increased during the Napoleonic Wars to the point where it handled 65 per cent of the nation's trade, and in 1799 Parliament authorised the construction of a large dock in the Isle of Dogs and gave the new company a 21-year monopoly of the West India trade. This walled dock, still in use, protected the valuable rum and sugar cargoes from the depredations of mudlarks and river pirates; it also provided customs clearance and extensive warehousing so that highly seasonal commodities could be stored *in situ* for distribution to retail markets throughout the year. In its early years the West India Dock Company was successful and ten more companies were founded by 1864 to develop the Surrey bank for Russian and Baltic trades, and the North bank from the Tower of London towards the mouth of the Thames estuary.

In spite of rapidly growing trade, London was overpopulated with dock systems and the companies were brought to the verge of ruin by the competition for business. They tried to cut back on operating costs by amalgamation and in 1864 all the North bank companies, except the newly-formed Millwall company, came into the hands of two companies, the East and West India Dock Company and the London and St Katharine Docks Company. After the former committed its last resources to opening Tilbury docks in 1886, a joint management was set up between the two companies to assist rationalisation. But the decline was irreversible and it was documented by the Royal Commission of 1902. In 1859, 4·3 million tons net of shipping used the port; in 1869, 6·1 million tons; in 1879, 8·7 million tons; in 1889, 12 million tons and in 1899, 15·2 million tons. But operating profits had steadily declined and entrepôt trade had been lost to riverside wharves. The upper-river docks, extensively warehoused, had become liabilities as larger steamships moved to the newer docks in the Royal group, and at Tilbury regular shipping services obviated the need for warehouses in which goods could be stored to last the off-season.

The growth of the wharves was instrumental in undermining the companies. The expiry of the original monopolies, and then the Act of 1853 which allowed bonded goods to be stored outside the dock systems, exposed the companies to fierce competition. Moreover, the wharves enjoyed an inestimable advantage in the 'free-water' clause which was established in the 1799 Act and incorporated in successive dock charters; this allowed lighters and their goods free access to all enclosed docks and let wharfingers take delivery from ocean-going ships overside and land them at wharves more cheaply than on the quays which were subject to company charges.

By the turn of the century, London was split into a bustling down-river port and a decaying, barely-mechanised, up-river group of docks. The economic plight of the dock companies had an important effect on labour. Up to 1889 the companies had established an un-challenged monopoly to do their own quay work and all discharging, but left the more skilled business of loading to independent master stevedores. They employed many thousand men and a significant percentage were given permanent status. In the East and West India docks, for instance, the average daily requirement was 1,311 casuals in 1887, with a maximum requirement of 2,355 and a minimum of 600, but a further 247 labourers were permanently employed. In the London and St Katharine docks, there were 420 permanent men and an average requirement for 2,200 casuals in a range of 1,100 to 3,700. In Millwall a fairly steady figure of 800 were employed, half as per-manent men. The figure of 19 per cent permanency achieved by the two big companies in the 1880s was not matched by the industry as a whole until 1953.

The 1889 strike, however, had a cataclysmic effect on the pattern of employment. The shipping lines had been clamouring for better ser-vice from the dock companies for some time and believed that they could do faster discharging through contractors. Half-way through the strike their quarrel burst upon the public when Thomas Suther-land, chairman of Peninsular and Oriental, wrote an extraordinary letter to *The Times*, announcing that ship-owners might build their own docks if they were not allowed to handle their own discharging. He accused the companies' joint management of eliminating ship-owner interests from their governing board as a sop to shareholders but at the expense of customers.

'It is no secret, therefore, that the principal shipping companies . . . have had and still have under consideration the project of constructing a co-operative dock for themselves on the Thames, which would enable them to control their business much more economically than they can ever hope to ensure in the hands of the present dock com-panies. . . . We are endangered by dock company monopoly . . . in the opinion, therefore, of many ship-owners a very slight addition to the charges now levied would place London at such a disadvantage that consideration of a co-operative dock would become absolutely necessary to prevent trade from leaving the port.'[13]

He went on to identify the ship-owner with the dockers themselves –

they 'alike consider they are sweated by the dock company' – and suggested that the strike could be ended simply by transferring the right to discharge ships to the ship-owners' shoulders.

His case was conceded by the dock companies and in November 1890 the joint committee gave up its discharging monopoly to shipping lines in the Royal Victoria, Albert and Tilbury docks but kept it upstream where discharge was closely linked to warehousing. Sutherland had performed a ruthlessly efficient feat of blackmail since the chairman of the dock companies' joint committee, Mr Norwood, was primarily interested in maintaining a united front against the strikers. But the transfer was not without logic since the stevedoring contractor was probably able to give a specialist service and it brought London's pattern of employment more closely in line with Liverpool, where the harbour board contracted out all stevedoring and portering. Also, it relieved the ailing companies of unprofitable operations which threatened further conflicts with the victorious unions.

But the transfer did much to weaken the bargaining strength of the joint committee and was an open licence to multiply the number of employers. Fifty discharging stevedores could be brought in to do the work of the two dock companies and this proliferation duly took place. The prospect of bringing the labour force under the control of a small group of employing interests in the foreseeable future was dashed and, to one school, this decision put an end to the hopes of erasing casualism from London. Sir Joseph Broodbank, writing in 1921, said:

'The worst result was not completely foreseen by anyone, namely, the effect on labour. What it has meant in this respect has been a continuance of casual labour as far as ship-owners' import work is concerned. . . . By allowing each ship-owner to be a law unto himself as regards the conditions and terms of employment, there was created a class of men receiving higher wages than the joint committee offered but working irregularly, with heavy overtime one week and idleness the next, in busy times competed for by ship-owners with surreptitious bonuses and in slack times left to fend for themselves. There will be no solution to the dock labour problem until the PLA reverses the decision of the joint committee and again undertakes all operations in the docks including stevedoring work and loading ships as well as discharging ships.'[14]

The ship-owners' victory in London was matched nationally by setting up a federation to protect their interests against the New Unionism. A prototype employers' association was formed in the North-East in 1887 after Havelock Wilson had founded the National Amalgamated Sailors' and Firemen's Union and in 1890 the Shipping Federation was formed with the express purpose of smashing labour organisation. Major liner companies like P and O, the Orient, Royal Mail, Castle Mail, General Steam Navigation and Shaw Savill and Albion were quick to join and launch an offensive against the unions. The Federation took the word 'Nemesis' as its telegraphic address and, in the words of its biographer: 'From the first it was founded as a fighting machine to counter the strike weapon and it made no secret of the fact.'[15]

The Federation's principal weapon was its ticket of employment, which did not disbar the holder from joining a trade union but required him to work alongside non-union labour. The ticket was directed primarily against seamen but it was occasionally forced on dockers.

The Federation also relied on a liberal supply of 'free labour' to replace men on strike and its industrial battles with the unions up to the First World War were bitter in the extreme. It used three ships, the *Lady Jocelyn* – a hulk – the *Paris* and *Ella*, to house blackleg labour and would bring them to trouble spots to break strikes. Often, it was successful. London dockers were beaten in 1900 by the import of free labour from as far afield as Swansea, Shields and Rotterdam, but such tactics came to be counter-productive as unionism entrenched itself after 1911. Running the gauntlet of pickets, collecting the blacklegs and sailing the three ships became more risky, even when the crews were accompanied by policemen and armed with French infantry chassepots to make a show of strength, albeit the weapons were obsolete and allegedly did not work. The strikes of 1911 and 1912 saw the last major use of the Federation ships; the *Lady Jocelyn* carried 2,000 men to the Bristol Channel in 1911, then proceeded to the dockers' strike in Liverpool and on to the Thames, where it was stopped by the Home Office from discharging labour because of the risks of violence. (At Cardiff the seamen claimed one of their major successes against the Federation when their organiser, the redoubtable Capt. Tupper, infiltrated a union sympathiser on board the *Lady Jocelyn* as cook and did not forget to arm him with 'certain substances' from a chemist's shop; the crew and blacklegs were duly laid low!)

The battles on the industrial front were reflected in hardening attitudes between capital and labour. A ship-owners' journal wrote of dockers that a 'turnip would answer for a head and a round of beef for brains' and a management textbook of 1926 asserted that men drifted into the docks 'as naturally as the drainage system of the country finds its way to the lowest level.'[16]

Against this background, the collective bargaining structure of the industry was formalised and it centred on the conflict between the ship-owners and the port authority in London, as well as the conflict with the unions. In ports where the controlling authority was not an operational employer, comparatively strong employer associations grew up which the ship-owner felt looked favourably on his interest. But, in London, the shipping companies wanted direct participation in negotiations because of the employing functions of the PLA and therefore, in 1912, the London Ship-Owners Dock Labour Committee was formed as a body responsible to the Shipping Federation. Speaking for most of the contractors in the enclosed docks, it soon had the most important voice in labour affairs, although it was only one of ten employer bodies which formed the global port association. The others were the PLA, the London Master Stevedores Association (LMSA) – an organisation which dealt only with the stevedores' union in upriver docks – lighterage and barge-owners, two wharfinger groups, coal-bunkering and the short-sea traders. Together, these groups were commonly known as the London Ten.

In 1920 the docks, like many other industries, adopted a national negotiating structure on the principles of Whitleyism. The local employer associations were made subservient to the National Council of Port Labour Employers and a national joint council was established as the topmost negotiating body with the unions. In 1944 the employers' council was re-named as the National Association of Port Employers (NAPE) and this machinery was in being during the Devlin era.

The direct involvement of the ship-owner in labour relations would not have happened without the battle in London against the dock companies and the growth of so many stevedoring companies in the 1890s. Opportunity to perform their own discharging as well as loading persuaded many shipping companies to set up their own labour departments, or to go into business as contractors themselves. The history of Scruttons is the classic example of a shipping company taking advantage of the times.

The Scrutton family owned ships in the Caribbean trade and their interest in dock labour was confined to loading their own vessels while the dock companies' monopoly lasted. Reorganisation began, however, when their eighteen sailing vessels were replaced by a fleet of steam in the 1880s; the sailing ships had made one round trip a year to the West Indies but the new steamers could make four, assuming an efficient turn-round in London. They organised the hiring of some stevedores themselves and contracted other work out to master stevedore undertakings. But, three years after the monopoly was broken, the family set up their own stevedoring subsidiary, Scruttons Ltd, which proved so successful that the family sold all its ship-owning interests to Thomas and James Harrison in 1920 to concentrate on stevedoring. Within a decade Scruttons was the largest private contractor, handling more than sixty services in London, including Cunard, Atlantic Transport, Houlder Brothers, P and O and Van Ommeren.

Most of the enclosed dock employers in London owe their origins to the period of ferment at the turn of the century. Furness Withy, Shaw Savill and Albion, Glen Line, the constituents of British and Commonwealth and Ben Line set up their own labour organisations; the Vestey Group created Thames Stevedoring as its subsidiary. The exceptions were the companies of the P and O group who used Scruttons except for tallying, where some had their own clerical organisations.

In the amalgamations of the past decade, Scruttons survive as a major company without ship-owner backing and it merged with T. F. Maltby, another independent, in 1965. Tom Wallis, a company which grew from humble stevedoring beginnings two generations ago, is linked with Ben Line, Thames, set up by the Vestey group, is linked with Shaw Savill and the last major grouping is Southern Stevedores, a 1967 amalgamation of the labour departments of British and Commonwealth, Glen and Furness Withy (partial).

Under casualism, even large port employers could survive with small resources and most compnaies were ill-equipped by normal standards to develop industrial policies for domestic negotiation, training, promotion, welfare facilities and output control. They were particularly weak in first-line supervision and the need for professionalism was accentuated by the technology of the 1960s.

Where the trend had been for ship-owners to take control of stevedoring subsidiaries, primarily to handle their own traffic, and single management control was well-fitted to the through-transport concept, it now appears that the advantage lies with the truly professional employer operating as a berth contractor.

At Tilbury, the container consortia, O C L–A C T, used P L A labour to man their berth for the U K–Australia trade and, at Southampton, their Far East container trade is being handled by the existing port employer, although the consortia initially applied to do it themselves. By the same token, Ellerman Line left its few remaining London operations in the hands of Scruttons–Maltby, not its subsidiary Hovey Antwerp, and companies like Southern, with 1,200 dockers, could not match the economies of Scruttons–Maltby, with 2,500, and in 1972 announced it would go out of business.

In conclusion, three features characterise the employment structure which was created by casualism. First, it was inefficient because the multiplicity of employers created illogical divisions in function between undertakings serving different sectional interests. In London, it is particularly marked, with the P L A handling all quay work, discharging in the up-river docks and some shipwork at the new berths in Tilbury, while the majority of shipwork has been the exclusive work of the stevedoring contractor. In Liverpool, the division between master stevedore and master porter remained important and this divided responsibility in the country's two main ports has provided a powerful argument in support of a single employer concept, or even nationalisation under single port authorities.

Secondly, conflicting sectional interest has weakened the employers' bargaining position on many occasions. Again, London provides the worst examples because negotiators, up to 1967, had to serve two masters – the Shipping Federation through the London Ship-Owners Dock Labour Committee and N A P E through the overall port association, with the P L A occasionally going its own way to add to the confusion. Finally, the haphazard development of the ports and the bargaining procedures – augmented, as we shall see, by problems of multi-unionism – has created totally different wages structures and working practices in each port, so that the scope for national action by the employers diminished as local custom and practice grew in strength.

Dockland trade unionism first took root among the more skilled trades of the ports. Under a casual system, any specialist knowledge increased a man's chances of employment and identifiable occupational groups were the first to band together in a protective capacity. It took years of practice to learn the stevedores' art of stowing goods in the cramped holds of sailing ships, to carry sacks of grain or planks of deal up and down swaying gangways. Working in warehouses in entre-pôt ports also required specialist knowledge in coopering and box-knocking or grading commodities like tea; then there were the shore-gangs which roped a ship at its berth, riggers who moved the hatches, cranemen, winchmen, coal-heavers, bargemen, tugmen and lighter-men: all valued their trade as a sign of status and a guarantee of employment.

Technically these were unskilled groups, except for the London watermen and lightermen who served apprenticeships, but their work had its own identity and was sufficiently well defined to allow asso-ciations to be formed, preserving their jobs from the encroachment of outsiders and establishing special rates of pay.

The corn and deal porters combined to control the hiring process, with the agreement of employers, and the stevedores won recognition from the L M S A to conduct their own calls, outside the dock-gate. Later the crane drivers, engine drivers and winchmen, hydraulic and boiler attendants, coal porters' winchmen and ballast heavers evolved their own organisations in London and the sectional organisations in other ports were nearly as numerous.

Like genuine craft unions, these societies were essentially restric-tive – the London stevedores, for example, charging an entrance fee of £1 (except to sons of members) up to 1963 – and their aim was to preserve the monopoly right to certain grades of work. There was little common interest between these organisations and the ordinary dock labourer who performed the despised tasks of discharging, trucking and sorting on the quays. This was a major obstacle to general organisation since there was always a fear that increased status for the labourer would erode the privilege of specialists.

In some instances, the specialist union tried to organise downward, if only to reach a *modus vivendi* with the labourers. The Coal Trim-mers in Cardiff, Penarth and Barry succeeded in becoming a general union in some areas and the London stevedores tried in 1909 to extend their organisation from pure stevedoring work – loading – to all ship-work.[17] But for the most part they had the same organising difficulties as the general unions when there was no occupational nucleus to build on.

There were three occasions when general unionism gained a powerful hold in the docks, in 1872, 1889 and 1911, but in each case initial victories were squandered by ill-judged strikes and organisational weakness, and finally it was the co-operative experience of the First World War which consolidated general unionism more than the massive strikes of 1911–13.

In 1872, boom conditions in London meant the level of dock employment was high and the men combined in the Labour Protection League to win wage increases in a succession of disputes with individual employers. The League never had a strong federal organisation but remained, even at its peak with 20,000 members, more a *confederation* of autonomous branches. It was to survive precariously on the South Bank of the Thames through the corn porters, and it gave birth to the Amalgamated Stevedores Labour Protection League, forefather of today's National Amalgamated Stevedores and Dockers.

General unionism achieved a stronger permanent foothold after the 1889 dockers' strike – a pivotal point in union history. For the first time, it brought the labourer who had no craft to use as a bargaining weapon but only the value of his toil, within the ambit of organisation.

New unionism was made possible by the stabilisation of the labour force at this period, but it also had strong antecedents in Socialist thinking. The theorists realised that general labour could not be fitted to the restrictive and inward-looking practices of craft unionism because an employer in dispute with unskilled labour could easily replace it. To preclude this form of black-legging, organisation had to be extended beyond the immediate work vicinity to the entire area from which strike-breaking labour could be drawn. Will Thorne set out this philosophy before the Royal Commission on Labour: 'If we should confine ourselves to one particular industry, such as gas-works alone, and if those other people in various parts of the country are let go unorganised, then, if we had a dispute with any of the gas companies, these men would be brought up to be put in our places.'[18]

Organisation in the docks was to be the real test of New Unionism since it was the most uncompromisingly casual of industries and day-to-day replacement of labour was common. The leaders of the 1889 strike, Tom Mann, John Burns and Ben Tillett, were united behind Thorne in the belief that their organisation would have to be vast, with all possible sources of labour enrolled and all sectional interests catered for. The victorious 'tanners' strike showed that a general organisation could be held together at any rate for the duration of one struggle, and it fired the popular imagination as no strike had done before.

Much was fortuitous about the success of the strike, not least its origins when Tillett was forced to call out his small Tea Operatives and General Labourers' Union because Thorne's gasworkers' union from Beckton had begun to organise down-river and were even trespassing on Tillett's home territory, the West India dock. The response to the strike call was by no means certain. Tillett had only enrolled 2,000 men in two years and, earlier in 1889, he would have abandoned his union, had he been elected to the general-secretaryship of the gasworkers'; the other imponderable was the reaction of the stevedores and lightermen but they ensured the success of the dispute when they walked out in sympathy. For the strike committee, the main concern in the five weeks of the struggle was that sectional settlements might cause a drift back to work; many groups were already being paid the rate of 6d an hour and 8d for overtime and the outcome hung in the balance when the committee split to pursue separate claims for deal porters, lumpers, stevedores, overside corn porters, quay corn porters, granary corn porters, steamship workers, weighers and warehousemen, trimmers and, of course, for the general labourers.

But with help from the London public, other unions and staggering contributions from Australia, the strike was financed and stayed solid until the Lord Mayor of London and Cardinal Manning mediated to effect a settlement. By this time, most dockers were enrolled in Tillett's union – which changed its name to the Dock, Wharf, Riverside and General Labourers (DWRGLU) – through the simple device of supporting the men not with money but food tickets, for which union membership was a prerequisite. Before the strike, the only organised general labour had been in the Tea Operatives and the surviving branches of the Labour League; now Tillett had 18,000 on his books and 25,000 a year later.

The sudden expansion was repeated all over the country. In Liverpool, where the first attempts to organise dockers had come from the American Knights of Labour, Sexton was able to build up the organisation founded by Richard McGhee and Edward McHugh from Glasgow into the National Union of Dock Labourers; the gasworkers organised Grimsby; Tillett moved into the West Country ports; the group of local associations which were to join the General and Municipal Workers' Union (GMWU) strengthened their basis around Newcastle; and a Glasgow union grew up to vie with Sexton for control of the Scottish ports. McHugh returned the compliment to the Knights of Labour by trying to organise the New York dockers in 1886 but his fledgling organisation collapsed. The US Atlantic ports were eventually organised by the longshoremen of the Great Lakes. The months after 1889 were heady times for dock labour and contemporary observers believed that organisation would rapidly solve the casual labour problem. Booth, returning to the docks in 1892, was representative of this optimism:

'In 1887 when dock labour was considered by us (namely by Beatrice Webb) the position was found to be very hopeless as well as very unsatisfactory. The employers were content and the men, although far from content, were entirely disorganised. The dock managements accepted the crowd at the dockgates as an inevitable phenomenon which happened to fit in well with the conditions of their trade. They could always be sure of sufficient labour and, although its quality might be bad, its pay was correspondingly low. The character of the men matched well with the character of the work and that of its remuneration. All alike were low and irregular. The vicious circle was complete. How should it be broken?

'In 1892 all this was changed. The unions, founded under the greatest difficulties in 1888, had a remarkable career . . . what the men had achieved through organisation was not to be measured solely by advantage obtained in pay or the conditions of employment. By organisation they step into line with other more highly skilled and more highly paid labour, and so acquire a position of great practical value. We see the effect of this in the changed attitude of the employers as to casual employment. It is now generally admitted by them that more regular work makes better labourers and that better labourers are more satisfactory servants even at higher pay.'[19]

But this optimism was ill-founded in regard both to the career of the unions and the impact of the 1889 strike on casual practices. With their objectives won, Tillett's membership drifted away and the erstwhile solidarity evaporated still further in the face of the dock companies' and ship-owners' counter-offensive which smashed unionism in Hull, in 1893, and in the North End of Liverpool. The DWRGLU hardly survived the 1890s and by 1910 its London organisation was being subsidised heavily by the contributions of the provinces. In Liverpool, the story was the same. Sexton tried to restrict hiring to men with a union button but was so badly supported that the button was hastily withdrawn. His branches lapsed into virtual autonomy, becoming in effect small clubs, mutually antagonistic and resentful of interference from union headquarters. In many ways the Liverpool branches were like the sectional associations of other ports which bore the stamp of benevolent societies, running sick clubs, Christmas clubs and paying death benefit. Liverpool coal-heavers had a society for each end of the port, one led by an Orangeman, the other by a Catholic; the coasting trades kept their own club, as did the salt-heavers, and they all formed part of a caste system which Sexton claimed was 'quite as powerful as India's.' It was bitterly difficult to channel money up to head office and even to get the branches to accept the principle of ballot-voting in elections.

It is little wonder that Sexton described his union as an unholy mess in the 1890s; that Tillett called the port of London the great unmanageable and that Bevin said organising in the docks was calculated to break the heart of the union official.

E. J. Hobsbawm aptly illustrated the diversity of union organisation, in his essay on waterside unionism, by tracing the voyage of a coaster down the Eastern ports. At Aberdeen, it would deal with the NUDL, in Dundee with the Scottish Union of Dock Labourers, in Leith with the NUDL, in Blyth with the North of England Teemers and Trimmers, in Newcastle with the GMWU constituents, in the Hartlepools with the Teemers, in Middlesbrough with Tillett's union, in Hull with practically all unions in the industry, in Goole with the NUDL, in Grimsby with the gasworkers and in Boston and southwards, with Tillett again.

This instability was partly an accident of growth, answering the interests of different occupational groups and the independent development of the ports in purely local terms. In part it stemmed from the natural response of the early union leaders to the problem of fragmentation. Tillett was an egoist with a tongue which could talk him past an angel, but listless in day-to-day administration; Mann had demonic energy but also preferred to operate on a broad canvas;

Burns drifted away from the docks and it was left to the lesser officials to create a healthy branch life which accommodated local interests to the good of the union as a whole.

The top leadership found it easier to create a centralised union structure – alien to the traditions of sectionalism – and then to feder-ate with other organisations in order to bolster their authority. Federation was doubly attractive since the theory of mass unionism was clearly breaking down in the docks. There was little point in organising all general labour when internal dissension meant that groups within the union could blackleg on each other and there were other organisations which might not support a dispute. Federation thus could bring all strategic groups into alliance as well as increasing the central power of the unions in relation to the branches.

Early attempts at federation between London and Liverpool broke down because of the disinterest of the Northern rank-and-file but, in 1910, Tillett's union took the initiative in forming the National Trans-port Workers' Federation (NTWF) and within a year a wave of trans-port strikes swept the country, involving 100,000 men and co-ordi-nated by the Federation. The seamen and dockers came out together in Liverpool; for a moment, it looked as if London would avoid a dis-pute when the Federation concluded the first port-wide agreement with an employers' committee headed by Lord Devonport, chairman of the PLA. But the provisional terms did not create a single port rate, they omitted some groups altogether and ignored the vital issue of union rights at the point of hiring. The deal was rejected by the men and Harry Gosling, the genial president of the Federation, had to perform a rapid *volte-face* in supporting the ensuing stoppage. A series of settlements brought peace after a month but introduced new anoma-lies to the wage structure and it was soon apparent that another con-flict was bound to follow.

The 1912 strike was led from the start by the Federation, but on the far more elusive ground of union monopoly. In 1911, the right for the call to be held outside the dock-gate was re-established and now Gos-ling's lightermen insisted that foremen should be unionised. It was a sectional issue *par excellence* and, although the dockers came out, there was always a hint of desperation among the unions. Even Til-lett's appeal to the dockers to remove their hats at Tower Hill while he called on God to strike Lord Devonport dead could not affect the outcome and the attempt to call a national stoppage was a fiasco;

13,000 blacklegs were working in London and the only provincial support came from the DWRGLU in the West. To the new generation of union organisers, the failure to capitalise on the success of 1911 was a failure of unity; amalgamation of the transport unions was thus to become the burning issue after the First World War. But amalgamation could not eradicate the factor which contributed most to unstable unionism: the nature of men's responses to the casual system.

Casualism forced men to adopt a host of expedients to lessen the severity of arbitrary engagement and these concentrated on the hiring procedure, as the point where protection was most needed. By the time general unionism was established, the unofficial loyalties, practices and malpractices of the men were rooted in patterns of behaviour which could not be built easily into the institutional framework of the unions. The union organiser could offer the formalised relationships of the branch, a grievance procedure and an official hierarchy but unless these could be harmonised with or improve on the informal and unofficial customs, the unions were not seen as a complete vehicle for the men's interests and plans to alter the nature of casualism would be resisted.

In many instances there was no harmony because custom and practice was antithetical to the collective principles of unionism; the casual attitude did not correspond to 'one for all and all for one' but was aimed primarily at setting one man, or one group, in a position of vantage over his fellows in the free-for-all of the call. The inherent selfishness of behaviour at the call is recognised by most dockers. A Londoner told me of the first day he applied for work after completing his national service. He went to the stand where his father was known and the foreman promptly gave him the last place in a gang, one of whose regular members was absent at the time. 'There were a good few people there who had been following the foreman for a long time to try to get into the regular gang and, when I was taken, they cut up a bit rough. "Who's this geezer? Why did he get in?" Then my dad appeared – he always turned up by taxi – and told them I had more right to the job than any of them because I was his f . . . ing son. They respected my dad who'd been around a long time and said that was all right then. Of course, the whole thing was not fair but that was the way it worked.'

In research carried out in Manchester docks in 1951, the same attitudes were found. One docker said: 'People would not say that dockers are solid if they saw us in the pen squabbling like a lot of monkeys to do ourselves a bit of good.' Another: 'Dockers are not really solid – it's each man for himself and the devil take the hindmost.'[20]

Overtly selfish behaviour embarrassed the men and a whole vocabulary grew up to condemn the imprudent display of self-interest; the phrase 'he'd take your ear off with his tally' survived until the last day of casualism although the metal tallies, which could be thrust too eagerly towards a foreman, were last used before the Second World War. Feelings of guilt helped to drive the open lobbying of the callstand underground, into the informal network of relationships within the dock community. Rather than jockey in front of the foreman, men relied on innumerable private arrangements to improve their chances of employment. This might mean approaching a foreman directly in a pub or getting to know the leader of an established gang in the hope that he would fit you into his team when he had a vacancy; usually, however, most reliance was put on kinship.

The tradition of son following father has been marked in casual trades where experience is more important than trained skills in knowing the ins-and-outs of a job and making it pay well. In ports there are always a large variety of occupations to follow – in work associated with shipping or small manufacturing processes using the commodities of local trade – but the docks have provided an unusually high ratio of kinship successions and many dockers today can count a dozen relatives in the same employ. The ties of kinship date back to the early influxes of Irish labour and to the sense of community fostered by the building of housing around the dock estates. Up to the Blitz and the slum clearance programmes of the last thirty years, the great majority of dockers lived within walking distance of their work and spitting distance of their colleagues. In spite of the dispersal of the dock communities, kinship played a more important role than ever in the ports after entry was restricted by the formation of registers of dock workers. The unions gave priority to the sons and relatives of dockers in selecting names for the register and, in Manchester, 75 per cent of the labour force in 1951 were sons of dockers. In the first eight years of the Dock Labour Scheme, when there was fairly regular recruitment, 3,369 out of 6,425 admitted before 1950 in London were dockers' sons and the proportion rose up to 1954, with the admission of 5,168 sons and 1,957 others (many of whom were probably lesser relatives).

Once job opportunities began to decline, kinship rights caused enormous trouble for the unions. For instance, London tally clerks objected to the transfer of dockers to their ranks, because it excluded their relatives from work. Similarly, London dockers objected to the transfer of lightermen. At Tilbury, where recruitments cannot always be filled by relatives, non-dock labour objected to the transfer of London dockers. In Southampton, the TGWU branch preferred to open the books to their sons than admit seasonal dockers to full-time work. In 1969–70, the pressure in Liverpool was so great when a recruitment was imminent, that stewards bravely tried to draw up a hierarchy of blood relations!

One of the most distressing examples occurred early in 1972, when Greenock dockers struck for nearly three weeks in an attempt to stop Glasgow dockers being transferred 20 miles down the Clyde in the place of green labour who could be recruited locally.

Before kinship became such a vital factor in recruitments, it had a somewhat different role in assisting men to cope with casualism and establishing links which could circumvent the lottery of the call. A father would 'speak for' his son, introduce him to a gang and teach him the tricks of the trade. Later the son would help to carry his father through heavy work. It was thus part of the process of self-interest which is so clearly recognised in the terminology of the docks. In London, the term was 'getting a good corner' and it occupied a most important place in the life of the men. Once found, they would go to enormous lengths to protect their corner, as the following incident reveals. The story was related by a tally clerk at Tilbury who used to follow the P and O in the 1950s. He was recognised as a good worker and the foremen were quick to reward his loyalty by selecting him early at the calls; this relationship, in fact, was his corner since it guaranteed him good employment.

'One day the charge clerk told me to go down into the hold because the marks on canned goods were mixed. I wasn't meant to go down but you did not argue in those days. When I was down I slipped on some dunnage and broke my ankle. I was lifted out by crane and left sitting on the quay, waiting for the ambulance to come. Then the charge clerk comes up and thrusts an accident report in my hand which says I fell down a companion way. That would have been above deck and would absolve the company from responsibility. I had to do a quick calculation. Was it better to collect a bit of compensation or sign the form and have a corner to come back to. I signed it. I was off for six weeks but I never felt I did the wrong thing.'

In this instance, the tally clerk could have expected compensation equivalent to six weeks wages since the order to go down the hold was illegal. But he preferred to keep his good standing and forsake the money, so that he would not be passed over on his return to work.

The line between the practices which dockers used to get their corner and the malpractices which were thrust upon them, as part of the unofficial hiring procedure, is narrow and it is made more difficult to distinguish by the myths which are incorporated in dockology. It was known, for instance, that many gangs were composed of Catholics, like the green-scarf gang at Mark Brown's wharf in London or the renowned Bustard gangs at Tilbury, but it was then assumed that entry was arranged by a Catholic priest. By the same token, it appeared as if casualism forced men to pander to foremen, when in fact the favours might not be asked but given, precisely to avoid reliance on the chance element in hiring.

Here, then, was a pattern of responses which unions found hard to incorporate in collective principle and, if they do not accord with the dockers' reputation for group loyalty and aggressive solidarity – a reputation which has gone unquestioned and unexplained in many official reports on dockland – the nature of this loyalty must be clarified.

The traditional view was exemplified in the Leggett report of 1951 which said: 'It appears to be incredibly easy to bring dock workers out on strike. We were given repeated instances of men stopping work almost automatically with little or no idea why they were stopping. In the words of one witness, himself a dock worker, "All that was needed was for a man to go round the docks shouting 'All out' and waving the men off the ships, and out they would come".' [21]

The Devlin Committee quoted this paragraph verbatim in 1965 and accounted for the 'exaggerated sense of solidarity' by the need to combat casualism and the fear of ostracism at work or in the tight home communities. These were valid reasons, as far as they went. The docks have been strike-prone and the spontaneous eruptions have come, in the main, from the shopfloor rather than the machinery of the unions. But reasons other than casualism itself and the compactness of the community have played a part in making the docker exhibit these characteristics more markedly than other groups of workers.

One is the élitist regard which the dockers have for themselves. It is a defensive élitism, corresponding to the self-esteem of the poor white in multi-racial societies, and derives from the stigma which is attached to dockwork and, in London, the sheer physical isolation of the docks from society at large.

However much architectural determinism may be discredited in academic theory, I am also intrigued by the possibility that the high retaining walls of the old dock estates – shutting out the public and shutting in the men – have shaped dockland behaviour. By contrast, dockwork in the old port of Antwerp, where promenades run along the top of quayside sheds on the River Scheldt, can be watched by the public and the effect of public scrutiny may have put pressure on dockers to work to socially-acceptable norms.

In Britain, the public's low regard for the docker, which was so evident in the nineteenth century, has survived to our day and an occupational grading published in 1950 placed the docker twenty-ninth out of thirty groupings, superior only to the road-sweeper. At that time, dockers were earning more than the national average wage and, today, when they are among the best-paid manual workers in the country, the feeling persists that they have risen above their station. For instance, Prof. Hugh Clegg has suggested that dockers should not be given further wage increases until poorer workers have caught up, if Britain is ever to adopt an effective incomes policy.[22]

Similar attitudes are reflected in many jokes at the dockers' expense. The 50p piece was called the dockers' threepenny bit. Or the docker, caught stealing a bar of gold, was punished by having its value deducted from his next wage packet. The jibes also perpetuate the image of a loutish, unskilled labourer. In one newspaper cartoon, two dockers point to their surly mate. 'Don't talk to him about containers, he hasn't accepted the crane yet,' one says. In another, some dockers watch a huge safe being unloaded. Says one: 'Blimey, Alf, it's your pay packet.'

Dockers have reacted to the sting of public scorn by identifying closely as a group and it was the policy of early union leaders to restore their social position. During the 1889 strike, Burns berated them for 'so conducting their lives as to be unworthy of the human respect he demanded for them – for beating their wives, drinking themselves silly, fighting like animals';[23] Tillett made sure they knew how to handle their knives and forks before attending a victory dinner; and Bevin based his case before Lord Shaw on the need to make the docker a better citizen. Latterly, the attitude of union officials has often been condescending and some talk of their men as if they could do nothing right – but this is a reflection of the conflict between rank-and-file and union authority. Since decasualisation, it is probable that the docker has developed a higher estimation of his calling but one still finds those who say 'I'm only a docker' as if they were social outcasts.

The conjunction of a hostile society, the system of employment and strong kinship bonds have had the effect of creating a sub-culture in the docks, a world of clannishness and resentment of authority, which was first recorded by Beatrice Webb when she described the peculiar attractiveness of the dock labourers, who might be morally and economically worthless, but were tolerant of each other's vices and drawn together by want into a 'communism' of share and share alike. 'As a class they are quixotically generous. It is this virtue and the courage with which they face privation that lend a charm to life among them.'[24]

The most striking example of the dockers' inward-looking society was the London march, in April 1968, in support of Enoch Powell's tirade against immigration. Although only a few hundred took part, it gravely embarrassed union officials and militants who liked to present their men as a vanguard of international brotherhood.

Shop stewards got clergymen to denounce the walk-out and Jack Dash, with members of his unofficial liaison committee, put out a circular – in a personal capacity – castigating Powell and warning men that any action unconnected with industrial issues was diversionary. 'We must keep our eye on the ball. The Tory attempt to lay a false trail should deceive nobody – least of all dockers who have suffered so much at the hands of these scoundrels.'

Because the London docks have not been a free labour market for so long, no coloureds work there and immigration posed no threat to dockers' livelihoods. What they did feel, however, was a threat to their community and, at the same time, a plea for a total and immediate ban on immigration, regardless of colour or race, was being processed through TGWU committees.

The nature in which dockwork is organised, by gangs and one-off jobs, is the other factor which contributed to group loyalty. After the call, hired men walked from the stand to the ship and, if the vessel had just arrived in port, the hatches would be uncovered and the gang would see the condition and stowage of the cargo. An experienced gang-leader could quickly size up how long it would take to discharge the hold with the equipment available and how much the job would yield in piecework; if he reckoned the yield would be inadequate, he would consult the gang and decide whether to ask for an extra payment from the foreman. At this point, the gang was in a very powerful position, if it could be sure no other dockers would work that hold in its place. It was an economic fact that the amount of money claimed seldom matched the cost of delaying the ship and, if the ship-owner wanted a fast turn-round, his stevedoring contractor was under strong pressure to reach a settlement.

In these circumstances, the lesson of solidarity did not take long to learn and, at times when the level of unemployment was low or following a union victory, the incidence of disputes at the hatch used to rise. After 1889, there were complaints of incessant small stoppages in London and the first use of 'ca'canny' (literally treading warily or, in modern parlance, going slow). In the boom following the First World War there was another spate of unofficial disputes; Bristol employers reeled off a list of stoppages to Lord Shaw, where the men demanded larger gangs for bushelling grain, bonuses of £1 a man to finish a discharge of cotton seed, and £1 again for one and a quarter hours' work on manganese ore; when extra payments were refused on another ship, the men contrived to spin out the discharge of 122 bags – half an hour's normal work – from 4.30 p.m. on a Friday, through a half-day on Saturday and into Monday morning. Tim O'Leary, the national docks secretary of the TGWU, recalled an incident of his youth to Lord Devlin when the whole of Regent's Canal dock in London stopped for two hours because one gang objected to a faulty winch which was blowing off water instead of steam; and, in the late 1940s, when unemployment in the industry was lower than ever before, a crop of disputes involving extra payments were initiated by militant gangs.

Often, the demands were justified: bags of antimony were torn, phosphate rock had got wet because of a leaking ship's plate, cotton seed cake was infested with flies and insects, maize meal in rotten paper bags had to be transferred to hessian sacks, bags of figs were sticky, and 250 tons of spelter (zinc) had to be extracted from below 100 tons of peanut butter which had melted from the heat of the ship's propellor shaft! While the claims were understandable, the significant point was the way the men dealt with them, often walking out without recourse to the grievance machinery and against the advice of union officials who were cast in the unhappy role of mediator when the men felt they could get their way by straightforward industrial pressure.

The gang as a bargaining unit has disappeared from almost all other industries, in large part because of the power it gave to small groups on the shopfloor. But this power gave dockers an elementary political awareness of the value of collective pressure which the bold gang-leader would be quick to exploit. This rank-and-file politicisation can be glamourised beyond its true worth but it is undeniable that the organisation of dockers into small bargaining units under the casual system, working on jobs which never repeated themselves, created a situation where solidarity gave power. This power was used so that men respected the disputes of their fellows and seldom undermined them – even to the point where a minority could dictate the behaviour of the greater part of the labour force. (In his autobiography, Jack Dash devotes an excellent chapter to the choices facing a gang at work (*Good Morning, Brothers*, pp. 98–104). Another excellent account of gangs, as an organisational nucleus, reconciling pressures between themselves, their workmates and management, is found in Solzhenitsyn's *One Day in the Life of Ivan Denisovich*, where the inmates of a labour camp work in gangs on a building site.)

These instances of loyalty used on behalf of small groups in dispute were, in part, an extension of pre-hiring attitudes, in so far as both were self-interested. Once developed, however, this loyalty could be turned to the disinterested objective of protecting the labour force as a whole from the effects of casualism, by the regulation of overtime and weekend working, unofficial fixing of piecework speeds and defining job continuity – all of which helped to spread work over the labour force as a whole. In the early days of union organisation, this form of loyalty was not highly developed since it cut across sectional interests. In London there was marked rivalry between dockers and stevedores for the same work – Tillett once went so far as to accuse the stevedores of blacklegging during a dockers' strike – and, in Liverpool, men were reluctant to give up the right, once hired, to work for as long as they were physically able, although the NUDL wanted to limit continuous stints to 24 hours, day and night.

One theory which tried to square the self-interested response with the traditional reputation for loyalty postulated that solidarity could be seen as *compensation* for the selfishness of the call-stand.

'The satisfaction they get from a public display of solidarity, particularly in support of a colleague they think has been victimised may, indeed, be due to the fact that such action helps them to get rid of feelings of guilt aroused by the selfish struggles in the call-stand. If this is so, behaviour of this kind may be regarded as compensatory rather than merely unreasonable and it follows that while the present (casual) system of allocating work remains in operation, dock workers are likely to continue to indulge in the aggressive behaviour associated with the industry.'[25]

But this does not ring true and it is unsatisfactory to explain social phenomena in psychological terms. A simpler answer suggests itself, once a distinction is drawn between basic behavioural responses and the points at which they occurred.

The first group of responses stemmed from the procedure for getting work and was self-oriented. The responses were for the most part individual, covering a man's relations with any other capable of influencing his chances of getting work; but they could be extended to a group of men who joined together to seek work and whose interests were common. Occasionally, they might be shared by an entire occupational group, if it exerted sufficient control over the hiring process – usually through organised work-sharing endorsed by management.

In such instances, the conflict was between one docker and another and was therefore internal. But the second category of responses – where the docker showed his solidarity – occurred after hiring had taken place. The enemy was external, the employer, and the responses thus were group-oriented; they might take the form of trying to control the job or securing a fair distribution of work among the labour force but they were as much the product of shopfloor strength as casualism itself.

The nature of group-protective responses to the external enemy changed in the 1950s and 1960s, when the dockers achieved greater security within the casual system. They took on a more restrictive role, increasing the inefficiency of port operations and accounting for the fast rate of wages drift. But they also retained a moral function in the desire to protect job security and it was a fundamental error, during the years of the Devlin programme, to assume that the dockers' aggressive solidarity represented solely a casual response to the casual system.

As we shall see, even after Devlin Phase I and Phase II had swept away casual hiring and inequitable payment systems, some of the old responses were left intact, because job opportunities were contracting so rapidly.

In the development of waterfront unionism, the importance of the responses to casualism, and the residual power of the rank-and-file, was the strain they put on union organisation. Collective action has been, in fact, a rank-and-file prerogative which waxed and waned more in relation to economic conditions in the ports than to policies emanating from union headquarters. The strikes of 1889 and 1911 were generated from the shopfloor, as were most of the major stoppages since; of the four national stoppages – 1912, 1924, 1926 and 1970 – the first and last were called through the constitutional machinery of the unions but with reluctant support from the top leadership. This is not to deny the important influence the unions have exerted; they provided a focus for shopfloor energy and gave the labourer faith in his ability to resist the employer, as well as providing the national framework which prevented employers playing off one port against another. They protected members in the smaller ports and also established normal secondary benefits relating to social and psychological security. But the weaknesses which emerged in the early years have dogged union organisation since – sectionalism and an inability to change casualism at its roots – because the unions could not replace the unofficial protections adopted by the men nor overcome their resistance to change.

Initially, the unions did make a sustained effort to dislodge casualism by fighting for control of the hiring procedure. Tillett launched the 1889 strike with the demand for the dockers' tanner low on the list of priorities. His main demands tackled the effects of casualism and they were conceded in the Mansion House settlement. Men in future were to be taken on by the half-day, not the hour, and there were to be only two times a day for the call to take place, so that men did not have to wander round the dock day-in, day-out looking for work. But the most important concession was the granting of a virtual closed shop, by letting the call be had outside the dock-gate under the surveillance of a union organiser. Inside the gate, the union official could be arrested for trespass.

This arrangement allowed a card inspection to be held and only paid-up union members to present themselves for work. The LMSA granted the same privilege to the stevedores' league, whose members got priority for all loading operations, and this was instrumental in keeping the league viable through the bleak years of 1889–1911. Similar power over hiring is the basis of union strength in the United States, where a theoretically casual system still exists, except that the unions control the distribution of work at the hiring hall and enforce agreements which guarantee work-sharing.

In London, however, the dock companies withdrew the hiring concession after thirteen months – as soon as they possibly could – since they feared abuses of the union privilege and, as Lovell points out, their fears were justified by the behaviour of the men in the flush of victory; the DWRGLU executive's efforts to make branches restrict the number of men going to the call, and to make sure that new entrants were fit enough to be good dock labour, were unavailing, as were Mann's pleas for the men to work at a proper stroke. In Liverpool the attempt to control entry with the union button also failed and the unions did not regain the right to take on general labour outside the dock-gate until 1911. The concession was won under duress and promptly withdrawn after the collapse of the 1912 strike as the ship-owners launched their counter-offensive. In fact, P and O, Orient, New Zealand and British India, with the help of Scruttons, succeeded in breaking the stevedores' preferential control although it meant Scruttons leaving the LMSA to do so.

With hindsight, the employers' action seems wrong, since they stood to benefit from strong union organisation. To retain the support of the men, the unions needed a *raison d'etre* in day-to-day activities and control of hiring would have provided just such a role, offering an alternative to unofficial practices through the involvement of the rank-and-file in work distribution. The exclusion of the unions from the hiring process held their influence in check but also kept them weaker than even the employers wanted. When the Devlin Committee had to choose the form decasualisation should take, the attractive precedent of the US West Coast Mechanisation and Modernisation agreement had to be ruled out because British unions did not have sufficient control over the labour force to educate it for change or the discipline to deliver what they agreed at the negotiating table.

The defeats of 1912 ended the only union attempt to deal with casualism in its entirety. In the next half-century, union leaders accepted that a casual margin was inevitable. Sexton's views were typical when he said 'You cannot decasualise dock labour at all, you can relieve it but you cannot absolutely decasualise' because he felt the men would not accept the crushing out of the margin as more permanent employment was given to the regulars.[26] Bevin was more positive in believing he could overcome the opposition of his members but he retained the essential assumption of casualism – that a margin would remain.

The Bevin era of dock leadership thus saw the consequences of casualism vigorously attacked and much success in increasing security. But by acquiescing in a margin, casualism was perpetuated with its hallmarks of low status, irregular earnings and underemployment. Men continued to see their salvation in the attitudes and practices which grew up in the nineteenth century and eventually enough people were cocooned by the unofficial practices to feel that any major changes to the system would leave them more vulnerable than before. In theory, the abolition of casualism was approved but the shopfloor never threw up a realistic programme for achieving it. This left the employers as the most likely source of change, once they believed that casualism worked more to their detriment than advantage.

The unions' early failure to control the hiring process and to persuade the rank-and-file of the need to abolish casualism has contributed in large measure to their weak hold over the membership. Bevin failed to bring all the waterfront unions into the amalgamation of 1922 and the TGWU suffered breakaways in the docks between the wars and unsuccessful splinters in the 1950s and 1960s.

Five unions survived to negotiate the Devlin programme – the TGWU, the GMWU, the National Amalgamated Stevedores and Dockers (NASD), the Watermen, Lightermen, Tugmen and Bargemen's Union and the Scottish TGWU. Although the lightermen amalgamated with the TGWU in 1971 and the Scottish TGWU re-joined in 1972, the rivalry between the main union and the NASD, representing a mere 8 per cent of the labour force in London alone, has still to be solved, as has the dockers' tendency to pursue sectional interests in defiance of the union as a whole.

Lovell's conclusion about organisation in 1914 is largely true today. He said unions far less cumbrous than the TGWU found it difficult to control the unofficial movements and narrow horizons of dockland:

'In this perspective the whole history of waterside unionism falls into place. The paradoxical situation of the pre-1914 period, with its massive strikes but weak and unstable unionism, and the problems of more recent years, with continuous organisation and disruptive unofficial movements form part of the same pattern. As a group, port workers have developed a great capacity for spontaneous and unofficial action, yet the extent to which trade unions have been able to harness and direct and control these forces has remained limited.'[27]

CHAPTER THREE

First Reforms

'While neither employer nor employed are really satisfied with things as they are, both are more fearful than hopeful of the effects of possible change on their individual interests.'   Eleanor Rathbone.[28]

The earliest attempts to reduce the margin of surplus labour without abolishing the casual pool were confined to two experiments in London and Liverpool. Both were palliative measures which accepted casual hiring as a principle but they chose different starting points. London's experiment was an employer's initiative, engineered first by the dock companies and subsequently the PLA. It sought to organise the rights of men at the call so rigidly that the truly casual fringe would be driven away from the docks. Liverpool's was a joint attempt by the NUDL and the majority of employers to reduce the margin but then allow free choice of labour within this limitation.

The London dock companies were able to embark on the gradualist road to permanent employment because they were large employing units and labour could be switched within and between departments to a variety of tasks on the quays. Compared with the stevedoring contractors whose labour requirement fluctuated with the arrival and departure of clients' ships, quayside operators in an entrepôt port had a much steadier supply of work, receiving goods for export, delivering imports to lorries or railway trucks and sorting in the warehouses.

The London plan was 'Mr Booth's scheme.' The companies' potential labour force was divided into four categories, beginning with permanent staff who were paid weekly, given a paid holiday, sick benefit and a benevolent allowance of up to 10s a week after fifteen years service; next came the *A* list (abolished in the First World War) from which the permanent men were recruited and who were guaranteed a week's employment at a time when accepted for work at the call; they had priority of employment over the *B* list, who were ordinary casuals but had a preference ticket and filled vacancies in the

A list. Finally, there was the *C* list, out-and-out casuals who only took the name if they followed a dock company foreman in the hope of getting a preference ticket by dint of loyal service.

The scheme was taken over in its entirety when the PLA was set up and charged in its founding articles to 'take such steps as they think best calculated to diminish the evils of casual employment.' The increased security of employment for high-listed men had been spectacular in the last years of the dock companies, for whom 19 per cent of the labour force were permanent men at the time of the tanners' strike; in 1894, 30 per cent were permanent and 34·9 per cent *A* men and in 1904 the proportions had increased to 41·2 per cent and 37·2 per cent for a total of 78·4 per cent in pretty regular employment. By 1913 the PLA had 3,000 permanent men, 47 per cent of its average daily requirement, and 40 per cent *A* men – a peak which was not to be passed again until the 1950s. During the First World War, however, the *A* category was abolished; the title was given to the permanent employees and the *B* men came next in line for promotion but continued to be hired on a daily basis. In the trade boom which followed the armistice, congestion in London was so great that the PLA had to take on all available labour. The number of permanent men increased to 4,000 and the *B* list to 2,800, but the proportion of regulars decreased in relation to the total requirement and the *B* man was never to have the security of the pre-war *A* man. In fact, in the Depression, some permanent men had to be put back on a casual basis and the *B* men had to chase work much like an ordinary casual. Col. Oram, in his days as a PLA superintendent in the 1930s, recalls them as a very mobile group of men with an extremely efficient grapevine. 'The *B* men had to keep their ears to the ground if they were to survive. How else explain the occasions – and they were several – when during the morning I would tell the foreman that we should need another gang at 1 p.m. and at 12.45 there would be several hundred men fighting for the thirteen jobs on offer.'[29]

The Depression put paid to any hopes that the PLA's example might ease casualism out of the port of London. In 1939 it still had 3,000 permanent men but it had hardly recruited any new men in the 1930s and it kept a ban on recruitment until 1948 when this part of its labour force had dropped to 1,649. There were, however, other basic difficulties in London's gradualist approach. First, the dock company programme was launched at a time of severe conflict with the unions.

The policy was linked to an attempt to break the power of Tillett's union on the assumption that the permanent man would not put his security at risk by joining casuals on strike, and it was introduced simultaneously with the transfer of discharging work and the breaking of union monopoly at the call.

The casuals were highly suspicious of permanent men; they despised their comparative respectability – Booth noted that the permanent men and foremen tended to live in more salubrious neighbourhoods than the dockers. They surmised correctly that the permanent man would easily be lost to union organisation and he got the reputation, inherited in our day, of staying at work through thick and thin. (*The Trade Unionist*, a journal which appeared sporadically to record the gains of new unionism, was particularly venomous in calling the permanent men people 'who would go to work for 2d an hour and a good kicking.')

The early unions thus opposed permanency as a threat to their existence and for a more basic reason: so long as permanency was partial, the work available to the casuals would decrease in proportion to the amount given to regularly-employed men. Permanency was regarded as contrary to the principles of unionism unless it was linked to a very strict control of the numbers allowing to compete for the outstanding work. Bevin explained this attitude cogently before the Roche Committee in 1919.

'Our difficulty is this, you cannot make them all permanent and as you increase your permanent staff there is a danger of intensifying the casual nature of the balance which is left . . . the more regular you make one set of men the tendency is to make the others more casual . . . The employer naturally says "This man is on my pay sheet, he is a permanent man, I must give him employment in order that he can earn his economic wage" and very often we have found that the casual man has been in consequence dismissed or stood off before a ship has been finished or before a task has been completed in order to make room for the permanent man whose liability the employer has undertaken to carry.'[30]

On the Mersey, few inroads were made against casualism as in London. While many foremen kept unofficial preference lists, only Cunard and White Star openly used a 'constant number' system, but London contractors began to follow the PLA pattern shortly before the First World War. In 1913, Scruttons, Atlantic Transport, City

Line, New Zealand Shipping, and Shaw, Savill and Albion made a joint offer of £5 10s a month, almost the standard hourly rate for four weeks at 8d an hour, to men who accepted permanent conditions of employment. Wages were to be paid at 27s 6d a week, whether earned or not, and at the end of the month surplus earnings – if any – would be paid in addition to the last week's wages. The conditions attached to the scheme were rigorous. Men would have to agree to full mobility to work at any part of the port, on wharf, quay or ship and it was understood that they would be interchangeable between the five employers; they would have to agree to work with non-union men and 'will make no stipulation that other men shall hold a union or Federation ticket of any kind'; a reasonable amount of overtime was to be worked, if required, and the employers reserved the right to summary dismissal. More generous points included a week's paid holiday, reduction of the number of calls to one a day and thirty days notice to terminate the agreement, later reduced to one week.

The Labour movement was quick to attack this offer, led by the *Daily Herald* under the headline:

AN IDEAL AGREEMENT

MESSRS SCRUTTONS PARENTAL CARE
FOR THEIR SERFS

Souls sold for 27s 6d a week.

'The ways of fat are like unto those of the heathen Chinee, as is shown by the most recent attempt to dragoon the men made by Messrs Scruttons Ltd,' the article began. 'We have seen some agreements but this one certainly takes the biscuit. Scruttons are undoubtedly acting as a decoy to see how well it will be taken by the men and if it is generally signed it will be imposed on the men by all the contractors and the PLA. The matter is vital and we publish the document in full and call upon the NTWF and the parliamentary committee of the TUC to take immediate action. If this agreement is allowed to stand, it means that the men have sold body, mind and soul for a paltry 27s 6d a week and a holiday when it is given to them. Every man who signs binds himself to be a blackleg all the time he is in the employ of the firm.'[31]

This scheme did not make headway until the 1920s and then in a form akin to the PLA terms for permanency, but its launching, in the wake of the 1912 strike, shows the burning issues of the day, flexible deployment of men across established sectional interests and union monopoly. The mobility clauses were still relevant fifty years later when Jack Dash quoted them at mass meetings in London to point to the iniquity of employers.

The real nature of opposition to his scheme, as to the PLA's, was the division of the labour force into a regularly-employed minority and an embattled majority and this friction remained sharp. In the late 1950s, when the proportion of permanent men was being built up again at all ports, the tensions of an earlier generation spilled over. In some cases, the unions imposed an upward limit on the percentage of permanent men and, in instances where no official limit was agreed, the rank-and-file applied their own pressure, sometimes good-humoured, sometimes ugly.

An old London quip was that the most durable hair-do a woman could ask for was the 'PLA perm which never came out.' Occasionally threats were used to stop people deserting the casuals' ranks and the decision to accept permanency was not lightly taken, but usually justified on the grounds that 'if I don't take the job, someone else will.' Feelings against the permanent man lessened in later years, because it was felt his loyalty switched more from the employer to his casual colleagues. But feelings could still run high.

In 1965, when the labour department of Shaw Savill and Albion was merged with Thames Stevedoring in London, the unions successfully stopped the amalgamated company taking on permanent men, and the tactics were unsavoury – as the following letter illustrates. It was written by a permanent employee to the chairman of one of the companies involved.

'It is with the utmost regret that I send this letter to you notifying that yesterday I terminated my employment. . . . This may seem peculiar coming from a person who had indicated by previous correspondence his willingness to join the new company and therefore think that an explanation should be offered to your good self. Up to 9.30 a.m. yesterday . . . I reaffirmed my decision that I wished to serve as a weekly worker with the new company. I also informed Capt. X that despite veiled threats and mutterings against me for daring to sign, I would not be intimidated by any man living, on things that I should or should not do.

'I considered that I owed a duty to the firm that had given me a good living for the past fifteen years and I was indeed looking forward to signing the new contract. However this was not to be, because at 9.20 a.m. yesterday information was placed at my disposal that certain elements in the docks intended to attack not only the exterior of my house but also would lie in wait for my wife returning from work, if I dared to sign.

'As I have said before, sir, I am afraid of no man living, I will not be intimidated or cajoled into anything. But when underhand threats concern my family and property, I think you will agree that it calls for more serious thinking.'

The legacy of rivalry between permanent and casual worker is so bitter that it clouds the ideals which lay behind the gradualist movement. The dock companies hoped that security would help men to better their condition and that the process of selection would bring the most able people to the fore, in an employer/employee relationship akin to other industries. But this type of reform was unrealistic while it left a large margin of men frozen out of the best jobs in dockland and the Liverpool experiment was a necessary and more fruitful avenue to explore.

Liverpool could not follow London's example since it did not have large employing units and the insistence of the men to choose how and when they worked was matched by the insistence of employers to control their own affairs. Liverpool regarded itself above all as a free-enterprise city. The Docks and Harbour Board made no attempt to interfere with the employing structure inherited in 1858 and, as a matter of policy, continued to 'refrain from interference in private enterprise unless absolutely necessary to the common good.'[32] Consequently, little attention was paid to the flood of recommendations about dock affairs which began in the 1890s, because they interfered with management prerogative.

In 1893, the City Labour Conference recommended cutting back the 150 call-stands, bringing them closer geographically and linking them by telephone, so that men could move easily between them and foremen could find where labour supplies were plentiful. The attempt to eliminate 'friction' was continued by Eleanor Rathbone, who commented wryly in 1904 that everybody knew what should be done but no one was earnest enough to submerge their own interest to the good of the port as a whole. She suggested that far more men sought a living from the docks than was arithmetically necessary; once the arithmetic was worked out in detail, the conclusions made reform imperative. In January 1912, a busy month in a busy year, 27,200 attended the calls per day, but the largest number taken on was 19,861 and the average was nearer 15,000. No one was getting more than four days work a week with any regularity; 70·2 per cent of the men got between three and four days work; 12·4 per cent between two and three; 5·4 per cent between one and two; and 11·9 per cent less than one day. But it was estimated that optimum organisation of the calling system and the elimination of unnecessary overtime could have provided six days work for 56 per cent of the men and between five and six days for a further 18·2 per cent.

This analysis, published three years after Beveridge's great work on *Unemployment*, proved its point by demonstrating how closely the number seeking work approximated to the theoretical maximum demand of each employer – whose combined possible demand in 1911–12 would have been 28,514, only 1,300 more than the number of men seeking work. But this was also shown not to be simply the supply of labour chasing a theoretical demand but demand creating supply. It cost the employers nothing to keep a large pool and there were instances of foremen insisting that regular followers attend their calls, even when the prospects of work were poor and the men would have been better advised to look elsewhere. This pressure, coupled with the men's tendency to specialise in one location and one type of work, had brought a high degree of voluntary immobility to the labour force.

As a result of the analysis, the Liverpool dock scheme was introduced in 1912. It had two interdependent aims: to regulate the overall size of the labour force by compulsory registration and to create a secondary hiring system to help the distribution of labour. To be registered, a man was required to get the signature of a trade union official and employer and, if he could prove he had worked in the docks before, he would be given a metal tally which accorded him priority at the stands over non-registered men. For the NUDL and employers, registration was a major discipline and, if anything, resented most by the employers. Robert Williams, the civil servant who administered the scheme, wrote:

'They fear that any system of organisation may tend to reduce the reserve of labour below the number necessary to work the port and that therefore business may be seriously interfered with. On the other hand, the men are desperately afraid of any system which involves decasualisation in view of the fact that each man fancies he may be one of those squeezed out.'[33]

Another contentious aspect of the scheme was the joint control which the union shared with employers in determining the size of the register. The men thought it gave too much power to their union officials and Sexton was once forced to flee from a stormy union meeting by a back window. To employers it also raised spectres of union authoritarianism and the usurpation of management prerogatives. But dual control was a *sine qua non* in 1912 and in all subsequent schemes, and registration would have broken down if the union at any point chose to ignore the tally.

The registration schemes failed to cut back the margin since, initially, far too many tallies were issued. The NUDL did not want to squeeze men out and the employers asked for the register to be re-opened at the first hint of a labour shortage. Part of the trouble stemmed from the Birkenhead dockers refusing to accept registration at all; they struck and the dispute was only ended by Sexton's offer of union protection to tallyholders willing to replace the strikers and by the import of blackleg labour, some of whom stayed on in the port, with tallies. Another difficulty was the men's custom of working for only so long as gave them money to make ends meet; thus on some days 10,000 men preferred unemployment rather than try for work at the stands.

Initially 31,300 tallies were issued, 4,000 more than the number already known to constitute a greatly over-inflated labour force. In the 1920s and 1930s, the register was repeatedly pruned back – to 24,300 in 1922 and 21,500 in 1929. But the onset of the Depression and bulk-handling of commodities cut back the demand for labour even faster. Between 1913 and 1929, the volume of Liverpool's trade dropped by 14 per cent and the demand for labour by roughly 20 per cent, so the margin stayed as high as ever.

Conservatism also undermined the supplementary hiring system. The original calling system was retained but fourteen surplus stands were created where men, who had not found work at the first call, would report. These stands were linked to clearing houses, one for each of the six dock areas, and foremen short of labour could ring to the clearing house for help; in turn the clearing house would dispatch the required number of men from the surplus stands. Or so it should have worked. In practice, men often did not bother to use the surplus stands, believing it safer to stay with foremen they knew whether there was work or not; they sometimes refused to be allocated to new sectors because of a vague notion that it would mean blacklegging and foremen, assured of labour from the clearing house, might wait for it in vain. Equally, many employers ignored the surplus stands. They were reluctant to take on men they had not chosen in person and they could resort easily to their informal hiring practices – finding men in the streets to complete a job. Even in 1930, one major employer admitted candidly that he operated two calls, one for registered men and the other for non-registered.

The surplus stands were dropped during the First World War and not replaced after the Armistice, although the 1920 Insurance Act gave the clearing houses a new function, stamping cards for unemployment benefit and, then, they could be used informally for the direction of labour to undermanned ships or quays.

The failures of registration and the stands attracted more opprobrium than the experiment, as a whole, deserved. Some successes were real enough. Wages were paid from a central office on Saturday mornings, thereby ending the man's trek from contractor to contractor to pick up his earnings of the past week. Payment of insurance stamps was correspondingly simplified and a wealth of statistical information, on earnings, fluctuation and underemployment, was gathered for the first time in any British port.

The conclusion of informed opinion in the 1920s was that Liverpool could have been worse off but for the experiment and the bar on the general influx of labour to the docks. 'It has overcome the violent opposition of certain sections of the men to registration and by doing so has prepared the way for further steps towards decasualisation. It has provided a valuable experiment from which precedents have been drawn for schemes in other ports.' [34] Lawrence Holt, Lord Mayor of Liverpool in 1929, said, in like vein, that the scheme 'has indeed mitigated the degree of casualness but it has not so far changed its nature.' [35]

For all its faults, the Liverpool scheme was significant for opening a path of reform acceptable to both sides of the industry and therefore easier to follow than the London path. As the PLA discovered, its method of decasualisation could not overcome union hostility while the casual margin was unregulated and before it could work it needed Liverpool's registration and better deployment of the margin.

Liverpool's experience also showed the difficulties which reform on a wider scale was bound to face. For effective control of the register, employers and unions would have to give up a large degree of autonomy and the 1912 scheme was fatally weakened by not embracing all employers in the port. The 65 companies who joined constituted a large majority of the employing capacity in Liverpool, but a minority was allowed to undermine registration by hiring in the time-honoured way. A clear distinction needed to be drawn between employers who would be compelled to use registered labour and those who could operate outside the scheme, and herein lay the genesis of the still-explosive issue of defining dockwork.

Finally, the participation of the union in fixing the register demanded a responsible exercise of power and the assertion of official authority over the rank-and-file. The portents were not good and joint control, however attractive as an extension of the union sphere of influence, would not work if joint decisions were ignored on the shopfloor. Sexton ran foul of the 'same old gang of malcontents' who appealed to sectional interests against union leadership.[36] In London, Tillett had little confidence that his membership could be led forward united, when the successes of 1911 had nearly been squandered by 'sectional unionism, overlapping trade unionism and trade union membership, the incapacity and indifference of the so-called unskilled unions and the selfishness of the better-paid class of workmen.'[37]

Effective reform demanded the tempering of union organisation into a more stable weapon and the choice facing Tillett and Sexton in 1914 was to see permanency introduced at the sole behest of the employers or to join in the attack on the casual fringe, albeit within a casual framework. The events of the First World War, however, swung the industry irrevocably behind registration and, afterwards, the man to build on these foundations, Ernest Bevin, had emerged as a major force in the union world.

CHAPTER FOUR

The Age of Bevin

'Officers would have to overcome the resistance of the men who would claim that their liberty was being interfered with. Being interpreted, the expression mainly meant "the liberty to go home with nothing".'
Bevin to union officials, 13 September, 1920.

For the trade union movement, the First World War achieved overnight what the industrial agitation of 1911–14 had failed to secure – recognition of labour as an essential part of the body politic and representation of the unions in the counsels of the nation. It was a response in part to the labour movement's jingoistic support of the war; men like Tillett, denounced as an agitator in 1912, were to tour the trenches in support of King and Country and the shopfloor geared itself, with little complaint, to the rigours of war production.

In the docks, it was also a response to necessity. With the labour force depleted by volunteers to the colours, it was clear in the early months of the war that the casual system could not cope with the emergency. Dockers were soon exempted from military service, then supplemented by 15,000 troops in the Transport Battalions and the flow of goods was supervised by national and local Port and Transit Committees. Initially, the unions were excluded from Committee representation but, in 1916, Gosling was appointed to the national body and the National Transport Workers' Federation was granted local representation, because of the complexity of using military alongside civilian labour, the handling of ships diverted from blockaded ports of the Continent and, at the height of the submarine menace, the wholesale diversion of imports away from English channel ports.

In some ports, registration schemes were started jointly with the unions and attempts were made to extend them after the Armistice, to cope with the anticipated influx of demobilised labour. It marked the start of a new era. No longer were the unions to battle for recognition, nor were the employers to claim the right of sole determination of hiring practices and working conditions. The attack on casualism was to become the product of what unions and employers agreed together, under the watchful eye of the Government.

During Reconstruction, the unions had to decide how to exploit their partnership in the affairs of state. To union leaders brought up in the belief that industrial action alone could achieve political results, it was difficult to adjust to the potential of extended collective bargaining. But it came quite easily to the dock unions because they were in no position to dictate terms on the industrial front.

Membership had declined between 1911 and 1914 and relations between the waterfront unions were strained, especially in London where stevedores and dockers were competing openly for jobs at Tilbury. Moreover, there was no national organisation with which to confront the employers on equal terms. The obvious solution was amalgamation of the unions, but to what purpose? Tillett regarded amalgamation as the means of winning larger strikes but, to Bevin and the younger generation, it meant the chance to win victories as much at the negotiating table as on the shopfloor.

Bevin's service on the Bristol Port and Transit Committee had converted him from his flirtation with the Social Democratic Federation to a belief in the possibilities of co-operation. His chance came with the dockers' wage claim of 1919, which had been drawn up by the Federation as an instrument to unite labour in every port. It was the first docks' claim to call for a national rate, in place of the myriad of occupational rates within a port and between ports. It called for 16s a day across the board – worth roughly 37 per cent on the industry's wages bill – but it was intentionally pitched high to keep pace with inflation and to rally the better-paid men behind the campaign. It also asked for a payment to 'maintain' men who were willing to work but not hired at the daily call and a standard working week of 44 hours.

Bevin was a bustling and obviously competent leader at the time but not a national figure like Tillett, Sexton or Gosling. He was national organiser – second-in-command – of Tillett's union and had a seat on the executive of the Federation. But his successful handling of the claim gave him immediate national prominence, the nickname of 'the Dockers' KC' and ensured him the eventual leadership of the TGWU. His first success lay in pursuing the claim through the new machinery of the Industrial Courts Act instead of by strikes. It was a bold decision since an enormous wave of industrial action swept the country in 1919, 1920 and 1921, with the number of work days lost averaging 40,000,000 in each of these years compared with 5,000,000 during the war; the railwaymen had embarked on a national strike in 1919 and the miners were simmering; but Bevin argued that the Federation, which made up the third wing of the Triple Alliance, would achieve, at best, fragmentary and patchy victories by a national dock strike. Rather than risk the fragile unity of the dockers he put his faith in a Court of Inquiry, set up under Lord Shaw of Dunfermline.

His faith was justified because the Shaw award conceded the claim in full and, for good measure, delivered a crushing condemnation of casualism. Bevin's advocacy was powerful indeed and his opening speech of eleven hours took two and a half days to deliver, but his tactics were determined by the need to strengthen the unity of the twenty-six unions in the Federation and to avoid conflict between the many occupational interests he represented. This accounts for his uncharacteristic approach. He could afford to be visionary, demanding maintenance and worker representation because these were new and exciting issues; equally he could indulge in malicious knockabout with the employers because all the dockers loved it. But his essentially pragmatic nature was subdued and his approach to the practical issues of registration and permanency was vague, precisely because he knew these were contentious areas among his members.

His argument hinged on the degrading effect of casualism and the need to give dignity to the docker before he could be expected to accept the roles of responsible citizen and honest worker. First he sketched in the background to the claim and the diversity of the industry; he moved on to the profits of the shipping industry (and the mood of the inquiry was caught in an interjection of Lord Shaw which tacitly acknowledged that there had been excessive war-time profiteering) and the ability of employers to pay the full demand. Then he turned to the casual system itself, which he said was retained chiefly because employers 'had at the back of their heads that economic poverty producing economic fear was their best weapon for controlling labour.' He went on: 'I do not think that civilisation built upon this is worth having. We believe in developing self-discipline as against maintaining control by economic poverty and economic fear.'[38]

Poverty had reduced dockers to a state of degradation which made inefficiency inevitable. If a man knew that by working hard he would only displace himself from work on the morrow, he was tempted to spin out the work as long as possible; if he ran along the quay with water squish-squashing out of his boots, he would not work as well as a man well-shod. In future, Bevin claimed, men would have to share control over their own lives if port transport was to improve and this meant registration, maintaining the labour force throughout the year and giving men representation on the governing bodies of the ports. 'The easiest thing to get rid of has been the human. He has not been sufficient trouble. If he had only been more audacious and more aggressive, then possibly (employers) would have found other means, but the reason why casual labour has been perpetuated is because it is the easiest way of dealing with shipping. . . . If the captains of industry who have claimed monopoly control for themselves, who have argued in effect that we are not capable of taking part in control, say that we are unable so to organise their concerns as to give us work for a decent standard of life, then I say they ought to lose their place as captains of industry in this civilisation. They stand condemned if their control of the means which have been placed into their hands either by fortune or by luck is inefficient.'

He reiterated again the need to satisfy the aspirations of working men, to give houses where they could study without having children on top of them, to give good singers, not music hall comedians. 'If you refuse this claim, then I suggest you adopt an alternative,' he concluded. 'You must go to the Prime Minister, you must go to the Minister of Education and tell him to close our schools, tell him that industry can only be run by artisan labour on a pure fodder basis, teach us nothing, let us learn nothing, because to create aspirations in our minds, to create the love of the beautiful and then at the same time to deny us the wherewithal to obtain it is a false policy and a wrong method to adopt. Better keep us in dark ignorance, never to know anything, if you are going to refuse us the wherewithal to give expression to those aspirations which have thus been created.'

A short silence greeted this rousing finale, then spontaneous applause broke out around the courtroom. The rest of the inquiry was inevitably an anti-climax. Bevin taunted Sir Alfred Booth, chairman of Cunard, about his profits and whether he could live and feed his family on the money paid to dockers; the unfortunate Prof. Bowley, called in to prove that men could live on £3 12s 6d a week, was mercilessly exposed when Bevin brought in plate after plate of the recommended diet and asked working dockers how they would react if the 'mouse's portion of cheese and the guinea pig's portion of peas' was served in their household; the court even had to adjourn after an acrimonious confrontation between Bevin and Lord Devonport – the bogeyman of the 1911 and 1912 strikes – over the issue of worker representation.

The employers replied with what, by now, are familiar arguments – the inability to pay, declining outputs and the danger of inflation. Sir Lynden Macassey, their KC, outlined differences of operation from port to port and refused to accept the union assurance that the 16s minimum would not lead to differential claims when, for instance, the current rate in Glasgow was 14s but in the PLA 11s 8d. Employers from Bristol documented a 22 per cent decline in output since 1917; from Hull, Brown Atkinsons, the ship-owners, reported a 33 per cent drop from pre-war standards; in Glasgow, men were refusing to work an electric grain-weighing machine for Thompson Lines since it would displace labour. Numerous instances were given of restrictive practices, bad time-keeping, piecework and overtime disputes.

But Macassey's main case was to allow regional settlements according to the circumstances of each port and the local cost-of-living. Standardisation of pay rates would tie the efficient port to the wage rates of the least efficient, he argued. The process would be uneconomic and uncompetitive and, for this reason, had been resisted in mining and the railways.

For all the mass of statistics produced in the twenty days' hearing, it was the emotion of Bevin's appeal which won the day. In the Court's report, the claim was conceded, with Frederick Scrutton and Sir Joseph Broodbank dissenting in a minority report, and casualism was attacked unequivocally. The danger of inflationary repercussions was discounted because of the special nature of dockwork. (Surely a foretaste of the Wilberforce award to miners in 1972.) The high rate of pay was said, in effect, to take account of the underemployment inherent in casualism. But the Court declared that still more was required to do justice to the dock labourer. The time had come for the industry to maintain its unemployed casuals. Although no guidelines were given for doing this, the case for maintenance was set out in a declaration of principle in a paragraph which was the most important to emanate from any report on dockland and which Bevin later confided to value far more than the wages victory. It was couched in language of messianic fervour. The Court said it would be shirking its responsibility if it avoided a pronouncement because a solution had to be found for casualism if peace was to be brought to the docks.

'Labour frequently or constantly underemployed is injurious to the interests of the workers, the ports and the public and it is discreditable to society. It undermines all security and is apt to undermine all self-respect on the workers' part. It is only among those who have sunk very far and whom the system itself may have demoralised that it can be accepted as a working substitute for steady and assured employment. In one sense, it is a convenience to authorities and employers, whose requirements are at the mercy of storms and tides and unforeseen casualties, to have a reservoir of unemployment which can be readily tapped as the need emerges for a labour supply. If men were merely the spare parts of an industrial machine, this callous reckoning might be appropriate. But society will not tolerate much longer the continuance of the employment of human beings on these lines.

'The system of casualisation must, if possible, be torn up by the roots. It is wrong. And the one issue is as to what practical means can be adopted to readily provide labour, while avoiding cruel and unsocial conditions.' [39]

The Court did not underestimate the difficulties of change. It realised that casualism had evolved injurious habits 'of mind and body' which would cause resistance, not least from men who prized working by the day as a sign of independence and liberty. It deplored 'ca'canny,' said to be as hurtful to the men in loss of self-respect as to the employers in loss of output; it estimated that bad time-keeping cost the ports 9,375,000 man-hours a year and that the simplest way to tackle declining output was through mechanisation and more piecework. The final recommendations corresponded almost exactly with Bevin's demands. In six points, it conceded 16s a day, recommended more registration schemes, maintenance, payment of wages by the week not daily; it called for a National Joint Council (NJC) for port transport to be established with full bargaining machinery at port level; finally, it proposed that the NJC deal with any points arising from the report which could not be ratified in direct negotiations.

(The minority report is no less interesting as a statement of contemporary employer attitudes. Scrutton and Broodbank reckoned that the 16s would add 37 per cent to the wage bill, not the 25 per cent claimed by Bevin, and believed that the settlement was bound to influence wages of ancillary grades like clerical staff, and industries where work overlapped with the docks, like the railways. Where railway porters at goods depots earned 57s to 61s for a 48-hour week, dockers currently had 64s 2d for 44 hours and the Shaw award would give 88s, increasing the differential in favour of the dockers to 60 per cent. They did not consider the NTWF had the discipline to enforce the national award without differential claims arising; nor did they think maintenance practical unless the dockers could be persuaded to accept a greater degree of mobility at work. They added a final lament; 'the award' would accelerate the loss of entrepôt trade to continental ports and drive up port charges to a degree which would be reflected in retail prices. They cited Lord Devonport's prediction that London charges, which were already 85 per cent higher than pre-war, would climb to a 140 per cent plussage. (In fact, they went up to 150 per cent!) They sought regional negotiation of wage increases and local costing maintenance schemes; once the price of maintenance was known, they suggested, it should be included in the new pay award.)

The Shaw award was immediately recognised as a charter for dockland. Even before it was published, Bevin told a union meeting at the Albert Hall that the Inquiry was not only a novel means of settling a wage dispute but a 'platform on which it has been possible to open a page of history that tells of the struggle of men and women we represent . . . to unfold the great human tragedy of men and women fighting year in and year out against the terrible economic conditions with which they have been surrounded.' When the time came for the big struggle against capital, he did not want 'a volcanic eruption of labour followed by a mere falling back into the same grooves . . . I don't want a mere blind struggle. I want it to have a very definite objective – that of achieving for those who toil the mastery of their own lives.'[40]

The collective bargaining machinery of the NJC and local committees was set up and the employers created their national association, independent of ship-owners. (Although the employers' association is an independent body, ship-owners have usually had a voice in its affairs through their participation in London negotiations and, since London was the largest port, more than half the chairmen of the employers association have been prominent ship-owners.) The monetary element of the award was sanctioned in a national agreement. But there the progress stopped, and the long-term implications of the Shaw report had become, by and large, a dead letter by the mid-1920s. The Depression quickly wiped out the financial gains; wage rates fell to 10s a day and did not reach the Shaw level again until the Second World War; registration schemes were launched in the face of apathy and occasional hostility from the men and maintenance was not achieved.

It is a record of non-achievement which hardly accords with the determination of Bevin's personality or his passionate dislike of the casual system. The fault, however, lay not in his convictions but in his approach. Bevin was trained as a union official in the Bristol docks and he knew the men's resistance to any dramatic form of change. His hope was to harry the employers into conceding maintenance and make the casual system so expensive that they would choose to discard it. This meant initially driving on with the amalgamation of the dock unions in order that registration and maintenance could be achieved rationally; but it also meant waiting for employers to take the initiative and, during a depression which kept a ready supply of cheap labour at the dock-gate, it meant waiting a long time.

Moving to amalgamation was comparatively easy, since he now had sufficient stature in the union movement to push all before him. He was not only 'the Dockers' KC' but the foremost leader of general labour, sitting on fourteen of the new NJCs in industries which had no previous bargaining machinery at national level. He had won his spurs while older men sat on the sidelines.

Within days of the Shaw award, he began wooing other unions of the Federation. In July 1914, a drafting committee had been set up to work out an amalgamation of Federation unions with those of the General Labourers National Council – they were overlapping bodies but the Council included Thorne's gasworkers and thus the nucleus of what was to become the second of the great general unions, the General and Municipal Workers – but the outbreak of war one month later had ended this initiative. In 1920, Bevin initially secured agreement in principle for an amalgamation ballot from thirteen waterside unions and then from seven in road transport. In December, the ballot went out and a massive campaign was launched on behalf of amalgamation. By March 1921, a majority was assured but three dock unions had stayed out, the Stevedores League, the Cardiff, Penarth and Barry Coal Trimmers and the Scottish dockers; it was an unhappy portent of the sectional pressures which assailed the TGWU's dock organisation in the first ten years of its life and which survives to this day.

Historically, the decision of the stevedores to stay out was the most fateful. Rivalry had built up before the war when the League had opened its books to all shipworkers but failed to establish itself on a wider basis. It had been prone to sectionalism just like Tillett's union, losing members at Tilbury and in the short-sea trades to breakaways, and now it was trying to preserve its remaining areas of privilege. But it was also becoming a focus for rank-and-file discontent against the new monolith. Bevin first fell foul of the rank-and-file during the war, when he was accused of ignoring short-term gains for the less tangible objectives of the Federation and his only opponent for the general secretaryship of the TGWU had been Tillett's London dock officer, Fred Thompson, campaigning on a slogan 'to challenge autocracy and protest against the building up of a new union around individuals instead of policy.'

Bevin's association with authoritarianism and the climb-down of the Triple Alliance in 1921 led to the first docks' revolt; his London officers resigned *en masse* for a while. The second revolt was more serious. London dockers walked out in protest at Bevin's acceptance of a wage cut (on condition that there should be a six-month moratorium on further depression of wages). Bevin stuck his chin out and the strike collapsed, but the lightermen left the TGWU together with many dockers to join the Stevedores League. By demanding no recriminations against unofficial leaders, Bevin healed the wounds for the time being. But Thompson, a Communist who thought Bevin was tinged with a streak of cowardice, remained an implacable enemy. In 1926, when Bevin was in America, he and another London official, Fred Potter, tried to organise a complete breakaway by the port membership, issuing cards under the name of the National Union of Transport and Allied Workers. But the men did not respond and, even without Bevin at the helm, the TGWU was able to hold its ranks.

The next year saw the split of the lightermen from the stevedores, thus bringing the union structure in London to the point where it remained until 1971. The NASD has survived as a substantial minority, priding itself on close contact with the rank-and-file and keeping one section to cater for old League members and the other for the TGWU dissidents of 1923. Colloquially, the NASD is known as the 'Blue' union and the TGWU as the 'White', supposedly because of the different colours of membership cards. However, the NASD issue different coloured cards each quarter to help keep a check on members in arrears with contributions.

In 1932, the TGWU suffered a final set-back with the secession of Glasgow dockers to form the Scottish Transport and General Workers' Union (STGWU). They had been the dominant branch of the Scottish Union of Dock Labourers who boycotted the ballot of 1921. However, their general secretary, Joseph Houghton, had taken the union into the TGWU five years later against violent opposition from men who resented the loss of autonomy, Bevin's known approval of registration and the TGWU rule of appointing rather than electing its officials.

Sound arguments for selection against election of officers can be made, if a union is seeking to get the best qualified person to fill a vacant post. But within union circles Bevin made no secret of his distaste for elections, which he knew could too easily be manipulated at branch level, and the Glasgow dockers believed him undemocratic.

What angered the Glasgow dockers was Bevin's obvious distrust of the ballot in union affairs. Bevin thought branch votes could be easily manipulated and he told the TGWU biennial delegate conference in 1937 that appointment was the cleanest, best and fairest method – although ballots might be preferable if human nature was more perfect. 'I am surprised when I hear of the very poor attendance of members at branches and then see the remarkable polls that come in in the returns sometimes. Let us be quite frank with one another. Trade Union ballots – and I would not say this in public – do not reach the standard of parliamentary election. Let us be quite honest about it.'

In 1930, the Glasgow dockers challenged the power of the TGWU executive to stop the annual election of the eight branch officials and won a court action. When Bevin tried to circumvent the decision with a change of rule, the branch seceded. Bevin fought bitterly against the breakaway unions at the start. He vowed the Glasgow dockers would 'eat grass', the NASD, lightermen and STGWU were not given seats on the NJC and the former two were expelled from the TUC for poaching Bevin's members. But, in 1945, the NASD and STGWU were readmitted to the NJC and the lightermen were readmitted in 1957.

But the battle with the stevedores was to re-erupt in the mid-1950s and London was to produce another abortive splinter movement in the 1960s, when Sid Senior tried to set up the National Union of

Port Workers, claiming the mantle of true democracy. The tendency towards sectional splits *within* the TGWU also remained, many centring on attempts by Tilbury or PLA members to dissassociate themselves from the overall London structure.

REGISTRATION

Had Bevin wanted to make a frontal attack on casualism, he might well have found his organisation too weak to follow him as a single body to the barricades. There was difficulty enough in getting registration schemes off the ground after the amalgamation and it was accepted that they were a necessary precursor to winning weekly maintenance guarantees and further decasualisation.

In addition to Liverpool, simple schemes were introduced at Aberdeen, Bristol, Grimsby, Hull, Leith, Newport and Swansea during the First World War. But most did not survive the return of servicemen to the labour market. Ideally, the genuine dock worker had to be protected from the influx of men with no claim to dockwork and the former docker, who had joined the ranks, should have a job to go back to. For most registration committees the problem proved insuperable. Anticipating the influx back to London, a committee under Mr Justice Roche was appointed and it called for a well-controlled registration scheme. By the time everyone with a claim to dockwork had been registered, however, 61,000 books had been issued although the average labour requirement was only 24,000 a day.

With a margin of this size, registration was pointless and the Ministry of Labour tried to impose better standards by issuing a 'model' scheme in 1919 which specified that registration be confined to men employed in the ports before the war and that no further tallies or books be issued for the time being. Round, square or triangular tallies were to be proof of registration, depending on the work the holder was entitled to perform, and they were to be withdrawn and reissued each quarter, to prevent malpractices. Where these conditions were attained, the Ministry offered to service the schemes by supplying officials, office equipment and buildings. The most far-reaching clause, however, was the suggestion that disciplinary powers should be vested in the joint registration committees, rather than the employers alone, for abuses of the scheme. This was the genesis of the joint control of discipline introduced in 1947 (see Chapter 5).[41]

As a venture in joint control, the registration committees were treated with suspicion from the start. But their failure to act as effective checks on the casual margin was caused primarily by the Depression. The total of unemployed tripled from 691,000 to 2,171,000 in the first six months of 1921 and was to fluctuate around 1,500,000 for the rest of the 1920s before rising to 2,000,000 and 3,000,000 in the 1930s. In these circumstances, the union side of the committees were reluctant ever to sanction cuts in the register which would deprive people, admittedly underemployed, of the chance to get any work at all.

There was further opposition to registration as a matter of principle from both sides of the industry. Employers saw it as interference in their legitimate business, especially when it was linked to revised hiring practices, like the central call-stands of Avonmouth and Swansea, or the central pay office in Liverpool; there was a corresponding fear that registration would give too much security to the men and outputs would drop once the fear of losing one's place in the labou force was lessened. For the men, registration meant discipline. It forced them to present themselves for work or risk losing their place on the register and to accept the authority of union officials on the registration committee.

In the Tyne and Wear ports and the Hartlepools, and in Kirkcaldy and Glasgow, opposition to the principle of registration prevented schemes being introduced for a long time. The argument in the North-East was that preference lists were a sufficient control of supply, but in Scotland, opposition was grounded in the mistaken belief that the union could control entry to the industry without joint action by the employers. Glasgow opposition to registration was apparent during the Shaw Inquiry when Houghton said the 'main objection to it is the fact that the men are afraid of losing what they call their liberty and their freedom so far as selecting their work is concerned. They are afraid that registration would mean they would have to go to the job they were wanted to go to, whereas at the present time they have the right to work or not as they like.'

In the 1920s, opposition to registration was interwoven with the fight for local autonomy and Glasgow dockers formed the Anti-Registration league in 1928 to castigate the TGWU. They declared:

'It is our opinion that, from the employers point of view, registration has long since resolved itself into a mere instrument of discipline and coercion and that from the point of view of our trade union officials, who are its insidious promoters, registration provides a solution to their vexed problem of stabilising the union amongst the Glasgow dockers and thereby providing them with the maximum security in the undisturbed enjoyment of their salaries and superannuations.'[42]

The STGWU believed naively it could enforce a closed shop and that hiring through the union ticket would give all men an equal chance of work. But their claim to control the hiring system was preposterous as the Irvine Inquiry of 1937 demonstrated. Investigation showed that, from a maximum daily requirement of 4,500, between 800 and 1,000 non-unionists were hired each day and, without fixed hiring points, the usual unofficial practices flourished with men being taken on at the side of the ship as they presented themselves.

For the most part, however, registration was accepted in principle and introduced individually at each port. After the national dock strike of 1924, fought over a wage issue and settled with the promise of a further investigation into decasualisation, a committee under Sir Donald Maclean reviewed progress to date. It concluded that there was little virtue in considering maintenance until an efficient system of registration was introduced to weed out the unnecessary surplus. Many early schemes had fallen into abeyance – at Aberdeen, Cardiff, Grimsby, Hull, King's Lynn, Leith, London and Middlesbrough – and needed reconstituting, but this could not be done by national action, as favoured by Bevin, because local variations in defining dockwork and types of control were already established.

The Maclean Committee, called in again by the Ministry of Labour in 1930–1, found that 31 major ports had schemes of which 25 were jointly controlled. In some ports, the unions had sole control of the register and distributed the work in rotation to ensure equal earnings between the men. In Grimsby, the employers had a majority on the registration committee and in Manchester the Ship Canal Company was obliged only to *consult*, not deal jointly with the TGWU. In deciding which categories of port worker should be protected by registration, most committees worked on a rule-of-thumb basis which kept port boundaries vague and respected local custom and practice. In most ports, coal-trimmers were excluded and, in some cases, shore gangs, timber porters and ship and boiler cleaners. Bevin saw registration as a means of 'drawing a ring around the port' but it was seldom tightly drawn, except in London where a full definition of dockwork was drawn up in the 1920s and the port experienced then many of the problems which were to become acute throughout the country under the National Dock Labour Scheme.

The last few steps to nation-wide registration were achieved painfully slowly in the 1930s. In 1932, schemes were brought to the Tyne and Wear; in 1933 to Falmouth and Kirkcaldy and in 1935 to the Hartlepools. By the outbreak of war, only Glasgow and Aberdeen, the strongholds of the Anti-Registration League, were holding out.

THE INSURANCE ACTS

The Maclean inquiries brought to light another factor which militated against efficient registration – the operation of the national insurance acts. Essentially, they were geared to factory conditions where a man was either employed or unemployed for weeks at a stretch, rather than to a casual industry like the docks where employment could be broken many times in a single week. Dockers were excluded from the unemployment provisions of the 1911 Act but were covered in 1920, when benefit was assessed under the complicated continuity rule. As amended in 1923, this stipulated that benefit would be paid when a man could prove three days' unemployment in each spell of six continuous working days. Thus, if there were only two days of unemployment, no benefit was paid but the third day brought entitlement to three days of benefit.

This gave rise to the widespread practice of 'getting the bulkhead in' or 'three days on the hook, three on the book'; men who had been unemployed for two days out of five would not seek work on the sixth in order to qualify for benefit yielding more money than they could earn at work. For instance, in 1930, the daily wage was 12s while the benefit for a married man with three children was 5s 4d; by stopping away from work on the third day, a man could thus pick up 16s in benefit instead of the time-rate of 12s on a week-day or only 6s on the Saturday half-day.

The system encouraged absenteeism and the men were accused of being subsidised by the state, but the system was perfectly legal under the terms of the act so long as they did not deliberately avoid work. More insidious was the injustice of the scheme which allowed some pieceworkers to earn more in three days, yet still qualify for benefit, than timeworkers might earn in a full week of work, and which encouraged the men to resist regulation if it interfered with manipulation of the insurance acts. Registration schemes gave the Ministry access to good statistics and surveillance of the call, since employment offices were often built near the stands. Without registration, it was much harder to keep records and stop the more flagrant abuses, such as the following which developed in Glasgow: men could pretend they had lost their insurance books and hiring foremen would then give them emergency issues, in which the period of employment would be recorded; frequently men would give a fictitious name for the emergency issue so that no true record was kept of his employment and he could present his original blank book when applying for benefit. An investigation of emergency books issued in 1937 showed that 3,100 out of 3,600 were made out to fictitious names!

Beyond encouraging registration, the employers could only suggest that the shortcomings of the insurance acts could be put right by relating benefit to the industry's contributions. But this sound actuarial basis contained its own difficulties since the employers would be moving towards maintenance if contributions were increased and it was obviously inhuman to cut benefit; yet between 1921 and 1929 the industry paid in £6,000,000 and drew £22,000,000 in benefit. In 1929–30, this deficit was increasing. While the deficit for all industries was 150 per cent (£30,000,000 paid and £44,000,000 drawn), in the docks it was about 500 per cent and in Liverpool, where contributions totalled £45,000 and benefit £352,898, it was almost 800 per cent.

MAINTENANCE

The inadequacies of the insurance scheme lent added beauty to Bevin's plan for maintenance which would shift the burden of casualism from the nation to the industry itself. His idea, as expounded to the Roche Committee, was to use a levy on all goods passing through the ports to set up a fund for paying unemployed dockers unable to get work, thus bringing their wages up to a weekly minimum. Primarily, each port would pay for its casual margin but part of the levy would go to a national fund to help ports dependent on highly seasonal trades or for emergency use, when unemployment might be exceptionally high because of a commodity failure somewhere in the world. Another reason for putting the scheme on a national footing was to ensure that all men were treated equally and that one port was not given a competitive edge because rivals took better care of their margin.

This plan was adopted by the NTWF in 1918 but was turned down by employers waiting to know the terms of the forthcoming insurance bill. After the Shaw award, Bevin worked out further details and disclosed them to London dock officers on 13 September 1920. He wanted the maintenance guarantee to be £4 a week – 91 per cent of the time rate for 44 hours – and estimated that it would cost £2,600,000 if the margin could be reduced to 10 per cent ('and if we and the employers cannot run within 10 per cent we can be ashamed of our organising ability').[43] A levy of 4d per ton would yield an estimated £3,000,000 and cover the cost of maintenance and administration.

Discussion of maintenance was shelved at the first meeting of the NJC and Bevin did not press it again until 1924 when decasualisation was included in the natural wage demand and Ben Smith, a union MP, put a private member's bill before the Commons designed to empower the Minister of Labour to approve and enforce registration and maintenance. The bill was dropped after the Maclean Committee was set up and the next union thrust came in 1930, when it was clear that the reform movement had ground to a halt over the intractable difficulties of stabilising the registers.

Three issues were notable in the new proposals. First, they sought to give statutory responsibility to the NJC to enforce maintenance. Secondly, they recognised the employers' case for cutting down the registers by suggesting the severance of all men aged 65 or over from the industry, with a pension of 25s a week, and by allowing more union control to enforce mobility of labour. Thirdly, a guarantee of only 50s a week was demanded, representing 79 per cent of the current time rate compared with 91 per cent in the days of Shaw.

The TGWU argued this case before Maclean in 1930–1 and argued further that the wages of permanent men were financed out of the income of the port, whether they worked or not, and thus the maintenance of casual men should be similarly financed. 'We should strongly object if a proposal so eminently suited to solve the port labour problem, which has baffled sociologists ever since the inception of the port industry, were put on one side on the ground that it was likely to call forth similar proposals on behalf of the casual worker.'[44]

In this plan, the seeds of the Dock Labour Scheme which Bevin was to impose on the industry during the Second World War, and subsequently to be embodied in statute in 1946-7, are to be found. But a fifth and final attempt to get voluntary acceptance of maintenance was to be made between 1937 and 1939, in which both sides made compromises and which thus came closest to success.

With Basil Sanderson (later Lord Sanderson) as chairman of the national port employers, the new initiative took Bevin by surprise. The union was about to launch a national pay claim for an extra 2s a day when Sanderson went round to Transport House to tell Bevin that the employers at last were amenable to maintenance, if the cost was met out of money which Bevin wanted for the wage demand. According to Sanderson, Bevin was cruelly moved by the dilemma. 'For the first and only time in my life I saw him really distressed and his eyes filled with tears. I remember the scene as if it were yesterday. He got up and walked around the room in silence for a little time while he regained control and then told me he felt heart-broken. That for almost twenty years "work or maintenance" (he still called it that) for the docker had been the summit of his hopes and ambitions and now that it was within his grasp he had to refuse it. That he had pledged himself to his union to secure the increased wage for which he now had asked and that he could not go back on his word.'[45]

Eventually a compromise was reached with the employers conceding half Bevin's demand and the NJC pledging to 'give effect to a scheme for the greatest possible measure of decasualisation of labour in the ports.' The employers assumed that the 1s they had saved on the wage demand would help finance maintenance and that the Government might chip in with a further £1,250,000, which was the excess over contributions which the industry took out of the unemployment insurance fund.

For the unions, the price of agreement at NJC level meant sacrificing the principle of covering the labour force with a uniform system of maintenance. Instead, the level of maintenance and the numbers covered were to be determined locally and the NJC confined itself to recommending two schemes, one covering all men with a single guaranteed rate and the other envisaging sliding rates of maintenance, with the possible total exclusion of some dockers in seasonal trades. In return, the unions agreed to prune the registers, retire the aged and infirm on pensions, and centralise hiring through labour bureaux, on the lines of the Liverpool clearing houses of 1912.

The level of suggested benefit was admittedly high. The NJC envisaged a minimum payment of four, four and a half or five days pay per week, organised on a monthly make-up. Each port would choose its level, depending on how well the register corresponded to the extent of actual employment, and the minimum guarantee would be paid for the first three weeks of the month and made up to full earnings in the fourth, with the addition of extra payment for longer hours of work, overtime and piecework.[46]

With difficulty, the union leaders could agree to trim the registers and the men could give up their access to unemployment benefit. But they could not agree to the exclusion of some men from maintenance and they also jibbed at the disciplinary clause which made payment of the guarantee discretionary on proper attendance for work at the call throughout the week. Had the passage of time brought concensus on these points, the consequences of such a potentially diverse and decentralised scheme are horrible to imagine; but the proposals ultimately failed on the question of finance. The Government refused either to adjust the insurance act to allow contributions to be channelled into guarantee payments – and it must be remembered that the guarantee would constitute income, so debarring men from state benefit – or to make a direct payment from the unemployment insurance fund towards the scheme. It pointed out that such changes would need statutory approval. But the real stumbling block was the amount of subsidy. The Ministry of Labour began costings in nine ports but the results from Liverpool and Middlesbrough alone showed that the cost would be far higher than the NJC's estimate of £1,250,000.

Failure was finally recognised shortly after the outbreak of war, when the NJC agreed to the payment of the second half of the 1937 wage claim and, in doing so, neatly circumvented war-time restrictions on wage increases.

For the docker, the Second World War like the First was the agent for vital change. Bevin became Minister of Labour and within eighteen months made registration compulsory and established maintenance for all dockers under the tri-partite control of Government, unions and employers. Embodied in post-war statutes, these arrangements fulfilled virtually all the ambitions voiced before Lord Shaw and by the time of Bevin's death in 1951 'work or maintenance' – the cry of the 1889 strike – had been achieved and, in a strictly technical sense, the docks were decasualised.

The change is so dramatic that the historian tends to dismiss the 1920s and 1930s as decades of much concern but little achievement, a period of marking time when the unions were too easily diverted from the attack on casualism by the easier target of conventional wage claims. But the transition from unfettered casualism to a degree of organisation, sufficient to identify and maintain the labour force, could not be achieved at a stroke. Unlike a wages claim, casualism could not be attacked by industrial action because the system was too deeply-rooted in behaviour and responses for any one part of the system to become a focus for discontent, and because a viable alternative had to be presented before the employers were prepared to move.

This was at the heart of the reformers' problem. Casualism had to be defined and, between the wars, the area for definition was set out port by port by area and occupation. Of course, the process of definition took an unconscionably long time but the pace of national progress was governed by the most dilatory port.

Ideally, Bevin could have used the authority of his union to get schemes accepted at progressive ports and force the recalcitrants into line. But the size of the TGWU belied its essential weakness in the docks. These were years of retrenchment for the union movement as a whole and the TGWU which had membership of 376,251 in 1925 saw the figure drop to 315,000 in 1928 and, after climbing back to the pre-General Strike figure, suffered further losses in the early 1930s; nor did it reach the financial security of having £1 per member in its accumulated balance until 1932. This was not a strong position from which to counter-attack and the fact that TGWU organisation survived, especially in the docks where sectionalism was most pronounced, was due in part to the tempering of policies to the line of least resistance.

The Depression also militated against reform, as the decline in trade outstripped all efforts to cut back the registers. The busiest inter-war year was 1929 when roughly 70,000,000 tons passed through the ports; by 1932 the volume was down to 52,000,000 tons and unemployment among dock labourers stayed consistently between 30 and 40 per cent in spite of sincere attempts to prune the labour force. (By 1931, registers were cut back from the 1925 figures by 17·8 per cent in

Bristol, 33·8 per cent in Cardiff, 12·9 per cent in Grimsby, 34·2 per cent in Hull, 36·2 per cent in London, 13·2 per cent in Liverpool, 14 per cent in Newport, 10·1 per cent in Southampton, 16 per cent in Swansea and 7·1 per cent on the Tees.) In the mid-1930s, trade hovered between 60,000,000 and 65,000,000 tons and only once, in 1937 when the employers launched their bid for maintenance, did it exceed the 1929 figure.

Commentators of the period, who castigated the employers for letting the burden of maintaining their casual fringe fall on the state, overlooked the difficulties caused by depressed trade and the high level of unemployment. In the 1930s, employers on the whole were prepared to offer more security to a limited number of men and the unions stood in the way. Even so, registration was not a failure, however hesitant and ill-operated. It set out the parameters in which the future dock labour scheme could operate and committed the industry to the definitions of casualism which were conceived in the First World War and came to fruition in the Second.

The other important development of this period was the growing intervention of the Government in dock affairs. Originally, the Government confined itself to ordering inquiries and letting industry draw its own conclusions from the reports. The Board of Trade started to keep records of strikes and lock-outs in 1888 and the immediate advent of New Unionism encouraged the Government towards intervention during disputes, as a mediator rather than enforcer of law and order. But Lloyd George burnt his fingers badly in the 1912 dock strike and concluded that direct ministerial intervention usually would be harmful to government prestige. The first Insurance Act and the creation of labour exchanges, however, brought the Board of Trade (and then the Ministry of Labour) directly into dock affairs. The Board backed the Liverpool experiment and the Ministry helped to run clearing houses under approved registration schemes, a power which was extended to paying maintenance under the 1934 Insurance Act. The most important step, however, was the reconstituting of the Maclean Committee as a permanent departmental committee of the Ministry in 1930, to report on registration and the operation of unemployment benefit. Recurring evidence of the industry's failures pointed inescapably to more government involvement. With the failure of the 1937–9 initiative – not least because of the Government's refusal to finance a scheme the employers approved of – the industry looked increasingly towards statutory control rather than the fumblings of its own institutions for effective reform. At the outbreak of war, the mood closely paralleled that of the industry when the Wilson Government planned to nationalise the ports: both sides recognised that something had to be done and however distasteful government action might seem, it was better than nothing.

CHAPTER FIVE

The National Dock Labour Scheme

'The scheme must now be regarded as part of the structure of the industry. It is no use threatening to destroy common property. Threats of this sort act as an irritant and disturb the minds of moderate men without deterring the extreme.' Lord Devlin, 1956.

When Bevin joined Churchill's government as Minister of Labour and National Service, the conditions preventing reform had been swept aside. Three-quarters of the population were engaged in the war effort. Bevin's greatest fear was that labour shortages in the docks and other key industries might reach chaotic proportions and there were rumours of companies hiring agents to poach men from one job to another. For the first time in twenty years, unemployment disappeared from the docks and the dockers' wages soon rose above the national average, thanks to the high basic rates, the spread of piecework to the Northern ports and long hours of work.

In order to mobilise the nation's resources, Bevin had no choice but to provide a permanent dock labour force; decasualisation was no longer a matter of humanitarian concern but of national necessity. The first issue was whether to demand a voluntary scheme from the industry or to impose measures under the Emergency Powers (Defence) Act. The advantage of compulsion was speed, but it carried the danger of undermining the institutions of the industry and giving rise to a rank-and-file movement against new measures, as happened in the munitions industry during the First World War. However, dock problems were now so large, with the need to transfer labour and perhaps to use troops again, that the issue was never long in doubt. Bevin decided within two months of taking office to browbeat and be blessed; but he also maintained the facade of voluntarism by seeking the prior consent of the industry to all compulsory measures. His first step was to make registration for dockers compulsory and require them to accept transfer between ports (June 1940). Dockers were, in fact, one of the first groups to be covered by a registration order, together with professional engineers, scientists, men in the principal engineering industries, chemists, physicists and quantity surveyors. But the dockers' order was unique in also requiring the employers to register; before the war, it had been open to employers to operate outside registration schemes, now they had to be licenced or disbarred from hiring and the definition of dockwork could be correspondingly tightened.

In the later months of 1940, two schemes took shape for the employment and maintenance of a regular labour force. The Ministry of War Transport produced the first for the North-Western ports[47] and then the Clyde where the Atlantic convoys were handled; this gave the men a guaranteed weekly wage of £4 2s 6d – the existing time rate – or 7s a turn; but any overtime or weekend work was offset against this guaranteed wage. Under the Ministry of Labour scheme, introduced under the Essential Work (Dock Labour) Order of September 1941, the guarantee was fixed at 5s and then 6s a turn so long as men reported for work, but without any further guarantee for the week or offsetting of attendance money from extra earnings.

The main difference between the two schemes was the form of control. In the Clyde and Mersey, authority was vested in a regional port director who was required only to 'consult' about the allocation of labour; in the remaining ports, dual control was introduced through a national corporation and local boards, on which employers and unions were equally represented.

Bevin's scheme had its drawbacks. The old port registration committees were not compelled to carry out the recommendations of the new boards; there were some thirty strikes in each of the war years, in spite of Order 1305 which made strikes and lock-outs illegal pending binding arbitration through the Ministry of Labour; and absenteeism grew as the war progressed, reaching 30 per cent on occasions in Liverpool and 13·5 per cent at the beginning of 1945 in London. (It was to counter absenteeism and the men's tendency to walk off jobs they did not like that the famous Continuity Rule was introduced in London in 1944, at the employers' request.) But the merits of dual control were also self-evident. The labour force had been successfully managed and the unions' had given their co-operation, not least by putting their rule-books in cold-storage for the duration of the war. Restrictive practices were eliminated at a stroke and the fertility of

British shipping – a Churchill phrase! – was improved to the extent that Bevin estimated one and a half days were cut from the average length of turn-round.

It was obvious that the industry would not return to the haphazard pre-war system of employment. In Parliament, Bevin had promised to end casualism[48] and the NJC began in 1944 to see how the wartime schemes should be continued on the expiry of the Emergency Powers. The employers were willing to continue the 'maintenance' payments but, to counter the disincentive effect, they insisted on regaining sole control of port schemes, while the unions would not give up the footholds they had won in administering the registers.

The difference had not been resolved at the beginning of 1946 and a special Act had to be passed (The Dock Workers (Regulation of Employment) Act) to extend the war measures until July 1947. At the same time the Government gave the NJC until October 1946 to produce a voluntary agreement, otherwise a statutory scheme would be imposed on the industry. Under a Labour Government, in which Bevin's voice was still dominant albeit from the Foreign Office, the threat of a government scheme did not frighten the unions and they duly resisted the further proposals of NAPE. A deadlock was reported in July 1946 to George Isaacs, the Minister of Labour, and he set up an inquiry under Sir John Forster (Lord Forster of Harraby) to examine the opposing positions. The Inquiry findings strongly advocated the continuation of joint control and were put to the NJC as a basis for settlement, but still the employers would not agree. So a government draft scheme was published in October which differed little from the war measures of Bevin. Two more inquiries followed, to examine objections to the draft under Sir John Cameron (Lord Cameron) and to fix the level of attendance money and weekly guarantee under Sir Hector Hetherington. Finally the Dock Workers (Regulation of Employment) Order was issued in June 1947 and ratified through voluntary machinery, two weeks before the expiry of the emergency powers. At the end of the month, the National Dock Labour Scheme thus came into being.

The 1947 Scheme must be examined with care since it remains little changed but to accommodate the conditions of permanent employment in 1967, as the framework within which the industry moved from chronic underemployment, through two decades of comparatively full employment to the upheavals of the container revolution.

Above all, it was used by the Devlin Committee for the modernisation programme, in spite of growing complaints that its ancestry meant it was unfitted for modern conditions.

The most important consideration of the Government, in drafting the Scheme, was to build on the existing institutions of the industry. There was no desire to supplant the voluntary bargaining agencies or the custom and practice of individual ports and it was recognised that success depended largely on both sides of the industry identifying with the Scheme and reaching agreement within its confines. There was an obvious danger that the weak institutional structure would atrophy further if authority was passed too much into the hands of the State. Just as Bevin had sought the co-operation of the TUC and industry before using his emergency powers to direct labour and stop strikes during the war, so the Scheme was built on a basis of consent, underpinned by Statutory authority and, although the new bodies were staffed by civil servants, decision-making was left in the hands of the unions and employers. This is the reason why the Government ignored the opportunity in 1946–7 of radically altering the process of decision-making or rationalising the host of conflicting local practices into a common national framework; as the Dock Labour Scheme grew to be more and more part of the furniture of dockland, the opportunity to legislate with a clean slate, as in 1947, was never to recur and the Scheme was notable chiefly for formalising local practice and autonomy rather than forcing through radical change.

This defect is apparent in the preamble stating the aims of the Scheme. It was kept loose and perfunctory with one important ambiguity – concerning the obligation to work overtime – which cost the industry dearly in later strikes. The preamble states the Scheme is designed to ensure greater regularity of employment, and an adequate supply of labour, to facilitate the rapid turn-round of ships and the speedy transit of goods through the ports. The scope of the Scheme is defined as covering only registered dockers in, or in the vicinity of, a port whose work is connected with the loading, unloading, movement or storage of cargoes, or with the preparation of ships or other vessels for the receipt or discharge of cargoes, or for leaving port. The obligations of registered men are simply to 'carry out his duties in accordance with the rules of the port or place where he is working; and work for such periods as are reasonable in his particular place.' [49]

Supreme control was vested in the National Dock Labour Board

(NDLB), consisting of a chairman and vice-chairman appointed by the Ministry of Labour and eight to ten other members, holding office for two-year spells. Of the ordinary members, four must represent the workers' side of the industry and four the employers', leaving the Minister the option of appointing two more independents, but this right has never been exercised. The functions of the NDLB are to govern the use of labour by control of recruitment and discharge from the port registers, of training and welfare and provision of amenities; these duties to be financed by a levy of up to 25 per cent of the wages bill paid to the men.

In practice, control of the register has entailed a twice-yearly review of the sanctioned strength of the dock labour force, with attempts to forecast the level of trade and the demand for labour at each port. The time-lag between authorising change and implementation at the ports, and the imponderable relation of trade fluctuation to labour demand, made accurate forecasting unusual, but the Scheme does allow non-registered men to be used in emergency and for severe seasonal fluctuations to be met with temporary registers, as in Southampton, where 200 to 300 men were taken on customarily to cope with summer passenger traffic.

The NDLB is also empowered to cut the port registers, but the Scheme does not specify how this unpopular step should be done nor does it provide sanctions, should such an order be disregarded at local level; not surprisingly, early attempts to remove aged and infirm men from the register were strongly resisted and the NDLB found it unrealistic to exercise this power. Prior to Decasualisation, a further function was to pay men's wages, national insurance contributions and holiday pay, for all of which employers would be billed in some form or other. This was always done at port level and employers can still avail themselves of the clearing house function; latterly the Board has undertaken to administer the national severance and pension schemes and it still collects statistical data on the industry.

Each port, or group of ports, has its own local Dock Labour Board, which must consist of an equal number of representatives from each side of the industry and must appoint a chairman from their ranks. The rights of the chairman are not specified, but, to maintain the principle of joint control, he is seldom allowed a casting vote (although Southampton is an exception) and no independent members can be appointed. The local board is the administrative arm of the NDLB, enforcing decisions passed down from national level. For instance, if the national review sanctions an increase in one port's register of tally clerks, the local board would decide how they were to be recruited – from men waiting to be reinstated to the industry, from fresh outside labour or from other sections of the register – and how nominations should be split between unions and employers. By the same token, in the unlikely event of a cutback, the local board would decide which men to dismiss, whether the least fit, the last to be recruited or whether to achieve the reduction by natural wastage.

Local boards were also obliged to operate a secondary hiring system, akin to the surplus stands of the 1912 Liverpool experiment, and to deal with discipline. In legal terms, all dockers were employees of the Board, up to 1967, until the moment they were hired by a company operating in the port. This distinction between the contractual and operating employer was largely abolished after full permanency but local boards are still responsible for men temporarily unattached to a regular employer – about 500 in 1970, but trebling in 1972. Under casual conditions, men who were not hired at the free call were obliged to report to the Board's 'pen' to find out if they were needed elsewhere in the port or else to get their card stamped, as entitlement to attendance money for the half-day. Under the 1947 transfer clause, men were also obliged to accept any suitable work in the port, or at another port, provided it was within daily travelling distance of home. The Board's power to allocate applies now only to the temporarily unattached.

Disciplinary powers were vested in the local boards and were subject to joint control. The 1947 procedure was for an employer to lodge a written complaint with the Board, which would acquit or mete out punishment. An offender then had three clear days to lodge an appeal, which would be heard by a tribunal of three to five people, none of whom could be members of the local board. Punishments ranged from dismissal from the register to suspensions for up to five working days. The appeal tribunal could only lessen and not increase the original penalty.

For an employer accused of offences under the Scheme – such as the employment of unregistered labour or making falsified returns to the Board – judgment would be passed by the Board and appeal against removal from the register was direct to the Minister of Labour.

In 1967, the disciplinary procedure was altered to give employers the first initiative. Instead of the board instituting proceedings, the employer was allowed to suspend for up to five days unilaterally but the alleged offender had a further five days in which to appeal. The appeal would be heard by the full Board, with a further appeal procedure to a smaller tribunal.

Finally, the Scheme underwrote the agreements of the NJC and local rules relating to pay and conditions. With the weekly guarantee and attendance money established by industrial agreement, these came automatically under the suzerainty of the Scheme, which listed conditions when they could be forfeit.

Each component of the Scheme embodied ideas which had been outlined before Mr Justice Roche, Lord Shaw and the Maclean Committee – compulsory registration, maintenance, national supervision and, through joint control, Bevin's concept of the worker taking his place at the helm of the industry he worked in.

But even if the inspiration derived from the past, the Scheme's aspirations were progressive. The Scheme was to be the instrument for governing the transition from casualism to permanent employment and the identification of the unions with decision-making was expected to bring industrial peace as well as greater efficiency in the ports.

Arthur Deakin, Bevin's successor as general secretary of the TGWU, voiced the mood of the times when he hailed it as a form of workers' control and a brave experiment. Indeed, the concept of industrial democracy lent to the 1940s something of the fervour of reconstruction in 1919 and the Labour Government's commitment to nationalise the basic means of production and essential services was an opportunity to secure representation for the worker in the management of industry, from which it was blithely assumed that harmony would follow.

When actually faced with the problem of making representation meaningful, the Government was to flinch from conceding more than nominal involvement. But the docks were different. Historical accident already provided a large area of joint control and the Dock Labour Scheme was the only radical attempt to institutionalise a high degree of genuine participation.

Even today, the power given to the unions in jointly regulating recruitment, dismissal and discipline is unique in having its sanction by statute and it approaches the initial stages of industrial democracy advocated by the extreme Left.

For instance, the Institute of Workers' Control's outline of the methods to be used in eroding managerial prerogatives is uncannily similar to what the dockers won in 1947. The Institute said:

'Workers' control signifies a struggle by workers and their organisations to encroach upon the prerogative of management and to cut back managerial authority in the enterprise and the powers of capital in the economy. It begins with the simple trade union demands for control of hiring and firing, tea-breaks, hours, speed of work, allocation of jobs and so on. It mounts through a whole series of demands (open the books for example) to a point where, ultimately over the whole of society, capitalist authority meets impasse.'[50]

In practical terms, the Scheme required the docks' industry to progress without one side or other imposing its will unilaterally. Management objectives of maximising profits or securing the best return on capital could not be set above labour's interest in protecting jobs, enhancing earnings or reducing the physical effort of job content. Divergent interests had to be recognised and progress made by common consent.

This obligation to find a unitary framework for decision-making in vital areas separates the docks from industries where common interest is defined in bargains which hold good only while mutually acceptable and can be revoked at the behest of either party.

To the labour movement, therefore, the docks still represent an important bridgehead towards industrial democracy and, when the Wilson administration was preparing to nationalise the ports, the extension of worker representation was just as important an issue to the TGWU as the failure of the 1969 Ports Bill to bring the smaller ports within the ambit of government control.

The Labour Party Study Group, which was set up in 1966 under Ian Mikardo, saw nationalisation as a golden opportunity to incorporate further representation in the industry.

'Without a substantial element of workers' participation, no scheme (for nationalisation) can hope to succeed. This industry is one in which the chance of extending the practices of industrial democracy is better than in most others, precisely because of the tradition and experience of twenty years of joint operation of the register and of discipline under the Dock Labour Scheme.'[51]

It proposed minority representation for dockers on national and regional port authorities and equal or majority representation in policy-making at the lower level of group operating committees. When the Bill failed to live up to these recommendations, a one-day dock strike was organised in March 1970 and, next month, Fred Mulley, the Minister of Transport, and Peter Parker, the chairman designate of the National Ports Authority, became the first outsiders to attend the unions' national delegate conference – the senior policy body for dockers – when they tried to reassure the men that the degree of joint control which existed under the Scheme would not be diminished after nationalisation, and might be increased if the National Ports Authority so chose. Mulley pledged that there would be dockers on port boards; if appointed full-time, they would of necessity sever their links as working men, but part-timers could remain rank-and-file dockers.

Had the Bill become law, there was a chance that the unions would have been able to negotiate a greater degree of representation for the ports than any other nationalised industry – a fitting legacy to the ideals of the Scheme.

When the first major review of the Scheme's functioning was undertaken in 1955–6, much was found on the credit side. An administrative machine of nearly 1,000 people was functioning smoothly and much progress had been made in uncontroversial matters like welfare. Moreover, little direct connexion was found between the operation of the Scheme and industrial unrest and an estimate of 13 per cent of days lost was attributed directly to dissatisfaction with the decisions of the National or local boards.

However, in its 25-year life, the Scheme has obviously not lived up to the high expectations with which it was launched. From the earliest days dockers showed an increasing propensity to strike. During the later days of the war, there had been major stoppages in London, Liverpool, Manchester and Newcastle which reflected exasperation at the onerous hours which dockers were expected to work. At the end of 1945, there was a six-week unofficial stoppage by 50,000 men in Liverpool, Manchester, Hull and London in protest against a wage award.

But from 1948 onwards, under Scheme conditions, there were major stoppages in most years. The zinc-oxide strike, which started in London and was supported in Liverpool, accounted for 200,000 man-days lost. The Canadian Seamen's strike, in London, Liverpool, Bristol and Newport, cost 400,000 man-days. The expulsions strike in London cost 103,000 and the unofficial wages protest of 1951 in London, Liverpool, Manchester and Glasgow cost 230,000.

There was comparative peace up to 1954, but then the inter-union rivalry between the NASD and TGWU caused a further series of disputes. The Blue union's insistence that the Scheme carried no obligation to work overtime led to a mammoth strike in London, with 530,000 days lost and sympathetic action in Southampton, Hull, Manchester and Liverpool cost 195,000 more. A straightforward recognition dispute for six weeks in 1955 cost 673,000 days lost. Thereafter, until the modernisation programme, the incidence of strikes remained high, but not as bad as during the first decade of Scheme operation.

In large measure because of the strike record in the docks, the Scheme has found no direct successors in other industries and, in one instance when the National Union of Seamen had the choice of pressing for joint control of administration of the Merchant Seamen Establishment Scheme (which set up guaranteed payment for 'established' seamen for time spent ashore between voyages) the union's negotiator, Charlie Jarman, declined to copy the docks' example. At the same time, however, private industry has gone a long way towards matching the provisions of the Scheme, in the development of joint disciplinary and dismissal procedures; this leaves the Scheme as a unique method of determination, but it has not kept its place as a front-runner with regard to the subjects determined.

Other undeniable shortcomings of the Scheme were, in casual days, the failure to maintain the level of guarantee as the equivalent proportion of basic rates (84 per cent) or of overall earnings, as in 1947; and, still relevant today, the failure to command the interest or respect of the rank-and-file in everyday activities, thus allowing board decisions occasionally to be flagrantly ignored.

The partial atrophying of the Scheme is important to our story, but a far more relevant factor is the remarkable odium which the Scheme has attracted and which, quite simply, is not warranted when judged by the known difficulties of harnessing rank-and-file energies to systematic organisation or of reconciling secure and stable employment with the inevitable fluctuating workloads of the industry.

To many employers, the Scheme has been seen as the root cause of dockland's labour troubles and they have pressed again and again for its abolition. Their criticisms followed distinct patterns and they can be summarised as follows:

1. That disciplinary procedures were inadequate.
2. That the association of union officials with management functions weakened their position with the rank-and-file.
3. That local boards were an artificial barrier to the emergence of a direct relationship between employer and employed.
4. That the size of the register was improperly controlled.

Before examining these criticisms, together with the Scheme's success in creating a climate in which casualism could disappear, the effect of the employers' recurring attacks must be considered, since their contempt for the institution, which the men came to regard as part of the furniture of dockland, made it much harder to operate the Scheme successfully.

THE BATTLE AGAINST JOINT CONTROL

The reluctance of employers to make joint control work stems from their fight in 1945–7 to exclude the unions from the basic areas of managerial prerogative. NAPE's plan in 1945 was to make individual port authorities the holding employer of dock labour, which would then be hired on the normal half-daily basis to operating employers. The authorities would pay the weekly guarantee, either from a levy on wages or from an extra tonnage charge. It was a logical plan, since port authorities already were accountable to Parliament and they could add the administration of labour to their other functions; also, NAPE believed that since employers were financing the guarantee (on top of paying insurance stamps), they should determine how their money was spent and not be burdened with a form of joint administration borne by no other industry.

The Forster Inquiry killed this bid. It accepted that Bevin's war measures had been only a qualified success but thought this derived from the failure to make the old registration committees answerable to the new boards. By amalgamating their functions, Forster hoped to unify the chain of command from national to local level. He was quite emphatic that the boards should be jointly controlled because of the historical precedent of registration committees and the impossibility of the employers administering the scheme without the co-operation of the unions. John Donovan, the TGWU national docks secretary, had told the employers: 'We will take our responsibility equally with you and we will fight our men if they are not playing the game, but if you try to put trade union officers . . . in an advisory position by your consent and goodwill and you take decisions which hurt our people and we have to stand the rap for that, we are not prepared to do it.'[52] Forster fully accepted that decisions about the register would court unpopularity and stood a better chance of being accepted if the unions were involved.

NAPE got a further opportunity to press its case in 1950, when Sir Frederick Leggett led an inquiry into the spate of unofficial strikes in London. His report concluded that the Scheme was in large measure responsible for unrest. Its benefits were disguised because of full employment and its obligations irritated men who hankered after their pre-war freedom to pick and choose a job. Concerning discipline, two problems were identified. The first was the employers' attempt to enforce mass discipline during unofficial strikes; this power resides in the Scheme but common sense dictated that it should be used no more frequently than in other industries. The second was the disciplinary procedure itself, which was slow and cold-blooded, with its written forms and tribunal hearings which resembled police courts. Finally, the report highlighted the plight of the union representatives on the Board, whose fundamental role was to defend their members, but who were sometimes cast in an obviously managerial role.

The conclusion was that 'because of the restrictions and limitations on freedom which it entails, the scheme presents itself in some ways as a worsening rather than an improvement in the way of life of some men'[53] and the suggested remedy was to remove discipline from the boards to local joint industrial committees, where the union official need not be cast in the ambiguous role of having to repudiate a decision he was party to as member of a board.

This report, together with the earlier Ammon report (which removed the interpretation of industrial agreements from local boards to industrial committees), made a powerful springboard for the next NAPE attack. Employers construed the Leggett analysis of the difficulties of joint control as justification of its abolition and, in 1951, asked Alf Robens (Lord Robens), then Minister of Labour, to implement the recommended changes. But the general election pushed the dock problems into the background and nothing happened until 1955 when the new Minister, Sir Walter Monckton, was asked to establish sole control by the simple expedient of removing all union representatives from the boards.

Lord Devlin, then a Queen's Bench judge, was appointed to examine this proposal and his report, of July 1956, was a scathing indictment of the employers' persistent refusal to work willingly within the Scheme's constraints.

After gratuitously reminding NAPE that the whole problem might have been avoided had the employers provided an effective registration scheme and a guarantee before 1939, Lord Devlin concluded that the root of industrial unrest did not lie in the nature of the Scheme, but in people's attitudes towards it. These attitudes, he said, would not disappear with a change in control, especially one which would be resisted violently by the men and would be, in all probability, impractical. The misconception that the Scheme was a concession granted to dockers and not the best means of solving the industry's labour problem had to be eradicated.

'The Scheme must now be regarded as part of the structure of the industry. It is no use threatening to destroy common property; threats of this sort act as an irritant and disturb the minds of moderate men without deterring the extreme' and 'The employers have in the past accepted the Scheme as something imposed upon them but they have not welcomed it as the right and just solution. There can be no wholehearted co-operation between the two sides if there is left the feeling that one side is still seeking a way of ousting the other. The same effort which the employers made in 1947 to accept the letter of the Scheme must now be made to accept it in spirit. The spirit of the Scheme is a partnership of equals. It is not for one side to confer benefits and the other to discharge obligations but for both sides to honour their bonds in equal measure.'

Finally he stated that there was little chance of sole control working in practice; whatever its merits, therefore, it was unrealistic and the employers' belief to the contrary had nothing to support it beyond 'wishful thinking' born of a misguided sense of frustration![54] That was the end of the road. Ten years later, Sir Andrew Crichton, speaking for NAPE, was able to tell Lord Devlin that employers did not seek any changes to the joint control of the Scheme, only lesser amendments to disciplinary procedure.

DISCIPLINE

In switching their attack to discipline, the employers concentrated on one of the most contentious fields of Scheme activities, where they felt emasculated by joint control and believed that union representatives on local boards sometimes shrank from administering just punishments when it seemed impolitic to set their face against the rank-and-file.

Employers cited these arguments in their early demands for sole control and subsequently in asking for stiffer sanctions. NAPE frequently asked for longer periods of suspension than five working days and for appeal tribunals to be allowed to vary penalties upwards as well as downwards; later NAPE tried to get a code of monetary fines superimposed on suspensions from work.

But the basic problems were, in fact, not so much in the operation of the Scheme but in the method of administering punishment within a casual framework. The usual guarantor of good industrial conduct was the threat of non-selection at the call, but this remained a threat only so long as there was a large pool of labour to draw from. After 1947, the pool contracted, payment of the guarantee reduced the rigours of unemployment and the secondary hiring system meant that an employer might be allocated – and could not refuse – a man passed over at the call on disciplinary grounds.

Furthermore, the only effective means of punishment lay in the removal of a man from the register. If a man was simply blacklisted by one company because of some offence, he might easily find work with another and thus go 'unpunished'; but if his registration book was removed, he could not attend the call and thus could not get any employment for the period of the suspension.

Temporary suspension was considered legitimate punishment but *dismissal* from the register was drastic since a man thus paid for an offence against *one* employer by forfeiting the right to work with *any* employer in the industry. It was on this account that discipline was made a matter of joint control in 1947 – a man had to have every possible protection before losing the right to follow his livelihood with any undertaking in the port.

Many of the complaints about the disciplinary machinery ignored these basic constraints and the recurrent attempts to alter it have been as great an irritant as the attempts to win sole control of the Scheme.

It was unfortunate that most attacks followed periods of unrest in the docks, especially the large unofficial strikes, and thus concentrated on mass indiscipline. Theoretically, mass indiscipline can be handled through the Scheme, but experience throughout British industry has shown that retributive justice simply does not solve crises or remove sources of grievance.

The Cameron report, and the Devlin report of 1956, showed that Scheme sanctions were as harsh as those of industry generally and, although port employers are prevented from dismissing strike-leaders without union co-operation, employers who have this freedom seldom choose to exercise it. Exceptions can be found, like Ford Motor's dismissal of seventeen shop stewards in 1963 or Pilkington's dismissal of strike leaders in 1970. But the common practice is to recognise that disputes stem from genuine feelings of grievance and to put these right at source. This lesson has taken a long time to learn in the docks.

One of the early NAPE proposals was to suspend the Scheme during an unofficial strike, so that men could be laid off, without guarantee payments, and unregistered labour used to move essential cargoes. It would have been a potent form of strike-breaking and it was turned down in the 1956 report on the grounds that the Emergency Powers Act of 1920 already allowed the Government to declare a state of emergency and use troops to move perishable goods. (These powers have been used five times in the ports since 1945. In June, 1948, troops worked in London during the zinc-oxide strike in the first declared state of emergency since the General Strike. Emergencies were also declared during the Canadian Seamen's strike, the Smithfield strike of 1958, the seamen's strike of 1966 and the national dock strike of 1970. But troops were not actually used on the last two occasions.)

The claim was dropped after 1956 but a more durable demand has been the right to lay off without payment of guarantee when men cannot be given work because of unconstitutional action by their colleagues or when they refuse to work normally. In most dock disputes, there is no need to lay off men except when specialist groups like tally clerks or crane-drivers withhold their labour. But, after Decasualisation, employers feared the problem could become more acute because the guarantee was lifted above the minimum weekly wage and the cost of paid, but unworked, hours rose sharply.

In the national agreement accompanying Decasualisation, NAPE stood fast by the right to lay off and the unions refused to concede it;

in consequence the agreement remained 'provisional' but the effect was to prohibit lay-offs since they would invite union retaliation. In 1968, still smarting from the stoppages which greeted Decasualisation, the employers secretly raised the issue again with Ray Gunter, the Minister of Labour, and were turned down in a very reasoned statement at a time when reason was in short supply. He told NAPE that amendment of the Scheme to enable employers to terminate employment without reference to the local board ran counter to the principles of joint control and was so controversial it might jeopardise the whole scheme. Although it might strengthen the hand of the union official *vis-á-vis* unofficial leaders, the unions would be bound to oppose the amendment. Finally, he was doubtful if employers would even use the power if it was granted to them.

'The real obstacle – and this applies to other industries as well – is that such action could lead to a serious extension of the stoppage and make the problem of reaching a solution and securing a return to work much more difficult. This deterrent would not in any way be altered by the change proposed.' [55]

After this rebuff, the London employers toyed with the idea of setting up a fighting fund to help employers beset by unofficial strikes, but instead they turned to Barbara Castle, Gunter's successor, to tackle the Scheme again. A new area of conflict was introduced with the second part of the Devlin programme. This involved reshaping the wages structure, in most cases through buying out bonus payments into a higher basic weekly rate; the new rate became the local level of guarantee and the need to ensure continuous working and high outputs was paramount.

Under piecework, the men were paid for the amount of cargo moved and the gap between the basic rate and overall earnings had widened steadily. Piecework thus provided its own discipline and if men chose to go slow, they were paid at the lowly national day rate (£2 4s 4d a day from 1966 to the time of writing), less than half of the likely earnings from work at a piecework stroke. This rough form of justice disappeared once the guarantee was raised above the day rate or the day rate was raised to a level which afforded decent security.

The realistic solution was to introduce work norms by industrial agreement together with the new wages structure but we shall see in Chapter 13 that few employers were in a position to do this. The alternative was to guarantee output through Scheme discipline and this was the London employers' aim in 1969. They were encouraged by a minor success in October 1968 when tally clerks were going slow and the employers threatened to suspend them without pay if they did not undertake work in the normal manner. Undoubtedly, union leaders supported this move, otherwise the 'no work – no pay' notices would have been challenged through the London dock labour board, and the go-slow quickly ended. Soon after, the employers put a draft plan to the unions calling for 'joint responsibility for output' under Phase II Devlin. Simultaneously they consulted their lawyers and the Department of Employment and Productivity about the possibility of enforcing norms of output through the Scheme. The unions realistically shied away from the plan, which would have committed their representatives to further management functions, and the Department, as well as the solicitors, confirmed that there was little chance of getting work-rates accepted as a form of misconduct liable to discipline with the Scheme as it stood.

The employers tried to tackle mass indiscipline again in 1969, after Jack Dash had called unofficial mass meetings in support of a pay claim. Some 2,000 men who attended one meeting were suspended for one or two days each but, when they appealed, the board predictably split five-five as to whether the penalty should be enforced and the whole exercise collapsed, as had every previous attempt to discipline on a large scale. The employers at that point put forward a four-point programme to change the Scheme and it included suspension for three days without right of appeal, laying off and the appointment of an independent chairman to the board and the appeals tribunal. Once again, the Department turned a deaf ear but the idea of an independent chairman has remained attractive to the employers. It appeared reasonable; instead of stalemate, issues would be resolved. But this proposal would strike at the root of joint control of the industry and in situations of genuine conflict decisions would rest with the independent chairman instead of with the industry itself.

In the event, only one additional disciplinary measure was introduced with London's Phase II agreement, when the unions allowed employers to exact financial penalties for bad time-keeping. These penalties were neither severe nor effective. Half an hour's pay was deducted for being up to thirty minutes late, one hour's pay for thirty minutes to one hour and, thereafter, pay for the entire shift was forfeit. In the London riverside agreement, time-keeping remained a matter for board discipline.

But the concession was important since it marked the first time that employers could act unilaterally and it was seen as a pointer towards the acceptance of firmer discipline, as advocated in the 1965 Devlin report. It also recognised the genuine desire of employers, following Decasualisation, to supplement their greater degree of managerial self-determination and moved in the direction of transferring wider powers from Scheme control to joint industrial committees at company level.

A strong argument can be made now for moving discipline into the ambit of joint determination between the permanent employer and his labour force. Only under casualism was it absolutely necessary to have discipline controlled by an independent agency because men were not working continuously for single employers. But the Scheme machinery was – and is – undoubtedly cumbrous and neither the men nor management like waiting several days, or releasing senior personnel for board committees, to deal with petty cases of misconduct.

In London, the employers' disenchantment sometimes resulted in them not bothering to fill board places which were theirs by right and, in the 1960s, they sent a declining number of cases through the disciplinary machinery. For instance, in 1965 the London board heard 518 cases which went to appeal, in 1966, the figure dropped to 249 and in 1967, up to Decasualisation, it was only 106. Subsequently, the number of cases heard has fluctuated between 56 and 91 a year, but a lot of petty misdemeanours are dealt with at company level and the men do not bother to appeal through the revised procedure.

In some companies, it was not unknown to rely on the unions to deal with minor breaches of working rule, through their internal procedure. For instance, under piecework and the gang system, one man's delinquency was often as harmful to his mates as the employer and it was simpler for both sides to 'branch' the offender than go to the board. Thus the TGWU could fine a man £5 (now £10) for disobeying a ganger's order, coming back drunk after lunch or 'pitching off a job without a by-your-leave or thank you.' Both the TGWU and the stevedore's section of the NASD were strict in enforcing the continuity rule through internal discipline.

Another recent trend in London is for employers to issue warnings for petty offences – against which there is theoretically no right of appeal – and to suspend only when they have built up a full case history, which will carry weight in the board appeals machinery. Similarly, the unions are willing to use their branch discipline rather than let a record be built up against a member.

THE SCHEME AND THE EROSION OF CASUALISM

In 1954, Lord Ammon, the first chairman of the National Dock Labour Board, spoke in the House of Lords about his disappointment in the Scheme. The 'largest social and industrial experiment in any part of the world' was bedevilled by the intransigence of those for whom it was brought into effect, he said. He went on to complain that every party using the Scheme was the tool of particular viewpoints and even criticised the Government for once countermanding a Board decision – during the Canadian Seamen's strike – in the interest of industrial peace.[56]

The main burden of his speech was that the National Board was not master in its own house and thus had failed in its implicit task of providing the medium for tackling casualism and increasing the security of the labour force. To the pioneers of 1947, it did not matter whether this was achieved by enlarging Board activities or by allowing individual companies to take the initiative to move towards permanency; the role of the Scheme, however, was to enable the transition to take place.

The theory of a gradual transition towards permanency demanded that employers would find it more economic to engage permanent men than casuals and that the permanent force could be slowly built up until the shortage of work for pool labour was so reduced that the switch to 100 per cent permanency would be inevitable. It was commonly assumed that the weekly labour force could expand to roughly half the total before the switch was made. But, in the first two decades of the Scheme, the industry never approached this ratio.

Appendix I shows the small degree to which permanent employment increased between 1947 and 1967. At the inception of the Scheme there were 9,879 permanent workers in the gross register of 78,458 men. This constituted about 12 per cent of the labour force. The number of 'perms' reached a numerical peak in 1957, with 17,122 out of 76,691 men, or 22·34 per cent, permanent. Thereafter the number slipped back but the proportion increased slowly up to 1963, when almost a quarter of the labour force was permanently engaged – 15,357 out of 64,597. There all progress stopped and by the time of Decasualisation the industry in fact was getting more casual, because men felt the point had come where greater permanency endangered job opportunities for the casual docker.

This comparatively stable national trend hid wide variations at port level. In Hull the number of weekly workers reached 40 per cent in 1960 but fell back to 35 per cent at the insistence of the TGWU; in London the 1964 figure was 35 per cent, in Bristol 18 per cent, in Liverpool 11 per cent and in Glasgow 8 per cent. The causes of such disparity were largely historical. Hull's drive for permanency was the employers' reaction to the turbulence of inter-union conflict in the mid-1950s and London's was spearheaded by the PLA. In Liverpool and Glasgow, opposition to permanency was deeply-rooted and embodied in port rules, especially among the STGWU whose independence grew from the attempt to control hiring and the distribution of work through the union card.

The Scheme had no direct means of controlling the permanent/casual ratio but it could be used to exert indirect influence. One such means was through the power to withhold registration from employers. It would not have been contrary to the spirit of 1947 to exclude companies which could not 'ensure greater regularity of employment for dock workers.' But in practice employers' registration was a formality and in the first twenty years in London only one employer was struck off the register: this happened in 1952 and the offence concerned the submission of late and inaccurate statistics to the Board, not the pattern of employment offered.

Another means of persuasion lay in fixing a levy, which discriminated against casual hiring and in favour of permanency, but this was never tried. Yet another lay in control of the register which could have kept so tight an overall margin that employers were forced to build up their own labour force, rather than risk being left short of men at the call. But, with few exceptions, broad margins were kept in each port – so much so, in fact, that some argued that the Scheme positively encouraged casualism by keeping a margin of labour for the small undertakings.

The effect of keeping a sufficient margin to suit all employing interests during the post-war years was to entrench casual attitudes and practices among the men and, in finality, blocked the path of gradual transition, since the vested interests of those who resisted permanency outweighed those who welcomed it within the casual context.

Three distinct types of casual docker have been identified. A large proportion chose to follow one employer as casuals, but on a regular basis. Usually they were hired as complete gangs and were given official or semi-official preference listings. They found the casual system highly lucrative and were the 'kings of the river', the 'flying 18s' and the 'blue-eyed boys', who were proud of their ability to shift cargo fast and confident they would be picked for challenging jobs. Their earnings made them the envy of other dockers and sometimes they were treated better than permanent men, whose tied status could be exploited by allocation to low-paying work.

The distinction between this group, which probably represented a third of the labour force, and 'floaters,' who operated on a purely casual basis, was blurred because both tried to choose the best-paying jobs. But the floaters tended to operate individually, rather than in gangs, and believed that high earnings were found by offering themselves at random, without attachment to the employers. The last group were 'drifters,' men who had no advantages of unofficial influence or physique and were invariably the last to be taken on at the call or allocation centres. They were the one group which valued security, but were the least able to achieve it and their earnings were correspondingly low.[57]

The significant feature of this categorisation is the preponderance of regulars and floaters in the labour force. The regular stood to gain little from permanency since he already had a high level of security and the floater positively disliked it since it destroyed a way of life he cherished and the informal practices which enabled him to pick and choose a job.

Between them, these groups exacerbated the feelings against permanency. In Chapter 3, the origins of the rivalry between casual and permanent workers were described and it was just as keen after 1947. The unofficial movement stirred up the conflict in 1949–50 and the attack was concentrated against Shaw Savill's recruitment to permanent ranks. Albert Timothy wrote in the *Portworkers' News*: 'I gave a warning to men who were so eager to take permanency that they would finish up cleaning windows. Well, it almost happened. The rider was: get a broom and sweep up. The men, I am glad to say, rightly refused. But it goes to show what you are in for when you agree to permanent jobs.'[58]

A remarkable analysis of the truly casual attitude was contained in the unofficial journal of the London riverside. A story printed as a Christmas fable hardly found a good word for 'perms.' The eldest were frightened men who remembered the old days and were thankful for regular employment, but chary of imparting their knowledge to the young. Entrants to the industry in the 1950s got a worse press. When jobs became scarce, some retreated into permanency and others stuck true to 'the freedom of the river,' i.e. casualism.

'The word perm was at last allowed into the docker's language. Not only was perm no longer a derogatory term, but with Irish logic – i.e. "If I don't go perm, the next man will" – the long-fought for and oft-spoken of freedom of the river was sold for pounds, shillings and pence.

'The principal "holders" who refrained from the pieces of silver lambasted those who, they said, had deserted. This tended only to make the perms withdraw within themselves and make more restrictive practices to keep the outsiders out. They no longer attend branch meetings and rely on apathetic trade union officials to pull as many strokes as possible.'

The newest intakes got even shorter shrift: 'Having taken little part if any in the struggle for better conditions, they easily sold out principles for money. Probably pushed by the little woman and knowing no better, they pressed for regular employment as a prize. No sense of freedom burns in their breast, therefore the attitude of rebellious outsiders (from the pool) is misunderstood by them as jealousy for their jobs.'[59]

TGWU officials, who approved of permanency in principle, could not hold out against this kind of pressure. In 1965, the TGWU and NASD supported the London dockers against the merger of Thames Stevedoring and Shaw Savill because the combined use of the 719 permanent dockers and 64 tally clerks would have meant less work for casuals. It was an ugly dispute (see above, p. 66) which broke out while the Devlin Committee was sitting and eventually the merger took place, with a greatly reduced permanent labour force, and London employers tacitly agreed to close their books to perms until the leap to 100 per cent decasualisation took place.

In 1960, Hull dockers staged one-day strikes against increasing permanency and a quota of weekly workers was subsequently fixed at 35 per cent. Union restrictions in Liverpool on the mobility of specialists effectively halted recruitment of perms in the 1960s.

It was inevitable that the path of gradualism should peter out at the point where the conflict between casual and weekly worker became acute, but no one expected that point to be reached at such an early stage. Unimaginative use of the Scheme contributed to the impasse; control of the register could have been directed towards the social end of eroding casualism but, in the next section, we shall see that the policy of the national and local boards was governed chiefly by the commercial criteria of adjusting the labour force to the levels of trade and transport technology.

CONTROL OF THE REGISTER

Up to the 1960s, when the demand for labour was comparatively stable, the NDLB was quite successful in matching the supply of labour to demand. Admittedly, forecasting was crude. Expansion of trade had to be set against new methods of cargo-handling and the Government could upset calculations by measures to protect the balance of payments. Many of the Board's reports protested at the difficulty of 'endeavours to ascertain prospects on which to build a realistic labour programme'[60] and it was sometimes simpler to use Bevin's rule-of-thumb which guessed the requirement and added 10 per cent as a margin against fluctuation.

For fifteen of the twenty-four years of the Scheme's existence, the average requirement was within 10 per cent of the live register – the NDLB's term for the average number of men available after deducting those on holiday, sick or unaccountably absent.

The worst year was 1952, when the disparity reached 16·4 per cent, but this coincided with the unexpected controls which cut back the volume of imports for the first time since the war. 1956 to 1959 were all years of high surplus but again this reflected the state of trade. Freight rates began to fall in the middle 1950s and, although the Suez crisis provided an artificial stimulus for some months, tramp and liner rates continued to fall and world trade as a whole dropped by 8 per cent in the first half of 1958, leaving 1,500,000 tons of shipping laid up in the UK, a post-war peak. The surpluses of 1961 and 1962 coincided with the Selwyn Lloyd deflation, but they also marked the first impact of unit-loading on dockwork – the start of today's over-manning problem.

This matching of the register was achieved without the initial help of employer reorganisation to minimise fluctuation and Appendix 4 shows that the pattern of fluctuation changed little between 1947 and Decasualisation.

The NDLB kept full statistics between 1953 and 1967 on the maximum and minimum demands for labour, and at national level the maximum requirement on the busiest day of the year exceeded the minimum requirement on the slackest by roughly 40 per cent throughout this period. In London, where there was some employer rationalisation in the 1960s and the development of specialist berths was a stabilising influence, there was a slight narrowing of the extremes and a fluctuation of 40 per cent was reduced to 30 per cent. But elsewhere the picture was appalling. In the South Coast ports, principally Southampton, the maximum requirement could exceed the minimum by five times; in Bristol it was never less than double and in Liverpool, where fluctuation ranged between 70 and 90 per cent in the mid-1950s, it widened to an exceptional 140 per cent in 1967.[61]

Often local boards were singularly dextrous in adjusting the register to average requirements and Liverpool provides a good example. The board chose to keep the margin tight rather than have a large surplus to maintain during slack periods. But the corollary was labour shortage when trade expanded and there was a regular deficiency from 1964 to 1969, made worse by a twelve-month delay in recruitment, authorised in January 1970, when the TGWU insisted on 100 per cent nomination of new entrants.

In the past decade, matching the register has been increasingly difficult as labour-intensive handling has been replaced by unitisation, pallets and containers, or bulk discharge. Each year the demand for men has dropped by 8 to 10 per cent and each reduction of the register has been overtaken by new labour-saving operations.

The difficulties of ridding the industry of surplus manpower, of keeping the right quality as well as quantity of men, and of meeting emergency situations with emergency measures, have provided employers with ammunition against the Scheme. This type of criticism has intensified in recent years as the conflict of interest has widened between the two sides of the industry. In the 1950s, the balance of advantage lay with the employers since the Scheme guaranteed them

ORDER FORM Please arrange with my newsagent to supply me with three consecutive weekly issues of THE TIMES LITERARY SUPPLEMENT free of charge. I understand that subsequent weekly issues will be supplied to me by him at the normal cover price, which I pay, unless I cancel this order before the end of the free trial period.

Own name and address	Newsagent's name and address
NAME...............	NAME...............
ADDRESS...............	ADDRESS...............
....	....
....	....
....	....

OCCUPATION...............

SIGNATURE............... DATE...............

The cover price is subject to revision from time to time. Also available on subscription.

No postage stamp necessary if posted in Gt. Britain, Channel Islands or Northern Ireland

2

Postage will be paid by Licensee

Mr F. Owen
Circulation Manager
The Times Literary Supplement
Printing House Square
London
EC4B 4TE

Meeting place
of minds...

a labour force in years of full employment; both sides of the industry were happy to keep a ready supply of labour and the precedent was then established of refusing to order compulsory cuts in the register.

The one attempt by the NDLB to sack men from the industry was so violently resisted that no further attempts were made. In 1949, the Board asked individual ports to prune ineffective workers – the aged and the sick – from the industry and, in London, thirty-three men were chosen. One was 82 years old and had only worked six turns in a year; another was 70, had difficulty walking and could not push a truck or do clerical work; a feeble 62-year-old was a danger to himself and had to be stopped from walking out of a loophole (the first storey doorway in warehouses); a man of 47 who had only worked a half-day in forty-seven weeks, suffered from tonsillitis, bronchitis, rheumatism, fibrositis and had weak legs. These men were all maintained at the expense of the industry, but dockers walked out *en masse* when their impending dismissal was announced. It was a magnificent display of solidarity and made the name of Maurice Foley, now the TGWU's leading lay delegate in London, who stormed to the front of a meeting, as union officials were justifying the Board's action, and demanded doctors for the men, not dismissal.

It was the first and last time that the unions consented to compulsory dismissal and underlined the basic divergence of interest over job rights. Subsequently the industry was forced to look for different solutions to the problems of the aged and overmanning and, however painfully arrived at, the measures which accompanied modernisation are a credit to the industry and to the spirit in which the Scheme was conceived.

The first target was to sever elderly men from the industry. Under casualism there was no limit on who could present themselves for work and the average age was consequently high. The nature of dockwork itself, requiring long years of experience to make an efficient worker with knowledge of the tricks of the trade and the best means of handling a variety of cargoes, and the nature of casualism, which favoured men with the most informal contacts, also tended to make the labour force elderly; the virtual stop on recruitment in most post-war years then reinforced the process. The importance of experience was emphasised by Stephen Hill, a sociology lecturer at Bedford College, London, during the 1970 national dock strike. He argued that dockers' skills could not be compared with those of other industries. 'Any fit man could do a docker's job after a fashion – slowly and dangerously; but it needs several years of arduous on-the-job experience to cope efficiently with the wide variety of cargoes and ships that a docker meets each working week.'[62]

In Booth's day the average age of dock labour was about 40, already a high average, and since the war it has varied between 45 and 47. The fitness of the labour force is also affected by the occupational hazards of a strenuous and outdoor industry and many men age prematurely, or get hurt. For instance, fatal accidents occur five times as often as in manufacturing and two-thirds of all accidents are caused by conditions associated with dock labour, such as falling, striking against objects or being hit by falling objects. In addition, a man's health can be broken by continuous heavy lifting or handling noxious cargoes. One man died from anthrax, contracted while handling a cargo of bones; many men have been bitten seriously by insects or rodents in infested cargoes; there have been cases of asbestosis and skin diseases from goods like red oxide. Rheumatism, osteo-arthritis and bronchial illnesses are all more prevalent in the docks than other industries and absences from sickness are correspondingly higher. In evidence to Lord Pearson in 1970, Jack Jones, as general secretary of the TGWU, elaborated. He could talk from personal experience of the hazards of hard peas spilling from sacks ('it is like walking on marbles') or the bouts of coughing and choking caused by dusty cargoes or by sweating from heavy work and then standing around in the cold waiting for the next load. It was slightly unfortunate that he presented the figures for the incidence of rheumatism to the Whitehall officials on a mimeographed sheet which shows that the disease was 50 per cent more prevalent among civil servants.

In 1960, the NJC introduced a pension scheme for the first time, linked to the compulsory retirement of men aged 70 and over at the end of 1961, 69 from the end of 1962 and 68 a year later. This followed the publication of Board figures which showed an alarming increase in the higher age groups employed. Where 40 per cent of the men had been more than 50 years old in 1955, the proportion had gone up to 45 per cent in 1960 and the percentage of men over 55 had risen from 21 to 25 in the same period.

A gap of six years followed before the retirement age was brought down to 65, in line with other industry; this recommendation of the Wordie report was implemented in 1969 with the increase in minimum pension payments from 25s a week to £4 10s financed by a 10s contribution from the men and 5 per cent on the wages bill from employers. The pension scheme was of profound importance in setting the climate for modernisation. The plight of the aged docker, whose earning capacity grew steadily smaller under piecework and who was a burden to mates in his gang, was a continuing source of grievance and a superb piece of doggerel – by Patchy of Liverpool – was published in the *Portworkers News* (Vol. 2, Number 4, 1951) on the subject. It ran:

> *Forty years I've served you without a word of thanks,*
> *Sweated, toiled the whole long day in freighters, barges, tanks,*
> *You've made millions from my body, even Deakin can't deny,*
> *And all I get when I am old is Die, you ——, die.*

> *I'm demanding now a pension from the profits that I've made,*
> *From the industry I've built up, from the volume of your trade.*
> *By virtue of the very fact I've given you all I can,*
> *I demand a decent pension to live just like a man.*

> *Pensions for the bankers, pensions for the spivs,*
> *For the civil service – but dockers, they don't live.*
> *They even pension horses when from out the shafts they come,*
> *But the docker when he's served his time, he just becomes a bum.*

> *Some action by our union, some profits from the boss,*
> *A grant from our Government, it would not be a loss.*
> *In return we'll lose some bitterness, a lot of strife will cease*
> *And, who knows, all over dockland, we may have won the peace.*

Prior to the pension scheme, the only attempt by the Board to induce men to leave the industry was the creation of a Temporary Release Register in 1957. Men who left kept their registration so long as they returned to their old jobs promptly when asked. It made a totally inauspicious start in Hull and the Tyne; fewer than twenty men had left at the end of the first full year but it was valuable in the 1960s in syphoning large numbers of London lightermen away from their declining trade.

In 1967, however, the NDLB helped finance a voluntary retirement scheme for over 65s. Up to £500 a man was offered and was accepted by 1,780 of the 1,942 men eligible. The Board also undertook to sever 900 men on the Dormant Register – the long-term sick who could not be allocated to permanent employment. The terms gave £1,000 to £1,500 per man, according to length of service, and were eagerly accepted, leaving only six men on this register by 1969 and one in 1970.

In 1968, a few more men accepted voluntary retirement, but more attractive incentives were needed to cope with a crisis in London. The PLA was closing down the London and St Katharine dock basins and the lighterage trade was declining fast. Both needed to shed labour but the London employers would not agree to a port-wide offer of voluntary severance payments, because the problem was sectional. However, they were frightened of single undertakings setting precedents for the port as a whole and sought to prevent unilateral action. But they failed. Thames and General Lighterage got rid of 103 men with flat payments of £1,250 a man, irrespective of age, position or years of service, and then the PLA stampeded the ocean trades employers by offering maximum payments of £1,800, if more than twenty-six years of service could be proved. Other employers could hardly offer less and the unions immediately asked for these terms to be incorporated in a national agreement. Reluctantly the employers agreed. It was a generous step in so far as the initial London scheme had been voluntary to both employers and the men but now it was compulsory for all employers to pay a national levy, even if they did not have a surplus. The unions were insistent, however, because they rightly foresaw that so long as the levy was voluntary, it could be withheld as a form of blackmail and they suspected that many London wharfingers, who were on the brink of shutting down their businesses, would try to wind up without giving their men the terms on offer in the rest of the port.

In 1968, London severed about 1,000 men, over half from the up-river docks of the PLA. The national scheme opened in June 1969, after a long delay before the Government consented to give a bridging loan of £3,500,000. It was financed by a levy of 2½ per cent on the wages bill, raised to 5 per cent for 1970 and 7½ per cent for 1972, and was offered to unfit men and those nearest retirement age. In six months, 3,006 men chose to leave the industry and, when severance was reoffered in 1970 after the Government put up a further

£1,000,000 loan, another 3,545 quit. Up to November 1971, a total of 8,095 men had been severed under the national scheme and 3,902 came from London. This proportion exceeds London's contribution to the scheme; any port or undertaking without the same labour surplus problem resented the subsidy but the most extreme example of payment without return was in London itself, where a stevedore had to give £66,000 in levy up to 1970 but only shed two men. All in all, the help given to London now can be regarded as repayment for the many years before Decasualisation when London contributions to the Dock Labour Scheme financed guarantee payments in ports with a higher level of unemployment.

To shed nearly 12,000 men at a cost of more than £16,000,000, through severance under the national scheme, the dormant scheme, the initial London scheme and voluntary retirement, was a remarkable achievement. Table 3 shows how the register at the time of Phase II agreements was nearly 50 per cent lower than at the start of the Devlin programme and that voluntary severance accounted for three-fifths of the drop. It also shows that recruitment was tightly controlled. In 1968 there were major intakes at Liverpool and Manchester but otherwise there was a virtual standstill until the advent of two-shift working in 1970–1. London then was authorised to recruit 750 men and more than 200 tally clerks and Liverpool 732 men to put right their chronic deficits. Column C shows precisely why the severance scheme was so important. It represents the proportion of the registered labour force who left the industry of their own accord, without financial inducement. Before 1968, the annual average had been 3·7 per cent but the promise of better conditions and improved wages under modernisation reduced the outflow to a bare trickle. It was this low rate of turnover which forced the scale of payments for severance so high and set a value on job rights which is not matched at industry level elsewhere in Britain.

Column H is also important, showing the number of men who worked on a temporary or seasonal basis to meet known fluctuations of trade. Employers have always complained of the inelasticity of the Scheme in meeting emergencies with emergency measures and, no matter how well organised the industry may be, there are always periods of unpredictable congestion or slack, for instance in the aftermath of industrial disputes, after Manchester's famous fog of November 1955, or in London and Liverpool during the winter of 1964 when

Table 3 Reducing the register in the Devlin years

	A No. of registered men	B Average age of men	C % leaving the industry voluntarily	D Overall outflow including those severed	E Overall intake	F No. severed	G Cost of severance £	H Temporary register
1965 (Dec. 31)	63,615	45·7	3·7[1]	6,072	6,256	—		1,287
1966	60,878	45·3	3·7[1]	5,498	2,600	—		1,026
1967	56,161	45·8	3·7[1]	5,598	423	1,780 }	c. 3,000,000	871
1968	54,481	45·5	1·4	3,550	1,870	1,900 }		1,254
1969	48,785	45·5	1·8	6,363	667	3,006	5,072,000	1,114
1970	44,588	44·8	0·5	4,802	605	3,567	5,839,000	1,035
1971	43,647	44·5	NA	NA	At least 1,600 authorised	1,540	c. 2,400,000	NA

[1] This figure represents the annual average for 1963–7 inclusive.

some ships waited several weeks for a berth. The NDLB allowed a very occasional use of non-registered labour to meet such crises or allowed transfer of men from port to port. But most reliance was placed on the temporary register where men would be taken on for only a limited period of time. This register reached its peak of 2,058 men in 1954 and next year a probationary register was started, to serve roughly the same purpose. Probationers had limited rights but got prior entitlement to places on the full register during recruitments.

These supplementary registers, however, were never popular. To the employers, temporary men were bad workers whose inefficiency was augmented by lack of commitment to their jobs. To the unions they represented a hidden source of casualism and caused great problems during recruitments. In 1970, the conflict between temporary dockers, who handled the summer passenger trade, and the regular labour force was taken up by James Hill, the Tory MP for Southampton West. The TGWU branch, which covers the regular dockers, decided in September that all future recruitment should be reserved for dockers' sons, thus excluding the 200 to 300 temporary men. Since this group was organised through another branch, their case was not heard and Hill considered they had a good case for entitlement. Ernie Allen, the union's regional secretary, replied that 'dockers have long regarded their ticket as the birthright of their sons; though unwritten, it has been a rigid rule for generations that dockers' sons take precedence.' A compromise was eventually reached, allowing the branch decision to stand for the time being but making the temporary register the future nursery for all dockwork.

With the advent of containers and the increasing uncertainty about future labour requirements, far greater use should have been made of supplementary men. Officials of the NDLB wanted all recruitment during Phase II Devlin to be temporary because they suspected that the need for new blood would not long survive the continuing erosion of jobs. In the Board's annual report for 1969, the general manager made a thinly-veiled plea for this type of recruitment alone. 'As the permanent register becomes more stabilised at levels appropriate for all-the-year-round employment, greater recourse to supplementary workers may become necessary to offset holiday absences in the popular months of the year,' he wrote.

But his words were not heeded. The use of temporary men in fact is declining although the recklessness of the last major recruitments has been proven; with the loss of trade in London and the financial difficulties of the Mersey Docks and Harbour Board, both ports have tried to stop their intake of men in 1971, before the authorised figures were reached.

Is this a record of incompetence? The industry remains overmanned; some 15 per cent of the labour force was still surplus at the end of 1971. But it was a year of particularly rapid job contraction and the volume of trade was fairly slack in general; 1972 will see further severe contractions as the Far East trade switches to containers, but thereafter there is a prospect of greater stability.

Job rights remain an area of fundamental conflict between the unions and employers at the mercy of technology and the achievements of the industry, under joint control, are in the long run more notable than the shortcomings. The decimation of jobs has been matched, albeit haltingly, by the shrinking of the register and the employers, under Phase II agreements, have made the all-important step of bearing the cost of underemployment themselves – they pay stable wages to the 6,690 men out of 44,648 who were surplus in November 1971.

The situation is not without hope. First, the pace of technology may be tempering itself to the problems of labour; for instance New Zealand trade is not longer to be wholly containerised in 1973. Secondly, the necessity for proper manpower forecasting has at last been recognised. The failure of the industry to plan its needs for modernisation and to equip ship-owners with detailed information of the likely service British ports would be able to provide was staggering. George Cattell, as chairman of the National Modernisation Committee, said in January 1970 that 'too much is now at stake to go on muddling through to modernisation without knowledge of our real needs.' NAPE had guessed that a labour force of 40,000 would suffice in 1970 but the calculation was not based on a detailed analysis of natural wastage, manpower requirements by skills, the age structure of the labour force or the proposals of ship-owners. Cattell said that progress in the ports would depend on a comprehensive programme of retraining, redeployment and rehabilitation taken through to 1980, and covering management, technical staff, supporting and ancillary workers, as well as registered dock labour. The Ministry of Transport now is trying to set up such an exercise and port employers, who refused government assistance earlier, are anxious to co-operate so that British ports can plan the future with the same assurance as ports like Rotterdam, which has used several consultants to make projections for the 'greater delta region' at the mouth of the Rhine up to the year 2000.

Thirdly, severance payments have been extended to younger men in the industry and the inducements to leave increased to a maximum level of more than £2,300. With average earnings now above £2,000 a year, the case for raising severance payments still higher is strong and may warrant special government assistance, as was extended to the coalmining industry, where men retiring early are given 90 per cent of average earnings for three years.

Finally, both sides of the industry have been forced to look to radical solutions. The search has not been fruitful yet – and the Hull dockers' idea of setting up their own stevedoring enterprise to mop up the port's surplus labour was fanciful – but the process of testing and discarding various plans at least serves to re-direct the exploration.

London employers set high hopes on using a loophole in the De-casualisation scheme – the Temporary Unattached Register (TUR). In spite of the similarity of name, the TUR is quite different from the previous temporary register which was used either as a 'nursery' or a source of strictly seasonal labour. The TUR was created as a transit park for men switching between employers and they received the guarantee payment while awaiting reallocation.

Until Phase II, it served this function but in 1971 it was used more as a permanent pasture for men who were offered little prospect of getting back to full-time employment. Rank-and-file hostility to the TUR began to build up after the winding up of Hovey Antwerp operations in the Millwall docks. After John Hovey had negotiated London's Phase II agreement, his father found himself paying £80,000 in wages to men for whom he had no work, during the first eight months of 1971; consequently, the company's 240 men were returned to the TUR.

Shop stewards argued, justifiably, that the TUR was contrary to the spirit of permanent employment and when this register crept past 1,000 men, in spring 1972, they began to organise national resistance to this abuse. While traditional dockwork contracts so rapidly, the most promising solution to the problem of surplus labour will lie in finding new forms of work for dockers. But the industry is still looking to voluntary severance; the Government put forward a loan to finance higher severance payments as soon as there was a hint of trouble in London about the size of the TUR and it is possible that the industry will demand a larger contribution from container operators – either in the form of a higher Board levy or a tonnage royalty – to pay more towards the human problems they created.

THE SCHEME AND RELATIONSHIPS AT WORK

Two further arguments against the Scheme need cursory examination: the extent to which it stands between the employer and his men, preventing the emergence of a normal employer/employee relationship, and the extent to which it drove a wedge between the union official and the rank-and-file.

The first argument can be quickly dealt with. It was used most before the Devlin programme and essentially was a *cri-de-coeur* against casualism itself.

The kind of relationship between employer and employee which is common to other industries could not exist with casual hiring. Men could not be motivated by a pride in their work, or by career advancement, when they had a variety of employers and little prospect of promotion unless they were permanent men. Instead, the casual docker more than most men relied for satisfactions on relationships within the gang and the working community and regarded the work situation primarily as one of conflict in which he 'gave the boss his due and kept the rest for himself.'

By comparison, the division of employing function caused by Board control of discipline and the register was unimportant and, if employers had seriously wanted to stabilise relationships at company level, they could not cling to casualism as well. The option of reorganising into units capable of employing all or most of the labour force permanently was always open but it was not accepted until the attraction of casualism disappeared with the container revolution. Latterly, the case may have more force since full permanency has made employers take on a greater range of management functions and it would seem natural to transfer discipline to joint industrial committees within each undertaking. But most employers have a long way to go before they can claim to have perfected the standards of management achieved by a few companies like Olsen or some sections of the British Transport Docks Board and this issue is no longer pressed.

The contention that the Scheme put union officials in an impossible position with their membership was a major plank in the employers' case for reforming the Scheme in 1955–6. They argued that dockers could not accept, psychologically, that their interests were safeguarded by officials participating in port management and consequently the rank-and-file was alienated from the official organs of the union.

In one instance, this case was borne out. In 1949, Dickie Barrett, the general secretary of the NASD, sat on the NDLB when it decided to expel ineffective men from port registers. He was therefore party to the decision even if he disagreed with it. But his union executive subsequently forced him to lead an official strike against the order. He therefore lost his seat on the Board and the NASD has not regained national representation.

But the argument derived chiefly from the employers' frustration at the weakness of the unions and the power wielded by unofficial committees. It ignored the obvious reason for alienation – the failure of union leadership to provide the service which dockers wanted. In Chapter 2, the historical weakness of union organisation in dockland was explained, particularly of the TGWU. The early need to weld together the amalgamation justified Bevin's creation of a powerful central organisation in which the general secretary had wide powers and the national executive was responsible for the appointment of officials. But when Arthur Deakin, a sincere but lesser man than Bevin, inherited this structure and aligned the union behind the Labour Government and the TUC in seeking to control the growth of wages, the dockers rebelled. Their position was immeasurably more powerful in conditions of full employment and they followed readily men who filled the vacuum created by the Right-wing stance of the TGWU.

The most important organisation to fill the vacuum was the NASD. It sought a following in London by emphasizing its democratic structrue and, in August 1954, was invited by leaders of an unofficial strike to form a branch in Hull. The implications of the incursion into Northern ports, where the union had no previous membership, was fully known to the union executive. Some belonged to the Revolutionary Communist Party, a Trotskyist group, and regarded it as a chance to discredit TGWU leadership and break its organisation. Bill Lindley, the lightermen's leader, was party to the early decisions and tried to dissuade the stevedores.

'My organisation did what it could to stop the stevedores going the way they did. We actually told them that if they did what they were intending – and we were listening to such phrases as "Manchester will fall tomorrow and Hull the day after" as though a whole army was walking through the country, it was ridiculous – they would offend the rest of the trade union movement, they would finish up outside the TUC, outside the NJC. That was the only possible way we could see it ending . . . unfortunately, what we saw transpired.'[63]

The stevedores quickly established branches in Hull, Manchester and Liverpool and its overall membership shot up dramatically from 6,354 to a claimed 14,383. But in 1955 the TUC ruled that the union had broken the Bridlington agreement, which governs inter-union poaching, and ordered the return of members to the TGWU. The NASD accepted the ruling but, perhaps too readily, accepted a subsequent verdict, in a court case brought by F. Spring against the union, that its rules did not include the power to expel members in these circumstances. This judgment ended the temporary reconciliation, although no one doubted that the case had been brought with exactly this result in mind. The TUC retaliated in September 1956 by directing the NASD not to act on behalf of its membership but to transfer all servicing to the TGWU. Once it was clear these conditions were not being fulfilled, the union was expelled from the TUC in 1959.

This episode showed all too clearly how weak a hold the TGWU had over its membership. Before the Devlin Inquiry in 1965, the NASD still claimed to have 2,500 members in the Northern ports and, although the figure was probably exaggerated by the inclusion of retired members, it was a sufficient following to embarras the TGWU and make the basis of a claim for representation on local boards and industrial committees. 'We couldn't help what happened,' a former NASD executive member said. 'We only had to unbutton our coats and a rabbit jumped in.'

In Hull, the six Blue branches, centred on a thriving social club, were more active than the TGWU's and the challenge was only beaten after a ten-month purge of TGWU organisation in the port. In Liverpool, however, the NASD organisation was a law unto itself with decidedly tenuous links between branch and head office. None the less, when the TGWU tried to drive out the remaining Blues in 1962 and 1969 with a 'one union clòsed shop,' it was not supported by its own membership. Many men refused to show their union cards at check-points or to accept jobs they considered belonged to Blue members and the employers were forced to withdraw their support for the TGWU campaign.

Political organisations also found the docks a vehicle for agitation. Not only were the docks vital to the economy of the country, but there was never a shortage of grievances to be pursued at rank-and-file level.

Most of the complaints about 'sinister political influence' and 'wrecker activities' can be supported in the sense that organisations have a following among working dockers and some salient individuals may well have planned disruption. But the number of politically-committed dockers is few; Dash estimated that there were 100 members of the Communist Party in London in 1965 and groups like the Socialist Labour League and International Socialists today probably have considerably fewer members. Even if the influence of such men exceeds their numbers, little attempt has been made to see their role in perspective or to understand the ordinary men's reaction to them. Why, for instance, did the dockers support the Canadian seamen's strike which was obviously political in origin? Why are such a proportion of officials in the minority unions allied to political groups? Why did the Communists denounce NASD involvement in the North but support the London liaison committees?

Even now, the labour movement does not like to look these issues in the face. The idea of workers' attitudes being shaped by any influence other than the official union movement invariably has frightened the establishment and the reaction has often been to regard the working man as the unwitting tool of subversives, whose aims were fundamentally different from the aims of labour.

Again and again, the dockers have attracted this emotive response. In 1951, Deakin wrote of the 'duplicity and diabolical plan' of world Communism to disrupt industrial and economic life: 'Let me remind our members that we know perfectly well . . . that appointments to official positions within the union and to the branches were listed and circulated amongst the Party members. It was also well-known to us that before our executive council meetings took place, the agendas and other documents were circulated at headquarters level of the Communist Party, then marked as a brief with instructions to Party members on the executive council to take a certain line.'[64]

He went on abrasively to tell the dockers that their loyalties had been exploited in a 'dastardly' attempt by international Communism to achieve its purpose. The Leggett report said that unofficial leaders were 'more concerned to disrupt the working of the port (of London) as often and as seriously as possible than they are to improve dock workers' conditions.' The 1956 Devlin report was more reasonable in concluding that dockers did not regard a vigorous leader as disqualified from expressing their grievance because he was a Communist. But the 1965 report, otherwise so sanguine, classified all men who used the docks as a battlefield for the class war as wreckers – with the rider that some might be traitors in thought if not in deed.[65]

In the early 1950s, the TUC also published pamphlets explaining the nature of Communist involvement in the unions and a young official, Victor Feather, wrote about the use of trade councils as a medium for party policy. It was one thing to explain the workings of the political organisations and to warn unionists of tactics which offended democratic principles. It was right that ballot-riggings, techniques for swaying mass meetings or caucus policy – none of which are exclusive to organisations of the extreme left – should be exposed. No harm could result from talking openly about the problems of the labour movement. But it was short-sighted to imagine the problems would disappear with denunciation and to ban Party members from office in the TGWU, just as it was stupid to castigate men who had been on strike without asking the reason why.

An elementary knowledge of the history of the Left explains much of the 'politics' of dockland. The Communist Party decided in the 1930s to work through the unions and to establish an industrial power-base by representing the rank-and-file in the labour movement. The process was called 'boring from within.' Thus the party did not seek to break the authority of the TGWU but to swing it to the left by shop-floor pressure. Banned from office after 1948, Party members either went underground or were forced to work outside the union structure. In the NASD and WLTBU, however, many gained a high standing and a quarter of the 28-man lightermen's executive were Communists in the 1960s. After the denunciation of Stalin it was easier for the Trotsky groups to claim the mantle of true revolution but rivalry with the Communists kept them out of many of the existing unofficial committees. Therefore they looked to other available power-bases and the NASD in Liverpool was an obvious choice: in London they have been somewhat frozen out but have some support in the shop stewards' movement.

Many of the militants who formed the nucleus of the liaison committees in London were Party members but in most cases they had a genuinely representational role since casualism prevented the creation of a shop-steward structure. For the most part, they were regarded as champions of the dockers. For instance, Ernie Rice belonged to the Party during the years he worked as Dash's right-hand man in the Royal docks. But Dash valued him, not as a revolutionary who would be first on the barricades, but as an indefatigable organiser who ran welfare funds and established a sickness scheme before the employers took over this responsibility.

At a time when branch life was moribund, many rank-and-file activists gave valuable time and energy to making unionism work at the grass roots. Before the advent of decent sickness and accident pay, they would run lotteries and collections for colleagues out of work and some of the funds they organised handled vast sums of money. In London, the occasional 'bucket' or 'kite' collection at the dockgate for men in distress were replaced by self-organised welfare clubs and, in Southampton, shop stewards built up the 'banana fund' with the men's earnings from a productivity deal in fruit-handling for welfare payments. Even when the activists moved too far ahead of the membership, this was regarded as a justifiable counter to employers who had their own 'unofficial' means of influence in organisations like Moral Rearmament and the Economic League.[66] But this support was not given blindly and, with the accession of Frank Cousins to lead the TGWU, many unofficial leaders were persuaded to work through the union committees. Such a split occurred in London after the Cohen's Wharf strike of 1961, when it was felt that the strike-leaders had made an issue of a case which would have been better dropped. Similarly, the amount of misrepresentation in the campaign against Decasualisation was found distasteful by many, and the liaison committees never succeeded in calling out more than a third of the port.

When the unofficial committees sprang up – in London in 1948 and in Liverpool and Manchester in 1950–1, dissatisfaction with the TGWU was at such a pitch that they found a ready audience. Through the sporadic publication of bulletins and journals, and the frequent use of mass meetings, the unofficials established better lines of communication than the TGWU. They could claim, dubiously, to be democratically-elected at the dock-gate and were definitely inter-denominational, representing Blues and Whites. Moreover, in their Charters, they had programmes which were militant but not hope-lessly unattainable and they could make enormous capital out of identifying the Right-wing TGWU with the bosses' interest. (Most of the demands of the 1963 charter were met by the time of Decasualisa-tion. Later Dash made the mistake of predicting the future of the industry as he wanted to see it. He told the BBC that this included a basic wage of £30 a week – and this was £6 a week less than the unions achieved a few months later in London!)

Under Deakin, the charge of poor leadership was well-based. No dock strike was declared official and rank-and-file consultation was neglected. In the first issue of *Portworkers News* Deakin was accused of wanting to exterminate the NASD because its rank-and-file, not the general secretary, dictated policy. In 1954, the same journal said Deakin was a bosses' man and during the inter-union recognition dispute of 1955, the NASD continued this line of attack. 'The attitude of the TGWU was now to ensure that the Scheme worked, even if this meant it worked against the men.' 'For years now the employers in this country have disciplined the workers through the constitutional-ists and Right-wing leaders of the trade union movement' and 'In practice the T and G has become an instrument through which em-ployers carry out their policy.'[67]

But one fundamental fact must be remembered. Throughout this period, it was the union official who carried the burden of negotiating with employers. Although the unofficials had power at the dock-gate, they did not have the ultimate responsibility for delivering the goods and this divorce between rank-and-file agitation and the reality of the negotiating table has always pursued British trade unions.

But the TGWU's mistakes in the 1950s are widely recognised by now. It was too authoritarian, it paid too little attention to the shop-floor and its organisation was creaking. Worst of all, it seemed to regard each new disaster in the docks as a visitation of the plague upon the righteous and did nothing about it. This was at the heart of union weakness, not the Scheme, and it was this which made a senior lay officer recently remark, 'Thank God for the NASD in those days; otherwise we'd have had nothing.'

In many ways, it was the employers who felt most imposed on by the inadequacies of union organisation. They could observe but not influence, except in the area of joint administration. Thus, in stressing the potential difficulties of dual control, they were reacting at the one level which was not obviously internal to the unions.

It is significant that union leaders did not feel any dichotomy in their position on the boards – in 'swapping the cloth cap for the bowler.' They roundly condemned the NASD for putting Barrett in a position where he had to renege on a Board decision and neither they, nor the rank-and-file, ever wanted to give up joint control.

Obviously, the unions could not support the idea of alienation in public but it is significant that they believed it groundless, even in private discussion. They felt their position acceptable so long as they had the support of the rank-and-file. Without that support, there would always be difficulty in administering the Scheme but that would then be a reflection of their own internal problems, not of the nature of the Scheme.

CHAPTER SIX

Containers and Dockwork

'If they ever build the Channel tunnel, we're going to have a portcullis right in the bleeding middle of it, manned by a registered dock worker.' London docker, 1970.

To a rapidly changing industry, the ability to move men freely to the point where their labour is needed is as important as the size and quality of the labour force. In manufacture, this area and type of flexibility is readily defined by the boundaries of the plant or the nature of the process; in service industries, the efficient deployment of labour is more complicated, since it is dictated by the needs of the customer and labour has to be as mobile as the service demanded.

For example, if an office-cleaning contractor wants to stay in business, he may have to follow custom from a declining part of town to a developing suburb and he must arrange for his labour to follow the work or, of necessity, hire afresh. So it is in port transport. Dockwork is essentially a service which supplies one link in the carriage of goods between two points and it becomes inefficient as soon as it impedes the free flow of goods.

However, dockwork is singled out from other services because the Scheme not only defines what work the docker must do but also what he may *not* do. The ring is drawn around the ports and, inside it, the registered docker alone can handle cargo but, outside it, he has no legal rights. This causes immediate difficulties in the container age, when cargo-handling is no longer confined to the waterfront. Instead, the dockers' accustomed work is moving out of the areas in which he is allowed to do it.

An employer may always choose to use registered men outside the port vicinity, but this does not prejudice his right to revert to non-Scheme conditions and dockers know that their high level of earnings, the joint control of the labour force and the industrial relations record, makes the chances of voluntary hiring unlikely. Thus, if new methods are introduced or trade routes change, the dockers find that their automatic entitlement to work has become virtual disqualification.

The definition of dockwork is the part of the Scheme hardest to reconcile with modern requirements. Its *raison d'être* was casualism and the need to supply and maintain a pool of labour in orderly fashion. The scope of registration had to be delineated and it was the local custom and practice of individual ports which became the definitions enshrined in the 1946 Act and 1947 Scheme, brought up to date in 1966 and 1967.

So long as conditions were stable, these definitions caused little difficulty. In the first ten years of the Scheme, when the register dropped by less than 3 per cent, only two kinds of dispute occurred over definitions. One concerned which ports should be included in the Scheme. The unions wanted the few hundred dockers at non-Scheme ports put on an equal footing with the bulk of the labour force and pressed for their inclusion; by the same token employers tried to exclude ports where they thought registration and maintenance would kill trade.

Thus, of 319 ports where dockers were employed, only 82 – admittedly the largest – were included in the 1946 draft scheme. Lord Cameron added Birkenhead and Newcastle at the union request but refused to add Campbeltown or delete 29 small ports for which the employers sought exemption. In 1955, the unions asked for the inclusion of Holyhead, Milford Haven, Portsmouth and Ridham, which employed about 1,000 men between them, it was claimed. No action was taken but Lord Devlin suggested that another inquiry should be set up and this followed in 1960, under the chairmanship of Hugh Lloyd-Williams.

Tested by the criteria of whether dockwork actually took place – i.e. the handling of cargo as a service rather than by a manufacturer dispatching or receiving his own goods – and whether the Scheme would ensure greater regularity of employment, thirteen ports were kept out. Amble, Littlehampton, Norwich, Shoreham and Watchet were deemed too small. At the railway ports of Newhaven, Dover and Folkestone, the Channel ferries were worked by the National Union of Railwaymen on a permanent basis and the residual element of casual work was minute. As Dover was excluded, Ramsgate had to stay out because its irregular trade required grouping with nearby ports to exchange labour. Felixstowe already gave permanent employment and its men would not have benefited from the Scheme. But at Portsmouth, where 68 casuals regularly sought work and fluctuation could be met by transfers with Southampton, Lloyd-Williams recommended inclusion.

The effect of this last recommendation was startling. The Portsmouth employers, rather than accede to Scheme conditions, immediately gave permanent employment and the Government did not bring Portsmouth within the Scheme then or in 1967.

Before Decasualisation, the Forster Inquiry of 1961 and the Honeyman Inquiry of 1966 allowed the issues of exclusions to be aired again. Bo'ness was removed from the Scheme in 1961 after all cargo handling was shifted to Grangemouth and, in 1966, NAPE sought to exclude Charlestown, Great Yarmouth, King's Lynn, Par, West Cornwall, Whitstable and Wisbech on the grounds that the seasonal nature of trade would make permanency an intolerable burden. While sympathetic to the exclusion of Par, which was essentially a private port for English China Clay, Sir George Honeyman recommended no changes until the effects of permanency could be studied.

The other areas of recurring dispute in the early years were the fringes of dockwork, like warehousing, timber, coal trimming and fish-handling. Here the rights of dockers were governed by a variety of case law and were most problematic where the strictest definition was applied – in London.

Many waterfront businesses grew up with the capital's entrepôt trade, specialising in sorting and storing imported goods prior to release to the wholesale or retail market. Meat was a case in point and many riverside cold stores handled home-grown carcases as well as South American and New Zealand imports, transhipped from the enclosed docks by barge. Under war-time requisitioning, the cold stores were taken over for meat storage by the Ministry of Food, bringing them within the Scheme. But many tried to withdraw in 1959 on the grounds that rival stores at Smithfield, outside the vicinity of the ports, were excluded; that the percentage of domestic storage had risen against imports; and that the supply of pool labour was ill-suited to their needs. In spite of sympathetic hearings in 1956 and 1959, none were excluded.

Equally, the distinction between manufacture and cargo-handling was very fine at many premises on the riverside, especially in timber where the employers felt that timber handled by dock labour in the enclosed docks should be exempt at the wharves where it was cut up and milled for inland distribution.

These disputes were irritants and seldom led to stoppages of work. But the picture changed in the 1960s and definitions became one of dockland's greatest problems. The main reason was unconnected with the operation of the Scheme or the attitudes of the docker himself. It was the changing methods of handling cargo in the short sea trades. Since the war, mechanisation had continued in a leisurely manner, concentrating chiefly on automatic discharge of bulk commodities and better lifting gear for conventional goods. Mechanisation was opposed on principle, but could usually be introduced through good management and the knowledge that the expansion of trade would compensate for the jobs saved.

The development of roll-on/roll-off services across the North Sea, however, was momentous. These services concentrated on East Coast ports which offered the quickest sailing time to the Continent and also on the Irish routes, and they virtually dispensed with dock labour altogether. A lorry from Birmingham could drive to Hull, board a ferry and unload in Denmark thirty-six hours later; or it could detach its trailer which would be stowed on board the ferry and picked up by a tractor at its destination. By 1967, there were over fifty roll-on/roll-off services operating to the Continent and they multiplied, so job opportunities declined and the retention of fringe work became doubly important. In London, the position was worsened because the loss of this trade also removed entrepôt traffic from the wharves, especially dairy goods which had made the Upper Pool 'the bread-basket of London.'

The impact of containers was even more dramatic, because it made twin inroads into the dockers' livelihoods. Only a handful of men were needed to move the container on and off ship and the most labour-intensive part of dockwork, packing and unpacking, was often taken right outside the area of the port.

Europe was almost a decade behind the United States in recognising the potential of the container but by the mid-1960s the rush to invest in new ships and port facilities was fast and furious. There were early instances of bulk carriage in containers in Britain. Jacobs' biscuits were shipped through London from Ireland in cubic boxes in the 1920s and the railways introduced transferable freight boxes, which could be lifted from flatcar to ship or lorry, in 1928.

But the real pioneers were the US armed forces in the Second World War and in Korea. US ship-owners remembered the CONEX military box when they sought to cut down the increasingly expensive and unproductive time which vessels spent in port. In 1956, Pan-American (to be renamed Sea-Land in 1960) started to plan routes along the East Coast seaboard with containers carried on the deck of conventional vessels. By 1960, Sea-Land was operating to Puerto Rico with special container gantries there and at New Jersey, and Grace Line opened a container service to Venezuela. On the Pacific, Matson Lines inaugurated a container service between San Francisco and Honolulu in 1958, when the *Hawaiian Merchant* sailed with twenty containers on deck and the first proper container ship made the voyage two years later.

Then in 1966 Sea-Land sent the *Fairland* on the first all-container voyage across the Atlantic, with a cargo of 226 containers and 3 bulk-liquid containers, to Rotterdam, and later extended the service to Bremen and Grangemouth with connecting feeder services to Antwerp, Hamburg, Felixstowe, Hull and Tilbury. At the same time, US Lines began sending containers as deck cargo into the Royal Docks in London.

For the British docker, the early 1960s was a lull akin to the Phoney War. The battles over job entitlement were fought against the mechanisation of processes which speeded up work in the port but did not take work out of their hands altogether. Packaged timber berths were opened in London, sugar was bulked in Liverpool, wine was delivered from the ships by pipe at Millwall. More mechanical equipment was introduced – forklift trucks, stacker trucks and cranes with greater lifting power – all processes which diminished the labour content without removing it.

But the container was designed to pass through a port without being opened; even Customs clearance could be arranged inland. The entire conception was of a door-to-door through-transport service in which goods were uninterrupted by human handling. Containers were boxes of eight feet by eight and a half feet by twenty, thirty or forty feet. Traditional quays were quite inadequate for handling them. The conventional berth was built around the requirements of the docker. The distance from ship to shed was governed by the distance a man could carry goods on his back or push them by truck; later facilities were geared to the forklift truck and the better reach of crane jibs. But containers needed space on a grander scale. Sheds were superfluous since the box itself protected goods from the elements and much larger cranes and mobile carriers were required. The new kind of terminal needed easy access by road and/or rail, and a large backup area for marshalling the boxes and heavy lifting gear; it might also contain a depot for stuffing and unstuffing part loads but this work could be done inland.

In most ports these facilities could not be provided by mere alteration to existing quays. If container trade was to be won, old berths had to be written off and totally new developments begun.

At container ports, the dockers' hope was to maintain access to the work of stuffing and unstuffing the boxes (which was little different to the traditional work on conventional trades) and ancillary work common to entrepôt ports, like sorting to marks, sampling, storage and preparation for distribution. But, for container operators, there were strong incentives to remove these operations from the port area, where warehouses were old and traffic congestion notorious. So the work tended to move inland, although it is exactly the same as dockers have always performed.

To chase container work inland, the docker must give up the security of registration and port-negotiated rates of pay and to date he has shown extreme reluctance to put this security in jeopardy, even if he recognises that a job in an expanding container base offers far better prospects than continuing to work in declining sectors of port transport.

The advent of the container coincided with two further changes which exacerbated an already touchy situation. First, the duty on tea was lifted in 1964, precipitating a rapid move by the tea-warehousing industry away from the docks to inland depots. When dutiable, London tea had to pass through bonded warehouses along the Thames and, even when Commonwealth preference exempted empire tea from duty, the entire crop still had to travel the same way for the Customs to determine the tea's country of origin. When the duty was lifted, it was much more economic to store inland. Tea no longer had to be lightered up-river from the enclosed docks but could be driven direct to single-storey warehouses, away from congestion in the City.

Secondly, the 1966 Docks and Harbours Act changed the method of determining disputed cases of dockwork.

INDUSTRIAL TRIBUNALS

From 1947, disputes were referred for decision to tripartite committees of unions, employers and the Dock Labour Board and unresolved cases went to magistrates' courts for settlement. This system had been satisfactory in cases involving the operations of an existing port employer, but it fell down in instances of completely new work, not covered by existing agreement. Consequently, the 1966 Act made industrial tribunals the determining authority, with appeal through the High Court and ultimately to the House of Lords.

Cases before the Tribunal are presented by lawyers and this abruptly changed the climate of determination from industrial negotiation to legal exactitude, undoubtedly to the detriment of the docker. The solutions of the tripartite committees were often compromises and were doubtless riddled with misinterpretation of the law; but at least they were solutions. The Tribunals on the other hand have sought the technically-correct definition and in most instances the written law does not correspond to unwritten custom and practice.

Towards the end of 1971, seventeen cases had been heard by Tribunal and five more were pending. Four related to container work, four to timber, four to new forms of work and two to inland tea warehouses. Of these cases, three were settled out of court and twelve went against the men, leaving one decision shared and one victory yielding a handful of jobs driving the container gantries at the Tilbury freightliner terminal.

Of themselves, the losses of work are not of great importance but the premises used in reaching these decisions are momentous and could virtually exclude any new port investment from inclusion within the Scheme. In some cases, the 'vicinity of the port' has been taken to exclude land adjacent to the dock estate; the definition of 'cargo' has excluded second handling and a most significant ruling has been given about the work 'ordinarily done' by registered labour.

The argument runs on good semantic lines. The Tribunal does not have to decide whether work is *dockwork* or not. It must decide whether it should be dockwork performed by *registered men*; and one of the governing factors is whether such work was ordinarily done by dockworkers under the Scheme. *Ipso facto*, new types of work which the dockers lay claim to cannot be given to them, because they did not do it in the past. The implications of the argument are that any new port investment, entailing new forms of work, could be removed automatically from Scheme conditions and by that token the entire container operations of Tilbury or Seaforth could be given to unregistered labour.

The lawyers are aware of the contradictions and three of the seventeen cases have been taken to the Court of Appeal and one to the House of Lords, where Lord Donovan stated that 'the relevant statutory provisions are a maze.'[68]

This case, where the NDLB asked for the operations of seven Cardiff timber merchants, who picked up discharged timber from a wharf and took it to their yards in or outside the dock estate, to be classified as registered dockwork marked the triumph of legal purity over common-sense interpretation. First the tribunal dismissed the application, then the Court of Queen's Bench decided that the work was neither in the vicinity of the port nor could it be regarded as cargo.

But at this stage, a dissenting note was added by one of the three judges, Lord Chief Justice Parker, who believed that the timber remained cargo and should have been handled by registered men had it stayed within the vicinity of the port. He said a docker was a man 'Who works in connection with the unloading and loading, movement or storage of anything which has been carried or is to be carried in a ship or other vessel. I ask myself upon what canon of instruction it is permissible to add some such words as: so long as they retain the character of a cargo or so long as the sea transit continues and the transit on land has not begun.'[69]

In the Court of Appeal, the Tribunal judgment was upheld by 2 to 1, with the Master of the Rolls, Lord Denning, maintaining that the statutory distinctions were a nonsense and conceding the Board appeal on both counts of 'vicinity' and 'cargo.' 'It would be absurd to draw a distinction between the men who do the "preliminary stacking" and those who do the "first piling",' he said. 'The work was the same; if the one group are dockworkers, so are the others. Indeed, the same men may be employed on both operations at different times in the day. They are dockers all the time.'[70]

The dockers finally lost the case in the House of Lords. But they received a worse shock in their attempt to list ore-handling at Port Talbot as registered work. The ore for the Steel Company of Wales–British Steel Corporation plant at Margam used to be unloaded in the old harbour, which could not take vessels larger than 10,000 tons. This was classified as registered work in the South Wales definition, but when the tidal harbour was built, accommodating 100,000 ton ore-carriers, the BSC sought to use their own labour.

The industrial Tribunal gave a fraction of the work to registered men but the decision was unanimously reversed at Queen's Bench by a panel of judges headed again by the Lord Chief Justice. It was the turn of the Corporation to appeal and the Appeal Court duly found in the Corporation's favour by 2 to 1. The clash between the narrow and broad view of the law came most clearly into the open at this hearing. Lord Justice Sachs and Lord Justice Buckley decided the new port was more an extension of the steelworks than the old harbour and that the South Wales definition of 1941 limited dockwork at Port Talbot solely to the dock estate. Lord Salmon, however, argued that the narrow definition of 1941, perpetuated in 1967, excluded the possibility of extending the port within the Scheme. 'There were no doubt sound industrial reasons in the 1947 and 1967 Schemes to treat these matters as what . . . has been described as "frozen",' he said. 'It is quite another thing to say that the physical boundaries of the ports and wharves shall be deemed to be treated by the Schemes as frozen. So to treat them would make no industrial sense.'[71]

With industrial sense running a poor second to strict legality, dockers soon gave up hope of extending their working rights through the law. They saw ship-owners and port employers building container groupage depots just outside the vicinity of the ports and employing non-registered labour; their predictable reaction was to forsake the Industrial Tribunal and turn to industrial sanctions – picketing, blacking selected companies and strikes. It was to be more effective.

CONTAINERS IN THE UNITED STATES

Britain's difficulties in adapting dockers' traditional working rights to the container age are common to other countries. In a few cases, container services have been completely boycotted; Venezuelan dockers refused to work Grace Line's initial service to La Guaira and the Tilbury container ban can be construed in this light.

But these were not instances of mere Luddite intransigence; they were linked to a wider policy of job protection in a period of rapid change and, in London, the aims of the Tilbury ban were always clearly stated: it was to remain until a package deal was negotiated, providing security for all dockers in the port and, since London set the pace for negotiations throughout Britain, indirectly for the whole country. As such there are parallels with the protectionist policies of the International Longshoremen's Association (ILA) in the Atlantic and Gulf ports of America and the International Longshoremen's and Warehousemen's Union (ILWU) on the Pacific seaboard.

Containers came to the USA at a time when Teddy Gleason's ILA was still trying to secure single rates of pay and conditions in ports within its jurisdiction. Union policy thus had two objectives, to safe-guard the future against containers and to use container bargaining as a weapon in the fight for industry-wide terms.

By the 1960s, the ILA had established a single rate of hourly pay but the guaranteed minimum earnings level varied from port to port. For instance, up till January 1969, only New York, Boston and Philadelphia paid the guarantee of 1,600 hours' work a year and the · 2,080 hour guarantee, conceded by the New York Shipping Associa-tion as the equivalent to a full forty-hour week in the 1968–71 con-tract, applied at first only to Atlantic ports, not the Gulf of Mexico. Container terms, however, were added to the system of 'masterpoints' which had to be observed by all ports. The union wanted to share the benefits of mechanisation with all members, whether there were con-tainer developments in their home ports or not.

The union's first success came in 1959 in an arbitration award, which set up a royalty fund of one dollar (now two dollars) per ton on all containers passing through the ports, to help pay for longshore-men's benefits and to give some inducements to ship-owners to stick with labour intensive forms of conventional work.

A refinement came in 1962 with the creation of a fifty-mile circle round the ports, within which all container consolidation was to be done by union labour. If it was not done by union labour inland, the container would be opened and re-packed on the waterfront or, if shippers were caught sneaking a container through, they had to pay a 1,000 dollars fine. The effect was to keep container groupage largely on the quayside itself; this was the traditional element of dockwork, involving the package and unpacking of part-load consignments into single boxes. Any container emanating from outside the limit was not affected, although it paid the royalty, which has become, in effect, an imposition for the removal of work content from the longshoremen.

The fifty-mile radius did not apply to full container loads packed by the owners of the cargo, where the work had never been the long-shoremen's, but only to groupage containers and part-loads. Although smaller ports might not get container trade, there was every chance that there would be inland work for the men; thus, goods from Massachusetts might be stuffed by Boston dockers even if the containers were eventually shipped from New York.

Since all ports between Portland, Maine, and Hampton Roads, Virginia, lie within 100 miles of each other, a continuous corridor in which traditional dockwork was reserved for dockers was created for the main Atlantic trade routes.

The rigid definition was drawn up before the main burst of container investment and thus the battle for job rights at inland depots was largely pre-empted.

Essentially this was a protective agreement, which allowed port authorities to invest safely in container terminals, knowing that new trade would be handled. On the West Coast, the ILWU appeared far more ambitious. It ignored exact definition of dockwork but gave *carte blanche* for new investment in return for secure earnings and substantial pension payments.

This Mechanisation and Modernisation agreement was a phenomenal success in its first five years of operation and is certainly the best publicised agreement concerning dock labour. It took three years to prepare and had its genesis in a union caucus of 1957 when delegates decided that modernisation would come, whether they wanted it or not, and that the best policy was to secure a 'share of the machine.' Next year, the employers agreed to maintain the labour force at its current level for a year, subject only to natural wastage, while they developed a measurement system to assess potential man-hour savings. Subsequent study of the Conformance and Performance Programme persuaded them that the shared gains of modernisation could not be accurately costed and, rather than put a price on each restrictive practice, they offered to buy the union rulebook and have freedom to work exactly as they wanted. After final negotiations in the 'fish-bowl,' with dockers watching their officials in action, the terms were put to ballot and accepted by 7,882 to 3,695, with Los Angeles the only port where resistance was high.

The men got hefty pay increases and the employers agreed to pay 27,500,000 dollars over five and a half years into a jointly administered fund to provide an annual wage guarantee and a lump sum of 7,920 dollars to men who retired at the age of 65 with at least twenty-five years of service.

Between 1960 and 1965, labour costs fell, quicker turn-rounds were achieved and the expansion of trade meant that there was no labour surplus so natural attrition of the 12,500 labour force had to be made up by a recruitment of 2,000 men. Table 4 sets out a performance chart for these years.

In 1966, the agreement was renewed. The men had been sweetened by the disbursement of 13,000,000 dollars which had accumulated in the guarantee fund but was untouched and by a pension payment of 13,000 dollars at 63 and another large wages increase. But the new five-year contract was only accepted by 6,448 to 3,985 with the votes of San Francisco and the smaller ports outweighing the objections from Seattle, Portland and Los Angeles. The M and M agreement was turning sour; when it came to be renewed in 1971, the ILWU embarked on the first coastwide stoppage since 1948 and the ensuing strike was one of the largest in US history.

Table 4   Performance of first M and M agreement

	1960	1961	1962	1963	1964	1965
Tonnage handled (millions)[1]	19·9	18·8	19·8	21·7	23·4	26·3
Hours worked (millions)	29·8	29·8	26·7	27·8	27·8	30·1
Wages bill ($ millions)	124·4	124·5	126·3	137·9	143·0	162·1
Labour cost per ton ($)	6·26	6·43	6·39	6·35	6·11	6·16
Hours per ton	1·502	1·477	1·349	1·281	1·184	1·143

[1] Five tons of bulk cargo are equated with one ton of general cargo.
Source: 1966 annual report of Pacific Maritime Association.

Many reasons for this reversal in fortune have been put forward: that employers initially avoided capital mechanisation and did not take the physical load out of dockwork: that older men benefited more than the young; and that the deal was too favourable to employers who suspiciously stopped keeping statistics once it was clear the original deal was sound. (Max Kossoris, the US Government statistician who worked closely with the ILWU and the Pacific Maritime Association in the early years of the deal, claimed that employers believed they had saved more than 100,000,000 dollars in the first contract period, on top of meeting the special payments. The union estimate was strangely low, at 51,000,000 dollars!) [72]

But the essential problem was job rights. After the buoyant expansion of the early 1960s, containerisation bit into security and as container groupage moved inland, restrictive practices crept back to the waterfront, particularly with regard to manning scales and the insistence that all goods should 'touch the skin of the dock,' often involving double-handling. No agreement was reached with the Teamsters, the road haulage union, about rights on the quayside until a stoppage in 1969 and, even after the 1971–2 ILWU strike, the position regarding inland work is still undetermined. According to Joel Fadem, this was at the heart of the West Coast's problem.

'It was one thing when a new machine eliminates work outright at a specifiable point on the job or, conversely, when particular work drifts away and is assimilated elsewhere within the confines of "The System." But it's another thing for the longshoremen to see daily the containers moving clearly to and from distinct points away from the docks. Where is the point at which their job territory disappears? The problem is complicated by the fact that work associated with the stuffing and unstuffing of containers had frequently moved outside the jurisdiction of the dock employers, as well as the union. In fact, it could be maintained that work of this type is now outside the scope of the West Coast agreement itself.' [73]

BRITISH CONTAINER DISPUTES AND THE BRISTOW REPORT

If the ILA's grabbing of inland dockwork appears a crude use of the union's industrial strength, it had the merit of establishing a clear definition at the start of the container age. Britain, like the ILWU, is still struggling without proper definitions and the disputes in this country have arisen from attempts by dockers to nibble their way into new jobs.

Before 1972, the most serious stoppage came in the summer of 1969, when Liverpool shop stewards called a strike to get the work in Aintree container base, less than two miles from the port, reserved for registered dock labour. The Containerbase Federation had already negotiated a manning agreement for its six depots with the road haulage section of the TGWU, with the full knowledge of top union officials. It needed the personal intervention of Jack Jones to concoct a peace formula in Liverpool; it guaranteed registered dockers first option to new jobs and conditions which matched those in the port.

In Hull, there have been token stoppages against the use of unregistered labour at Humber wharves for timber discharge and in London lightermen struck against the movement of grain within the port in self-propelled barges manned by seamen members of the TGWU.

Then, in November 1969, a minor dispute over dockwork threatened to shut down London. It started as a protest against Hay's Wharf, the largest wharfinger employer, which was shutting down its entire port labour operations in the Pool of London and was widely suspected of wanting its river frontage for property development. The company's last months of operation had been acrimonious. Dairy trade had been lost to containers and Polish trade had switched to Ipswich because of unsatisfactory service at Mark Brown's wharf where Sir David Burnett, chairman of the Proprietors of Hay's Wharf, claimed the 300 men staged 123 unofficial strikes costing 8,308 man-days and go-slows for 6,800 man-days in the eighteen months after Decasualisation. Sir David wrote a stiff letter to Peter Shea, the TGWU's London dock secretary saying 'There has clearly been a complete breakdown of your Union's control of its membership and of your Union's ability to ensure that your members' obligations under agreements are fulfilled. . . . Either in the next few weeks we lay the foundations of a successful reorganisation . . . or all port transport work inevitably ceases in Tooley Street.' [74]

Sir David, of course, was right; the labour record was shocking. But there was another side to the coin. His managing director of the Tooley Street wharves was Bill Tonge, the chairman of NAPE, and some saw advantage in calling his personal husbandry into question; moreover, if the wharves closed down, the Proprietors still had other subsidiaries in transport and warehousing which could continue much the same work, but outside the vicinity of the port. Moreover, there was an element of truth in the dockers' contention that management wanted to force the issue of overmanning and industrial relations to a crunch. According to the *Observer*, Hay's Wharf had quietly acquired a third of its twenty-five-acre site since 1958 and were no amateurs in the property market. 'Old companies seldom die, they merely re-develop their assets,' it said.[75]

The strike opened in the last weeks of Hay's Wharf's operations as a port employer and the TGWU intended to confine it to company products and premises handling them, especially the company's Dagenham storage complex. But it quickly spread out of control, shutting down large sections of the port.

The Department of Employment intervened and Conrad Heron, the chief conciliation officer, chaired three meetings on 5, 6 and 7 November 1969. Government concern stemmed from the summer months when Phase II Devlin talks had broken down and the TWGU had made it clear that they were as concerned about dockwork as pay. Now a novel manner of settlement was reached. The Department agreed to sponsor a private committee, consisting equally of London port employers and union representatives, to re-examine the definition of dockwork in London. This formula was a God-send for the unions. The Committee would have the guise of official sanction, it would represent the views only of those already engaged in dockwork – who had nothing to lose by its extension – and it might establish a new target which could be pressed on the employers nationally.

With the appointment of Peter Bristow, QC, to head the Committee, the strike quickly folded and two months later the committee's report was produced.

The committee found that existing definitions resided in five pieces of legislation, the Dockworkers Act and Scheme, the Essential Work Order for London, the Port of London Acts of 1920 and 1935 and the register established for employers in 1940. In strict legal terms, the port did not extend beyond the high water mark of the Thames between Teddington and Havengore Creek, plus the premises of registered employers in the port or its vicinity.

The proposed new definition made a dramatic change to the nature of cargo, allowing any number of handlings by dock labour within the confines of the port, and a still more dramatic change to the 'vicinity.' This, it suggested, should extend throughout a corridor five miles wide on either side of the river. The union side also pressed for a ten-mile corridor for container handling but the employers would not agree. The effect was to give dockers access to a variety of premises in an area of 800 square miles for conventional goods and 1,800 square miles for containers, on the disputed clause. Also it brought all of

Foulness within the reach of London dockers and gave them theoretical rights to container work at Heathrow airport.

The Bristow report is an unnerving example of the long-term welfare of an industry being sacrificed to immediate needs. It had the virtue of settling a strike, but it promised a solution which the industry and even the Government was in no position to deliver. In short, it showed that the vested interests of port transport were prepared to sit down and carve out a larger sphere of influence – but that was hardly a surprising insight on human nature.

The idea of the corridor was derived from the East Coast agreement of the USA with the important difference that it did not just apply to containers but all forms of dockwork and thus intruded on many long-established businesses. To outsiders, the Bristow report was anathema. They were not consulted until it was published and the proposals had then become the minimum demands of the London dockers. Employers feared they might have to dismiss their own staff to take on dockers in the corridor and that wage inflation and all the worst aspects of dockland's labour relations would follow. Working men were also worried because it affected their job rights and the TGWU branch at the London International Freight Terminal at Stratford East threatened to tear up their union cards and join the National Union of Railwaymen *en bloc*, if dockers entered their depots.

To union leaders, the report provided ammunition in the fight for dockwork once they were ready to start battle. But first they needed to settle conflicting interests of different occupational groups and Jack Jones had to make the peace quickly between his road haulage and docker sections. In the meantime, they could easily be exposed to attack from within their own ranks for failing to secure the recommendations.

Many people blithely assumed that the Bristow recommendations could be implemented by Ministerial order within the ambit of the existing Scheme. But lawyers doubted this and it appeared as if the dockers could only get their corridor by putting a new Act through Parliament. The Labour Government was not going to move, while nationalisation was still on the cards, and, after the 1970 general election, no union leader wanted to offer up the Scheme to the hands of a Conservative majority in a climate so unfavourable to the docker.

Within days of the report's publication, objections started to stream into the Department of Employment. A group of London and Essex businessmen set up an Anti-Bristow Committee to keep dockers out of warehousing and haulage. The London Chamber of Commerce, the Shipping Council, the National Association of Warehouse Keepers, the Inland Tea Warehouse Keepers and the Road Haulage Association all took up the cudgels. In a circular, the Confederation of British Industry asked member companies to send in comments as soon as possible but did not neglect to make its own view clear: that Bristow meant joint control and joint control in the docks had undermined management functions and forced the unions either to lose the confidence of their members or to 'nullify effective management if they declined to do so.'[76]

By the time Peter Shea reported back to his regional docks committee, the time for euphoria was past. 'Everybody's objected except Mickey Mouse,' he told the grim-faced delegates.

DEFINITION AND THE FUTURE

The Bristow report was not implemented and the issue of definition lay fallow until the Liverpool crisis of March 1972. Then shop stewards laid claim to all stuffing and stripping of part-load containers, no matter how far inland the work was being done. They insisted that all the consignments should be brought inside the dock-gate and registered dockers would then stuff them. With import groupage containers, dockers would do the stripping on dockland premises.

While the Mersey dockers scored several successes in persuading Liverpool hauliers and warehousing companies to leave the work to registered men, many horses had bolted by 1972 and their principal victim, Heaton's Transport (St Helens) had modernised a warehouse for container-work, twelve miles inland, more than two years before the shop stewards retaliated.

Although container blacking became a national issue, the Mersey dockers were essentially chasing peripheral work. They accepted they had no right to work full container loads going to or leaving a manufacturer's premises, but they sought to prevent the proliferation of small contractors undercutting dock rates – the cowboys.

Unless the definition of dockwork is changed or ignored (mutually by employers and unions), it will continue to be a major source of trouble. When the Devlin Committee recommended that the Scheme be kept unchanged in its essentials, it was concerned primarily with the issues of joint control and discipline, which they rightly regarded as inviolable. Definition was still in the hands of tripartite committees dealing with the fringe areas of dockwork and the full impact of containers had yet to be felt.

Had the Committee sat five years later, it might well have concluded that the Scheme stood between the dockers and new jobs, especially when a legalistic interpretation could freeze dockwork within its existing limits, and in all likelihood it would have urged change, to give the docker working rights to the benefits made possible by modernisation.

As the Scheme stands, the unregistered worker is at great advantage over the registered docker, both in the distinction between Scheme and non-Scheme ports and in his access to container work. The hostility of dockers to the non-Scheme ports is already marked. Many ports were left out of the Scheme in 1947 because they were too tiny to sustain a regular labour force. They pottered through the next decade but the 1960 Lloyd-Williams report marked a watershed. It made it clear that very strong arguments would be needed to change the status of a port – and the volume of trade was not one of them. It said the main criteria for inclusion should be a port's *need* for the guarantee provisions of the Scheme to regularise employment. Thus any non-Scheme port which offered permanent employment – or a lesser degree of casualism than appertained in Scheme ports – was virtually certain of staying exempt. Undertakings which might have been dissuaded from investment lest the growth of traffic brought them within the Scheme, felt free to expand.

The statistics of port growth in the 1960s show that some ports benefited from their new 'safety.' The expansion of conventional trade in London and Liverpool tailed off and declined; the medium-sized ports varied in growth but the most explosive growth rates were found in small ports, many of them outside the Scheme.

Felixstowe is the most notable example. Its dock and railway company was incorporated in 1875 and, by the mid-1950s, it seemed moribund with little trade and only nine dockers. But the foresight of the Parker family and a new chief executive director, Ian Trelawny, enabled Felixstowe to capture trade from shippers disenchanted with the larger ports and to stake a sizeable claim to the burgeoning North Sea trade to EFTA and EEC countries. In 1959, trade had risen to

200,000 tons and the labour force stood at 90 men. Permanent employment was granted readily, along with pay and benefits far in advance of national rates; these included a pension, profit-sharing bonuses, life insurance and sick pay of thirteen weeks at basic rates. £3,500,000 was then invested in a container terminal which opened in 1968 and now is used by thirteen services. For a time, Felixstowe – 'that pokey little hole' as it is disrespectfully called in London – vied with Tilbury and Rotterdam as the largest container port in Europe.

In 1969, Felixstowe handled 1,939,000 tons of general cargo and other non-Scheme ports were also picking up a disproportionate share of new traffic. Shoreham won a large amount of the wine trade from London. Ramsgate, which could not provide fifteen hours work a week for twenty men in 1959, became the main port of entry for Volkswagen cars and handles 40,000 a year; and the fishing harbour of Whitby has developed a bustling little trade with 200 port calls by cargo vessels per year.

It is unconvincing to attribute these successes solely to geographical location, lack of traffic congestion or more dynamic management because, for every advantage, there are offsets. These might include poor road access, distance from main conurbations and industrial hinterlands, the shortage of deep-water berths or specialist ancillary services. Moreover, Whitehall pressure since the Rochdale Report has been for centralising investment, since Britain is overpopulated with ports.

The main point of difference, as the men and employers realised, was the functioning of the Scheme and labour relations. In a non-Scheme port, an employer could hope to provide a slightly cheaper service, assuming the cost of permanent employment before Decasualisation did not exceed the cost of the Board levy; he could also hope for more entrepreneurial freedom and relief from the disputes and delays of the major ports. These are sound and legitimate commercial considerations but the predictable result has been to increase the men's insecurity in Scheme ports and recharge the cycle which led to the original frustration. When the registered docker hears that a major container development is planned at Falmouth and knows that it could go to non-Scheme labour the frustration increases; and he is frankly afraid of the effect of the projected Channel Tunnel on his livelihood. The tunnel would remove the near monopoly he has on the movement of goods and – in the words of the Londoner which opened this chapter – he would have to man a portcullis to maintain this stranglehold.

To assert that the large ports have mortgaged their future because of the labour relations of the past is not a recipe for industrial peace. Ideally, all dockers should know that they compete on equal terms and that one group is not suffering at the expense of another.

It is not realistic to think that the Scheme could be extended to all ports – although many aspects of it which seemed most revolutionary in 1947 are now accepted by progressive managements – but a strong case can be made for requiring non-Scheme ports to contribute financially to the dockers' severance fund, since they have contributed in large measure to the national over-manning problem in the ports.

In the long run, however, it will be more important to help dockers stake a claim to new *forms* of transport work. The obstacles remain the boundary demarcations of dockwork and the unique character of registration and, in both instances, greater flexibility is required. It is manifestly absurd that today's inflexible definitions could lead to the virtual disappearance of dockers' jobs, leaving a diminishing number of men on the waterfront to handle a diminishing amount of non-unitised cargo in an area determined by obsolete definitions.

But mere extension of the dockers' working area, as in the Bristow corridor, creates conflicts with other work groups, like lorry drivers and warehousemen, who could legitimately ask for statutory protection of their rights, until all flexibility between work groups disappears. At the core of the problem is the concept of registration and it must be modified if a solution is to be found.

George Cattell, in a speech which coincided with the Bristow report, made this very point in trenchant terms. He said the Scheme had no place in an industry which had changed in form and content so completely in the last decade. Labour intensive dockwork was disappearing and the manual labourer was being replaced by skilled and salaried personnel, specialising in the operation of mechanical equipment, planned and integrated systems and administrative and control duties.

'Are we seriously to preserve a kind of closed shop for the sons of mechanical conveyor operators, for truck drivers, button pushers, systems analysts and container controllers, merely because their ancestors were registered dockers? Why not registration for the rest of the people who are employed in the ports and, if for them, then why not for railwaymen, coal miners, steel workers, post office employees and countless others? The question is a vital one and I pose it deliberately and without suggesting for a moment that the unions, specifically the TGWU, should abandon its bridgehead of joint control.'[77]

Cattell was one of very few people who could be so outspoken and still get a hearing. At Rootes Motors, he helped introduce measured daywork and establish the highest hourly rate of pay in motor car assembly. As head of the Department of Employment's manpower and productivity services, he had cast his eye over many industries and as chairman of the National Docks Modernisation Committee, he could see the momentum of sound negotiation receding because of the failure to question fundamental assumptions. He was not worried about joint control. It could be written into any agreement where management exercised authority by consent.

'But the principle of registration is an entirely different matter because it requires a definition of what is dockwork, or perhaps a definition of what is railwayman's work or what is motor industry work or road haulage work. And these definitions are going to prove increasingly difficult in a world in which manufacture or even agricultural products may be pre-packed at the factory or the farm and despatched to the other side of the world with attention from none but skilled mechanical operators, drivers and seamen.

'In this decade thousands of men who now regard themselves as dockers and enjoy special protection are going to find that there is no traditional dockwork for them. But there will be plenty of other work and enormous opportunities for acquiring new knowledge, skills and social benefits. The trouble is that it will not be what we now accept as traditional dockwork. Or will it? The issue that I am posing is that the implications of that question are not receiving enough attention. I don't believe they have been thought through by the trade union leaders or politicians . . . and it is high time that somebody paid attention to them or we shall be going into the future as blind as the ship-owners and the port employers were before the last war.'

The abolition of registration is as impractical and unlikely as the extension of joint control to all ports, and Cattell's vision of the specialist white-collar labour force in the docks is still a long way off. What, however, is needed is a new approach to defining dockwork which will be a bridge between the old and the new, and will overcome interoccupational jealousies and the dockers' intrinsic fear of change.

CHAPTER SEVEN

First Steps towards Modernisation

'Our proposals for decasualisation were successfully launched this morning and are still floating.' David Lloyd to Andrew Crichton, 4 September 1962.

If the chain of events leading to Decasualisation is traced back through the 1960s, the first link is found in the hands of an unlikely figure – a stocky London tally clerk by the name of Tom Roffey. As chairman of an unofficial strike committee he led a long stoppage in September and October 1960. The deep-sea trade of Britain's largest port was halted for nearly four weeks and the issues were incomprehensible to anyone unversed in the history of dockland.

The 1,600 tally clerks, whose job is checking and measuring cargo, are unique to the ocean trades in London; in other parts ordinary dockers work as checkers. Now they were short-handed and the London dock labour board instructed fifty dockers to transfer to the tally clerks' sub-register. For the dockers, the switch was to all intents and purposes promotion. They had already performed checking duties but now would get permanently the clerks' higher rate of pay, with the promise of more regular employment and less arduous work. But the transfer offended the clerks' sectional interest. The extra manpower reduced the scarcity value of their labour and, in any case, they would have preferred new entrants to be drawn from their kith and kin. Equally, transfer upset job hierarchies because ageing tally clerks did not want ageing dockers competing for the softer jobs – the corners they felt they had earned by dint of long service.

But the board's order was proper and was endorsed by the five union members, so it should have been obeyed. Instead the clerks struck, 13,000 dockers were made idle and the stoppage continued even when the Ministry of Labour ordered an inquiry. This strike angered a puzzled public and it folded without concessions to the men.

Roffey soon left the unofficial movement to become a full-time official of the TGWU and a group of employers realised that deteriorating labour relations could no longer be attributed simply to bloody-mindedness or the Scheme: something had to be done about the system of employment in its entirety and the docker had to be given more fundamental security of employment and earnings.

In David Lloyd, London employers found a man who would not shrink from the formidable task of reforming the casual system. He was a director of Ellerman Lines and later of Hovey Antwerp, the stevedoring company in which Ellerman had a 60 per cent interest. As such he could wear the hat both of the ship-owner and port employer, but primarily he was a ship-owners' man and his detachment from daily operations let him cut through the minutiae of committee work with an authority and urgency uncommon to the docks. It allowed him to concentrate on principle, without losing sight of the particular.

In 1960, Lloyd was the new chairman of the London Ship-Owners Dock Labour Committee and, shortly after the tally clerks' strike ended, he called in colleagues from the PLA, short sea trades and wharfingers to outline 'a fundamental proposal affecting dock labour relations in the port of London.'

The proposal was indeed fundamental. He described the vicious circle in which men were interested chiefly in the pay packet and avoiding unemployment, union officials were often disorganised and ineffective and harassed employers compounded these failings by indecisive management. 'Employers have often had to resort to the use of illegal payments and malpractices to obtain the movement of essential cargoes and the turn-round of ships, thus encouraging the men, discouraging the union and creating a vicious circle. Collectively their bargaining power had grown progressively weaker and indeed at present there is little hope of successful negotiation on such vital matters as mechanisation and mobility. In the docks there is a sense of frustration and indeed at times of apathy; in short we have lost the initiative; it rests not with us, not with the union but with the men and the agitator.'[78]

Lloyd's proposal for restoring the initiative to the official negotiating bodies was a package deal which would abolish the low fall-back guarantee and bring all men on to the minimum time-rate, whether they worked or not.

He did not minimise the difficulties of the proposal. London's example would almost certainly spread to other ports where the level of underemployment might make the cost prohibitive; it might spread to seamen who had a similar form of fall-back payment for time spent on shore and it would certainly result in union pressure to improve the time rate. But the main difficulty was one of principle. Were employers ready to set a precedent by paying men as much for not working as some men might earn when gainfully employed? To the old school, this was anathema and men like Lord Sanderson, who had led negotiations in the 1930s, were still powerful figures in the boardroom.

But the appalling strike record and London's belief that it had subsidised other ports through the Scheme were factors on Lloyd's side. For the past five years, London had paid far more to the Scheme than was needed to finance its own guarantee and Lloyd reckoned that £1,805,000 had been contributed to subsidising rival ports and the money could be better spent in tackling London's problems.

As a result, the proposal was well received and a Committee drew up two plans for implementing full permanency. Plan A was virtually a prototype for Decasualisation as it was introduced in 1967. In each sector of the port,[79] all registered men would be employed on a permanent basis and fluctuation in labour requirement would be met by flexible manning scales and inter-company transfer. Flexibility meant manning-up a gang in times of labour surplus and manning-down when men were short and the transfer clause was introduced primarily to help the Surrey dock employers, whose seasonal timber trade left them with a large surplus of men in the winter months.

Plan B envisaged the direct employment of all men by a 'holding' consortium of employers, one per sector. The consortium would not operate, but solely hire out men to existing employers and it was assumed that existing permanent men would have to be thrown into this employers' pool. The appeal of Plan B was that it ensured the survival of the small employer, drawing labour from the consortium in much the same way he drew it from the reserve pool.

The two plans were offered as alternatives which could co-exist in different sectors but not overlap. Either, it was felt, would achieve complete decasualisation and remove the insecurities to which so many strikes were attributed.

At this point, before either plan had been discussed with the unions, events at national level overtook London; and for three years Plan A disappeared from view, a victim of its own daring. It alone required the employers to decasualise as well as the men and by the time it re-emerged, the employers' initiative was blunted and the Government had asked Lord Devlin to point the way ahead.

It was the possibility of the Government ordering an inquiry into dock labour in 1961, concurrently with the Rochdale inquiry into port operation, which spurred the NJC into action. Harold Macmillan and John Hare (Lord Blakenham), his Minister of Labour, both favoured the second inquiry but were dissuaded by NAPE in January, after learning of the London proposals. Instead of a Devlin-type inquiry, it was agreed to make detailed changes to Scheme administration through an investigation under Lord Forster.

In May, however, London had blown up for the second time in six months. The Lower Oliver's Wharf strike, like the tally clerks', was a stoppage hardly comprehensible outside the industry; it began at a small wharf of Mr Cohen, a manufacturer, who took delivery of straw-board by barge once a month. The London dock labour board allowed him to use six of his own employees to cover this small amount of dockwork, giving the men 'listed' registration. But some militants felt that fully-registered dock labour should be used. They claimed to have seen Cohen driving a crane and his wife tallying and, in the en-suing strike, 15,000 men on the riverside and the enclosed docks walked out. The stoppage lasted more than a week before Frank Cousins secured a return-to-work.

In talks at the Ministry of Labour after the strike, the national movement towards decasualisation was born. Hare first prevailed on Cousins to review the machinery of his union in dockland and then asked Sir Andrew Crichton (then Mr Crichton), J. Morris Gifford, Bill Tonge and Lloyd what the employers would do to improve the situation. (These four were key figures in the negotiations of the 1960s. Sir Andrew was chairman of NAPE until 1964 and then was closely involved with the Tilbury container ban as chairman of OCL. Morris Gifford was general manager of NAPE and then director general of the National Ports Council. Tonge was chairman of the London Port Employers Association until he succeeded Sir Andrew at NAPE and Lloyd inherited the London Association until 1968.) Sir Andrew undertook to approach the union leaders to prepare the ground for a national campaign towards decasualisation.

Sir Andrew and Cousins were true to their word. On 6 June, the NJC launched a pilot study and in October it issued the 'Crichton–Cousins manifesto'.

The unions made much greater concessions than the employers in the directive. They admitted that casualism had bred attitudes which militated against the observance of agreements and the efficient use of manpower, and they conceded that the restrictive practices which had grown up over generations to give hiring and job protection should be scrapped before, or simultaneously with, the decasualisation of the industry. 'The real obstacle to more effective decasualisation has been the lack of flexibility in the deployment of labour in the most effective manner' and the remedy was for both sides of the industry to agree to mechanisation, rationalising the employing structure and flexible manning scales.

In the seven-point programme which local joint councils were asked to implement in three months, the union leadership sanctioned the scrapping of all such practices and the introduction of shift work, where appropriate. In return, the employers would keep the Dock Labour Scheme, hire most men on a weekly basis – but without compulsion on men or management to accept an offer of permanency – and, again without obligation, be prepared to recruit all new entrants as permanent men.

The influence of the M and M agreement is apparent. The employers hoped they could virtually buy the rulebook on the promise of partial decasualisation and, from that moment, the chances of winning rank-and-file acceptance began to fade. The 1965 Devlin report stated quite bluntly that the employers were trying to buy too much for too little and, not surprisingly, the men feared their leaders were committing them further than they wanted to go.

It is difficult to explain the selfless abandon of the union commitment without recalling the leadership structure of the TGWU. Even when Cousins swung the union to the left, the autocratic hierarchy remained and the leaders believed it was their duty to pluck back the initiative from the unofficial committees by choosing a platform so radical that it could not be negotiated from the shopfloor.

Cousins could take the helm because of the peculiar constitution of the NJC which made the general secretary of the TGWU a *de facto* joint chairman of the Council, irrespective of his experience in the docks.

For Bevin, this constitution had allowed him to stay involved in struggles he initiated before the amalgamation. But Cousins' background was in road haulage and he did not attend NJC meetings after his elevation to the general secretaryship until the time had come for reform. He retained a passing interest in dock affairs thereafter but it was his lesser officials, who had to negotiate decasualisation against growing attacks from the rank-and-file, who labelled the manifesto a charter for 'industrial dartmoor.'

O'Leary, as national docks secretary, was forced progressively to stiffen union demands. First, he said, partial decasualisation was unacceptable. 'It will be every man's right to be decasualised: this may take longer in some places than others, but it must be borne in mind that it is every man's ultimate right.'[80] The commitment to abolish all restrictive practices was also watered down. O'Leary said that working arrangements would no doubt lend themselves to change *as a result of* decasualisation – a far cry from the prior removal of all bars to full efficiency.

Local discussion of the manifesto was painfully slow. In Southampton it was rejected outright by the men; in Hull and Leith talks foundered on the union insistence on 100 per cent decasualisation; in Middlesbrough and the Hartlepools, proposals for manning scales and piece rates were rejected and at Plymouth the men refused even to discuss restrictive practices before full permanency was achieved.

Elsewhere talks began but little progress was made before the NJC's three-month deadline passed. Then local talks got submerged in successive crises over national pay negotiations.

In 1962, the unions claimed a $4\frac{1}{2}$ per cent increase and a reduction of the working week from 44 to 40 hours, at a time when government policy was to limit wage movement to 2 per cent. The 44-hour week had been given after the Shaw award and most industries had by now moved to 42 hours. But the employers were loathe to give up their right to Saturday-morning work because of the long-standing argument as to whether overtime was voluntary or compulsory. A national strike was called for 14 May, a Monday, and only called off the day before after long talks at the Ministry of Labour.

(On this occasion, Sir Andrew recalls, Macmillan flew back from Inverness to see the port employers at Downing Street and greeted him thus: 'My dear fellow, I am so sorry for you . . . the dockers are such difficult people, just the fathers and the sons, the uncles and nephews. So like the House of Lords, hereditary and no intelligence required, and so hard on the "Cousins", don't you think?")

The settlement conceded the wage claim but staggered the reduction of hours over two years, on condition that weekend overtime was freely worked. The railwaymen had won the 42-hour week earlier in the year and the dyke could not be held against the dockers; but the 40-hour week came earlier to the docks than industry as a whole and was to be a source of constant vexation during the Devlin years.

It was instrumental in bringing the next national pay crisis to a head in the autumn of 1964. The end of compulsory Saturday-morning work merely confirmed that weekend work was already being withheld in London and the employers were furious to be presented with a new national claim, even before the 40-hour week was introduced in July 1964 and when the terms of the 1962 agreement were being ignored. Now, however, the unofficial movement was at its zenith and local decasualisation talks had broken down in London and Liverpool. It was clear that the major inquiry into labour relations was in the offing. The Rochdale report had said that decasualisation was an 'urgent practical necessity' and, with a general election imminent, the new wage crisis threw the docks industry immediately into the political arena.

For Cousins, it was an extremely delicate position. Union leadership had to keep abreast of rank-and-file pressure and unofficial stoppages had already started. But a national strike before the election would discredit the Labour movement and Cousins' only course was to play for time. At a delegate conference, O'Leary appealed for calm. He and fellow officials often had to spend more time 'protecting themselves against unfair onslaughts from unofficial elements than they did negotiating with employers.' He could not stop unofficial pressure but he reminded delegates that 'you do not keep a dog and bark yourself.'

The vital delegate conference was held on 7 October and Cousins came with a formula which could buy him time: no increase on the cash offer of an extra 12s 6d a week instead of the 25s demanded but the promise of an immediate NJC inquiry into the wages structure and another attempt to tackle decasualisation. No vote was taken but the conference adjourned until after the election.

The situation was saved. When the delegates next met, Labour had its five-seat majority, Cousins was in the Cabinet and Ray Gunter, the new Minister of Labour, was on the point of setting up the Devlin Inquiry, first to settle the pay issue and then to report on Decasualisation and the causes of dissension in the industry.

The Devlin Committee was to draw heavily on the experience of 1961–5 in formulating their conclusions and it is apposite, at this juncture, to consider the progress of these attempts at self-sponsored reform.

The picture is one of apparent failure. Employers had put forward plans and they were spurned, the precarious authority of the unions had been further undermined by unofficial activities and what little goodwill existed had been dissipated by five years of frustrated negotiation. But in spite of the set-backs, the effort was not wasted. Both sides of the industry had been forced to examine what they really meant by decasualisation and they had been driven slowly towards common ground.

Employers often regarded decasualisation as a panacea for all ills. They accepted that it would involve some extra cost but they expected due reward in greater efficiency. To some extent, they and the union leaders also believed that it would destroy the power-base of the unofficial movement. But to the rank-and-file, permanency was meaningless if it removed the protective practices and pattern of informal relationships which brought a semblance of justice to casualism, without putting something better in their place. It was little advantage to replace the guarantee with a minimum time rate worth a few shillings more, if underemployment remained and the whole labour force was denied the security of a fair share of work and stability of earnings. If decasualisation could not be seen to provide this element of justice, it would not merit the sacrifice of practices associated with casualism.

The sparring of the early 1960s clarified these issues for the Devlin Committee and persuaded the employers that any scheme which did not give 100 per cent permanency stood little chance of success and that full permanency could not be achieved under the present employing structure.

FULL PERMANENCY

The 1961 manifesto had stated that decasualisation might be impractical for some ports because of irregular trade and that a casual fringe might have to be kept in all ports to meet fluctuation. Next year, the Rochdale report added its weight to this view, suggesting that 70 or 80 per cent permanency might be realistic.

The result was that no port volunteered to decasualise by allocating its *entire* labour force to operating employers. London promptly dropped Plan A and developed Plan B in slightly altered form. Operating employers would build up their own force of permanent men but the rest of the labour force would be held by the consortium – Port Employers (London) Ltd. – as 'unattached' men or 'rover perms'. The consortium consisted of all operating employers who wanted to draw labour from its pool. At first, consortium men were to be allocated at management's discretion but, in deference to the unions, it was later agreed that the free call could be kept, allowing men to go on competing for work on old-established lines.

It was a thoroughly untidy arrangement because the consortium was doing little more than replace the hiring functions of the Dock Labour Board, which continued unchanged in its control of welfare, discipline and the register. It would have perpetuated the division between the first- and second-class dockers, the cause of so much jealousy among the men, and it would not have brought many more people into a close relationship with a single employer. Ironically, the employers knew perfectly well that the scheme was a hotch-potch – all these faults were raised in a committee assessment – but it had the overriding attraction of allowing the casual employer to stay in business.

Liverpool's plan was even more complicated and, arguably, more wrong-headed. It was based on the assumption that some dockers liked the casual system and that men should choose whether to decasualise themselves. Four grades of docker were proposed. First were the men who were already perms, a tenth of the labour force, who would be called established contract workers. They would be joined by a new batch of perms – company contract workers – engaged on the same terms. Then a consortium would employ most of the residue, hiring them out to operators short of labour. Finally there was to be a reserve pool – the men who wanted to stay casual and new entrants to the industry who would have to be casual for a two-year probationary period.

Although it was planned to limit the pool to 10 per cent of the men, the disadvantages were obvious. Pool men would be as casual as in Sexton's day, but would not even qualify for work until the rest of the labour force was employed. People who chose to stay in the pool would be steeped in the attitudes of casualism and would pass on these attitudes to all new entrants. In fact this 'New Deal' not only offended the principle of equal treatment for all, but would have bred malcontents.

The only other ports where negotiations kept going were Bristol and Glasgow. In the former, employers were thinking in terms of increasing the percentage of permanent men from 18 to 25 or 33 per cent. In Glasgow, however, real progress was made and it exemplified the way the pendulum was swinging to full permanency.

The first two Glasgow plans were rejected but the STGWU was prevailed on to submit its own terms and these formed the basis of a 100 per cent scheme which might have been implemented but for the setting up of the Devlin inquiry and the return of talks to a national framework. The union document was responsible and the employers agreed to most clauses, including a local redefinition of dockwork. The only outstanding issue was pay, with the men claiming a basic rate of £15 for 40 hours, but it was accepted that the final figure would be related to national agreements.

The new mood took hold in London in 1964. Negotiations on Plan B had been deadlocked for a year and progressive employers were desperate to get talks re-opened. Their motive was by no means selfless because they feared that continued failure would lead to an unacceptable decasualisation scheme being imposed by whatever Government won the election. They most feared a scheme administered by the dock labour board in place of the consortium. This would extend the area of joint control and had been advocated by the unofficials and, tentatively, by the TGWU. To Labour MPs, toying with the possibility of ports nationalisation, it could present an attractive half-way house in preparation for buying out the private employers. (The 1964 Labour Party manifesto did not mention the ports but in 1966 the party committed itself to 'end the inefficiencies and delays in cargo-handling and help to cure the chaos of the casual system by making each port authority ultimately responsible for all port operations within its area, including stevedoring, and by extending the present valuable experience of joint participation.') [81]

Lloyd and Robin Hampson, the managing director of Scruttons, considered asking the PLA to take over the role of the consortium and had opened talks with Dudley Perkins, the Authority's director general, when a sudden new initiative came from the tally clerks, based on full permanency.

As a vignette of dockland negotiation, the history of these talks is unmatched. The clerks had voted in 1961 to press for total decasualisation and when Roffey took over as the TGWU's clerical officer in the summer of 1964, he went to a lunch party and began private – and quite unconstitutional – talks with a director of Scruttons, Alec Jeffery. By September, their plan was sufficiently advanced for the employers to hope it could be a pilot project for the port as a whole. The plan was put into the official negotiating arena with the NASD and there the fun started.

Dick Smith, the NASD negotiator, personally approved the scheme but it was opposed by his largest and most militant branch. As a result no joint meeting between the rank-and-file of both unions was held. NASD clerks rejected the plan by 178 to 18 but 1,008 TGWU clerks approved it and signed application forms for permanency. At this point Roffey might have been able to take the TGWU forward unilaterally but the situation became farcical, with both unions threatening to call strikes unless they got their way. As Roffey told Lord Devlin: 'The Blue union . . . did not accept and if any attempts were made to go forward with negotiations on 100 per cent decasualisation, their people would walk out of the docks. It knocked Mr Jeffery back. I replied, just to make perfectly clear that if the employers burked the issue at this particular stage, I would walk the TGWU tally clerks out of the docks, if they did not have the go-ahead.'

But the next step was that the TGWU clerks refused to go ahead without the Blues and discussion ended. To the Devlin Committee, the situation was unbelievable. They made the point that there was no division of interest between White and Blue clerks and it was a historical accident that 400 belonged to one union and 1,100 to another. 'The distinction between the two bodies on this issue is no more significant than if 400 men wore blue suits to work and the other 1,100 wore grey; and the point now reached is as absurd as if the 70 per cent who wore grey suits decided to give the 30 per cent who wore blue suits a veto over their proceedings. A social satirist with the power of imagination of Swift in *Gulliver's Travels* could not invent a more fantastic way of settling an issue on which the livelihood of 1,500 men depends.'[82] Roffey's verdict was concise but equally to the point. 'The dog was being wagged by two tails.'

Before these negotiations got uncontrolled, Lloyd had drawn up a similar plan for dockers. It was never discussed with the unions because the Inquiry was set up within a month of its airing, but it is significant for showing how employer attitudes were changing. He asked the employers to recognise the errors of the consortium plan and offer full permanency, even if it offended employers in other ports and even if it drove some London employers out of business. In effect, he reverted to Plan A. He pointed out that union attitudes throughout past negotiations had been coloured by comparison between the haves and have-nots, between attached perms and unattached perms. 'This led to them imposing safeguards and being far more conscious of what men were going to receive when not at work, rather than when in employment. It is extremely doubtful if the Port Employers (London) Ltd. scheme would have produced happy working in London and, in this respect, it is perhaps best that it now rests on ice.'

When the employers came to give evidence before the Inquiry, the lesson had been learnt. Full permanency was so much the vernacular of the day that it was surprising it had been so seldom offered in the past five years.

EMPLOYER STRUCTURE

The need to change the employing structure was a more difficult pill to be swallowed but it was closely linked to the acceptance of full permanency. The concept of free competition had changed little from Victorian days and a reduction in the number of employers was equated with monopoly and the danger of inefficient bureaucratism. Even large employers, who stood to gain by the elimination of rivals, saw them as a valuable counterweight and as providers of necessary specialist services.

Robin Hampson, of Scruttons, was to become a firm believer in full permanency but in 1961 he still thought it essential to keep his smaller brethren in business with a reserve pool. Full decasualisation would mean 'a monopoly of labour by the larger interests resulting in an assurance of business which they had never had before. This was bad in principle and would encourage the growth of malpractices in respect of the retention of labour and excessive payments,' he said.

But it was gradually recognised that the free employing market could only survive under casualism and the employer who relied on casual labour would also rely on casual management. He had little capital tied up in his business and might not be able to provide the equipment to man a job efficiently. Once the employer was inefficient, the men were discontented since the employer's shortcomings could affect their earnings.

Moreover, the casual employer had no commitment to his men once a job was finished and in a dispute situation his easiest course was to give in. His concessions then made it harder for the larger companies to stick closely to the letter of an agreement, if the men could point to precedents where the agreement already was broken. Thus the policy of evasion became the standard for the port.

The 1961 manifesto blamed casual employment, by undertakings which 'only engage labour intermittently but all of whom are entitled to call for labour at any time,' as much as casual labour for the inefficiencies of the docks; but it was the Rochdale report which made the first, blunt call for a reduction in employers' numbers. It suggested that small employers should either amalgamate into units with a stable labour demand or, if they were companies whose dockwork was secondary to other activities, they could sub-contract this part of their operations to out-and-out stevedoring companies. It also called for more rigorous licencing of employers to be built into the Scheme and the criteria for granting a licence could be the prospective employer's financial stake in the port or his ability to give regular work.

The process of reduction was already starting in the early 1960s as a result of mechanisation, which lessened the fluctuations in labour requirement. For instance, in London the most casual conditions were found in the Surrey docks, whose timber was only a summer trade. But the packaging of Canadian and Baltic timber and the construction of special timber berths at Tilbury brought greatly reduced manning.

The number of employers was already falling before the Devlin report urged drastic reductions and, as a consequence, modernisation was changing the essential problem of dock labour from one of fluctuating demand to permanent surplus. Rationalising the need for a more coherent structure was not such a difficult step when the exigencies of trade were getting the job done already. But David Lloyd was still ahead of the times when he said, in 1964, 'If an employer has not sufficient work in volume and continuity to enable him to stand alone, then he must consider joining with another employer or group of employers; *otherwise, very baldly, he must quit.*'

METHOD OF NEGOTIATION

An equally important lesson was the need to negotiate with the confidence of the rank-and-file. This was especially pertinent in ports with strong unofficial movements and inter-union rivalry. It was not only a question of what was said at the negotiating table but of the method in which the message was put across, of finding the proper framework in view of the known weakness of the unions and the radical nature of the proposals.

Great care had been taken in the protracted preparations for the West Coast M and M agreement to keep the membership informed and to educate them as to the fundamental objectives of the deal, culminating in the fishbowl talks. In Britain, however, the TGWU decided that the safest policy was to negotiate in private until concrete proposals were ready – and in London and Liverpool the effect was disastrous. By demonstrating that the leadership had little confidence in the membership, what confidence the men had in their officials was dissipated.

The gulf was widened by the failure of the leadership to enunciate a clear statement of their aims following the 1961 manifesto. O'Leary's few pronouncements after 1961 were confined to watering down the manifesto and spreading the general gospel of decasualisation – for instance he circulated much of the text of the Shaw award and Bevin's briefing to dock officers in 1920 – but gave little *specific* guidance to local negotiators. Cousins and O'Leary were at fault in letting the employers make so much of the running for it put their membership on the defensive. O'Leary's only explanation to the Devlin Committee was that the union was happy to let employers offer what they thought fit; he was not going to start hares he knew he could not catch!

The absence of leadership initiative from the NASD was equally reprehensible, but understandable since the union operated chiefly in reaction to the TGWU and its tradition was to bind the negotiators to rank-and-file decisions, usually the result of mass meetings, which do not constitute a flexible bargaining position.

It is amazing that the TGWU during this period never declared nationally what the price of decasualisation should be or which working practices should be bargained away and which retained. This was left to port negotiation and the unofficials were quick to make good the deficiency by issuing a new Charter as a national policy.

The Charter emanated from Dash's Royal Docks liaison committee and ostensibly it rejected decasualisation. Implicitly, however, the Charter was seen as the militants' price for permanency.

In its eleven demands, it called for nationalisation, the retention of the Scheme and for the register to be kept at its present strength, the inclusion of every port within the Scheme, a £15 a week guarantee, which excluded overtime from guarantee entitlement; better piece rates, sickness and accident pay; a pension of £4 a week and a retiring age of 65; a 40-hour week and three weeks' holiday a year with free or reduced fares for dockers on all ships. Its other clauses related to the fairer distribution of work, asking the union to enforce a 'no soliciting' rule and for the number of permanent men to be frozen or even reduced by wastage.

The hour of the unofficials came in London when negotiation turned to restrictive practices. Lloyd had launched Plan B (modified) in September 1962 and was pleasantly surprised that the scheme was still 'afloat' at the end of a day's discussion. A year later he presented a formidable list of alterations to working rules to the unions and insisted these were thrashed out sectionally before an absolutely final cash offer was made for the port.

The proposals were a negotiating document, asking for more than the employers would have settled for eventually. As such, the employers wanted them kept secret and the TGWU was able to fend off inquiries for some time.

When pressure from the rank-and-file mounted, however, the union printed a circular which was thoroughly evasive, admitting the document had been tabled but stating that 'it is not our intention to issue a leaflet containing the employers' proposals in current terms, knowing it to be a complex document, with the idea of seeking popularity or for propaganda purposes. To enter into this field would, undoubtedly, have a detrimental effect on the purpose of these discussions.

'As a responsible organisation, acting on behalf of its members, and whose committees are elected by its members and give freely of their leisure time, we will continue to act in your interests. Decasualisation in the docks is essential and sufficiently serious to require special attention. When a suitable document is acquired following further negotiations with employers, couched in terms which can be easily understood and are likely to be acceptable to you, careful consideration will be given to its wider circulation.' [83]

Conceivably, dockers might have bowed to the paternal concern of the TGWU had it been the only union in the talks. But the NASD insisted on keeping its membership informed, even at the risk of breaking confidences. On 10 March 1963, Dickie Barrett told a mass meeting of the Blues many of the employers' proposals and, from that point, the talks were doomed. The employers believed the Blues had committed deliberate sabotage and Lloyd tried to retrieve the situation by issuing a letter to all dockers, spelling out for the first time the state of negotiations.

It was quite an elaborate exercise blessed by Shea and kept secret from the NASD unless it also 'leaked.' The letters – printed on different coloured paper in the hope that men would be curious to see what their mates had got – explained that mobility, manning scales, overtime and night work were all matters which had to be *negotiated*. But the damage could not be undone.

Shea had no alternative but to refuse discussion of working practices until he could tell his suspicious membership what the *quid pro quo* would be, and the employers insisted on getting broad agreement to conditions before putting a final price on the package.

The myth grew up that London was on the brink of settling when the break-down occurred. NAPE had authorised the London employers for the first time to raise the guarantee above the time rate by a premium of 16·4 per cent, equal to a guarantee of £11 a week. For low-earners this could mean an increase of up to 40 per cent in minimum pay but the overall cost was reckoned to be less than 8 per cent on the wage bill. The TGWU was asking for a £12 guarantee, a premium of 27 per cent, and the NASD for £15 but London held firm on the request of NAPE which feared repercussions in other ports. In reality, with working conditions still to be negotiated, the sides still had a lot of talking to do.

Secrecy of negotiation was also at the heart of Liverpool's troubles. The TGWU district secretary, Alderman P. J. O'Hare, was an autocrat who did not see fit to keep in touch with head office let alone his membership. He negotiated the New Deal personally and, with the employers, launched it on the dockers in a blaze of publicity, in the form of an eight-page booklet distributed simultaneously to the City Council and the men.

The reaction was a fiasco. The booklet was meant to be the basis for discussion at the branches but it had the air of a *fait accompli*. The employers never got a formal response from the TGWU and were not even informed that every branch had rejected it. Only the unrecognised NASD made a detailed – and hostile – answer to it.

It was later said that the Mersey deal might have stood a better chance, if it had not carried O'Hare's signature on it, since it would have appeared more as a negotiating document without commitment. This is probably true and the presentation was another case of bad judgment by the union. Fortunately the Devlin programme was to take away the opportunity for such fundamental errors to be repeated.

CHAPTER EIGHT

The Devlin Inquiry

'We hope first and foremost that your report will be as fundamental and emphatic in its views as you can make it. Because, if it is not, we shall simply be where we have been with previous reports in relation to this industry; we have had brilliant analyses, a great grasp of our troubles and then we have been left to continue to flounder in the bogs of the docks industry.' Sir Andrew Crichton to Lord Devlin, 24 February 1965.

When the members of the Devlin Inquiry were named in October 1964 it was apparent that the Government had brought together a powerful team. They were to make three reports in all. The first, produced in three weeks, examined the national wages dispute and provided a compromise settlement which was widely regarded as a sweetener for the more important task of mapping the route to de-casualisation. The main report was issued on 5 August 1965, and was expected to end the Committee's work. But in April 1966 the committee was reconvened to put a price to modernisation and the third report was published six months later.

Lord Devlin was well-qualified to head the inquiry. He was now an Appeal Court judge and his association with the docks dated back to 1955–6 when his findings on the Scheme revealed a stern moral propriety and an exceptional analytical ability in separating the emotional response to casualism from the actual problems which the system generated.

Although the unofficials campaigned against Lord Devlin, claiming that a plumber should no more be used to mend a car than a lawyer to cure the docks, the attack was not personal and, arguably, the employers had more to fear from him than the men. In the course of the inquiry, Lord Devlin was to assume two roles: the independent chairman who questioned all and sundry with the detachment – even the incredulity – of a man in the streets and the conciliator who sought to chide and cajole the parties into positions from which a fresh start could be made.

The role of auxiliary harrier was left to Hugh Clegg, then a fellow of Nuffield College, Oxford. He was prominent in that school of industrial relations which looked to the institutions and payment systems of industry to discover the sources of grievance and he was on the threshold of a career in public service, which gave him a seat on the Donovan Royal Commission, the Prices and Incomes Board, the directorship of the Social Science Research Council's industrial relations unit, the chairmanship of the civil service arbitration tribunal and made him professor of industrial relations at Warwick University. His persistent questioning of the employers' costing and of union attitudes was hardly designed to court popularity and resulted in the TGWU successfully objecting to his inclusion on the Committee for the third report.

The other two members were Jack Scamp and Sidney Ford, both to be knighted later. Sir Jack, too, was at the start of a distinguished record of government service. Since leaving school, he had worked in personnel management and now sat on the board of General Electric, one of few major companies at that date to carry a director solely responsible for labour relations. This was the first of twenty-six inquiries he sat on and he considered himself a political innocent, never having met Gunter when he accepted the post and subsequently only meeting Harold Wilson once, in a celebrated all-night negotiating session during the 1967 Liverpool dock strike.

Sir Sidney was president of the National Union of Mineworkers and had led his members through a revision of the wages system which replaced piecework at the coal face with regional day rates – one of the major accomplishments of labour relations in a strike-prone and insecure industry.

The committee saw witnesses in private, to give them a chance to speak freely, and took evidence from employers, union leaders, rank-and-file dockers, shippers and even the Church of England industrial committee! It also gathered details of employment practices in the USA, Rotterdam, Antwerp and Hamburg.

POSSIBLE FORMS OF DECASUALISATION

If full permanency was an idea whose time had come, the industry
was still at a loss how to receive it. There were six basic forms it
might take. First, all men could be employed by the NDLB on basic
time rates and allocated to operating employers. Second, the NDLB
could become the sole operating employer, which was tantamount to
nationalisation. The third and fourth proposals were similar, but with
port authorities replacing the Board as either holding or operating
employer.

Fifth was the proposal that a consortium should be holding employer and, sixth, that all men should be directly allocated to those
employers who could maintain men on a permanent basis.

NAPE swayed between the latter two alternatives at the start of the
inquiry and the National Ports Council (the 'nudging' organisation set
up after the Rochdale report) saw virtue as well in the third – with
port authorities holding labour and leasing it out.

Both the official and unofficial union leaders favoured Board control but the Committee had difficulty extracting exactly what they
meant. Eventually O'Leary explained that he favoured full allocation
of men to employers but with the Board supervising any transfer of
men *between* employers. When the unofficials advocated Board control they wanted it to be the operating employer and this was a highly
theoretical solution while the issue of public or private control of the
industry was unsettled. Moreover, it might be disruptive in the short
term since the Board had no operating experience and would depend
on the private companies for management expertise and equipment.

A variant supported intermittently by the union side was to return
all men to the Board which would then allocate them on a work-
sharing basis to port operators. But this, as the Committee pointed
out, was 100 per cent casualisation, not decasualisation, and was
grossly unfair to employers and permanent men who had been together, in some cases, for many years.

The Committee was not concerned with theoretical solutions. It was
looking for the system which could be suited to the industry with least
trouble and, to that extent, it sought the line of least resistance.
('Concerned as we are to see the speedy introduction of a reform that
has been too long delayed, we naturally favour the least interference
with the existing structure,' 1965 Report, para 258.)

Thus the hiring practices of the USA were ruled out because they depended on union control of the hiring hall, where union officials allocated men to work by rota in accordance with employer requirements. British unions were patently too weak to enforce this form of work distribution although it had been a basic aim of the early waterside unions.

Rotterdam's division of the labour force into two-thirds company perms and one-third in a consortium pool was equally inapplicable to British conditions, because of the different labour market and wages structure. In Holland, dockers' wages were broadly in line with outside industry and the turn-over of labour in Rotterdam docks was high; sometimes it produced acute shortages – Moroccan gangs were used and occasionally casuals picked up from the streets. Thus pool men were usually assured of work and, in addition, Rotterdam was not a piecework port so by fixing the guarantee near to the level of the time rate, pool wages were little less than normal earnings.

The Devlin solution was to recommend 100 per cent allocation but to retain the Board intact in all its main functions, including responsibility for inter-company transfer. This was close to the employers' later position but the formula was neatly packaged to reassure the unions that the Scheme was intact and that the Board had not been reduced to the status of a 'medical specimen in a jar of spirits.'

METHODS OF IMPLEMENTATION

The 1961 manifesto had been a loose framework which allowed a large degree of freedom to individual ports and it was vitally important for the Committee to decide how much local autonomy was really needed.

NAPE was bitterly divided on this issue and a furious quarrel sprang up between London and Liverpool during the hearings about the obligation of one port to heed the interests of others. It was clearly preferable to impose minimum conditions for modernisation on all ports but London was more than willing to go-it-alone with wages and conditions suited to its needs.

London was the port with the least fluctuation in labour demand but the most entrenched working practices and the principle of flexible manning was therefore attractive to the employers. In theory it would employ the entire labour force all the time, by adjustment to gang sizes, and full employment meant that little recourse would be had to the guarantee, which could therefore be high.

But there were dangers which Liverpool employers were quick to point out. Lindsay Alexander, their chairman, was sure that flexible manning would prejudice negotiations for 'realistic' manning and norms of output. Each job had an optimum complement of men, he argued, and manning up or down would reduce optimum output; regular over-manning, moreover, would set a new standard for the job and make it harder to negotiate below it.

The worst effect, however, would be on ports which could not afford a high guarantee because of their wage structure or the degree of underemployment. Liverpool was particularly vulnerable, because the men had never taken up piecework like London. In 1964, the piecework *bonus* in London was four times as high as in Liverpool where the docker generally was happy to have lower take-home pay but supplemented earnings by padding out work into overtime. The result was that an increase in basic rates had far more impact on earnings in Liverpool and the disincentive effect of a high guarantee on output during normal hours was also feared; if men could keep themselves on the guarantee during the day, they would rely more and more on overtime, at double pay.

Liverpool employers claimed that they could not survive a guarantee higher than the time rate and hinted darkly of leaving NAPE if London was given the freedom to negotiate a deal with expensive spin-off at other ports. Alexander consequently became the champion of an entirely new approach to pricing decasualisation – a special payment common to all ports which would buy goodwill without upsetting the precarious inter-port balance of the wages structure. The idea intrigued the Committee and they turned to it in 1966.

The London–Liverpool quarrel brought the best from Lord Devlin. He wanted NAPE to understand, voluntarily, the need for national control and feared the ports would still be fighting, if he imposed it on them. He therefore asked NAPE to produce its own revised plan for decasualisation on the assumption that the employers would draw their own conclusions about the division in their ranks. When Sir Andrew later put the outlines to the Committee, the issue had been resolved. The employers agreed to tighten national control and the Committee willingly endorsed the decision.

Once this framework was agreed, other problems fell into place.

The institutional weakness of the industry demanded an element of independent supervision and a boldly-stated programme, if the industry was not to slip back into its morass, as Sir Andrew feared.

The report set out a 10,000-word plan of action in minute detail. The most important recommendation was that modernisation should be split into two phases, the first giving full permanency, eliminating the casual employer, strengthening union leadership and buying out only those wasteful practices which could be associated with casualism; the second was to review the wages structure, buying out remaining restrictive practices and introduce mechanisation and shiftwork.

Quite simply, the reason for 'divide and simplify' was the extent of the changes envisaged. The employers needed time to reorganise and the unions to reassert their authority. This could not happen overnight, nor could the ordinary docker understand the need for discarding the protective cloak of casual attitudes without a considerable time to adjust to the aims of full permanency.

The Committee had taken to heart the evidence of the late Bill Hegarty, a general secretary of the Blues. He told them how his union was swamped by the massive changes proposed by London employers in 1962–3. 'We were given too much to handle at one time. We found in the (proposed) working conditions there were arrangements which had been reached by agreement after twenty or thirty years of negotiation and it was put in front of us on a plate, every one an alteration in every one of the working conditions, such as the manning of derricks and things like that, which it had taken us a long time to beat them on; an increase in piecework rates takes five or six weeks on one individual rate.

'I did suggest we get over the first document, the terms of employment, get the decasualisation scheme and then let us sit down and give us three years to talk about all these agreements it had taken us thirty years to get. It was too much to take to the councils, it was too much of a big job for anybody to handle, to place on one document. If it had been given to us a little bit here and there we could have carried on. We have other business to do apart from negotiations. These chaps work on the docks all day and give up their evenings to attend committees. We would have had them there every night and Saturdays and Sundays as well.'[84]

The initiatives following the 1961 directive had all collapsed because of the enormity of the problem and because of false assumptions by the employers about what they could get away with. In a nutshell, they had asked too much for too little; the national directive had tried to buy the rulebook and abolish casualism, and pay for one with the other. But decasualisation could not be regarded as a gift which the employers were bestowing on the industry, since they wanted it as well. 'It should be looked upon as a change which is being forced on the industry by the need to adapt itself to conditions of full employment; and as a change which, while it necessarily imposes financial obligations on the employers, also inevitably results in certain practices, excusable under a casual system, *ipso facto* becoming obsolete' (paras 318–19).

The first step in the plan of action was for the NJC to issue a new directive setting out the aims of Phase I. Then it had to form a special negotiating committee to implement both parts of the programme. Two conditions applied to the formation of the committee, that a seat should be offered to the NASD and a strong independent element should be included.

The concession to the Blues was a bold step but Lord Devlin believed their members could stymie any talks in London, should they wish, and their co-operation might be secured by national representation. But the offer was sternly hedged. The Blues would have to negotiate in conformity with the new directive, observe the protocol of negotiation and not break confidences whatever the normal practice of reporting back to the membership; and they would have to abide by a majority decision on any scheme put to the vote, to avoid repetition of situations like the tally clerks' in 1964.

The inclusion of independents was deemed necessary by the lack of compulsory arbitration in the industry, at national and local level. It was simpler to set up a new committee, as the headstone of national and local negotiation, than tamper with the existing machinery and this had the added attraction, to a Government about to embark on comprehensive control of prices and incomes, of allowing its own appointees into the negotiations on one of the most scrutinised areas of industry.

The report then turned to action for employers, unions and the NDLB. Predictably, employers were instructed to prune their numbers drastically. They would have to decide which companies could survive as economic units, with proper supervision, equipment and welfare facilities, and be able to provide work for their men for at least

80 per cent of the year. Licencing was to be started with the National Ports Council as final arbiter of an undertaking's fitness to employ. This role was withheld from port authorities because it was considered a dangerous principle to allow authorities, themselves employers, the power to decide who their competitors should be. Examples of the sort of reductions envisaged are given below:

	No. of employers 1 January 1965	Reduction recommended
London enclosed docks	35	10
Liverpool	114	10
Hull	90	10
Glasgow	14	6
Bristol	77	8

The union problem hinged on the TGWU, which had to restore its authority in London, Liverpool and Hull, and the first essential was better communications. Dockers had to be educated to the purpose of decasualisation and this indicated a review of the quality and number of officers, more equipment and a series of dock-gate and lunch-hour meetings where the officials could challenge the unofficials on their home ground.

Before permanency, it was difficult to make more concrete proposals but this did not diminish the urgency of the problem. 'There is need for action now and by now we mean today. The national employers, whatever their shortcomings in the past, have struck their tents and are now on the move. At the moment the future depends on the T and G' (para 286). After Phase I, however, a priority would be to establish a shop steward system fitting into the existing chain of command. The Committee played down the complaints about the numbers and low pay of officials, since the ratio of officers to men was already higher than in most industry and the level of salary was not a problem peculiar to dockland unionism. It emphasised the lack of grass-roots vitality and the breakdown of decision-making because of the rivalry with unofficials and the NASD; it hoped that shopfloor relations between the unions could be improved by shop stewards and that definite spheres of influence could be agreed at port and national level. The logical alternative, the report warned, was to exclude the Blues from all areas except the traditional stevedoring section in London.

Responsibility for welfare and amenities was kept with the NDLB. It was instructed to find out at once what facilities were needed and devised how they should be provided and at whose expense – anything to prevent the existing evasion of responsibility which accounted for the appallingly low standard of toilets, washing and changing rooms and canteens.

The report carried a final sting. It said that, if the NJC failed to issue a new directive or to form a negotiating committee, or if the independent element reported an irreversible breakdown in negotiations or the wrecking of an agreed plan by minority groups, the Government should impose a scheme in the industry, just as Isaacs had in 1947.

CHAPTER NINE

Decasualisation at Last

'The employers are paying money as an earnest of their intentions to share with the men the benefit of change; they are entitled in return to an earnest from the men of their intention to accept change.' Devlin Report, 1966.

After Lord Devlin had drafted the report personally at his Wiltshire home, it was published on 5 August and immediately hailed as a blue-print for the industry. Sir Andrew called it the most important document since the Shaw award of 1920. The TGWU, in spite of the trenchant criticism, welcomed it in a four-page broadsheet as the clearest statement yet made by an impartial authority on the need for permanency.

The report was indeed a *tour de force*. It contained a brilliant analysis of casualism and was clothed in the most incisive terms, sparing none in its criticisms and ending with a precisely-stated plan for action. Nothing here of the drab Whitehall fustian which has condemned so many government reports to the pile of cast-offs nor of those well-meaning but woolly conclusions which are eminently easy to ignore.

Phase I of the Devlin programme was implemented twenty-five months after the date of publication and the sequence of events is simply told.

On 9 August, Ray Gunter met the employers and unions and agreement was reached in principle to follow the Devlin plan. A month later the NJC issued a new directive which was far more realistic than the 1961 manifesto. It guaranteed to keep the principles of the Scheme and promised that modernisation would not lead to the discharge of men from the industry. Employers would be licensed, pensions reviewed and sick pay introduced. Of the clauses relating to working practices, only those which were essentially a feature of casualism would be abolished, inter-company transfer was accepted, as was work-sharing, in principle.

The negotiating committee was then set up as the National Modern-isation Committee (NMC), with seven members from each side of the industry, including the general secretary of the NASD, and with four independent members. The choice of chairman was solely Gunter's. A telephone call to Machrihanish golf club, in the Mull of Kintyre, got him in touch with Lord Brown, the chairman of Glacier Metal. A few days later the prime minister tried to entice Lord Brown away from the docks to be secretary of state at the Board of Trade and eventually he was persuaded to accept both jobs.

On the NMC, he was joined by Tom Claro, the Ministry of Labour's chief conciliation officer, Sir William Garrett, former president of the British Employers' Federation, and George Doughty, general secre-tary of the draughtsmen's union.

Lord Brown was a controversial figure, a keen sympathiser with Labour, dynamic, inexperienced in the docks but well able to look beyond the industry's parochialism. He was known best as the arch-enemy of wage incentives, after switching his factories successfully from piecework to hourly rates in the late 1940s and early 1950s and publishing *Piecework Abandoned* in 1962. His strong view on wages was both the strength and weakness of the NMC, because the docks, *par excellence*, were the industry where a complex and fragmented bonus structure was out of control and because wages reform was not within his immediate brief, but in the second part of the Devlin programme.

The role of the NMC for Phase I was to introduce permanency within the existing parameters of the industry. But Lord Brown saw that greater security after Phase I could bring new inflationary pressures which the wages system could not contain and he believed that basic wage reform would have to accompany Decasualisation. There simply was not time to do this – it would have repeated the mistake of 1961 in trying to do too much too soon – and the NMC consequently got bogged down in wrangling over payments. It was a minor tragedy since it encouraged unions and employers to revert to their old institutions as a bargaining forum. When Phase II came to be negotiated and wages were under review, the NMC was a dis-credited body, useful chiefly as a listening post for the Government, but not influential over negotiations which had switched to port level with little national co-ordination.

In 1965, the NMC had to sanction some sort of payment for Phase I and Lord Brown insisted that the alternatives be costed by an examination of earnings at London, Liverpool, Newcastle and Southampton. This was undertaken by Urwick Orr and Partners and duly revealed the staggering disparities which would result from any change to the basic rate or piece rates. A minority still wanted movement on the basic rate on a non-offsetting principle but NAPE was now aligned behind Liverpool's idea of a modernisation payment. Only London objected but its weight was enough to prevent agreement; it sought the high guarantee, while the unions wanted a simple increase on minimum time rates.

With the employers divided between themselves and against the unions, the Devlin Committee had to be recalled. Their package was announced in October 1966 and conceded the modernisation payment *and* the high guarantee. It was worth an estimated 16 per cent, a tempting inducement since the six-month wage freeze was still in force. Ten per cent of the deal derived from a 1s an hour modernisation payment, 2½ per cent from bringing all men onto the minimum time rate and a fraction more from raising the guarantee above this level to £15 a week, with a £1 differential for London; and 3½ per cent from the cost of a sick-pay scheme and improved pensions.

Also in 1966, the NMC defined which wasteful practices should be abolished with Decasualisation, and these concentrated on restrictions on mobility and overtime. At the same time legislation was needed to license employers and amend the Scheme. The 1966 Docks and Harbours Act officially provided for licensing but reversed the Devlin Committee's recommendation in making port authorities responsible for issue. This was the result of pressure from the Docks and Harbour Authorities Association and the indifference of the National Ports Council; as it happened, the arrangement suited the Government well because its embryo plans for nationalisation vested this power in regional authorities and, in the meantime, the Council remained an advisory body without executive teeth.

Gunter issued a draft order amending the Scheme in March 1966 and objections were heard by Sir George Honeyman. Most of the changes were incontestable and provided the administrative machinery for permanency. Control of the register was unchanged, but boards were also required to supervise the allocation of men to licensed employers and to arrange inter-employer transfer. If an employer quit the industry, the local board was empowered to take his men back, into a pool of temporarily unattached men, and then re-distribute them among the remaining operators. The NDLB was also to administer collective benefits – holiday, pension and sick-pay arrangements.

The changes in discipline, however, excited opposition and the bulk of objections before Honeyman centred on the new clauses. (The exact nature of these changes and their implications were explained in Chapter 5.) It is significant, however, that NAPE foresaw the difficulties which would emerge from the hearing of appeals at Board level, where it was not possible to give a casting vote, and the unions realised what capital the unofficials could make out of conceding the initial stage of discipline solely into the hands of employers. The unions claimed this contravened the spirit of joint control but Honeyman opined that employers had slightly less power as a result of the amendments.

'It seems to me not unreasonable, as it seemed to the Devlin Committee – subject to the right of appeal to the Board – that the employer of the permanent workers should be given power to take minor disciplinary action. Some of the individual objectors claimed in general terms that the disciplinary power of the employers had been increased in the draft scheme. In my opinion, taking the draft as a whole, their powers have been reduced and the authority of the board extended.'[85]

Events were now moving rapidly. The price for Decasualisation was set and accepted by the Government as compatible with the criteria of severe wage restraint which would be operating in 1967. But Gunter insisted that the independent members of the NMC be satisfied first that enough wasteful practices had been negotiated out of existence to make Phase I a copper-bottomed productivity deal.

This was exactly the position which London employers had tried to avoid in 1963. The wages settlement was known before working conditions were agreed and little could stop the stampede towards Decasualisation. All the pressures were for a quick settlement after the national unions accepted the Devlin pay package by 57 votes to 26 at a delegate conference.

This vote was important because London and Liverpool rejected the terms but were outweighed by the smaller ports, and the unofficials, campaigning against Decasualisation, claimed correctly that half the dock labour force, in the two main ports, thought better terms were obtainable. To bolster the union negotiators, London employers at this point conceded another £1 on the guarantee, making a £2 differential over the outports. The cost of the improvement was marginal in London but it caused a furore in the Cabinet and in NAPE, who both knew that it could not be contained to London and would lead to claims for another £1 all round.

Incomes policy had already been stretched to accommodate the 16 per cent increase at a time when the norm for the country was meant to be stationary. The London offer was rank defiance and Gunter proceeded to block it through pressure on the NMC. 'Government endorsement in principle of the pay changes recommended by the 1966 Devlin report . . . was given on the basis that the London guarantee, if it differed at all from the national guarantee of £15, would not be more than £16,' he told Lord Brown.[86]

The London Modernisation Committee was persuaded to shelve the extra payment for the time being and the Government subsequently let it through three months after Decasualisation. It was really no more than a tempest in a tea-pot since the cost of the extra £1 was accepted as no more than £60,000 a year – less than 0·25 per cent on the London wage bill – and in many industries payment of London weighting yielded a differential of more than £2 a week in earnings, let alone a minimum weekly guarantee. But it did lead to the raising of the guarantee correspondingly in other ports and the real damage of the dispute was to the attitudes of the rank-and-file. Dockers were convinced, at the militants' dock-gate meetings, that they were the martyrs of incomes policy and the position of negotiators, who had backed down before government pressure, was undermined.

The summer of 1967 was a trying period. Both sides of the industry wanted to introduce Decasualisation quickly and risk a once-and-for-all showdown with the militants. Then the tally clerks in London, who had come so near to sectional agreement in 1964–5, announced they would wait no longer and would strike unless a firm date for permanency was given.

Gunter capitulated. On 1 June, he announced that D-Day would be on 18 September and subsequently the NMC independents – conveniently stretching a point or two – announced that a sufficient number of wasteful practices had been conceded in negotiation. But the licensing of employers and the allocation of men to the employer of their choice was still going on, against bitter opposition from the militants, who tried to persuade dockers to tear up their application forms for permanency.

By mid-July, the militants had lost this battle. On 8 July, they reluctantly told Liverpool dockers to sign, lest the unofficials were isolated by their intransigence and, in London, Peter Shea was able to tell his members that 13,000 out of 22,351 application forms issued had been returned and the remainder were flooding in fast.

In August, the amendments to the Scheme were approved by Parliament and only two issues were outstanding – the inter-union settlement for sharing work between dockers and stevedores in London and wrapping up the whole package in a mutual agreement. The first was sorted out three weeks after Decasualisation but the NJC stayed deadlocked over one clause – the employers' right to lay off. Because permanency would increase the cost of idle hours, the employers insisted on incorporating the following: 'Where a dockworker is unable to work because of a stoppage of work by other port workers due to a trade dispute, the employer may suspend his employment forthwith, provided that he shall be paid a guaranteed weekly payment break for the first week of such suspension.' The unions would have none of it and a typical dockland solution was found. Both sides agreed to disagree and Decasualisation was introduced on the strength of a provisional agreement.

D-DAY

On 28 September 1967 the port transport industry paid its debt to the early union leaders, to Beatrice Webb, Booth, Rathbone, Lord Shaw and Bevin. Casualism no longer existed and it remained to be seen if it could be torn up by the roots.

Gunter, with due sense of history, welcomed D-Day as the basis for new efficiency in the docks, greater union strength and more stable industrial relations. As the minister most closely involved with incomes policy, he also hoped that permanency would mark a triumph for productivity bargaining and he associated the reform of the industry largely with the possibility of higher output. 'We are laying the foundations for improving the conditions of work, the productivity and the rewards of individual dockers that could never have been achieved under the out-dated casual system which at last we are bringing to an end.'[87]

Two standard thus were set for judging Decasualisation; as a humanitarian reform which was meant to eradicate casual attitudes and as a bargain in which improved conditions were inseparable from increased returns for the port employer and the economy as a whole. This dualism was inherent in the Devlin programme but it was accentuated by the attempts of the Government to place all industrial bargaining within a wider structure of national interest. In many ways the coincidence of Decasualisation with the few months when the Labour administration was trying seriously to make a success of an incomes policy was unfortunate. The docker was being given something he mistrusted but which his leaders had cherished for more than half a century and the gift was tainted by its context in which an economic price was the top principle.

In its first months, Phase I showed little promise on either count and was greeted by a rash of unofficial strikes. On D-Day, men at London, Liverpool, Manchester and Hull struck. Most drifted back within the first week, but Liverpool dockers stayed out solid, totally rejecting the new working conditions and asking for a 50 per cent increase in the discharging bonus and 100 per cent on discharging rates.

The Mersey strike could largely be explained as a battle for higher earnings. The TGWU had agreed that the 'welt' – the practice of men working turn and turn-about to spin out jobs – should be abolished and the men, in effect, were demanding an accompanying change to the earnings structure, to make incentive bonuses more attractive.

The strike lasted six weeks and was settled after a government inquiry, headed by Sir Jack Scamp, went some way towards meeting the men's case. Sir Jack agreed that the welt could not be eliminated without radical improvement to the bonus system, since it was often used to increase overtime potential, and his formula was to guarantee a minimum bonus level of £4 a week.

He conducted the inquiry in a highly individual way. On Wednesday, 18 October, he finished taking oral and written evidence and then offered to mediate between the unofficial strike committee, the unions and the employers *before* writing his report. The employers thought this quite unconstitutional and demurred, so Sir Jack returned from Liverpool to London and, on Thursday, told Gunter of his fruitless initiative. The minister then gave Sir Jack government blessing for mediation and, on Friday, Sir Jack travelled back North and began to thrash out his formula in conciliation talks.

Again, it was the employers who liked least the emerging concept of the bonus guarantee, predicting that it would be impossible to remove once established. The talks dragged on into the early hours of Saturday morning and when Sir Jack eventually got to bed at his hotel, he was woken at 4 a.m. by a telephone call. It was Harold Wilson on the line; he was on a constituency visit in Liverpool and wanted to know the state of play. Sir Jack gave him a quick briefing and then snatched three hours sleep before returning to the negotiating table. The formula was approved by a hurriedly-convened meeting of NAPE's executive and put to a mass meeting of dockers by Jack Jones. The men cheered their leader enthusiastically, but promptly voted to stay out.

But the breakthrough had been made. Sir Jack stayed up to watch Match of the Day, then made up for lost sleep; four days later his formula had been accepted and Liverpool's 12,000 men began working for the first time under permanent conditions.

London, however, was to be a much more complicated test of casual attitudes and union authority, since the unofficial committees had been campaigning for two years against Decasualisation.

For a few days after 18 September it appeared that the unofficials were beaten. The men had been called out by Jack Dash and Terry Barrett, the leaders of the Royal Dock and West India dock liaison committees, with mixed results.

On D-Day, the unofficials were unsure of their ground. They said their demands were the extra £1 in fall-back, better pension and sickness terms and a No Redundancy guarantee (which had already been given). The committees were split tactically and weakened by the resignation of Charles 'Buck' Baker, who wanted an immediate up-standing weekly wage. On the Friday before D-Day, when Dash came to his 'moment of truth', he was given a 2 to 1 majority for a strike on Monday in the Royals. But the West India meeting was hopelessly confused. Dash spoke in support of Barrett and the first split vote was declared to be in favour of a stoppage. The men, however, objected and Barrett was asked to divide the crowd into two groups to get an accurate count. It was then clear that the strike was beaten, but Barrett would not give in. Still defiant, he shouted 'All those who support our brothers in the Royals refuse to go in on Monday and picket the gates.'

At the end of the first week, Dash had to recommend a return to work for want of support. From September 25 to October 3, the port worked normally but then Dash held another mass meeting to review the operation of Phase I and to give a platform to the strike leaders from Liverpool. Again, contradictory resolutions were passed; the men would stay at work, but they supported Liverpool and a new issue had emerged – the mobility clauses. The old London rule was that a docker moving cargo on and off ship stayed on the job until it was finished but this had been modified to suit permanency. When a man transferred to another employer, he had to break 'continuity' once the borrowing employer had enough of his own men to put back on the work. In an atmosphere less charged this would have been recognised as the only logical way of working inter-company transfer. But a case was raised at the mass meeting where Tom Wallis had borrowed men from Thames Stevedoring (65) and returned them half-way through a job. Dash had found his issue and, at a mass meeting the next day, the strike was re-launched. It lasted seven weeks in the Royals, with partial support from the up-river docks, the West India, Tilbury and the South side.

At the peak of the Decasualisation strikes, 8,000 out of London's labour force of 23,000 were out as well as the 12,000 in Liverpool. It was a disastrous start. More than 500,000 working days were lost, morale in the TGWU was severely dented and the Government had launched a new 'red scare' and devalued the pound before the ports were back to normal.

The Decasualisation strikes marked the beginning of three years of increasing industrial strife in the docks, in which the number of recorded strikes more than doubled and, although many of the stoppages were minor, the men showed a readiness to use their industrial strength rather than the official grievance machinery.

Phase I was also a period of rapid wages drift. Average earnings before D-Day were £23 os 5d a week and they rose to £29 8s 6d by the end of 1968. This 27·5 per cent increase in fifteen months was offset by an 8 per cent increase in tonnages handled and a reduction of the register from 58,515 to 54,481, so that the actual increase in the industry's wages bill was only 15·5 per cent.

But this was a much higher figure than anticipated in the third Devlin report. The Committee assumed that wages would only rise to £25 a week (from a starting base of £21 7s) and that savings from increased efficiency would offset much of the increase in overall costs. In fact, the report was quite specific in stating that the wage increases, to accompany Decasualisation, should be regarded as a sweetener for improved efficiency and thus could be sanctioned during a period of Incomes Policy which prohibited payments in advance of savings yet to come. The report justified its generosity on the grounds that employers had to choose between refusing to pay until they could assess what they were getting – and thereby run the risk of getting nothing – or paying for what they might never get.

'Whether it be called an investment, an advance payment, an earnest, a sweetener, or just a gamble, both sides of the industry are agreed that it is essential to the success of the scheme that (the men) should be given a cash send-off of some sort. . . . The employers are paying the money as an earnest of their intentions to share with the men the benefit of change; they are entitled in return to an earnest from the men of their intention to accept change.' [88]

The apparent conclusion is that the employers did not get their earnest and that the practices of casualism outlived the casual system itself. Indeed, the London strike of 1967 has been interpreted in this way – as the last kick from that group of men, the floaters, who were committed most to the free call and picking and choosing their work at random.

But the problems of Phase I lay, at heart, in the achievements and failures of the two years' preparation following the publication of the main Devlin report. The industry had been charged with the reform of its institutions, the identification and removal of important wasteful practices and the ultimate reform of the wages structure. However well these tasks were accomplished, the effects could not manifest themselves overnight and, within the two-part programme of reform, it was implicit that the first stage would need time to make its impact felt and the act of Decasualisation could not live up to heady expectations of immediate peace and prosperity for the industry, any more than the launching of the Scheme in 1947.

As it transpired, the preparations – although more thorough than any previous overhaul of the industry – left much to be desired and continuing structural difficulties within the unions and employers' organisations, together with the continuation of a flawed payments system, ensured that casual attitudes died hard.

CHAPTER TEN

The TGWU Reforms

'Of course we consider that you should get £50 a week, £25 a week pension, £10,000 severance pay and three months holiday a year but this is impossible to obtain and the higher we put these fancy claims, the nicer it sounds. What counts is that the union will obtain the best it possibly can.' Peter Shea to London dockers, 1967.

Devlin criticism of the unions applied mainly to those ports where the TWGU had lost control – London, Liverpool and Hull – and to the NASD. The three unions with the smallest membership, the STGWU, GMWU and lightermen, emerged from the Inquiry with some credit and the TGWU had no exceptional shortcomings in the smaller ports. This section, therefore, deals with the attempts of the TGWU to re-assert its authority in the large ports and reach a *modus vivendi* with the Blues.

The TGWU's problems were of policy and structure and the immediate task was to regain the confidence of members. The accession of Cousins was a step in the right direction but, from 1965, a special brief was given to Jack Jones to supervise dock affairs. He then ranked third in the union hierarchy and had started his career as a docker in the South End of Liverpool. His father and uncles were dockers before him and he had been christened James Larkin Jones after the labour leader who had organised in Liverpool docks and led the Irish general strike in the year of his birth, 1913.

Jones had a highly militant past, as the youngest councillor in Liverpool at the age of 23, as a volunteer with the International Brigade in Spain and then in a remarkable spell organising for the TGWU in Coventry. His commitment to shopfloor democracy was partly moulded by his knowledge of the docks and partly by the years of Deakinism which had seen the stultifying of life in the lower echelons of the union. Just as Cousins marked a revival of hope on the shopfloor, so Jones articulated the energy and aspirations of activists who previously felt bound to work outside and against the union.

By vesting authority in the national organisation of the union it was possible for Jones and O'Leary to take decisions which would have been unpalatable within the trade group.

HULL

This was most true in Hull where the TGWU officials were refusing to handle grievances if they felt the NASD was in any way involved. The Blues had capitalised on this high-handed approach towards the men; they had established six branches and claimed a fifth of the port's membership.

With this degree of penetration, it was clearly fanciful of the TGWU officials to pretend that the Blues were not 'honest' trade unionists. Another important factor of the Blues' success was the social club they opened in a converted warehouse, with billiards, fruit machines and evening entertainment; this club still exists as a centre of social life.

After the Devlin report's criticisms, the TGWU sent Tom Cronin, one of the ablest London officers, to Hull for ten months to restore union authority. He reorganised the branches and established shop stewards and sent a startling report to London headquarters. Jones did not shrink from the task of sacking the three full-time officials and replacing them with better men, although it had no precedent, and the TGWU's authority was slowly restored. Many of the leading Blues rejoined the TGWU once they felt it was properly supporting the membership.

LIVERPOOL

In Liverpool, the union's task was simplified by the death of O'Hare in 1964. The new district secretary, Lew Lloyd, acted more as a servant of his membership but he still had to work in a structure which had changed little since the amalgamation of 1922. As recounted on page 47, the branches of the NUDL had been virtually autonomous clubs, whose secretaries had great power to confer or withhold favours from the men. Lloyd inherited twelve branches, each covering a geographical area of the waterfront and the branch secretary was usually the full-time officer for the area.

Before the Scheme, the official's power rested on his control of the union ticket, without which men stood little chance of acceptance by the registration committee. The linking of registration with production of the union ticket had been fundamental to TGWU organisation in Bevin's day. Ports like Dundee, Ardrossan, Ayr and Troon, Greenock, Barrow, Bristol and Garston insisted on TGWU membership prior to application for registration; Middlesbrough distributed registration books through the TGWU office; Port Talbot, Newport, Cardiff and Barry, which used tallies rather than registration books, would not issue them without a certificate of approval from the TGWU; Grangemouth and Leith gave TGWU men preference at the call; and ports like Plymouth, Llanelli, Gloucester and Ipswich discreetly encouraged the TGWU to establish a closed shop.

While major ports like London, Hull, Southampton and Liverpool did not specify favours to the TGWU in their registration schemes, the TGWU on the Mersey had established special rights through the 1912 experiment. It had joint control of the committees which issued and withdrew tallies and thus any man who chose to be a non-unionist at times when the register was being continuously cut back ran an increased risk of not getting his tally renewed.[89]

Registration schemes thus proved to be a means of keeping a captive membership and, after 1947 in Liverpool, the same official control was perpetuated in the local scheme which required entrants to be in good standing with the TGWU.

Not surprisingly, the men often felt unduly accountable to their officials – who did not face periodic election – and a common Merseyside complaint was that officials only pursued such grievances as they chose.

Thus, dockland organisation was characterised in Liverpool by a type of 'bossism' uncommon to British trade unionism but – as pointed out by Stephen Fay[90] – akin to another port with a large proportion of Irish labour, New York.

In New York, the power of the union boss rested in his control of hiring practices and this could spill over into racketeering and gangsterism if the ship-owner was prepared to accept corruption in return for quick turn-round. The union boss could manipulate the rank-and-file and Daniel Bell's description of ILA locals could easily be applied to the old Liverpool branches. 'Each little local around a pier or neighbourhood was a molecular world of its own with its own traditions, prerogatives, cliques and jealousies. Each war lord knew his particular world and felt at home there.'[91]

The reaction of the Liverpool docker to such autocracy in the 1950s was either to turn to the NASD or, more likely, to decide that neither union was worth bothering with and in the mid-1960s a third of the men were non-unionists.

The harnessing of shopfloor energies in Liverpool was not achieved before Phase I, in spite of the co-option of militants on to the local modernisation committee. This was not a fault of structure, but confidence. Compared with London, the branch system was logical, with two delegates being elected to the district committee which was the top decision-making body for the port. The branches were well-placed and communication was direct, so long as negotiators chose to use it and men to listen.

The lack of confidence accounts in large measure for the ready disavowal of the negotiated terms of Decasualisation and the subsequent divorce between the shop stewards' movement and the branches. As elected representatives in the workplace stewards were in close touch with the men, but the events of 1967 prevented their integration.

The success of the 1967 strike was rightly attributed to the unofficial leaders rather than Jones, O'Leary, Cronin and local officers who tried to secure a return to work before re-negotiating the bonus element in the wage packet. This 25-man committee provided the nucleus of the shop-steward movement and many of its prominent members had a bone to pick with the TGWU. Some, including the chairman Jimmy Benbow, were Blues; others were declared Communists or Trotskyists who could not hold office.

In the aftermath of the strike, Jones sought to establish shop stewards and encouraged them, as workplace representatives, to stand for branch election and thus take command of the formal negotiating structure. This was a direct expression of his faith in shopfloor democracy and, ideally, it would have married the task of negotiating wages to the administrative task of running the union – which is the primary function of the branches.

This initiative, combined with the priority given to TGWU cardholders in allocation to permanency, went far towards breaking the challenge of the Blues. The shop stewards now sit with the district committee for important decision-making and their resolutions can be placed on the committee agenda without being processed through the branches. It is an unorthodox procedure, but it works. Power has been passed down the line and, in cases where the union officially disapproves of rank-and-file action, it has a direct line of communication with the elected representatives of the rank-and-file.

However, the drawback is that the shop stewards – ever since their victory in 1967 – see themselves as an autonomous force, rather than a parallel negotiating body. In 1969, they flexed their muscles against the union hierarchy in the Aintree container-base strike and, in 1972, they could organise the container blacking campaign and keep it going on the strength of shopfloor support, irrespective of the official instructions passed down from London and the TGWU's regional committee.

LONDON

In London, the TGWU's difficulties stemmed from the sprawling size of the port and the heritage of multi-unionism. In the 69 miles from Teddington to the Nore the variety of rates and working conditions was so disparate that an extra stage had to be used in union policy determination and this inevitably slowed the speed of decision-making and communication.

From the branches, six divisional committees were responsible for their own areas, but overriding policy was controlled by the regional trade group committee, consisting in 1965 of two delegates from each division and one from the South-East outports. It was known as the Number One Docks Group because London is the first geographical region of the union.

Compared with the two tiers of Liverpool, and the one tier of Manchester and Southampton where most policy is decided by a single branch for the port, the London structure was cumbersome and union difficulties were compounded by the decay of branch life after the Second World War.

The phenomenon of apathy was not peculiar to the docks and has been attributed variously to the domination of branches by political activists who alienated ordinary members, the failure of established unionism to provide the social and psychological satisfactions found in the crusading days of the labour movement, and to the response of permanent officials who tended to usurp rank-and-file functions which would have been carried out from the grass-roots, had there been greater participation. (These themes are more fully developed in *The Dockworker*, Chapter 6, and in Joseph Goldstein's *Government of British Trade Unions*, p. 223, where he stated – on the strength of his experience in one branch – that intervention by permanent officials 'nullified in every way the functions of a branch meeting both as an instrument of communication between the official and the member and as a device for creating a real sense of participation in policy determination'.)

To restore the role of branches in the union structure presupposed that their distribution suited contemporary working conditions and in many cases it did not. This was a legacy of casualism; when hiring was by the hour or half-day, when members seldom had a regular place of work and organisation could not be built around the work unit. The constituent unions of the T G W U consequently set up most branches on a geographical basis around the home communities of dockers and these branches were kept intact after the amalgamation.

The result was an overpopulation of branches, reflecting the distribution of the community at the turn of the century. With the dispersal of dockers into new housing estates after the Second World War, this structure lost much of its relevance. Many branches were virtually moribund but kept alive by the faithful few who attended meetings and used the branch as a channel to higher committee appointments.

This structural problem severely taxed the T G W U after the Devlin report. How were decisions to be communicated when branches were lifeless but remained the constitutional means of communication? Two weeks after the report's publication, Bert Fry, the London regional secretary, put a plan to the Docks Group which envisaged the reduction of branches through amalgamation, the re-grouping of membership so people were attached to branches in the sector where they were permanently allocated, and the ratification of the prospective shop-steward elections through branch machinery in order to make stewards, in effect, ancillary lay officers of the branch.

As far as it went the plan was sound, but it was fiercely opposed in the old sections of the port and the riverside branches of Number Five Division refused to countenance change. Elsewhere mergers did take place and the 80 London branches have been cut back to 52.

The important failure, however, was to link branches to the place of work and hence to the shop-steward system. Before Decasualisation, there was a logical case for not doing so, since people feared it would increase sectionalism and allow small groups to bargain with employers, independent of the senior committees. There was always antagonism against the PLA permanent men, the only group stable enough to have shop stewards and workplace branches; for instance, one resolution from the Royal docks early in 1967 called for the dissolution of these PLA branches and the transfer of members to branches peopled by casual dockers in the sector. The Docks Group defeated this resolution but passed instead a demand 'that the practice of the PLA permanent men to see themselves as a separate entity concerning rates and manning should end.'

After Decasualisation these objections disappeared but the integration of branches and shop stewards still did not take place. The main obstacle was the existence of the NASD whose stewards might represent TGWU men but who simply could not process a grievance through TGWU machinery. Consequently stewards sought as full powers as possible to process grievances without reference to the machinery of one union or other.

Another grievance was the TGWU's political proscription which held up the election of shop stewards in the Royals for many months. It had been agreed that one steward should be elected for every 250 men up to 1,000 per company, and one for every 400 thereafter, but the stewards were required to sign the normal affidavit, vouching they did not belong to a proscribed political organisation.

Early in 1968, the election of stewards in the Royals saw many members of the unofficial committees returned and five, at least, were associated with the Communist Party – Dash, Rice, Buck Baker, Ted Kirby and Danny Lyons. Their fellow stewards refused to see them excluded from office and resigned *en masse* when the Docks Group Committee tried to enforce the union rule.

It was a chaotic position since the stewards in other parts of the port had signed but in Bristol and Liverpool the proscription had been waived in deference to the known preferences of the shopfloor.

The impasse was referred to the TGWU executive, where opinion was divided about the relevance of the ban but united in the desire to protect the officials. Fortunately, the precedent of Bristol and Liverpool provided a loophole. It was decreed that the ban need not apply so long as Communist stewards did not take office on constitutional union committees. The stewards were then established and the ban was rescinded in 1969.

This little fiasco did little to bridge the gap between the new stew-ards and the union hierarchy and the hostility of some employers to the stewards – they thought the system merely canonised the former unofficials in respectable garb and left them free to roam the port, causing trouble – hardly helped them to settle in.

In the formative months, therefore, the stewards sometimes tried to pursue grievances, irrespective of merit, and to secure their position by broadening the scope of domestic bargaining.

In the enclosed docks, stewards felt frustrated by the employers' power to refer disagreements to an area committee, where the men were represented by two full-time officials not lay members, or to the port labour executive committee, where again there was no lay repre-sentation. After Phase II, area committees were replaced by arbitra-tion panels with stewards taking over the former role of officials, and the scope of company bargaining was widened, so this problem dis-appeared.

But a new bone of contention arose in 1968 and caused a second delay before the steward system could work. This concerned the facilities to be afforded to the stewards. Employers wanted them to be working men, released for union duty only when disputes occurred. As such, they were prepared to pay £5 per day to stewards on duty, but the stewards' place in the gang would not be made up. The stewards wanted half their number to be seconded permanently from the gangs and 'pro rata' men to replace them.

The stewards held out until 1969, but their fight was not supported to the hilt by the rank-and-file who believed that life could get too easy for their representatives. But the approach of Phase II persuaded the employers to compromise and, as soon as the shop-steward system was fully operative, the liaison committees – which had always repre-sented themselves as unofficial organs made necessary by the absence of shop stewards – were wound up, in accordance with Dash's promises.

The creation of the shop-steward system helped to solve the prob-lem of workplace representation but it could not help the T G W U re-store its authority unless communications within the union hierarchy improved. While stewards processed grievances without reference to constitutional procedures there was bound to be conflict and this occurred when the stewards tried to force employers to pay a daily earnings guarantee, with the use of one-day strikes, and when the

Hay's Wharf strike of 1969 was spread beyond the mandate of the Docks Group, thanks to the enthusiasm of riverside militants. (The riverside had had a semi-official system of work-place representatives for many years but they were not meant to deal with disputes outside their immediate place of employment. During the Lower Oliver's Wharf strike, they were threatened with union discipline for acting for the wharves as a whole and in the up-river enclosed docks.)

Fry's programme of 1965 foresaw these difficulties and tried to improve communications further by extending the authority of the main committees *downwards* towards the shopfloor. He felt that more contact was needed between the 'faceless' committees and the men and tried to brighten the image of the Docks Group Committee.

Before the Devlin programme, it had little role to play because negotiations were sectional and seldom covered the port as a whole. The negotiating committees were elected from the divisions – and remained so throughout modernisation – but now the top committee was used increasingly to co-ordinate terms.

The Docks Group Committee was strengthened by an intake of former unofficials during this period – Brian Nicholson from the riverside and Buck Baker from the Royals – and it encouraged militants to stand for election to its ranks. For a short time, Vic Turner and Wally Harris, two ex-liaison committee members, joined but they preferred in the end to operate from nearer the shopfloor. Indeed, precedent for returning to the shopfloor was set by Maurice Foley who gave up a position as paid official in 1961 to work as a lay delegate.

Fry and Shea were keen that the tradition of anonymity should end and asked the Docks Group Committee members to hold mass meetings themselves at the dock-gate, promising loud-speaker equipment to match that used by the liaison committees. Four more cars were given to dock officers (although it took an unconscionable time for the regional executive to release them) and the officers promised to act more as trouble-shooters.

Within weeks the new directive was seen to be inadequate and the Docks Group Committee met again to analyse why they were losing ground to the militants. The result was an attempt to improve liaison with the Blues and the lightermen, more frequent meetings and a faster report-back procedure through mass meetings of the divisional delegates; in addition, eight committee-men were appointed as 'commandos' who could attend any union meeting and present docks group policy.

This was the sum of reform and, in the light of the Decasualisation strike, it was obviously inadequate. There was insufficient effort to cut through the maze of committee work and there was, ultimately, a failure of nerve in not tackling the militants on their home ground, the dock-gate meeting. But it was not easy to go further. The Docks Group was subjected to severe criticism within the union for cutting out traditional methods of reporting back, especially from branch functionaries who were by-passed when information was issued at mass meetings. It was also hamstrung in 1965-6 by the National Modernisation Committee's decision to negotiate in secret, which left them little to tell members while secrecy was honoured.

There is no question that the Committee and officials toiled extremely hard with few resources to get Decasualisation accepted. The delegates worked in their own time and were weighed down by a mass of pettifogging detail which arose from the lack of workplace representation and the sectional differences of the divisions. They lacked adequate clerical assistance and also had to attend divisional and branch meetings in their own time.

This workload was quite excessive and it is little wonder that delegates felt personally slighted by the strike which mocked their labour. Examples abound of unnecessary burdens carried by the Docks Group and they are worth retelling, if only to give perspective to the conditions under which British unions are expected to work.

There was the lack of secretarial help which forced Shea – the officer responsible for negotiating dockland's most important labour agreement in Britain's largest port – to spend many weekends personally running off mimeographed bulletins because there was no other way of speedily disseminating information and no one else to do it. There was lack of research facilities and inadequate servicing with documents. Delegates had to buy their own copies of the Devlin reports and they could not get a copy of the US West Coast agreement, until John French, a delegate, found one by private means.

Roffey, during the tally clerk recruitment of 1969, had to undertake personally to teach new entrants the necessary arithmetic for checking duties; and it was left to a divisional officer to help the illiterate son of a docker learn reading and writing, so that he could sign an application form to join the register. (This young man's cause was championed by delegates at branch, divisional and Docks Group level and the amount of time devoted to helping him provides an illuminating insight into the dockers' concern for their kin and the continuing sense of moral duty within the union movement. The episode also reveals the men's attitudes to their calling in remarkable manner. A divisional resolution protested at the man's exclusion from his family's traditional occupation and asked the Docks Group 'to agree that the argument of illiteracy has no bearing on the man's capability as a docker.' However the Docks Group felt that literacy was important, for identifying goods and sorting to marks.)

Perhaps it was the very burden of work which blinded the union committees to the most pressing recommendation of the Devlin report – that officers *meet and overcome* the challenge of the unofficials.

With hindsight it is apparent that the battle for control of Decasualisation was lost within weeks of the report's publication when the militants launched a campaign and were not countered on the spot. In part, the problem stemmed from the ambiguous relationship between the official and unofficial bodies, in which union delegates were happy to use militancy for their ends, but frightened it might swamp negotiations, if misdirected. Thus, delegates used mass meetings solely to report back to the membership and they never dare put the progress of negotiations to a vote. They then lost face when the unofficials took over the platform and called for a show of hands to back their Charter and thereby discredit official policy.

Few officials had the charisma of rank-and-file leaders and they could not match Dash, Lyons or Terry Barrett in the techniques of handling a mass meeting. Without control of the dock-gate arena, the initiative was lost and the ordinary docker relied more and more on the unofficials for information. This was fatal. The information put out frequently bore little relation to what the union was negotiating.

THE LOAD OF TOFFEE

Shea called it drivel and Lindley a load of toffee, serious charges but not difficult to substantiate. The men were told time and again that the Scheme was being destroyed and once the seed of doubt was sown, it was a formidable task for the union to persuade them otherwise. Another area of distortion concerned redundancy – a genuine source of worry since the men feared that the unattached register could become a parking ground for surplus men and that average earnings might be cut back if the full labour force was used without the old protective practices. But there was never any question of men 'being thrown on the scrapheap' or militants being excluded from work, as the liaison committees maintained. The 'No Redundancy' guarantee was given in the 1965 directive and repeated by Gunter, and control over allocation to companies rested with the Board, not employers.

Phase I plans were sometimes put in such a one-sided light that it was tantamount to malicious distortion. This extract speaks for itself and should be contrasted with the findings of the Honeyman report, quoted on page 184. 'Did you hear about the modern five-day suspension rule in the fine modernisation scheme? It goes like this. If the boss does not like the colour of your eyes or the way you mutter under your breath, he can suspend you for five days!! Of course you can appeal (hurrah for British justice and democracy) but while you are waiting for the appeal you don't get paid for one week. Oh yes, it is suspension without pay by the bosses. Didn't you know? That's part of the modernisation. What's that? You didn't have it explained that way by the nice man from TGWU headquarters? Well, well, perhaps he doesn't understand either.' This account omitted to mention that suspension could not be enforced before appeal and that the Board could order restitution of wages.

The cavalier attitude of the unofficials to Decasualisation was heightened in London by a growing split between the left-wing factions in the port. The Trotskyist Socialist Labour League labelled Dash 'the pearly docker' and denounced him and the Communist party for being too conciliatory. This pushed the liaison committees into more extreme positions on the assumption that the faction which pitched camp furthest to the Left could claim the greatest purity. The fact that London did not strike over pay reflects the ordinary man's scepticism towards the spiralling demands of the unofficials. As Shea said: 'Anyone who knows our industry accepts that there will be many problems, changes are taking place, new methods of loading and discharging are being introduced throughout the port industry. We must face these changes cautiously but not afraid and obtain the best for our members.

'Of course we consider that you should get £50 a week, £25 a week pension, £10,000 severance pay and three months holiday a year but this is impossible to obtain and the higher we put these fancy claims, the nicer it sounds. What counts is that the union will obtain the best it possibly can for its members.'[92]

It is wrong, however, to judge the role of the liaison committees by the worst excesses of the Decasualisation campaign or to assume that they deliberately misled the rank-and-file as a matter of principle. They were filling a shopfloor vacuum and the more the union leadership tried to freeze them out, the more difficult it was to get accurate information. Much of the misrepresentation in 1966 and 1967 resulted from an ignorance which the unions were happy to prolong.

If the unions felt they could not beat the unofficials on their own ground, it was still open to come to terms with them. Early in 1966, this course was tried half-heartedly. Dash, Terry Barrett and Charlie Cole, the Tilbury leader, were summoned before the Docks Group and the Dockers' Charter was discussed point by point. It was emphasised that most of the claims of the Charter were being pursued by the union, but the unofficials were not persuaded to close the ranks. Later the unions sponsored mass meetings but made little impact on hostile audiences which interrupted speakers with occasional bugle-blowing and well-aimed eggs.

It was also open to the TGWU to provoke an out-and-out confrontation with the unofficials and their relentless attacks on the union, although purported to be in its best interest, provided ample grounds for discipline. But the strongest action taken was to warn Terry Barrett to look to his future conduct and even this mild stricture was not publicised for fear of making him a martyr. The general feeling was that stronger punishment would only strengthen support for the unofficials and might even provoke a dispute similar to the expulsions strike of 1950.

The only remaining course was to accept the militants with resignation and hope that the membership would rally behind the union on D-Day. It was the reaction of men whose confidence was broken and their sense of helplessness was highlighted during the big strike. The grievances were batted to and fro between branches, the Royals divisional committee, the enclosed docks joint group, the Ocean lay committee, the PLA lay committee, the Docks Group, and the NASD and TGWU executives. Amidst this frenzy, the only constant factor was the frustration of officials and delegates who felt themselves rejected at every turn, by the membership, the press and even Cousins and O'Leary who delayed a meeting of the TGWU national committee to talk to Dash. To give preference to an unofficial leader above so senior a committee (it advised the delegate conference) seemed the final insult and it earned O'Leary a recorded rebuke, after he persuaded the committee not to walk out in protest.

None of the toing and froing had an effect on the strikers' membership and, once clarification of the working conditions was achieved, it was symptomatic of union morale that Dash was asked to put the official terms to the strikers. The stoppage continued for another fortnight but nothing more was achieved than the union had already negotiated.

This breakdown of morale obscured the importance of one area of policy where the Docks Group had carried the port united. This was a ban on sectional agreements from August 1966 to June 1967 and was a prototype of the container ban.

Quite simply, the ban gave the Docks Group a weapon which the militants could only approve of and which cut across the sectional interests. The first ban was not used as a lever to secure a port-wide deal but its successor was. Once a sanction, which only the Docks Group had the power to remove, was linked to modernisation talks, the union found it had vested itself with a degree of control which structural weakness and unofficial activity could not diminish.

COMING TO TERMS WITH THE NASD

The final area of post-Devlin reform was the relations of the TGWU with the NASD and in this area reform was the most successfully accomplished. On 17 August, 1965, the Blues agreed a seven-point programme to implement the Devlin report. The Blues got their seat on the NMC in return for a definite attempt to clear relationships in the Northern ports. This meant abiding by the TUC verdict of 1956, a stop to all recruitment and immediate identification of all Blue membership. Once the exact position was known, the Whites were prepared to consider how the Blues should be represented but, meanwhile, servicing on local committees was to be through the TGWU.

In November, Jack Jones met Dickie Barrett again. Peter Kerrigan, the NASD branch delegate in Liverpool, seemed unaware of the London concordat and was still campaigning against the TGWU. Kerrigan had been 'disowned' by Barrett before the Devlin Committee and it was clear the national executive of the Blues had little control over his activities; now Jones was much tougher and insisted that the NASD co-operate in a card-show at Liverpool before any further talk about representation. The situation simmered down at that point, with the merging of militants from both unions in Liverpool in the unofficial movement, and the only overt dispute between the unions broke out in the summer of 1969, when the TGWU tried to enforce a card-show at Birkenhead and members refused to back their union. (This was one of the last disputes led by Benbow before his death; his comment was that White stewards were so inflated with their own power that they needed a 'bigger size in hats.')

In Hull, TGWU reorganisation brought the two unions much closer and in London the problem was not one of representation but of job rights between the TGWU and the stevedores section of the Blues.

For Decasualisation to work, the old distinctions between steve-dore and docker had to disappear. It will be recalled that the steve-dores used to be the skilled ship-workers and their agreements with the Master Stevedores Association had given them exclusive work rights in certain areas. While the stevedores tried to continue this élitist distinction long after it had any functional significance, there were powerful reasons for agreeing to a common register after per-manency. The stevedores were established in old parts of the port and had never been recognised by the PLA or in Tilbury. But the old docks were rapidly losing trade in the 1960s. The London and St Katharine docks were closed in 1968, the Surrey docks in 1970-1 and many berths in the West India and Millwall systems are now being shut down.

The opening of the main packaged timber berth in Tilbury and the move of the India–Pakistan conference lines – which had provided many stevedore vessels up-river – to Tilbury greatly reduced job openings. The existing practice was to man a stevedores' ship with men from that section of the NASD and to use dockers only if there was a shortage of stevedores in the sector. The employers' proposal, which was supported by the TGWU, was to merge the separate registers of the stevedores and dockers; to keep the distinction was already waste-ful but it would be insupportable when companies had to deploy their own men rather than pick up the appropriate denomination from the pool.

It was a perfectly reasonable plan but the stevedores were reluctant to give up the last vestige of their separate identity. Resistance was finally broken when Fred Olsen Lines moved their traffic from Canary Wharf, Millwall, to a £500,000 berth leased from the PLA inside Millwall dock. This transfer was within the same sector but the work at the wharf was done by TGWU dockers while shipwork in the enclosed dock was the traditional prerogative of stevedores. Both unions were prepared to strike to make the work available for their men and the NASD refused to back down when an arbitration panel awarded the work to the Whites, on the grounds that men followed work when it moved within a sector.

In October 1966, the NASD called a strike throughout the enclosed docks on this issue and a Court of Inquiry was appointed at once. The chairman, Sir Roy Wilson, upheld the arbitration award and made a plea for agreement on the common register. He noted with some surprise that no one had mentioned this problem before the Devlin Committee and concluded that continuing demarcation was indefensible.

By persistent prompting, Shea was able to frame an agreement which made all port work available to all men and allowed the NASD representation on the PLA, wharfinger and short sea trade joint committees. It only remained for the NASD membership to accept but they stalled throughout the weeks leading up to D-Day. By now Gunter was hinting that a common register might be imposed compulsorily but ten days after Decasualisation a mass meeting in the Surrey docks at last saw the stevedores accept.

The distinction between the two sections of the NASD now was meaningless and, but for the greater financial assets of the old stevedore branches, the two halves might have been fused by now.

The distinction between the two unions, however, remains and there is little prospect of it ending in the near future. This is not logical but it is understandable. The *raison d'être* of the NASD is to be an alternative and it has never been much more since stevedores lost their wage differential with the Shaw award. The NASD must be what the TWGU is not and its strength waxes and wanes inversely to the fortunes of the TGWU. With the common register and the movement of the TGWU power-base closer to the shopfloor, the NASD is currently in search of a special identity but even White dockers do not take kindly to suggestions that the Blues should be amalgamated. 'This union has done a lot for our industry,' Maurice Foley said. 'They were for many years the backbone of the union movement as far as London was concerned and I am always annoyed when I hear people attacking them.'[93]

The one Devlin recommendation directed specifically to the NASD was to give more power to negotiators but it is difficult to discern progress because of the very nature of the union. It is too small and too poor to be judged by the same standards as the TGWU and its reputation rests chiefly on the extent to which officers are accountable to the rank-and-file. Membership has declined from a peak of 14,383 in 1955 to 8,087 in 1960 and 6,381 in 1969 but this figure is probably inflated by the inclusion of retired members who still contribute to the funeral benefit fund. It has £26,500 in its general fund and £8,000 in branch funds which is insufficient to finance an all-out stoppage for any length of time; in fact only £54 has been paid in dispute benefit since 1951 and the officers are kept on the London release register to qualify for pensions which the union cannot afford to pay on its own.

Its organisation is distinguished from the TGWU's by two features, the triennial election of officers and the use of mass meetings rather than the branches for reporting back to members. This imposes severe constraints on negotiators. The mass meetings are characterised by a surfeit of democracy and have often tied officials to inflexible mandates. However, the Blues gave no cause for complaint during the Phase I negotiations, such as accompanied their performance during the 1964–5 tally clerks' talks, and the union largely opted out of talks on Phase II.

The overall impression is of amateurishness. Since the days when Dickie Barrett, as general secretary, reputedly went hop-picking while members were on strike, spectacular stories of the NASD's waywardness are harder to come by. But they still exist.

In January 1965, a mass meeting was convened to discuss the Devlin programme only for Barrett to announce that the executive had not yet read the Devlin report of November 1964. In 1966, another meeting tried to discuss Scheme amendments but had to be adjourned when Greenwich town hall was filled to capacity and the gallery was in danger of collapsing as men stamped their feet; on resumption at a sports ground, Mersey delegates caused confusion by haranguing the platform and were threatened with a fist fight by a London executive member!

Disorganisation of this kind lessened the stature of the union in negotiation and it embarrassed the leadership. The long ban on week-end overtime, for instance, cost the union dear as 780 men gave up their cards in order to free themselves for this lucrative form of work. Leaders tried to get the ban lifted many times but failed and a simi-larly tough mandate, opposing shiftwork, forced negotiators to ignore most of the Phase II negotiations. But finally the membership rubber-stamped the agreement which the TGWU had negotiated and in-cluded two-shift working.

So long as the Blues are prepared to accept minority status, the industry will not suffer by their shrinking from responsibility at the negotiating table. But there is always the possibility that the Blues will not go on endorsing White agreements, if they can cause embarrass-ment by holding out for better terms, and the situation described by Lord Devlin, of men in identical jobs but wearing different coloured suits, applies as much as ever. It is no more right now than it was then for a minority to dictate to a majority and for the industry to be dis-rupted because of the colour of a man's cloth. If tradition rules out amalgamation, a just solution could be found by the unions balloting jointly on all port issues and accepting the *joint majority verdict*, irrespective of how their own members voted.

In conclusion, strenuous efforts were made by the TGWU to im-prove its performance in the Devlin period, but some of the initiatives have not been followed through to logical conclusions.

The main obstacle remains the TGWU's structural inheritance. The shop stewards have yet to be integrated into the docks structure and the problem has gained urgency with the predictable emergence of a national shop stewards' committee, under the leadership of a militant NASD Londoner, Bernie Steer. It contains the seeds of a separatist movement for rallying dockers on major issues of principle, like the definition of dockwork or abuse of the Temporary Unattached Regi-ster, and could be a powerful ginger group in wage negotiations. In the past, its power has been limited because of the hostility of TGWU stewards in Northern ports to accept NASD participation, but with the re-emergence of the container dispute in 1972, the unofficial com-mittee was presented with a ready-made platform.

The committee played a large part in keeping the container crisis on the boil and it was instrumental in forcing the TGWU to launch itself towards a national strike. The fact that it attracted powerful figures like Vic Turner, then sitting on the number one docks group, to its ranks showed the ultimate failure of the TGWU to sustain itself as a vehicle for effective decision-making, as it undoubtedly was during the period of the container ban. Between 1970 and the time of writing, the TGWU has lost ground and its difficulties were multiplied enormously by the rulings of the NIRC.

The Court stopped the union behaving in its accustomed manner – i.e. *reacting* to a manifestation of shopfloor grievance – by deeming the blacking of lorries in Liverpool an 'unfair industrial practice.' Had the union *anticipated* the strength of feeling and been the first to call official action, all might have been well. But the Court cut off its only escape route by requiring it to enforce compliance with the law – even to the point of sacking its shop stewards. No matter what the union wanted to do, it did not have the structural means of pushing through such a decision, without the support of the membership.

The court ruling highlighted what union leaders have found out by trial and error – that a union can only govern a powerful rank-and-file by expedients which suit their interest. In 1972, the TGWU was asked to re-adopt the authoritarian manner of a Bevin or a Deakin, although their styles of leadership had broken down in the docks. It was an impossible demand.

Jones and his senior dock officers are quite aware of the ideal solutions to union structure. They would like to see branches linked to the place of work and shop stewards automatically becoming the senior representatives of the branch, combining administrative and negotiating duties. The higher committees would then be composed entirely of shop stewards and the national docks committee would be a constitutional national shop stewards committee. But this cannot be realised while the old branch structure survives and while the NASD remains an independent bargaining unit. In London, the continuing difficulty for the TGWU is to communicate upwards through its elaborate committee structure while in Liverpool it is to communicate downwards, because of the independence of the stewards.

One other factor has passing relevance to the differences between the union leadership and the rank-and-file in the Decasualisation period: the bogey of political influence which the Government raised during the 1967 strikes.

During the 1966 seamen's strike, Harold Wilson alluded to subversion in the ranks of the National Union of Seamen. Now Gunter spoke of the Communist party entering into unholy alliance with the Trotskyists to plot a winter of disruption. Lord Carron, the right-wing leader of the Amalgamated Engineering Union tried, erroneously, to link the London and Liverpool strikes as a deliberate attempt to embarrass the nation by a suicidal strangling of trade.

'Surely it does not require a genius to see the linkage between events divorced in geographical location but identical in nature and expression. The docks, building sites and other spheres of activity bear the same stamp and have the same origins. This situation will continue and get worse so long as those in authority continue to bury their heads in the sand and refuse to face the realities of this accelerating development of peace-time fifth-column activities.'[94]

Many of the strike leaders were political activists and a few had been ruthless in campaigning against Decasualisation. But they were not followed out of the gates for political reasons, but because the dockers believed this was the best way of looking after their own interests. Conjuring up a red scare was not the kind of talk which brought settlement closer or bolstered the authority of the unions, who merely became associated with the men's detractors since both were trying to secure a return to work. To men who might be disturbed by the stand they were taking, it was simple to assume Gunter had been talking chiefly for the benefit of foreign bankers and they tended to close ranks behind those who had led them out and still showed faith in them.

CHAPTER ELEVEN

Wasteful Practices

'The continuity rule has been regarded by Britain's registered port workers from its inception right up to the present day as their most treasured possession. They will guard it with the same intention and purpose as the Guards Brigade give to the crown jewels in the Tower of London, to keep it safe from the thieving hands of the employers.'   Jack Dash.[95]

In preparing for Decasualisation, the need to remove restrictive practices associated with casualism had caused immediate problems of definition and the Devlin exhortation came to be interpreted very differently from port to port.

The confusion is illustrated by the argument whether they should be known as restrictive or protective. Many were originally designed to increase job security, rather than stand in the way of efficiency as such. Lord Brown attributed these with a crude morality, but, to avoid being partisan, Lord Devlin chose to call them all 'time-wasting'.

One type, which includes inflated manning scales, controls on the hiring process, restrictions on working hours and the continuity rule, were aimed at spreading available work over as much of the labour force as possible. A second group covering contingency payments, *pro rata* payments and rules of precedence for working in the hatch were meant to spread earnings fairly between men who had secured work. A third group originated in safety requirements, such as restrictions on the size of sling loads, and a final group, which includes bad time-keeping, extended tea-breaks, spinning work into overtime and the welt, were the response to rank bad management.

By the Devlin era, the original purpose of most restrictions was lost in the distant past and, in any case, had largely disappeared with the poverty and underemployment of pre-war years. They became essentially bargaining counters in day-to-day negotiation and, as employers lost control of the wages system, so the restrictive element increased over the protective.

Whatever the cause, the effect of wasteful practices was the same. They slowed down the pace of work and restricted the effective hours when a ship could be worked in port. If the men were to ignore their 'cherished' rights to help the employer in need, the price he offered had to be high. Consequently the cost of stevedoring increased, the increment was invariably passed on to the merchant or ship-owner and, the greater the pressure for fast turn-rounds, the more such practices were decried by port-users.

In many national agreements, the unions had consented in principle to their removal by local negotiation and from 1945 onwards the unions were committed in theory to the acceptance of nightwork and shift-work and efficient manning throughout the country. But it was un-realistic to imagine that practices, which in themselves were often lucrative to the men, could be bought out for the small sums which employers at local level were free to offer without running foul of NAPE. The 1961 national directive, however, gave employers *carte blanche* to buy out any practices they wanted and port after port presented the unions with formidable lists.

London demands were contained in five closely-typed pages and concentrated on new manning scales and mobility. It was a detailed document, for instance, asking for ships to be started at the weekend, early morning starts on a ship's last day in port, all sorts of transfers on the job and the lessening of quay gang strengths as shipworkers went overside or the hatches were nearly empty.

In Liverpool, employers were most concerned with time-keeping and the welt but also tried to remove restrictions on the size of the sling, the refusal of men loading ships to land a second sling until the first load had been stowed away, restrictions on the use of bogies and the reduction of certain manning scales by up to a quarter.

Priorities varied from port to port but many were anxious to get better conditions for mechanised handling. In Cardiff, where more than 900,000 tons of iron ore were handled annually by grab, only one man was needed per hatch, but the gang strength remained at six. Bristol was troubled by constraints put on mechanisation. Men insisted on keeping four hold trimmers during bulk discharges by grab; the discharge of refrigerated meat was grossly overmanned. Even the reductions of two men per gang when forklift trucks were used was seldom achieved. Hull had the same problem with forklift trucks and wanted quay gangs cut from six to three men. In Swansea, sectional rivalry between crane drivers and dockers prevented the introduction of such aids in shed operations.

Restricted sling-loads were a prominent problem on the Humber and Mersey. In Hull, load restriction was a common tactic during piecework disputes and the men might cut bag cargoes from seven or eight per sling to five. In Liverpool, there were theoretically no restrictions on slings, subject to the overriding safety of the gear, but men could always bring pressure, when dissatisfied with the earnings potential of a job, by reducing the load and appealing to superceded agreements 'which seemed to have as many lives as a cat.'

Glasgow employers wanted discretionary shiftwork and smaller gangs and Southampton wanted to place gangs at the employers' discretion and a more rigid definition of necessary overtime, so that jobs could not be artificially prolonged.

With such a varied list of priorities, the National Modernisation Committee was hard-pressed to define a programme to suit the needs of individual ports when it gave guidance on the Devlin order to remove wasteful practices associated with casualism. Of necessity, the NMC could not be exact and in March 1966 it defined Phase I practices as:

'1. Restrictions on mobility within working periods, whether between different points or between different operations. The aim must be to facilitate the maximum flexibility of working. Continuity rules which inhibit such mobility will require modification so as to ensure that the full benefit in terms of production is assured from all hours of a shift.

2. Unreasonable restrictions on, or conditions attached to, overtime working.'

It was left to local modernisation committees to decide how these principles should apply in each port and it was assumed that employers would put their own house in order to stamp out the wastage of bad organisation and ineffectual management.

In the event, London employers concentrated on the first clause of the NMC directive because they were chiefly worried by the continuity rule and Liverpool saw it as a mandate to remove the welt. The scope of negotiations had been sensibly narrowed by the directive and it was to be limited even further by the time the talking was over. The essential point, however, was how well the employers could enforce the agreements they secured.

THE WELT

Liverpool's Phase I agreement was the eighth attempt to get rid of the welt which cost the port more man-hours lost than all stoppages put together. It was the practice of half a gang absenting itself from work for an hour or more and the other half leaving when the first returned. In some form or other it was known in Glasgow, Hull and Southampton and it is common to dockwork around the world. In Australia men welting are known as judges – since they often 'sit on a case' – and on the US West Coast as witnesses!

The remote origins of the practice were in turn-and-turn-about working in refrigerated holds and this is how it survived in Southampton. But in Liverpool the habit got out of control during the 1940s, abetted by the war-time practice of allowing breakfasts in working hours. Employers recognised they were largely to blame for letting the welt become so ingrained in working practices. Their efforts to remove it – all backed by the TGWU – were based on no more than exhortation to enforce discipline, collectively if necessary, against absentees, but they all withered away through fear of retaliation. Companies which did enforce discipline were subject to reprisals in other forms of go-slow, while those which turned a blind eye at least maintained a certain level of output.

The welt was also sustained by the wage structure in Liverpool which paid double for overtime hours and allowed men to earn as much between 5 and 7 p.m. as they could for half a day in normal hours. The result was that Liverpool was, *par excellence*, the overtime port, with an average of four more overtime hours worked than in ports which only paid time and a half or time and a third.

The consequence of the welt unchecked was to breed indiscipline, since in most cases foremen connived in allowing it, to slow down turn-rounds and thus to underutilise the capital assets of the port. The Devlin report did not associate the welt with casualism as such and, in tackling it with Decasualisation, the employers ignored the extent to which it was the product of the wages system. They hoped, however, that shop stewards would side with official union policy of condemnation and, in part, this happened.

The welt has not disappeared in its entirety but the more organised form, when men left the ship altogether to go home or to a pub, appear to have disappeared while 'on-ship' welting continues. Evidence suggests that the welt has been cut back most in operations with good first-line management. In one instance, for example, a company refused to discuss special award payments with a gang unless all men were present and since most awards related to discharging, where piecework bonus was hardest to attain and consequently welting was most prevalent, it proved to be a simple and effective means of keeping men on board ship during difficult operations.

THE CONTINUITY RULE AND TRANSFER IN LONDON

London employers sought their *quid pro quo* for Phase I primarily in mobility clauses but also in better hours of work. The Decasualisation strike focussed attention on the amendments to the continuity rule and, in spite of the stoppage, this proved to be the most successful part of the package.

The rule was drawn up in 1944 at the employers' insistence and stipulated that the movement of cargo on and off ship should be completed by the men who started the job. Thus all shipworkers and their complementary quay gangs were covered, but tally clerks and lightermen were not, nor warehouse jobs and movement between sheds and road or rail. Exemptions allowed stevedores from the appropriate sections of the NASD to replace dockers on stevedores' ships in the middle of continuity work, and riverside and short-sea shipworkers to return to their normal place of employment, if work was available.

The original purpose of the rule was to force men to stay on unattractive jobs instead of switching to easier or better-paying assignments. As such it was resisted initially by sections of the men but, with the accretions of time, it became, in Dash's oft-repeated words, the dockers' 'most treasured possession.'

It could be seen to be just and it was as strictly enforced by the unions as the employers. But it was also the cause of difficulties. For instance, riverside men resented working on continuity jobs which might be a long way from their normal wharf and nobody from London liked transferring to Tilbury into continuity on the allocation of the local board. Not surprisingly, all sorts of tricks were tried to break continuity in these circumstances and the most common was for transferred men to take an inordinately long time travelling, in the hope that the foreman would connive in breaking continuity and look for better local labour on the morrow. Equally the rule was a headache to men on preference lists; for instance a PLA man might lose his priority if he was absent from too many calls and if he got stuck on a continuity job with another employer he might well 'blow out' to maintain his corner. For the unions, such circumstances made discipline difficult. But the stevedores section of the NASD strictly enforced the rule since it helped preserve group identity and both unions were tough on breaches attributed to plain venality – for instance a man who walked off a wine-discharging job for a better-paying assignment on tea was fined £5 by the TGWU.

The nature of the rule changed between 1944 and 1967, developing an increasingly restrictive function. From being a guarantee of labour it became a bar to many forms of mobility within a turn. The definition of 'job' was drawn tighter until transfers from hatch to hatch were banned in the same work period, quay gangs could not switch when shipworkers turned overside to work lighters and a man who finished work during a turn, even if it was within minutes of the start, could not be re-engaged until he attended the next free call.

The Devlin Committee was fascinated by the rule since it exemplified a wasteful practice operating in three ways. The first element was neither protective nor restrictive but designed to ensure that men got the rough with the smooth in any job. The second was protective under a casual system, since by preventing transfers in mid-turn it ensured that blue-eyed boys did not get all the good work; and the third element, which defined the job so narrowly, was restrictive and indefensible.

Two case histories were cited to show the rule at its worst. In one a ship was forced to sail out of trim because the ban on inter-hatch transfer resulted in 40 tons being stowed forward and 115 aft. The other was more extraordinary.

On a vessel bound for North Africa, general cargo and eighty-nine cars had to be loaded into two hatches. At the end of the first day, eighty-four cars were loaded into Number One hold and there was still room for the remaining five. On the second day, the stevedore was not prepared to employ a full gang for the half-hour needed to stow the five cars in Number One hold when he would be unable to employ them again until the second call but would nonetheless have to give them stand-by payment. So he put a gang on the second hatch and hoped there would be room for the five cars as well. There was, in fact, only room for one car and the gang refused to transfer to Number One but compromised by agreeing to lash the last four cars to the hatch covers of Number Two.

'The choice therefore lay between taking the four cars as deck cargo or holding the ship for half-an-hour's loading . . . on the following morning. The captain reluctantly accepted the four cars as deck cargo. Again, it is impossible to give any explanation that does not reflect discredit on the workings of the port, of why four new cars have to be taken to North Africa upon an exposed deck when there is good stowage for them under cover.'[96]

For Phase I, significant changes had to be made. It was agreed that the continuity rule would apply generally when men were working for their own employer, although any form of transfer had to be accepted on completion of a job within a work period or when there was more urgent work elsewhere. But for men on transfer, continuity could be terminated by the borrowing employer if the transferred man prevented his own employees from working or by the contractual employer if he would otherwise have to borrow men on the following day.

It was this which led to the strike. The clause was elaborated in further negotiation so that transferred men were put into non-continuity work *where practical* and in this manner the transfer clause was operated with considerable success until Phase II. It was estimated that the abolition of all continuity restrictions could save 5 or 6 per cent of the wages bill and this may have been achieved in spite of minor troubles on hatch transfers.

A more serious weakness was the transfer clause and the trouble stemmed from a predictable cupidity among employers who released their least able men for transfer.

From the start employers were chary of borrowing men since they had to pay a 33 per cent fee to the contractual employer, on top of wages (later reduced to 24 per cent), but they baulked at accepting the slowest of their competitors' gangs. Scruttons Maltby was the first company to complain of getting the 'dregs', and infuriated the unions by allegedly turning transferred men away in Tilbury after announcing a shortage at the sector meeting. Another Tilbury company, Metropolitan Terminals, had exactly the same problem. Work in its delivery shed was non-continuity and had to be given as priority to transferred men. But it found that the quality of borrowed labour was so poor that it put two of its own gangs semi-permanently on deliveries to avoid shed congestion. It then found it could not borrow men for shipwork unless the delivery gangs were broken up because of the priority rule.

The consequence was that London employers made progressively less use of the transfer facility. While this helped develop a greater sense of permanency between men and their contractual employers, it squandered the most important concession on mobility in the Phase I agreement and was tantamount to accepting many of the worst pre-Devlin practices. For Phase II, inter-company transfer was dropped and the main reason was not the hostility of the unions but the employers' disinterest.

OVERTIME

The history of overtime in London during Phase I was even more depressing. The 40-hour week agreement of July 1964 had committed the unions to the provision of reasonable weekend overtime and the Phase I agreement confirmed the need for weekend work and night-work on any day of the week to finish a ship. In neither instance was the agreement honoured and London remained the port with the most severe restrictions on the hours of work between 1964 and 1970.

The overtime issue had a long industrial history and centred on the degree to which the Scheme made it compulsory by requiring men to work 'for such periods as are reasonable in his particular case.' Employers argued that the need to clear berths or catch tides was unpredictable and that some overtime had to be worked at short notice, although it remained voluntary in principle. To the men, who might have social arrangements for the evening, it was inconvenient to work late without knowing in advance; even under Phase I the employers could wait till 4 p.m. before asking for the two extra hours between 5 and 7 p.m. and men who wanted to avoid overtime were expected to find their own substitutes.

The 1951 strike in Manchester and the NASD strike in London in 1954 both stemmed from the insistance that all overtime was voluntary and the Evershed Inquiry provided a temporary solution only by allowing the two sides to agree to disagree.

But common sense was on the side of the employers and the men were hard put to uphold the voluntary principle if they condoned compulsory bans on overtime. Future trouble might have been avoided if overtime had been used for its original purpose of meeting emergencies, but it became the norm in most ports. For the country as a whole, the average working week has fluctuated since the inception of the Scheme between forty-four and forty-seven hours a week. But because there always was a degree of underemployment during normal hours, it will be realised that the number of overtime hours worked was higher than is at first apparent. In Liverpool, where the use of overtime was built into the wages structure, eight to ten hours of overtime was common and in London it averaged between five and eight hours a week, until the respective Phase I agreements began to bring these figures closer together.

In London, dockers used restrictions on overtime not only as a bargaining weapon but as a justifiable protest against the built-in use of overtime for some, while other men were proving attendance, i.e. not working at all. Dickie Barrett used to tell his men that the forty-hour week had not been achieved while this amount of overtime was worked. 'We have had the taste of leisure and we are not going to be robots,' he told a mass meeting in 1965. 'Perhaps the employers want all the top sheds turned into dormitories.'

Within a week of the July 1964 agreement all weekend overtime was effectively halted, although there was a normal requirement for between 2,000 and 3,000 men. The trouble started with petty disputes over interpretation by Blues and tally clerks and the employers retaliated by deciding not to ask for any Saturday or Sunday work in the hope that men who needed the money would put pressure on the minority to lift their sanctions. This ploy backfired since the Royals liaison committee promptly imposed their own ban and spread it to Tilbury. While the Devlin Committee sat, the TGWU was asking its members to honour the 1964 agreement but the Blues kept the ban first by 260 votes to 234 and later by 463 to 227, in spite of appeals from the Government to clear congestion in London.

After Decasualisation, the weekend ban remained at the instigation of the Blues and, as had always happened in the past, White dockers refused to accept orders which Blue members had refused. Thus the amount of weekend work was minimal during Phase I in London and this was a major cause of dissension between the unions. Hegarty and Ron Webb of the Blues claimed that men only cut their own throats by working overtime and leaving less work for normal hours and Shea argued that unemployment in the port was the product of such short-sightedness and not offering a proper service to ship-owners. However, until Phase II, London could only offer two hours overtime a day and a maximum working week of fifty hours, the shortest of any British port and pitifully low compared with Continental ports where shiftwork was standard.

When NAPE reviewed the progress of Phase I agreements in the summer of 1968, it found little of cheer. Manchester had incurred a heavy increase in costs without a compensating increase in productivity. Liverpool was pleased with the decline of the welt, but was under great pressure from piecework claims. Hull had gained no benefit and discipline was bad. The Tyne had trouble with overtime, the Tees was worried by the disincentive effect of the new guarantee and Bristol had seen a falling in throughputs.

But there were successes in Southampton and, in particular, Glasgow where there was full mobility and where spelling – the local term for the welt – and restrictions on sling loads had disappeared.

London's position was paradoxical since little was going right but the leading employers wanted to press on towards Phase II. The transfer arrangements were not popular, restrictions on overtime remained and men in the Royal docks were refusing to accept overnight orders, which meant they could not be directed to new work before the morning on which it started and work was thus delayed at the start of the day.

But the new generation of London negotiators, John Kiernan and John Hovey, felt nothing would be gained by clinging to a mediocre agreement, although men like Lindsay Alexander wanted to see positive benefits from Phase I before embarking on a further round of bargaining. They also felt there was little chance of making Phase I work as a productivity deal after buying out wasteful practices, but allowing many of their causes to remain.

This was at the heart of Phase I difficulties. As the Devlin report realised, the underlying cause of casual attitudes was the lack of job and earnings security and, even under permanent employment, the increased level of security could not be meaningful while one man could take home £50 one week and £16 the next.

Although no general statistics exist, individual instances suggest that the fluctuation of earnings remained as wide as ever during Phase

I. The Devlin report had tabled examples from London and Liverpool which showed a range of £11 to £47 for a high-earning docker and it was hoped that Phase I would see a degree of equalisation between these extremes. The report had even suggested special measures for equalising earnings potential, but it recognised that the difficulties of easing gangs who enjoyed high-paying work away from this accustomed privilege were acute.

'To meet the general desire for equalisation of earnings it is inevitable that the man with the big pay packet will have to sacrifice something. But the range of weekly earnings is so wide that a sudden descent from the top to near the average might cause hardship. On the other hand, most dockers' earnings vary so much from week to week that even high-paid dockers may prefer the greater stability of earnings that work sharing should provide. In these circumstances it might be said that the higher-paid worker should accept the loss for the common good and for the compensating advantages which it has to offer him' (para 314).

The report suggested that high piecework potential might be bought out – just as it was to be in the motor industry at Cowley – with a once-off cash payment when work-sharing was introduced.

But almost no regard was paid at national and port level to the problem of equalising earnings in the negotiation of Phase I, although a firm statement of principle might have assuaged the men's misgivings and forced employers to institute domestic arrangements to spread work fairly and thereby counter protective attitudes.

The result was that the gradations of privilege and status which divided dock workers under casualism and determined which men got the pickings of piecework were hardly touched; men in declining trades still got work which, in all probability, required a high degree of effort but did not give a good bonus yield while 'blue-eyed' gangs were given the work which needed a fast throughput and carried high earnings potential.

The one major difference of Phase I was the raising of the minimum cut-off point from £11 to £16 or £17, so a degree of extra security was given at the bottom end of the earnings' scale. However, Figure I shows that the narrowing of the earnings range after Decasualisation was only proportional, with the lowest sum constituting a higher percentage of the top. In cash terms, the difference may have increased. In the 1964–5 fiscal year, the earnings of a docker with an average income of £870 a year in Liverpool ranged between £11 and £26 a week. In 1968, a Liverpool porter-holdsman had a range of £17 to £35 – a widening of the cash difference from £15 to £18 a week.

In London, fluctuation was worse than in Liverpool. A medium earner, averaging £1,166 a year in 1964 had a weekly income range of £11 to £31 and a high earner (£1,479 a year), £11 to £47 a week. Four years later equivalent figures were £17 to £44 and £19 10s to £50.

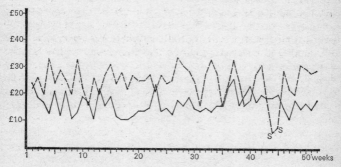

——— Weekly earnings of docker with annual gross earnings of £870 11s 8d (average) in 1964-5 fiscal year. The range is from £11 to £26 a week.

— — — Weekly earnings of porter-holdsman for fiscal year 1968-9. The range is from £17 to £35 a week.

S = Sickness.

Figure 1   Fluctuation in earnings in Liverpool.

During 1968 and 1969, such progress made towards equalising earnings was largely the work of progressive managements assisted by shop stewards. In Scruttons–Maltby, for example, work was allocated between gangs so that the great majority of men earned within £300 a year of each other, but as mechanisation increased, the disparity between good- and bad-paying sectors tended to widen again. In 1968-9, 74·2 per cent of the men were placed within an earnings range of £24 to £35 a week and 48 per cent between £29 and £35. Next year, the numbers in the equivalent groupings were down to 72 per cent between £27 and £38 and 41 per cent between £30 and £36.

The stage for Phase II was thus set soon after Decasualisation, as the problems of the wages structure were made manifest; the men were much better off but still displayed the attitudes of previous insecurity. Some employers believed this was caused by the payment of a higher guarantee, which removed the moral pressure on men to look after their colleagues' earnings and allowed the classic piecework syndrome of 'chasing the fastest penny' to emerge with a vengeance. But most looked to the growing difficulty of linking increases in bonus earnings to a corresponding increase in effort. They saw dockers' earnings rise by roughly 40 per cent in the two years following de-casualisation – a period when no pay increases were conceded at national or port level – and concluded that the wages system, inherited from casualism, was out of control. It was wages drift pure and simple and the longer the wait for reforms under Phase II, the worse the drift became.

CHAPTER TWELVE

The Wages Structure

'*In many cases, the existing wage arrangements are so complex, irrational and varied that the task of sorting them out would certainly be long and difficult.*' Lord Pearson, 1970.

Dockland's wages structure was determined by the insecurities of casualism. The Shaw award set the pattern for pre-war years by giving a high basic rate on the assumption that overall earnings would be offset by underemployment and the figures in Table I (page 19) showed how favourably dockers' rates compared with those for engineering and building labourers but how weekly earnings tended to be lower.

Fuller employment post-war completely reversed this position. As earnings potential grew, employers at national level tried to retard wages drift upwards by pegging back the national time rate, to which port piecework tariffs were linked. The effect can be seen in Figure 2 and Appendix 20. While the industry's basic rate was still high in 1947, it declined steadily in importance and now constitutes a very small part of total earnings, while the bonus yield continued to grow. In 1947, bonuses and overtime added some 50 per cent to basic rates but, in the last years before the reform of the wages structure, they added more than 300 per cent and accounted for the dockers' superiority in earnings above the national average, especially in the upward surge after Decasualisation.

This gulf between the minimum rate and average earnings was the root cause of insecurity and the increasing complexities of the wages structure. For men burdened with mortgages and hire purchase commitments, the sum they could be sure of taking home was low and the surplus, in Lord Devlin's words, was jam on the bread and butter; thus their main preoccupation was to manipulate the bonus system to give a *consistently* high surplus and there were too many ways to do it, without regard to output, for the employers to keep wages drift in control.

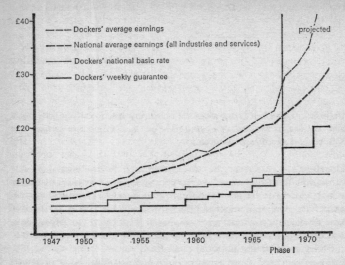

Figure 2   Earnings and the guarantee.

Phase II reforms inevitably centred on increasing security through the basic wage and rationalising the bonus structure according to local needs. At most ports, this meant a thorough re-examination of *piecework* which was by far the most important element in the pay packet.

In early days, piecework was never wholly popular with the unions – although preferred to the 'contract' and 'plus' systems – because it was seen as a means of driving men, without regard to health and safety, and of narrowing the prospects of employment for the labour force as a whole. But Lord Shaw had recommended its extension as a means of guaranteeing outputs and it was widely adopted in London during the 1920s. The PLA introduced a tariff for quay work in 1921, designed to yield a third above basic rates, and other ocean trades employers devised their own systems, heedless of each other's practices. The discrepancies were so marked that the main concern of the 1930s was to standardise payments and Lord Sanderson succeeded in introducing the Red Book discharging tariff in 1932 into all the enclosed docks; but it did not cover all commodities and tea, for example, could be discharged still under fourteen different rates.

The Second World War brought the next major extension of piece-work, principally in the convoy ports where London employers like Scruttons set up operations. In the years of the Scheme, virtually every port used piecework but the yields were different in each locality. Just before Decasualisation, it was reckoned that 90 per cent of jobs in London were piece-rated with a yield which justified working at a piecework stroke. In Southampton the proportion was 86 per cent but in Liverpool, although 95 per cent of jobs were rated, the men only achieved bonus on 62 per cent because of a lower incentive element.

While port tariffs as a whole were moved by national negotiation in proportion to movements on the national time rate, the fact that tariffs were essentially accretions of local custom and practice allowed a large amount of flexibility and local pressure could occasionally change a tariff on a departmental basis and often on individual commodities.

As piecework became more prominent, so did the opportunity for men to exploit their inherent strength on the shopfloor. This power was built into the nature of gang organisation but it was encouraged by the method of piecework *calculation*. Most ports paid commodity rates on a gang-day basis, with earnings linked directly to the tonnage handled. This was London's original system but a war-time agreement introduced an alternative payment by measurement (the Western Front agreement), thereby relating yield to the volume of goods as well as the weight. Liverpool initially made loading payments 'ship-co-operative', rewarding men for their share of the deadweight tonnage input for the operation as a whole and not allowing the bonus yield to be ascertained until the job was finished; payment for discharging and delivery in Liverpool was similar to London until 1965–6, when the system was altered to give the bonus on top of a time-rate payment which was boosted by a higher yield once a threshold was passed.

Throughout the industry, however, the most common feature was daily payment to the gang. It was admittedly the simplest form of calculation but it allowed issues of payment to be raised on every day of an operation and increased the potential frequency of disputes.

After piecework itself, the most important bonus element was the *contingency award.* This was essentially a fixed sum, paid when work was dirty, dangerous or obnoxious or when the earnings potential of piece workers was affected through no fault of their own. Cargo might shift in transit, it might be damaged by sea-water or be wedged in the wings of the hold and, in such instances, there was either a recognised 'con' or one would have to be speedily fixed through the grievance machinery.

Such one-off payments were a ready source of malpractices by employers and men alike and the records of London's area committees, in which union officials and management supervisors gave on-the-spot awards, show how frequently trouble arose. The committee was called as soon as a gang refused to accept the small payments which foremen were authorised to give on top of normal rates. Usually London companies restricted first-line supervision to awards of 10s a day but claims rose to as much as £5 and the area committees tended to compromise in the interests of speedy settlement.

When trade was brisk just after the war, the men often resorted to the committee procedure and there could be four determinations per working day. When underemployment was higher in the early 1950s, the number of committee awards dropped to as low as 342 but in the 1960s the average was between 500 and 1,000 a year.

Each committee evidenced the dockers' willingness to engage in a naked power struggle and the greater their security, the more ready they seemed to do it. During Phase I, the level of committee awards was consistently high and the result was to increase the importance of the special payment in relation to piecework earnings. Liverpool underwent exactly the same experience during these years; the Scamp award of 1967 opened men's eyes to bonus potential and employers' resistance to this pressure resulted in a host of petty stoppages.

The last element in the pay packet was the *time-rate payment* itself. Some work, usually a shed involving the arrangement rather than the movement of cargo, could not be put on a bonus basis and remained timework jobs. A minority of men, usually the medically unfit, relied on this work alone but the time rate was also important to piece workers through overtime calculations and stand-by payments.

The overtime premium was invariably based on the time rate rather than on an increment to piece rates and, before Devlin, this form of bonus was far more important to the Liverpool docker than piecework, constituting 25 per cent of his earnings while piecework bonus yielded only 10 per cent. This was why Liverpool was always regarded as a timework port and the Mersey employers readily admitted that incentive payments had never really caught on and men preferred to spin work out into overtime to build up the pay packet. To both the TGWU and the employers, this situation was a headache. O'Leary was often berated by Liverpool delegates for winning national increases in the piecework tariffs instead of greater increases on the time rate and he could only remind them that they were not the only fish in the pond. 'If Liverpool men really wanted conditions like London I can supply their district secretary with all the information required, but Liverpool must then supply people who would work in accordance with these details. But in the present circumstances, they cannot expect to be compared fairly with everybody else all the time they maintain a system which is different.'[97]

The stand-by payment, as its name implies, originated under casualism as compensation for piece workers hired but unable to work on account of weather conditions, traffic delays, shortage of essential equipment or plain managerial faults. It theoretically was no more than the minimum hourly rate but, as this declined in proportion to overall earnings, stand-by hours were often boosted or used like contingency payments to bring earnings up to an acceptable level. Any statistics on these payments are suspect because they were often fictitiously contrived; most dockers could produce wage slips where their piecework tonnages would have been impossibly high, had the hours paid as stand-by been true.

However, so long as piecework was used in an industry whose workflow was uncertain, the stand-by payment had to exist to give the same protection to men hired as the guarantee and attendance money gave to men not engaged at the call.

With full permanency and the elevation of the guarantee above the time rate, payment for idle hours became a source of growing friction. Because the guarantee was paid as a weekly calculation, men seldom benefited from its level of £16 or £17 per week during odd hours which were calculated on the time rate basis of £11 1s 8d per week. The situation was eased after November 1969 when NAPE agreed to convert the guarantee from a weekly to a daily basis, but the issue of stand-by hours remained one of the most vexing in the wages claim which led to the national dock strike and Pearson settlement of 1970.

The complexities of this wages structure were highlighted by the strike and showed how limited was the scope for any reform at national level, without worsening the anomalies and opening the way to further wages drift. The relative importance of the constituent parts can be judged from Table 5, which gives a breakdown of earnings in one London company during the Devlin years.

Table 5   Analysis of total gang earnings, excluding terminal operations

	1965–6 (Oct.–Sept.)	1966–7 (Oct.–Sept.)	1967–8 (Oct.–Sept.)	1968–9 (Oct.–Sept.)
Cargo piecework	61·24	62·55	58·71	55·85
Cargo daywork	1·38	1·16	1·00	0·54
Contingency payments	1·13	1·12	1·42	1·66
Area awards	1·74	1·63	2·59	2·87
Delays	20·86	19·87	20·75	21·18
Extra payments	2·65	3·02	4·81	7·40
Overtime	10·65	10·40	10·72	10·40
Total	c. 100%	c. 100%	100%	100%

For the employers preparing for Phase II, the warning signals stand out clearly in the growing importance of payments unrelated to output, listed under area awards, extra payments and contingency payments. Whatever their philosophy of a new wages structure, they dared not ignore that rank-and-file pressure had succeeded in cushioning the incentive system so that bonus had to be paid even if work was not done.

In the piecework debate of the 1950s, when the concept of securing output by financial motivation was seriously questioned and the successors of Elton Mayo looked beyond Economic Man for social and psychological influences on behaviour at work, a strong defence of wage incentives could be mustered by managements which exercised strict control over production and their piecework schemes. In Britain, payment by results had spread to a third of the working population in the 1960s and it received the qualified blessing of the Prices and Incomes Board, which refused to condemn plant-negotiated incentives although admitting they contributed largely to wages drift.

Even the advocates of piecework, however, demanded careful control of workflow, if the cash nexus was to outweigh loyalties to collective principle and social status, and it was ironical that employers in the docks, where the non-repetitive nature of work made control most difficult, were among the most ardent supporters of the incentive system.

Their faith in piecework was in part a symptom of casualism, since the inherent self-discipline made supervision easy and fitted their role as providers of a labour-only service. But, still more ironically, the Mersey employers who had never succeeded in getting piecework to operate fully presented Lord Devlin with the most detailed defence of incentive payments for dockwork. They admitted that: 'Men will work hard for one employer and not for another – on the same cargo; they will go for piecework when working cargo in one trade but not in another; they will damn one commodity, indistinguishable in handling qualities from another rated the same, on which they will have a go.' But they found no objections to the principle of piecework itself, although there were frequent shortcomings in its application. They argued that it was possible to perfect piecework to eliminate friction between men and management and still keep a necessary reward for men who were prepared to work hard.

The other school, which began as a small minority among port employers but went from strength to strength as Phase II negotiations progressed, conceded it was theoretically possible to rationalise piecework into an ideal system but thought that the practical chances of doing so were remote. The faults of piecework were so intertwined with the faults of casualism that one could not be abolished without the other.

Their primary argument condemned piecework as a cause of dissent, partly because of anomalies between rates, partly because of pressures to lessen fluctuation in earnings. In London, with the competing rates of different sections of the port, the anomalies could not be eradicated and the incentive effect of many rates virtually disappeared while others, like the rate on motor cars, were unduly lucrative. There were many distortions. For instance, the PLA's intended yield of 33 per cent bonus had disappeared in many areas while the ocean trades employers tried to fix a 70 per cent yield against union pressure for 100 per cent above time rate. Arguments over rate-fixing could be dragged out for many weeks and it was more common to correct anomalies by *ad hoc* payments or extra time-rate allowances based on coercive comparisons.

Secondly, piecework created tension among the labour force, fuelling jealousy against the 'blue-eyed boys' who were thought – with considerable justification – to be favoured in the allocation of work and earnings. When the difference between a thick or thin wallet on pay day rested not on the men's willingness to work but on the arbitrary flow of goods and choice of gangs, the reaction of the less-favoured was to seek payment irrespective of output, if not actual work-sharing. London employers found that most area committee awards went to the least able gangs and it was the same men who pressed for the strictest interpretation of rules on manning and flexibility.

Thirdly, piecework imposed huge strains on management. Most disputes were settled on the spot, before reaching the grievance machinery or the proportion of a strike, but this involved management literally in many hours of negotiation per week and the burden of this ceaseless debate prevented the exercise of more important managerial prerogatives. In theory piecework may have been self-disciplining but, as Lord Brown knew, it also made supervision less possible. Foremen had little answer to men who chose to be inefficient on the grounds that they paid for the misdemeanour out of their own pockets and the prospect of pieceworkers 'going daywork' was always a nightmare.

Men maintained they could legitimately revert to a pace of work befitting the low hourly rate of pay and this could be dreadfully slow since piecework had been used as a substitute for the harder managerial task of establishing proper work norms. (As is the case in most industries, the rank-and-file developed their own unwritten rules about what constituted a fair day's work for a fair day's pay. In London, going day-work usually involved phenomenally low throughputs. In the dispute which led to the closure of Millwall wharf in 1968, throughput of auctioned tea from barge to quay dropped to one ton a day!)

The following schedule for such a work-to-rule was issued unofficially in London but, if all the thirty-seven clauses were enacted, it is not difficult to imagine how output would decline!

WORKING TO RULE

Ships gangs

1. No rigging of gear or placing of derricks.
2. No work until all faulty hatches are refitted and placed.
3. All ladders in ships' holds must be static and in good order.
4. All gangways must be secured and all handrails in place.
5. All cargo in slings to allow for reaving.
6. All boards loaded to ensure the utmost safety.
7. No winches, even with the slightest fault, to be worked.
8. All cranes must plumb the centre of the hatch. (No bonds under combings.)
9. No winches to be worked unless blocks behind drivers head have preventors.
10. No tea breaks on ship. Mobile (canteen) surroundings to be clean, if not go outside (the dock area).
11. In no circumstances must piecework be attained.
12. All wires, ropes, boards and slings to be in tip-top condition.
13. All lightermen to be in attendance of craft and all barge shunts and shifting of same to be done by lightermen only.
14. All ropes for securing craft fore and aft to be applied, guy lines must not be used.
15. Safety nets to be used down the holds all the time, including all handrails round tween-deck combings.
16. Ensure sufficient walking way round tween-decks containing cargo for other ports.
17. No gangs to work short-handed.
18. Working times from 8 to 12 and 1 to 5. (No plugging before and after.)
19. Special attention to be paid to vision of all winch drivers.
20. All beams to be made secure and bolted.
21. Where protective clothing is supplied all washing facilities to be made available.
22. No sorting of cargo and no books or papers to be held by any member of the gang.
23. All cargo to be worked in the interest of safety.
24. Make sure proper lighting is available at all times.
25. All craft to be worked to gunwale height only.

Quay gangs

1. Before commencing work ensure that red flags are displayed at both ends of shed.
2. All barrows inspected as to wear and tear.
3. All mechanised bogies, fork lifts and mobile cranes thoroughly inspected.
4. All quays inspected for potholes and jutting railway lines.
5. All lorries to be loaded or unloaded in bays and not in sheds.
6. No splitting of gangs.
7. No overloading of ropes, slings or boards. (Reave all sets.)
8. All delivery gangs to draw out at four hour periods for re-allocation.
9. No delivery under cranes which are in motion.
10. Essential, no splitting of striking gangs.
11. No lorries on quay except for ships' stores and then only one at a time.
12. All non-continuity men to draw out at four hour periods, this includes gearers, needlemen, coopers' shop, etc.

We do insist that all men be allocated to work, to protect our
members from the ugliness of victimisation
This means mass allocation

Finally, there was growing doubt over the ability of piecework to provide good outputs at all. Figures from the turn of the century when no bonus was paid were staggeringly high for some commodities. A gang of 17 men and a boy regularly could discharge 1,000 bales of cotton a day with steam winch and split-gear relay transfer from hold to deck to quay. In 1969, a gang of 24 using married gear for direct purchase from hold to quay might average 500 bales a day, in spite of bonus and mechanised quay transport. Such comparison is not fair without recalling the pressure under which men then worked – 'economic poverty producing economic fear,' as Bevin termed it. But it does show that the financial incentive was not of itself sufficient to guarantee high output as men's expectation of a *reasonable pace of work* altered, and most supervisors recognised that outputs were largely controlled by unofficial norms which gangs set for themselves and which could be institutionalised in semi-official understandings.

The relevance of piecework was even more questionable with the unitisation of cargo, because yields were automatically distorted with mechanisation and the pace of work was no longer dictated by individual effort but by the cycle of the machine. The simpler forms of mechanisation could be met, within the piecework structure, by revision of targets and manning scales and the PLA registered some success in de-manning when it introduced fork-lift trucks and pallets in the movement of export cargoes from road or rail conveyance to shed and then to quay. But this was made possible by having a stable labour force and the PLA's success was not matched by stevedores reliant on pool labour.

The real difficulties came with roll-on/roll-off and containers, where 20 men could do the work of 250 in a day, rather than a week, and the throughput per man year of 1,000 tons in a conventional berth was replaced by 10,000 to 20,000 tons in a container operation.

Piecework simply could not be adjusted to this scale of output and the new docker had to be given a wages structure akin to his status as a salaried technician. So long as the old and the new methods of dockwork co-existed in a port, and many of the best-paying piecework commodities were most readily containerised, the security of the new docker was bound to increase dissatisfaction among men labouring under the uncertain earnings of piecework.

The force of these arguments was recognised by a growing number of ship-owners and employers during Phase II negotiation and also spread to the unions. Initially, rank-and-file attitudes to upstanding wage rates were ambivalent. Piecework provided good wages to some men and even those who were not 'blue-eyed' did not like to see slackers rewarded on equal terms with men who 'tore their guts out.' Furthermore, piecework was an attractive bargaining weapon; it had given the principle of shopfloor mutuality and established the strength of shop stewards in many industries, since bonus levels had to be adjusted by mutual consent on the shopfloor; it was also a powerful means of raising levels of earnings between major pay settlements.

But union principle demanded that all men be given the opportunity of equal earnings and that men, whose capacity to work well was undermined by age or ill-health, should not be stigmatised after giving long years of service to the industry.

The upstanding weekly wage, without any form of bonus, was the simplest way of giving equal treatment to all men and the TGWU gradually moved towards this position in the London enclosed docks negotiations. At first, they did not object to a large bonus element, then they suggested it should be no more than 5 per cent of earnings, and then plumped for full security through the basic rate. In other negotiations, however, union attitudes were not so clear-cut. On the London riverside, the men wanted to retain a bonus structure and in Liverpool, where the shop stewards put forward the preposterous claim of £60 for 20 hours work, they eventually chose to retain piece-work.

To abandon incentives altogether was a leap in the dark for the industry. The upstanding weekly wage essentially meant putting the whole labour force on a system of payment required for mechanised operations alone and the men had to exchange the really high earnings of a few for everyone's security, while employers had to trust they had the expertise to maintain outputs on conventional dockwork without the piecework carrot.

In the first year after Decasualisation, the issue between the two types of wages structure did not crystallise quickly. The most pressing problem for employers was to get rid of surplus labour through voluntary severance and progress was slow, because the Government withheld finance.

They also had to decide the extent to which Phase II should be controlled from national rather than port level. The employers were seriously divided. They recognised the differing needs of individual ports but were frightened that the devolution of negotiating power would escalate all local settlements to the level of the highest; this form of leapfrogging would make Phase II expensive and also remove the tenuous authority of NAPE as a negotiating body over the conflicting interests of the ports.

The National Modernisation Committee should have given a quick lead towards Phase II, but it was dormant for most of 1968. Lord Brown had resigned and Gunter was waiting for the Royal Commission on Trade Unions to be published before committing the docks to a pattern of negotiation which might conflict with its findings.

In this vacuum, NAPE stated its interest by issuing guidelines on how the outstanding recommendations of the Devlin programme – the review of manning scales and of wages structure – should be implemented. It wanted the normal hours of work, annual holidays, pensions and sick pay to remain issues for national determination – as expected. But it also wanted to keep the national time rate and national guarantee as part of any local settlement. Local committees would be free to alter piecework rates, overtime and shiftwork premiums, manning scales and the system of payment, but these were to be tacked to the two planks of national control. 'Where bonus schemes are introduced which involved timework payments, it is desirable that the excess payment over the national standard time rate should be expressed in terms of a special timework differential rather than as part of a new port basic rate.'[98]

NAPE was fighting to preserve its influence at the instigation of Liverpool and smaller ports who feared London would move faster than the rest of the country towards modernisation because of its acute labour surplus and the container ban. But by the end of the year, NAPE's stand had been broken.

The NMC was reconstituted under Cattell (and without two of the independents) and it took heed of the main conclusion of the Royal Commission – to recognise the importance of decentralised negotiations and move away from the façade of industry-wide negotiation. In December, it issued an important policy statement defining the aims of Phase II agreements. These aims were to vary from port to port and between employers within a port, to let companies 'modernise their operations to the fullest possible extent in order to improve the economic performance of the industry.'

The NJC was allowed to control the minimum levels of pay in agreed areas but local negotiators would be self-sufficient in varying the lengths of the working week, if coupled to the introduction of shift work, and in improving upon the national time rate without couching the excess in terms of a local differential. The rest of the directive set out basic principles of productivity bargaining and defined the procedural roles of local modernisation committees, the national body and the NJC. The significant point, however, was the independence given to the localities and the emerging attitudes towards new wages structures.

This directive envisaged the retention of the bonus. 'It will be open for the two sides locally to agree on a move away from piecework and towards the introduction of enhanced time rate payments *supplemented by bonus payments related to productivity*' (my italics). In February 1969, however, a supplementary directive spoke in terms of possible time rate systems of payments, not linked to bonus.

No employers' association had yet proposed an upstanding weekly wage, least of all London, but the change of tune reflected the growing pressures from outside the industry. One important source was the ship-owners who knew that foreign ports paid by the hour, not the piece, and often preferred their service.

Rotterdam paid no bonuses, except through the strictly graded increments to basic rates which rewarded skills and experience. Similarly, all US ports operated on time rates and already one or two operators in London, who significantly refused to join the employers' association, were moving in the same direction.

The Government itself became an indirect source of pressure. Perhaps it was coincidence which placed miners' leaders – Sir Sidney and Will Paynter – on the most important dock inquiries of the 1960s. But it was no chance that Lord Brown and Cattell headed the NMC and that much of the servicing of Phase II negotiations was carried out by the DEP's manpower and productivity services, also under Cattell's leadership. These men were associated with the removal of piecework in their own industries and, by 1969, civil servants at the DEP were leading advocates for its abolition in the docks. With each successive crisis in the London negotiations, they exerted more pressure to switch directly to the upstanding weekly wage.

To see the conflict between the two philosophies of wages at its most acute, we must follow the negotiations for the enclosed docks in London. Not only did they set the pace for many ports, but the pendulum swung agonisingly between a flat rate and retention of bonus up to the very last minute.

CHAPTER THIRTEEN

London Modernisation and the Container Ban

'*My men do not understand your London dockers. We will handle any ship at any time and we are happy. But your men seem crazy.*'

Antwerp port employer, November 1969.

One fact above all others shaped the negotiation of Phase II Devlin in London – the ban on new container work, imposed by the TGWU Docks Group Committee on 3 January 1968. The ban was to last twenty-seven months until April 1970 and was lifted only when TGWU members had accepted new wages deals for the enclosed docks and riverside wharves.

As a tactical weapon, it was totally effective and each improved offer from the employers followed the Committee's refusal to open Tilbury to new container trade. But it was a disaster for national prestige. It kept most berths at the £30,000,000 Tilbury container extension empty and drove Britain's largest container consortia, Overseas Containers Ltd and Associated Container Transportation (OCL–ACT) to Rotterdam and Antwerp for half its duration, as well as deterring foreign shipping lines from using the largest British container facility.

The Tilbury extension was conceived in 1962 and the first of the ten berths – seven for containers exclusively and three for packaged timber – was ready in 1967, a few months after Rotterdam opened its Europe Container Terminus and three years after the New York Port Authority opened Port Elizabeth, the largest container development in the world.

Before the ban took effect, the PLA got four berths operating, under the 'peninsular agreement,' one for US Lines, one a common-user berth for short-sea hauls to the Continent and two for package timber. By the time it was lifted, Rotterdam was fully established as the European terminus for deep-sea container traffic and had garnered the trade of Sea-Land, Atlantic Container Line, Moore-McCormack, US Lines, Hapag/Lloyd and Canadian Pacific.

It was not simply a matter of losing the advantage of an early start at Tilbury. There was a serious danger that the ban would shake the confidence of ship-owners and alter decisions on their choice of port and routings. Some deep-sea container trades are bound to need port-calls at Continental *and* British ports but, for others, the decision to use one port or two can hinge on very marginal calculations. It can be cheaper to sacrifice one port-call and tranship to other destinations, in order to get maximum use of the main container carrier, and lack of confidence in British labour could tip the balance irrevocably to Europe.

The PLA's fear was that the ban might play a decisive part in such delicate economic equations; and if British ports were deprived of revenue from the large container ships there would be less money to invest in good facilities, more deep-sea traffic would be carried by foreign shipping and the transhipment of UK-bound containers from the Continent in small feeder services would scatter the already-diffuse investment in container terminals over an even wider area in Britain.

The National Ports Council voiced the same fears in 1969 and stressed that no port could rely on its hinterland as a catchment area for container traffic; if the port did not provide an efficient link in through-transport services, container traffic could easily be diverted to different routes. 'Delay or slower working at UK ports resulting in slower ship turn-round compared with a Continental one could have a significant result in deep-sea vessels on certain trades by-passing the UK. Delays at UK ports would affect the US traffic first, since this has the shortest round-voyage time. For fast ships with a fourteen-day round voyage an effective rate of working at UK ports of 90 per cent or less of the Continental rates would be sufficient to tip the balance and make the UK direct call uneconomic. For slower ships on a twenty-one day round voyage, an effective rate of working at UK ports of 70 per cent or less of the Continental rate would tip the balance.'[99]

The Docks Group imposed the ban with little regard to its long-term implications since the thirteen delegates had no access, inside or outside the union, to accurate forecasts on container development or the industrial experience of foreign ports which had faced the same scale of job loss through mechanisation. They frequently asked for information, particularly about the future of London, but none was forthcoming at this stage and their decisions were taken in an emotive atmosphere, charged by such information as was widely publicised – like McKinsey and Company's report for the British Transport Docks Board that containers could eliminate nine-tenths of all dock jobs!

They were guided chiefly by the success of the prototype ban of 1966–7, which was imposed for ten months while Phase I was negotiated. Its purpose was to stop sectional agreements while the more important objective of full permanency was achieved and it was directed against parts of the port most remote from Docks Group authority – Tilbury and operators outside the aegis of the main wage negotiations.

The resolution of 1 August 1966 read: 'We are not prepared to negotiate on any new methods of discharging or loading or any mechanised operation that involves a reduction in the number of men employed as against the conventional method of these operations. On the introduction of 100 per cent decasualisation we are quite prepared to discuss and negotiate on the above matters.'

The ban was never quite solid because senior union officials did not want an all-out challenge to modernisation during the launching of the Devlin programme. On the riverside, some wharfingers secured better working arrangements and Olsen was allowed to transfer from Canary Wharf to P Shed Millwall, because of the TGWU's interest in preventing the NASD getting the work (see page 207).

Because the Tilbury container extension was still unfinished, the ban attracted little publicity but its observance was sufficiently enforced to show the Docks Group how their authority could be exerted above the heads of the unofficial committees.

The ban was withdrawn in curious fashion – to accommodate the two largest employers who refused to join the London Port Employers Association. In early June 1969 the Docks Group learnt that Shea and Bill Munday, a full-time official, had negotiated with Samuel Williams, a wharfinger operating from Dagenham dock, to make more than 200 men full-time dockers with a high basic wage and abolish piecework. It appeared as if this deal contravened the ban, but the situation was complicated since some of the labour previously was unregistered.

The Docks Group was reserving judgment when a far more important case emerged – a new agreement with Olsen. Since the Wilson Inquiry gave the bulk of work at Millwall to the TGWU, Olsen had been plagued with labour troubles and the men had struck against a plan to build up a permanent work force, provoking David Lloyd to remark that the 'unparalleled, ill-advised, wanton' action seemed bent on losing the work that the same men had been prepared to strike for, in order to get it.

Now Olsen wanted to put all 240 men on to a basic wage of £27 a week with an operational bonus of £2 10s and threatened to leave London altogether if he could not get these terms. He was in a strong position, one of the first ship-owners to operate a leased berth and the principal carrier of goods between Britain and the Canary Islands. He asked to meet the Docks Group to explain his predicament and they consented – the first time an employer was admitted to their deliberations.

Olsen and his managers used the opportunity to argue on two fronts. They said they recognised that the union wanted to protect jobs but their stand was driving trade away; also Olsens should really be treated as an ally because they were committed to palletisation, with the vessels worked by forklift trucks through side-doors in the hull, not to containers. This was modernisation in humane form, efficient but not devoid of labour content like container-handling.

They pointed out the paradoxes in a situation which encouraged the use of outports in preference to London and would forfeit the few available jobs in container handling, by driving depots inland. 'If the container adventure succeeds, both dockworkers and dock officials will be out of business. Further, the existing docks and existing tonnage will be obsolete. It is difficult to see the sense in this. For an outsider it looks like a man-made crisis, where the bodies involved are doing their utmost to accelerate the development and finally commit economic suicide.

'No doubt the crisis within the dock industry could have been avoided by more far-sightedness, but even today quite a lot can be saved. We have to remember that the main object of introducing containers has been to reduce loading/discharge cost and time in port.

'By abolishing restrictive practices in the ports, existing vessels can operate more economically than new container carriers, provided a fair amount of modernisation (flush decks, sideports, unit loads, etc.) is implemented. Further existing berths can, with a minimal expenditure, be excellent berths for unit load ships. By choosing this policy a fair amount of work will be left to the dock industry, practically no investments will be needed and, maybe most important, instead of having a revolution the dock industry will undergo a sound evolution.'[100]

In a question-and-answer session, Olsen said he could not wait for D-Day before getting a decision from the TGWU. A tough Norwegian who did not mince words, he said that the alternative to accepting his trade now in London was for him to look for another port.

This exposition was, in fact, close to the views of the union moderates, especially Shea who saw another good reason for accepting the Olsen and Samuel Williams agreements: they would set a precedent for the kind of conditions he wanted for the whole port and these would be more easily achieved if proved to work in these two instances.

Shortly after the Olsen team left the meeting, the delegates withdrew the ban and instructed officials to start negotiations 'for a policy of a higher basic wage plus incentive payments.' In the next six months, several sectional agreements were negotiated, particularly for Tilbury, and the PLA was putting the finishing touches to a deal for the container berths – the peninsular agreement – when a new crisis was produced by the problems of the up-river wharves, which were beginning to close rapidly as warehousing moved inland and the flow of lightered goods up the Thames contracted.

The wharves had thrived on the free-water clause and on London's entrepôt role in the commodity trades. But increasing labour costs of double-handling from the enclosed docks now offset the savings on quay charges and many of their specialist short-sea trades were the first to be containerised or switched to lorries and roll-on/roll-off ferry services. 8 wharves closed in 1967 but the figures jumped to 17, 15 and 14 in the next three years and, by the end of 1971, 70 had shut down since Decasualisation and only 74 remained as places of employment, with a labour force of 2,100 dockers instead of 5,500. The most accurate means of measuring this decline is in the tonnage figures of the London lighterage trade, which ferried goods from the enclosed docks to the wharves – and they tell a sorry story.

At the end of 1967, it was clear that New Fresh Wharf, which handled mostly fruit, was in difficulties. At the first meeting of the Docks Group in the New Year, it was therefore a riverside delegate, Brian Nicholson, who asked for a repetition of the early ban. He moved

Table 6   Lighterage in London

Year (Dec. 31)	Tonnage handled	No. of men on lightermen's register
1963	13,093,469	3,327
1964	12,515,180	3,169
1965	10,663,413	3,028
1966	9,559,478	2,915
1967	7,900,284	2,799
1968	7,435,994	2,471
1969	6,780,020	2,050
1970	5,774,364	1,734
1971	4,893,311	1,606

that: 'We the Number Five Divisional Committee on investigating the situation at New Fresh Wharf ask the Docks Group not to negotiate any new methods of discharging, etc. . . . until the whole of London is included in the package deal as is the policy of the Docks Group Committee.'[101]

He was well supported by delegates from the up-river docks but opposed by Tilbury and Shea, who felt that none of the arguments which applied to the removal of the first ban had changed. Also, there was little likelihood of achieving one deal for the whole port let alone the kind of wage structure which progressive employers might concede in individual negotiation. But Nicholson won the day and the ban was on.

The unity of the TGWU only just survived the ban, which polarised the conflict of interest between the old and new parts of the port. Riverside dockers were particularly bitter at the Phase I agreement, which allowed inter-sector transfer and meant that a stable nucleus of men could not be kept to work the wharves. The transfer clause was vital to the distribution of labour as a whole, but was regarded as the death-knell for the river.

Tilbury's case to be treated independently from London was also strengthened and Harry Battie, an ebullient man hall-marked by his warm grin and flat white cap, led the movement to remove the ban constitutionally within the Group. But even Tilbury was not united against the ban; there was an influx of dockers from the older part of London during Phase I who objected to local separatism and the most vociferous crusaders against the ban were PLA employees, who stood to gain most from new agreements.

The independence of the PLA negotiators was always troublesome to the union and, in the spring of 1968, there was a protracted row over the negotiation of the peninsular agreement. The PLA officer and his lay committee claimed it had been negotiated in finality one day before the ban came into force, while the Docks Group maintained it had not been sanctioned properly by *all* the membership at Tilbury. This quarrel lasted five months but the peninsular agreement stood, allowing a handful of services into the container extension.

However, it was succeeded by other disputes of overlapping jurisdiction. First, Stanley Turner, the PLA's industrial relations director, negotiated severance terms for PLA employees ahead of the ocean trades. The terms were as much a shock to other employers as the unions, since they established the top level of payments which were to be adopted nationally in 1969. But the Docks Group was infuriated that the terms had been reached without reference to themselves and that Shea should defend the constitutional right of a lay committee to negotiate for its members, although Group policy was port-wide.

Shea bravely said that, in like circumstances, he would again authorise officers and committees to go on negotiating sectionally and the Group retaliated by voting him out of office, pending a regional investigation of where ultimate union authority lay.

But the crisis passed quickly. Within minutes, Bert Fry refused to consider Shea's 'dismissal' but agreed to hold an investigation, if necessary. Later, the PLA severance terms were accepted by all employers and the storm died away.

While the content of the PLA agreement benefited the union, the procedural implications were decidedly threatening. If a sectional agreement on severance was valid, why not one on container-handling? This was just the problem which arose next, when the Belgian national line (now part of Dart Containerline) asked to switch from conventional trade to containerwork in Tilbury. While PLA members of the union seemed willing, the Docks Group refused to depart from the ban and the trade was soon lost to Southampton.

At this point, union morale was low and Turner saw the opportunity for a new initiative to get the ban removed. Early in September, he talked to the Docks Group, reminding them of the loss of this traffic and of Atlantic Steam Navigation – the company started by Col. F.

Bustard pioneering roll-on/roll-off from Tilbury with war-time tank landing ships – to Felixstowe. Maurice Foley, the Docks Group chairman, made an important concession to Turner, on which the next six months of negotiation were to hinge. He said that if the employers submitted a letter of intent – something positive, not just bare bones, with detailed outlines of Phase II proposals for the entire port – his committee would review the ban.

The employers turned to this task, producing a first draft two months later, and in the interim there was a minor relaxation of the ban to help Buchanan's Wharf, the only large undertaking to keep tea on the riverside, and to open the new PLA grain terminal at Tilbury. This was a convenient stick for PLA members to beat the Docks Group with again. They complained of insults to their committees and of the anti-PLA attitudes which were strangling the port; on the quiet, they also continued to negotiate with Turner on possible Phase II terms for the PLA only. Once again, the content of these talks was irreproachable to the union, since it involved a higher basic rate than John Hovey was offering for the enclosed docks, but the Docks Group was even more worried about a fragmentation of negotiations since the date – March 1969 – was fast approaching when OCL–ACT was to inaugurate its UK–Australia trade and 39 Berth at Tilbury, which it had leased specifically for the service, was covered by the ban.

The Docks Group faced strong pressure from many sources to lift the ban, at least for this prestige service. It had moved a little way from its original position; it was mutually recognised that a single deal for the port was a non-starter and different arrangements were needed for the enclosed docks, the wharves and lighterage; the occasional deal had been let through already and the issue of defining dockwork was being introduced into the bargaining situation. Further, the ban was to be reviewed on receipt of a satisfactory letter of intent.

This last concession, however, proved ephemeral because the union found it impossible to accept the outlines of Phase II without knowing the price and, once the price was stated, acceptance would prejudice future bargaining. But the definition of dockwork provided a new area for compromise. The bone of contention was the Orsett container-base, a few miles from the dock estate at Tilbury where some containers for the OCL–ACT trade were to be stuffed and unstuffed, and the railway freightliner terminal in the dock itself.

Crane-driving at the freightliner terminal was conceded to dockers by the Industrial Tribunal – and, having won the work, the Docks Group could hardly refuse to perform it – but there was little prospect of winning Orsett through the Tribunal machinery. This was the one card which Sir Andrew Crichton, as chairman of OCL, had up his sleeve, but he could not play it prematurely. While he accepted privately that dockers could work Orsett, he was not going to concede the work until he was sure of getting his ships into Tilbury.

At the end of January, Sir Andrew had to advise caution. He told his board that there were plenty of volunteers for the 54 jobs at the OCL berth and that men had been informed of the planned rates of pay for this work. The difficulty was that a sectional agreement would probably be vetoed by the Docks Group and if the veto was ignored by the men, London would almost certainly erupt in a major strike.

'Whatever the outward attitude of the Docks Group may be, there is mounting evidence that the members of this group are becoming embarrassed over the consequences of continuing their present action for too long and do realise a solution must be found. It is fair to say that they are under pressure themselves and . . . it will be intolerable if British and major operations such as ours are frustrated when an American operator and two Swedish operators have enjoyed special arrangements since the middle of 1968.'[101]

In February the pressure intensified. O'Leary pleaded for the ban to be lifted for 39 Berth, Shea thought a bargain could be struck by removing the ban in return for winning work at Orsett and introducing Phase II for the port by a given deadline, and the DEP summoned the Docks Group to explain their position.

John Kiernan, the new chairman of the London Port Employers, wrote at length to the Docks Group asking for special dispensation for 39 Berth and 46 Berth, where Seaboard Pioneer Terminals were excluded.

'I think everyone is fully aware of the danger to the port as a whole if these agreements cannot come into force at the proper time and both of these cases are now extremely urgent.

'All of us working in the port are at the mercy of these modern innovations and I am sure that the majority of us realise the full implications if we do not try and keep up with them. We fully appreciate all the fears of not just the possibility of the loss of livelihood but also the apparent anomalies created by different systems of payment. . . .

'I do not think that it is fully appreciated all the work which both sides, London employers and London unions, have put in during the past year in order to try and get Phase II off the ground. Had it not been for the work done in this way, against national pressure, there would quite clearly have been a stalemate and even further unrest than is current at the present time.'[102]

The Docks Group was at last told about the future prospects for London trade when Dudley Perkins, the director-general of the PLA, attended a meeting of the committee. He believed fully in the need to consult men, with trust, about their livelihoods and he told them just how bleak the future looked.

He pointed out that the Atlantic trade was mostly containerised already, that now it was the turn of the Australia trade, and that next it would be the Far East and then New Zealand. In East and West Africa, where unit loads and palletisation were being introduced, there would probably be future development into containers and some of the residual trade might be carried by LASH ships – the vessels which carried pre-packed lighters aboard and off-loaded them by gantry at each port of call, giving a phenomenally quick turn-round potential since the carrier ship was not involved in dockwork at all.

A final appeal came from the port newspaper demanding the recall of Lord Devlin – or another mediator of his standing – to lead intensive discussions on Phase II, as Leonard Neal had just done in railway productivity talks at Windsor.

But the ban was not lifted and in the first week of March, OCL's *Encounter Bay* sailed for Australia from Rotterdam, with 900 full containers which had been transhipped from Harwich. The cost of the diversion was about £100,000 per round voyage and OCL–ACT were soon forced to put a 10 per cent surcharge on export containers from Britain.

THE PHILOSOPHY OF MODERNISATION

When the *Encounter Bay* began her maiden voyage, the container ban had pushed London into the vanguard of modernisation talks and the basic aims of unions and employers were clearly delineated. The ocean trade employers had listed their targets early in 1968 as:

1. Manning and method of payment for
   a. Conventional vessels – balancing of piecework tariffs.

   b. Conventional vessels where mechanical appliances are used.

   c. Terminal berth agreements.

2. Shift working and/or a system of a ten-day fortnight.

3. Redundancy.

The need to improve discipline was implicit and this meant both tightening the Scheme, perhaps with the use of an independent chairman on the local dock labour board, and the broadening of Scheme functions to include maintenance of output levels. Many hours were spent trying to persuade the DEP and NAPE that discipline and redundancy – by which they meant voluntary severance – were *sine qua nons* for a new wages structure; and the attempts to impose mass discipline and to isolate and punish unofficial leaders like Dash in 1968 and 1969 must be regarded as wilful attempts to demonstrate the shortcomings of the Scheme. While the need for severance was recognised, the argument for more disciplinary power got a distinctly sceptical response from the Government, which realised the impracticality of changing the Scheme as such but supported the exercise of proper managerial functions.

The London employers' frequent journeys to the Department ended only when it was made clear that unilateral action by London would have national repercussions and the issues of discipline and severance were removed to national level.

The unions responded with simpler but more radical demands for the new wages structure. Instead of the three tiers, they wanted one higher basic rate for the port. On 28 February 1968, Shea asked for:

1. Higher basic rate.

2. Increase in sickness and accident pay and extension of the period for payments.

3. Increase in pensions.

4. Increase in holiday period.

5. Payment for voluntary severance.

In return, the union would agree a free manning clause and a more modern service commensurate with new methods of work.

In September, the NASD submitted essentially similar demands, although more precisely stated and more ambitious than the TGWU's. In both cases the issue of bonus payments on top of the weekly wage was left unclear, but the crucial factor was the TGWU's willingness to trade restrictions on manning and hours. Shea's document was considered thoroughly responsible by the employers and it left them free to choose the service needed to match the efficiency of Continental ports and, once these decisions were made, to negotiate the price.

However, it took the employers a long time to decide what type of service they should provide. Modernisation hinged on turn-round times and there was a substantial, but scattered, amount of research from management consultants, ship-owners and the National Port Council to assist decision-making. All showed that the proportion of operating costs in the shipping industry attributable to cargo-handling had been increasing steadily.

W. MacGillivray, the managing director of Prince Lines, had illustrated this growth in an analysis of his general cargo costs in the pre-war and immediate post-war period. Port and stevedoring charges had averaged 38·5 per cent of operating costs (excluding capital charges) in the fifteen years up to 1939 but rose to 51 per cent in 1946–7, while running costs, including crew wages, victualling, stores and insurance, declined from 31 to 27 per cent and bunkering costs fell from 15 to 7 per cent.

The best anlyses of the 1950s covered US shipping, but showed the same trend, with cargo-handling alone accounting for 37 and 55 per cent of costs for a C2 cargo vessel on long and short voyages in 1958. In 1964, R. O. Goss estimated that cargo-handling represented 25 per cent of costs for operating a 10,000 ton cargo liner with a crew of forty-two, compared with 11 per cent for crew, 9 per cent for port dues, pilotage and custom fees and 5 per cent for fuel. This breakdown included depreciation charges of 24 per cent and, if these are excluded to compare with earlier figures, the cost of each item is raised by roughly a third.

The avid switch to unitisation and containers was the consequence of this growing cost of non-productive port time and the potential savings in cargo-handling were so great from a berth which could achieve a throughput of 500,000 to 1,000,000 tons a year compared with a conventional throughput of 100,000 tons that the requirements of modernisation for the two types of trade were very different.

When a fully-equipped container berth cost in the region of £5,000,000 and needed 50 to 100 men to man it round-the-clock, the cost of the labour content was secondary, so long as full utilisation was achieved. It was desirable but not vital to pare the labour content down to an absolute minimum; in New York gangs of seventeen men are still used while some Rotterdam operations were cut to three and most British operations range between these extremes. The first task of the Phase II negotiators was, therefore, to get the principles of container-manning accepted in a broad sense but at the same time get a much more efficient service on conventional work, which still constituted the bulk of port traffic.

The room for improvement in conventional handling was enormous and in Chapter 12 the shortcomings of the wages structure were discussed. But the problem was not only the wages system; restrictions on mobility and manning and the available hours of work were equally important for achieving quick turn-rounds.

No general statistics exist on the pattern of productivity in the 1960s but figures exist for particular trades. For instance, the Benson report on the New Zealand trades showed that the number of freight tons discharged per day in British ports averaged 423 in 1959 but fell to 313, 359 and 333 in subsequent years up to 1962. Figures of the New Zealand Meat Producers Board show a worse picture after Decasualisation in London – which was nonetheless considered more efficient than Liverpool. The average length of turn-round increased by more than 40 per cent while the tonnage handled rose by one-tenth.

Table 7   New Zealand meat discharge in London

	1967	1968	1969
Number of port-calls	106	106	104
Total tonnage discharged	226,000	250,000	247,000
Total working days	681	883	974
Tons discharged per gang day	90	84·36	77·7
Average no. of working days per vessel	6·42	8·33	9·37
Gang days per vessel	23·66	27·99	30·63

While the causes of delay are not known, it is wrong to assume that the increasingly long turn-rounds were caused by dock labour alone and isolated evidence in other London operations show varying results. One ship-owner in the East African trade reckoned that in the first quarter of 1967 about 14 tons per ship-hour in port were moved and 47 tons per hour worked, giving a rate per gang-hour of roughly 12·75 tons. Three years later, these figures had dropped to 8·6, 32·2 and 7·2 tons respectively. But some PLA shed operations in the same period maintained constant levels of output with little increase in cost and specialist operations like Swedish Lloyd at 26 Berth Tilbury and Olsens at Millwall showed large increases in output with labour costs.

The lesson of the success stories was readily apparent since they related to operations where workflow was guaranteed or labour was easily distributed. The second aim of the negotiators thus was to get an agreement on conventional handling which allowed systematic working – a question of management organisation – and complete flexibility of labour to avoid delays when work was available.

There was no difficulty on the latter issue after the TGWU had agreed to free manning. But the kernel of the problem was to increase the *effective working hours per ship in port*. With one-shift working and no weekend overtime, London could only offer fifty hours work per week and the chosen solution was to increase the available hours by the introduction of shiftwork, linked to the fullest possible utilisation of hours paid.

SHIFTWORK

The argument for shiftwork had a long industrial history. The National Association had tried to buy it in 1945 but it was never established nationally as a matter of right. In 1962 in London, a committee under Stanley Turner re-examined the port's requirements and then concluded that shiftwork was not required on a regular basis.

For ship-owners using London as a terminal port, turn-round was dictated as much by the needs of their market and the repair or victualling of vessels as by the time taken for loading and discharging. But for those using London as one of many ports of call, the speed of cargo-handling was all-important. In the first case, shiftwork was attractive as an emergency measure but in the second it was wanted as a matter of course. Other considerations were the inevitable shortening of shifts to fit the practical hours of regular work between 6 a.m. and 10 p.m. – producing at most a fourteen-hour day after the deduction of meal breaks – and the splitting of the labour force into smaller units per shift.

The Turner committee plumped for a partial nightshift because it would give longer hours of work, when used, and because it could be extended from small beginnings if the demand arose.

But, by the time of Phase II, many factors in the equation were changed. Foremost was the advent of permanency and the constant labour surplus, which could be absorbed by permanent shiftwork. Secondly, all ship-owners wanted faster turn-rounds to increase the earning capacity of new generation cargo vessels; and thirdly, the area of potential disputes could be minimised by eliminating overtime rates and, if overtime was abolished altogether, it was possible to stop the tendency to spin work into the more lucrative earning period.

By opting for a two-shift system without weekday overtime, the enclosed dock employers committed themselves to a course which was theoretically sound but fraught with practical difficulties, the chief of which was to maintain outputs during the shorter hours worked per man. This made it all the more essential to ensure maximum use of each hour paid.

EFFECTIVE USE OF HOURS

Several analyses of the amount of *actual* work performed during the working day were undertaken for the London employers and the results were staggeringly low.

One showed that, during a six-week period in the summer of 1968, an average of 9·2 hours per day were 'attended' by men in the enclosed docks. Of these, 2·2 hours were lost from avoidable causes like bad time-keeping, extended meal-breaks and disputes and a further 0·9 hours were lost unavoidably from weather, lack of facilities or equipment and gear break-down. This left 6·1 hours worked per day and it was estimated that wasteful practices which had survived Phase I reduced effectiveness by nearly a third, so that only 46·5 per cent of the hours attended were fully productive. A more detailed analysis was prepared by Scruttons-Maltby on one ship in 1968. The main purpose of these figures was to show the amount of extra timework hours which men were paid when unproductive, but I quote them in full because they spell out clearly the kind of delays which were endemic to dockwork and how fifty-three gang-hours in a four-day loading operation could be lost.

To make a success of shiftwork, the employers had to switch their 10,000 men in the enclosed docks from working 9·2 hours a day at 46·5 per cent efficiency to roughly 7 hours with virtually all restrictions, avoidable and unavoidable delays, eliminated. The ship-owners

Table 8   Analysis of Scruttons–Maltby delay sheet

Date of operation : April 29 to May 2 (inc.), 1968.
Total tonnage : 1,276 deadweight.

Delays	Time taken		Day work paid	
	Hours	Minutes	Hours	Minutes
Preparing	3	20	5	30
Changing stow	4	35	10	30
Rain	14	50	14	00
Gearing		45	1	00
Await craft	1	20	1	30
Tomming asbestos		35	—	
Shunting vans	1	00	—	
Shunt and berth craft		45	3	00
Dunnage (over drums, for car stowage and over broken scrap iron stow)	9	10	16	30
Await PLA crane	4	15	4	30
Tank lids (raise and lower)	2	05	2	30
Quay congestion	7	35	10	00
Await HMC		35	—	
Mechanical hatch break-down		45	1	00
Sorting forecabin cargo to port		30	—	
Crane break-down		35	—	
Allowance for working over broken scrap iron stow	—		6	00
Allowance for long runs in shed	—		6	00
Total	53	00	82	00

realised that it was asking much of stevedores, who had operated so long on a labour-only basis, to acquire the expertise to do so easily. The delays which emanated from scheduling or lack of equipment could not disappear overnight nor would it be easy to enforce good time-keeping, when men were accustomed under piecework to treat time as their own because they lost earnings by stopping away; it was going to be doubly difficult if their earnings potential was unaffected.

Initially, the ship-owners suggested two shifts of 8 working hours but this was impractical since it demanded an overall span of 9 hours per shift and a daily coverage of 18 hours, which could not be served by personal transport for the men and ancillary services. Thus the employers' original target was to get 14 working hours, but in negotiation this was whittled down to $12\frac{1}{2}$ with $6\frac{1}{4}$ per shift.

It was here that the plank of reason broke. No matter how efficiently labour was organised, ships could not be turned round on conventional trades as quickly when the labour force could work a maximum of 312,500 hours per week, plus weekend overtime, compared with 460,000 under Phase I. Added to the imponderable effects on output of removing much or all of the wage incentive, the prospect of achieving the 30 per cent increase in productivity which AIC management consultants demanded to make Phase II self-financing, was remote from the start and much depended on the degree to which individual employers could gear themselves for change.

EMPLOYERS' STRUCTURAL REFORM

Progress towards modernisation in London quickly exposed the flaws of the employing structure at port and company level. The unique role of the ship-owners in negotiation, the multiplicity of employers and the historical division of employing interests between ship and quay labour all served to weaken the authority of the London Port Employers' Association (LPEA) as a bargaining agency. It had no ultimate power over its constituent bodies and, in turn, they had little authority over their member companies.

To negotiate a sound agreement, the employers required an organisation which vested authority in the users of the port as well as the employing companies, was well-financed and staffed and capable of assessing a variety of options and enforcing its choice down the line.

This was a far cry from the LPEA as it existed. It had no written constitution and its total staff was a hard-pressed manager, two assistants and two typists. Its minute budget precluded any activities beyond the collation of the simplest statistics and lateral communication between the constituent associations, the ocean trade employers, wharfingers, PLA, lighterage and ship-owners.

Julian Badcock, a barrister by training, not only had to manage the Association but devote a considerable portion of his time both as secretary of the lighterage association – which owned the LPEA's cramped premises in the City – and as secretary of the tug-owners. The burden of policy formulation and negotiation fell of necessity on the senior personnel of the Association's executive council, all holding down jobs with their companies and not always experienced in industrial relations. The executive was powerless to enforce common policy for the port and constant divergence of sectional interests was the main reason for setting up the separate committee structure, as an offshoot of the National Modernisation Committee, for both phases of the Devlin programme. The London 'mod' was responsible to the national parent and, when it was divided into sectional sub-committees, these also were accountable. This at least established a chain of authority and Kiernan, who inherited the chairmanship of the LPEA from David Lloyd in 1968, wanted a similar command extended to the normal institutional structure.

Kiernan, a marine lawyer with Furness Withy, was backed to the hilt by ship-owners. Their joint plan was to strengthen the LPEA by appointing a full-time director with support staff, responsible for long-term planning of labour relations, collation of information – especially on productivity – and education in management techniques. Above all, the director would take charge of negotiations instead of the amateurs who were burdened with an increasing amount of bargaining and liaison work during Phase II.

Under a new constitution, the governing body was to be a council representing port-users, ship-owners and port employers, from which a smaller executive could be drawn. But the most radical proposal was to make council decisions enforceable, with the possibility that any irregularities could lead to the revoking of the offender's employing licence. In Kiernan's words: 'Despite inadequacies on the part of the unions, their officers are fulltime paid officials and have some training in industrial negotiation. None of the permanent staff of the LPEA, or its member associations, are capable of carrying out the kind of negotiations necessary. This aspect is left entirely to the chairman and executive committee, all of whom are untrained, and in any event, have their own jobs to perform within their own companies.'[103]

For two years, the Kiernan plan hung in the balance but it was ultimately defeated by the smaller associations who refused to give up their autonomy. Conceivably the ship-owners and enclosed dock employers could have forced it through on their own, bearing the entire cost, but they chose an easier path by building up the organisation for the ocean trades alone, at the expense of the London association as a whole.

The London Ocean Trades Employers' Association (LOTEA) was set up by the ship-owners to represent the private employers, many of whom were ship-owner controlled, in the enclosed docks. Its prime function was to negotiate, but it was obliged to consult the London Ship-Owners Dock Labour Committee on matters of policy.

Its creation marked the withdrawal of ship-owners from the front line of negotiation in London for the first time since 1912 and the timing was curious, since it was chiefly ship-owner interests at stake during modernisation. But it was logical to change the line of command from the British Shipping Federation to the port-employers' structure and it was designed to set the stevedores on their own feet as they approached full permanency.

But LOTEA had important flaws, chief of which was the exclusion of the PLA. By retaining the right to independent negotiation, the PLA kept 5,000 of the 13,000 men in the ocean trades separately represented and throughout the Devlin programme the employers suffered the identical problem of sectionalism as the TGWU.

For a while, it appeared as if all other major employers would join LOTEA but, after a tentative application, Olsens also opted for independence – a vital factor in persuading the dockers that modernisation would create first- and second-class citizens unless the demand for a single package deal was backed by sanctions. (It is of interest that two of the most progressive wharfingers, Samuel Williams and Victoria Deep Water Terminal, also refused to join the Association, in order to secure their own terms and conditions of employment.)

Another difficulty was liaison between LOTEA and the ship-owners. Delay was inevitable in reporting back from the negotiating table but it was worsened by the shipping companies' reluctance to spare top personnel for the Dock Labour Committee. The strain of negotiating Phase I undoubtedly had blunted the ship-owners' enthusiasm for labour relations and Kiernan noted caustically that there was 'a certain lack of continuity of attendance at meetings of the LSDLC.' Later, however, some improvement was effected when ship-owners set up a senior panel, which included the chairmen of P and O, Furness Withy and R. A. Vestey, to intervene when crises were reached.

Finally, LOTEA suffered like the LPEA from under-staffing and lack of finance. While piecework remained, much of its energy was devoted to monitoring payments and area awards, and even some of these statistics could not be processed during the hectic years after Decasualisation. After Phase II, however, LOTEA could offer advisory service on management techniques and work study.

In seeking a better bargaining structure, the employers' achievement fell far short of their best intentions. The same was true at company level where many undertakings had to evolve a new structure suited to modernisation and decide on the best way of dividing or unifying their employing functions.

Phase I had not given employers the exact labour force they wanted. Two-thirds of the men were allocated to the company of their choice and these allocations were usually in the mutual interest of the employer too. But some companies, notably wharfingers like Hay's Wharf, had got far more men than they wanted and in view of the obligation to accept them, stability was to be achieved by adjusting function to the labour supply.

Unfortunately the threat of nationalisation drove the employers to emotional, not objective reactions. Early in 1969, the Government followed up the recommendations of the Labour Party study group by issuing a white paper on nationalisation, based on a single employer per port, arguing that the existing structure remained 'exceedingly complex, leading to divided responsibilities, the fragmentation of operational control and unreliability of service.'[104]

While ports handling less than 5,000,000 tons were not to be taken over and operations which were vertically-integrated parts of other industrial activities could be exempted, most common-user services like stevedoring, wharf-operating, lighterage and towage were covered. Consequently private employers struggled primarily for survival and, whatever their personal views, would not contemplate reforms which bolstered the case of the nationalisers.

Some employers publicly stated the need for national co-ordination of port investment but not for the single employer concept, whatever its merits. They said competition was still the guarantee of good service and that the ship-owner, who was responsible for cargo-handling on vessels, had the right to choose who was best qualified to do the work. While quay transit followed regular patterns, stevedoring requirements varied from ship to ship.

Ship-owners, however, were more forthright – especially about

London. They saw little virtue in the provision of quay labour by the PLA and ship labour by contractors and even less in the shed and quay agreement, whereby the PLA gave up its right to discharge, where sorting requirements made the land facility an extension of the hold, in return for a fixed payment per ton to a stevedore and proceeded to recoup the cost handsomely in the charge on delivery from shed.

They wanted a single employer to control a berth, if not a sector of the port. This, they said, could either be achieved by the PLA giving up its labour and the ship-owner renting or leasing a berth with full working rights, or by the PLA contracting to perform all labour.

With Kiernan as chairman of the LPEA, they had a staunch ally but he outwardly had to support the employers' interest. In a public statement in July 1969 he placed responsibility for reform only on ship-owners.

'Ship-owners should increasingly accept the responsibility for the speed and degree of mechanisation which can be introduced. The rental, wherever possible, of terminal berths with composite ship and quay operations . . . is an obvious improvement and a necessary part of any integrate system of transport.' [105]

In private, he went further by saying this process could be begun by port employers too. He wanted the ship-owners, PLA and contractors jointly to decide how the traditional horizontal system of handling goods by a variety of undertakings during transit could be integrated. Terminal berths like Olsens should be set up, with manageable labour units and payments reflecting the operation, not the price of port operations as a whole. This theory could be extended to common-user berths, under one contractor, and would immediately improve the cash-flow to the port authority as well as committing stevedores financially to the premises they worked.

'The division of control within the enclosed docks . . . whereby men from different employers work side by side engaged in what is one operation does not in modern conditions lend itself to efficiency. Anomalies must arise which lead to industrial trouble. Moreover it is not in keeping with the modern trend towards through-transportation.' [106]

Such changes ran counter to the vested interest of undertakings to preserve their traditional toeholds and offended the historical but diminishing differences between dockers on ship and quay. Ocean trade employees did not regard themselves as interchangeable with

PLA men and certainly did not want to lose the higher earnings potential of shipwork by going on the quays, while PLA men were only too happy to extend their jurisdiction.

But the real obstacle was the refusal of port employers to invest in port facilities – which hitherto they paid nothing for – when it looked as if they were soon to be nationalised. They wanted the PLA to continue to bear the cost of quay installations rather than become a mere landlord like most continental port authorities.

Nonetheless, the terminal berth system has spread slowly in London, particularly in unitised trades. Olsens, Swedish Lloyd and OCL-ACT are examples of companies leasing their own premises and providing all the labour themselves of through contractors. At common-user container and package timber berths in Tilbury, the PLA has provided all the labour and, in the Royals, Southern Stevedores took out a long lease on quay space, although the split between their own and PLA labour persists.

Such progress is modest and undoubtedly the uncertainty over the future of the industry between 1967 and 1970 retarded further rationalisation. The same uncertainty also accounts for the lamentable failing of port employers to adapt their internal organisation for Phase II.

This was the area where the practices of casual management died hardest. Management based on selecting labour at will and reliance on the payment system for outputs had a child-like simplicity which was reflected in the attitudes and abilities of first-line supervision.

Under casualism, the role of the foreman was primarily to distribute not *govern* work and the post was filled from the ranks of dockers, usually permanent men. They knew the hiring procedure and saw the selection and allocation of gangs and their chief responsibility. Under Phase I, however, permanency reduced this function and it took the extra responsibilities of Phase II to restore a higher level of job satisfaction.

Supervisors were recruited largely from outside the industry and most commonly from the merchant navy – a good qualification for exercising discipline but not for management expertise. The weakness of this structure was the lack of role definition especially at the lowest level, where it was difficult to define where purely managerial functions began. Few companies could spare foremen to supervise each hatch and organisation of work often fell on the gang-leader who was both the leader of the men and management's representative. It was a division of function which the setting-up of shop stewards helped to overcome but it would not disappear until proper role definitions were made for the management team as a whole.

The most complete attempt to study job activities and evaluate a supervisory training programme was undertaken by Olsens and the results have been adopted by the National Ports Council as an exemplary case study.

Olsens made the switch to free-manning and high basic wage in 1967 and soon discovered that resistance to the *implications* of these changes was as marked at supervisory level as among the men. But it was able to identify the source of problems largely in terms of communications and the inexact concepts of function at each level of the organisation. This was put right by exhaustive meetings, sometimes with the labour force as a whole, and slowly the makings of a team, in which problems were channelled easily upwards and downwards, emerged. In the first fifteen months, there were more than sixty conflict situations – two-thirds involving breaches of discipline and one-third poor outputs – but all were resolved without stoppages. And the effort was further rewarded by increasing outputs.

Here was an example of the kind of management techniques which Phase II would demand in the enclosed docks. Irrespective of the final shape of the wages deal, productivity levels would depend on a company's ability to teach all levels of personnel how to deal with problems and maintain work flow.

Once the proper managerial framework was established, the next need was the most effective use of resources through method study and work measurement. The PLA had some experience of these techniques but it is a sorry fact that little was done in the three years preparing for Phase II to begin these essential tasks. The agreement itself gave the right to begin work study generally, but measurement is a long process and it should have started as negotiations opened.

The port which tackled Phase II in the most professional manner was Middlesbrough, where the Tees and Hartlepool Port Authority, the sole employer of labour, began *within a month* of Decasualisation to examine the abolition of piecework. While inter-port rivalry prevented the ready dissemination of the findings, they were well-known to the National Ports Council which in turn could advise other ports.

At Middlesbrough, it was soon apparent that the confusion of piece rates precluded any move towards modernisation except through total revision of payments and the Authority appointed AIC early in 1968 to draw up a new bonus system based on work study.

At a mass meeting addressed by Geoffrey Robinson, the port's senior executive, the consultants and the district secretary of the TGWU, the men agreed to set up a productivity committee, on which the rank-and-file was represented, and the next six months were devoted largely to building up confidence in the aims of the new deal. Only in the latter half of 1968 were talks begun on such items as rostering for work, preparation of ships, use of hatch-tents during rain, transport arrangements for the men, absenteeism, hours of work, safety, manning levels, mechanisation and differences in earnings which were not related to the criteria of effort and skill.

In February 1969, trials were started and the whole port was brought on to new conditions in January 1970. The agreement provided for savings to be shared between the men and the Authority on a 60 to 40 basis, with work norms set by productivity officers to reflect the nature of the commodity handled, the type of ship, the manning level and capacity of gear. Guaranteed earnings were £30 a week, with target performance paid at 17s 9d an hour and standard at 22s 2d. Two shifts of seven working hours were used, with the obligation to finish a ship on any weekday night up to 11.45 p.m.

It was not all roses, but extensive training had narrowed the areas of conflict and greater mechanisation, good outputs and the reduction in gang sizes from, on average, 15·6 to 11 men could be set against the 31 per cent increase in earnings, from £31 5s 5d to £40 16s 9d a week.

Middlesbrough provided a breakthrough in the industry by getting work study accepted, but the lesson was that it could not be done overnight and the success of Phase II lay in the close consultation with the men over two years while the wage negotiations continued.

This level of preparation was hardly attempted by many London employers who preferred to see what deal emerged before adjusting their operations and, even in Southampton, where the Phase II agreement bought out all bonuses and made a successful start, no norms of output level were set; the employers relied on the tacit co-operation of shop stewards to maintain productivity and the subsequent declines in output were predictable.

There were two areas of re-organisation where the London employers were more successful. First was the provision of decent amenities for the men. In many ports, facilities like washrooms, toilets and canteens simply were not built because employers had no permanent labour force to look after. But, the position was deplorable in London because the employers, PLA and dock labour board could not decide who should pay. The Devlin committee were 'appalled' at what they saw and found the employers' squabbling pitiable; to the men, lack of amenities was living proof of the employers' iniquities and Dash could always make capital by describing the stinking urinals as 'unfit for Prince Philip's polo ponies.'

The PLA at last undertook to finance new amenity blocks on behalf of contractors; the first stage cost some £500,000 and catered for 4,000 men and, with additions, the employers are now committed to repayments to the Authority of £60,000 annually for twenty years.

Improved communications was another necessity for Phase II, to explain the issues of modernisation and port bargaining. Company journals were inadequate for the task; few were more than occasional broadsheets, tending to be parochial and evasive. The unions also had no permanent channel. The TGWU was asked periodically to provide a publication for dockers alone but invariably refused because of the expense and the reluctance to give special privileges to one trade group, already better serviced than the others, in terms of the ratio of full-time officers to the number of union members.

The National Modernisation Committee was aware of the problem but its bulletins were rare and could not bridge the gap between national policy and its impact on the shopfloor. The PLA, however, came to London's rescue by financing a newspaper for London dockers.

The Port was started in April 1967 and has been a resounding success in bringing alive the details of negotiation and comparing London's problems with other ports. It is essentially a journal of industrial relations and has achieved high readership in the docks' community. Predictably, employers claim that it sometimes is too much a platform for the militants and militants see it as the tool of employers. But it is managed by a board of trustees which includes representatives from both sides of the industry and independents, and the very fact of such criticism is proof of its independence.

ON TO PHASE II

When London employers opened the main round of Phase II negotiations in 1968, dragging NAPE and the DEP behind them, their aim was
to shake off the container ban and to get a severance scheme off the
ground.

The first five meetings of the London Modernisation Committee
dealt with severance only and when the London seal was approved on
26 June the employers moved on to frame a letter of intent.

The first wage offer was hurriedly prepared and was essentially a
holding position, with a basic rate of £21 10s a week and an envisaged
tonnage bonus of 50 per cent.

The terms had been formulated – at NAPE's bidding – as specific
additions to the national time rate of £11 1s 8d a week; roughly £8 a
week was to replace all special payments and obtain flexibility, and
£2 was the modernisation payment, while the bonus replaced piecework.

The offer envisaged some form of shiftwork to be determined sectionally, and stiffer discipline if only to ensure an effective rate of work. By
adding a shiftwork payment of £2 10s a week into basic rates, the offer
was easily adjusted to give a minimum of £24 a week and a 33 per cent
bonus and John Hovey, in charge of the LOTEA negotiations, made
this improved offer early in 1969.

Meanwhile, consultants made costings on behalf of the LPEA for
fringe benefits (which were largely under national aegis) and alternative pay structures. It is noteworthy that AIC's objections to this first
offer corresponded in great measure to the TGWU's. AIC accepted that
piecework had to be abandoned but felt that any bonus system similar
to piecework was likely to perpetuate the attitudes and wasteful
practices of the existing wage structure. They also felt that the employers could not rely on maintaining output by forcing union co-
operation through the Scheme since this merely encouraged slipshod
management.

AIC's main concern, however, was to open employers' eyes to the
magnitude of reform needed at company level. Again and again, their
reports stressed that insufficient attention was being given to the
meaning of a new wages structure, to collecting control data and to
formulating precise objectives.

'A wage structure or a productivity agreement is not a substitute for effective management and supervision. They are merely devices or procedures to assist management to secure the performance and behaviour from employees which it desires.

'There would appear to be a need to substantially improve the effectiveness of management and supervision, especially first-line supervision, to ensure a reasonable degree of success from any new wage structure and productivity agreement.

'First-line supervision is the only level of management which can ensure compliance with agreed new working practices.

'Experience in many industries has shown that a considerable and sustained effort is necessary, to improve the effectiveness of supervision and bring them into a closely-knit management team with supportive relationships.'

In its final report, AIC set out as necessary objectives much the same kind of programme as Middlesbrough used. Each company had to establish specific targets of performance and develop managerial practices to achieve them, with the proviso that the men should know that they would win an equitable distribution of the overall benefits achieved. While the Letter of Intent was studied, Hovey was left to find a formula which recognised the managerial shortcomings of the employers. While AIC had suggested a target of a 40 per cent cut in turn-round time, Hovey knew that his work by itself could never achieve it. At most, he could produce a framework within which companies could seek their own salvation and he had to produce a deal which placed the least possible strain on management resources.

This realisation drove him towards the upstanding weekly wage and flexible manning, with common hours of work throughout the enclosed docks. He saw company bonuses on any substantial scale as a source of friction and coercive leap-frogging, while the high basic rate accorded well with the men's desire for equal reward for the willingness to give equal effort.

In February 1969, the unions agreed that 'one deal for the port' could be superseded by sectional deals so long as minimum standards, unstated but tacitly understood to mean a basic wage of at least £25 a week for all dockers, was achieved. The Letter of Intent was then abandoned.

Sectional negotiation immediately brought the hitherto private dealings of the PLA into the open and Turner was thinking in terms of a £29 minimum for his labour, topped with a small bonus and shiftwork. The TGWU then formulated more specific aims of a £35 minimum for a 30-hour working week, plus a small bonus, and negotiations progressed into summer with Hovey offering a range of all-in payments of £24 a week for timeworkers, £31 10s for quay workers and £34 for shipworkers, all on equal shifts of 32½ working hours, while Turner followed suit with £24 for timeworkers and £29 and bonus for the rest of his staff.

In terms of overall earnings, neither the PLA nor Hovey were being particularly generous, since wages in the port had risen to roughly £32 a week. But the package gave enormous increases in hourly earnings; dockers currently had to work 47 hours to build up their pay packet and the new level accrued from 32½ hours.

The natural tactic of the unions, to get the bidding pushed higher, was to present shiftwork as an odious intrusion on the men's leisure and the NASD at this point pulled out of the talks, rather than discuss shiftwork at all. (During this period, a copy of the well-known picture 'When did you last see your father?' was posted on the wall of a canteen in the Royal docks and the boy was shown answering 'Please sir, not since my dad started shiftwork for Scruffy-Maltbys.') In retrospect, the objection to shiftwork was an artificial issue but vital as a bargaining counter. The working day was only being extended by an hour at the start and two and a half hours at the end and, in reality, it enormously increased leisure time available to the men.

But shiftwork became one of the issues which produced the crisis of June 1969 when the Olsen agreement came up for re-negotiation. To buy two shifts of six working hours, Olsens agreed on 14 June to pay rates of £26, £34 and £39 a week – more than Shea was even asking for in the enclosed docks' negotiations. Olsen in fact was on a safe wicket; he was anticipating a 50 per cent increase in traffic and by buying out all bonus pay, overtime and Saturday work, he persuaded the DEP that earnings would not rise above the 3½ per cent pay norm. But Hovey was completely undermined and he refused to countenance any further negotiation until the container ban was lifted.

It was a tactical decision based on intuitive understanding of the Docks Group, which had just returned from a tour of Antwerp and Rotterdam organised by the PLA. Of Shea's original five points, three had been won. Better pensions and three weeks holiday had been conceded nationally and London had agreed a severance scheme. In every sector of the port, there were minor productivity deals awaiting ratification – not least the new Olsen terms and those for Victoria Deep Water Terminal, a wharf at Greenwich which had been re-equipped to handle short-sea container traffic.

The doves felt enough have been done to lift the ban, especially if the employers would set a target of three months to introduce Phase II and conceded Orsett to registered dockers. More important, the PLA was known to be negotiating with six shipping lines willing to use Tilbury if their containers would be worked and the most important by far was OCL–ACT's Far Eastern trade, due to be fully containerised in 1972. The PLA had quoted for this work but the chances of getting it were slim while the ban remained. (In fact this trade was based on Southampton, a decision taken as much for the commercial desirability of spreading investment as London's particular labour problem.)

While these decisions hung in the balance, the hawks' case for keeping the ban to *safeguard* trade appeared ill-founded and even more so when the largest riverside employer, Hay's Wharf, began to shut down all its wharfing operations in the Pool of London.

Finally, there was the danger that the Committee would lose control of negotiations to the shop stewards if a settlement was not quickly reached. The rank-and-file were demanding guarantees of £6 a day (£8 with overtime) in Tilbury and the Royals and, for some operations, individual employers had given in. If unofficial pressure could secure £30 for a 40-hour week under the existing wages structure, the unions would have to pull something quickly out of the bag to warrant a Phase II Deal.

The month of July was tense. The DEP called in the Docks Group, senior employers and ship-owners to re-state the problems and the conciliation officers discovered that the union delegates were now more concerned about extending the definition of dockwork than achieving the single package deal. This provided an important loophole, since the DEP was already talking with the NDLB on a more satisfactory way of referring issues to tribunals; now Sir Andrew offered work at Orsett to dockers as soon as the ban was lifted and the union agreed to reconsider the ban, not when the whole port was covered, but as soon as agreement was reached with the TGWU only for the enclosed docks and riverside.

Hovey said that the employers would offer a wages structure with bonus or without – whatever the union wanted – on the understanding that 'There was joint acceptance of the need to maintain satisfactory levels of output and for joint sanctions to deal with the small proportion of men who might not be prepared to accept their responsibilities in this respect, should an upstanding weekly wage be chosen.'[107]

By the end of the month, the ship-owners told Hovey to climb-down. On August 6, he wrote to the TGWU: 'The employers still consider this ban should have been lifted before any further negotiations took place, but they feel that in the interests of the national economy and the future of the port of London, they are prepared to resume negotiations on Phase II. It must be clearly understood, however, that any agreement will not be implemented until the ban is lifted enabling all new agreements to be worked effectively.'

In September and October, negotiations resumed and the price of Phase II rapidly escalated. The ship-owners were wavering between the two types of wage structure but Hovey and the DEP now wanted the simplest possible terms. The TGWU then raised its demands to £37 10s for a 30-hour week with shift-working, and £28 for men only fit for light duties; the PLA and LOTEA at last combined their proposals and offered a basic rate of £33 10s to all fit men, with a £2 10s supplement to shipworkers and £25 to unfit men, for a working week of five 6¼-hour shifts, i.e. 31¼ effective hours. Two important points had been agreed – that the old distinction between time workers and piece workers should be abolished and the only grading of basic rates should be between men capable of *all* dockwork and those who could only manage lighter tasks; and that weekend work at double time should be introduced on a rota basis to any men who fancied a maximum of twelve hours work at roughly 50s an hour.

In November, the TGWU put this offer to ballot among PLA and LOTEA members, without any recommendation to accept or reject. Out of some 10,500 employed, the union thought it had 8,500 in membership but only 7,100 proved to be fully paid up and eligible to vote. Of these, more than 5,500 returned their ballot envelopes to regional headquarters and, in spite of support from PLA members and Tilbury, the result was a rejection by 3,090 to 2,442.

The decision to ballot was unprecedented in the London docks. One of the lessons of Phase I was the need to ensure rank-and-file approval and Dash had harangued the negotiators in 1967 for not using the 'democratic' channels of the mass meeting to vote on

Decasualisation. So long as the unofficial committees controlled the dock-gate, it was unthinkable for negotiators to use this medium and, in 1969, they still felt that a mass meeting would produce an emotional response instead of allowing men to express their feelings without fear or favour.

Although the use of the ballot was to cause problems within the Docks Group with Tilbury again pressing for sectional agreement, the exercise was completely effective in persuading the employers that a new deal had to be made. What it did not show, however, was the reason for rejection and many employers felt it was because the high-earners wanted to retain a bonus element.

Consequently a group of senior managers from Scruttons-Maltby and officials from the DEP set to work on a bonus structure which was presented to the TGWU early in 1970. Seeing how quickly it was prepared, it was a remarkably thorough document and reflected the principles of the Middlesbrough agreement. The basic wage for all fit men was to be £29 0s 10d a week (£25 for light-duty men) contingent on a target output of half-standard performance being achieved. For standard performance a bonus of £7 11s 3d was to be paid, giving an earnings figure of £36 12s 1d.

Hovey, however, did not want to be associated in any way with the offer. His view was that the schedules of target and standard output, with fixed manning scales, would all have to be thrashed out on the shopfloor and that different practices could easily arise between companies. Similar terms took two years for one employer to introduce at Middlesbrough and the local negotiation might take just as long in London. Fortunately for him – since he was prepared to resign over this issue – the TGWU never expressed much interest and, within a month, Hovey had revised the autumn offer, with £1 a week increases all round, and this was put to a second ballot of the TGWU. This time, 6,442 papers were issued and 5,954 returned and the offer was accepted by 4,137 to 1,800. The way was clear for removing the ban.

It was high time for the Docks Group to get off the hook, since it barely maintained a united front throughout the winter. The Tilbury delegates, who had loyally supported the ban in public, had been called to account by their divisional committee in November, after the first ballot, and a mass meeting was arranged to take a vote – the first since 1968 – on the container ban. The understanding was that, should the ban be overthrown, Battie and George Hughes would have to resign from the Docks Group. However, union policy was upheld by a very narrow majority and all was well until the new year, when the Docks Group refused to re-elect Battie to the London Modernisation Committee.

He and Hughes promptly stalked out of the meeting, claiming it was a deliberate slight which had been pre-arranged and that it was a vote of no confidence in Battie by the rest of the committee. Thus, in April, there was little question of the ban being kept. Even before the riverside deal was accepted the Docks Group agreed by six votes to five[108] to lift it at the end of the month on condition that Orsett work was given to dockers, that Phase II was introduced on 1 June and, of course, that the riverside vote was favourable. It was. By 2,299 to 647, the men accepted a deal which gave a weekly wage of £27 10s for 40 hours, company bonuses and optional shiftwork.

In the first week of May, the 36,850 ton *Thorbjorg* slipped into 46 berth to discharge package timber from British Columbia, the first vessel to bring new trade to the container extension at Tilbury since the ban was imposed 28 months before. Two weeks later it was the turn of OCL–ACT. Its equipment had been taken out of mothballs and the 54 men, whose terms were £42 10s for a 34⅔-hour working week, with two or three shifts working, began training. The first ship to arrive was the 27,000 ton *Jervis Bay*, fresh from her trials after being delivered one year late by UCS, and work at 39 Berth began. Battie presented Nicholson with one of his white caps as a token of reconciliation.

So the ban was lifted, but London was still a long way from implementing the Phase II deal and the TGWU, without the sanction which had maintained its authority, immediately was plunged into the feuds which characterised the first part of the Devlin programme.

One trouble was that agreement had still to be reached with the Blues, the tally clerks, foremen, lighterage and all the ancillary services which had to be re-patterned around two-shift working. The Dock Group's reaction was to try to storm its way to modernisation, insisting that the June date be kept regardless of the NASD. It was a piece of crude blustering and the shop stewards openly defied the Committee by refusing to enter Phase II without the Blues.

When the NASD sat down again with the employers – with the boycott on shiftwork still in existence, theoretically – they were more interested in the free manning clause than money. Les Newman, the general secretary, believed that manning scales should be written into the deal, instead of leaving their determination to individual employers. Had there been no change during the summer months, the impasse could have reached frightening proportions. A NASD mass meeting might have forced the Union to come into line with the TGWU; but it would have been unlikely. The TGWU could have tried to go-it-alone, using the threat of revoking the common register (thus restricting Blues from many jobs) if the Blues objected; but they would have needed the support of employers to achieve it. In all likelihood, had the TGWU tried to enforce its will, its membership would have rebelled and London would have been thrown into a mighty dispute.

The face-saver for the NASD was the national dock strike, which erupted in mid-July and resulted in a complicated settlement, giving London employers the excuse to add £2 a week to all rates. At a mass meeting in West Ham stadium, Newman claimed that it was Blue pressure which had won half this sum; even so, it was not clear until the last moment if Phase II would be accepted. Finally, in a manner befitting Victorian melodrama, Newman was left with two resolutions – one for and one against the deal – and had to decide which to present first. The motion opposing Phase II was chosen for the first vote and it was defeated by 515 to 746, betokening acceptance of the deal. Dockers have a habit of defeating resolutions at mass meetings and, had the other gone first, the result could well have been different.

Four weeks later, Phase II was implemented. Enough of the ancillary negotiation had been completed and on a clear September morning, Walter Lewis, the new chairman of the LPEA, walked aboard the S.S. *Orita* in the Royal docks to watch the start to modernisation.

What he saw was hardly auspicious. Many gangs, meant to report to the ship's side at 7 a.m. had gone, in confusion, to muster points; no lighters appeared; there were few lorries; the first crane did not swing until 8.30, foremen at Scruttons-Maltby debated whether to work at all because they felt their differentials were so eroded by the pay deal; and, worst of all, PLA quay gangs heralded modernisation by leaving their mechanical equipment in the sheds and pushing out hand-trucks, in protest at their failure to secure wage increments like the shipworkers and other specialists.

But these were teething troubles. By mid-morning, Lewis was

cracking jokes with men working at a good stroke. 'Once we've got this lot sorted out, you won't see us for dust,' he was told.

Compared with Phase I, the troubles of the second D-Day were minor. But, as Lewis and Hovey well knew, Phase II was very much an act of faith by which the skeleton for modernisation had been provided but individual employers had to make it work effectively. Whether the men would continue to work with goodwill, while so much else in the port was in disarray; was another of the 'imponderables' which had so often bedevilled their calculations.

CHAPTER FOURTEEN

The National Dock Strike

'We need this strike and Jack Jones is doing a good job – none of this cap-in-hand and "how's your uncle" stuff.' Brian Nicholson, London docker.

A final upwards twist on the price of modernisation came in July 1970, with the national dock strike – the first since 1926 – which shut down the ports for nearly three weeks. The strike was a remarkable feat of opportunism by union militants because there was little logic in pursuing a national wage increase simultaneously with local Phase II deals at port level. However, the door had been left open by the employers and the union leadership could not stop their men marching through.

In October 1968, when NAPE was still trying to retain national negotiating power, the claim for a substantial increase in the national time rate was lodged at the NJC. Had the employers anticipated then the extent to which Phase II would decentralise negotiations, they could have insisted that national talks applied only to ports not covered by actual or impending modernisation agreements.

But NAPE could not maintain its case for keeping control if it refused to consider a national claim. Employers therefore hoped to put off answering the union claim until it was made irrelevant by the progress of local deals; they played for time and, in 1969, conceded no wage increase as such, although giving a third week's holiday, improved pensions and converting the guarantee from weekly to daily application. Meanwhile, the unions priced their claim first as an improvement in time rate from £11 1s 8d a week to £16, then to £20.

Once the claim was recognised, and by failing to shut the gate in 1968 it was automatically validated, it was inevitable that a showdown would come: union leaders do not thrive on constant rebuff. In 1970, the employers still hoped to be saved by the advent of local agreements, but Tonge was cruelly disappointed by the protraction of London talks (where employers had once envisaged settlement within *three to six months* of opening negotiations) and by the reluctance of regional ports to settle in advance of London. By summer, he knew some national wage offer would have to be made.

When the crisis was reached in July, only Middlesbrough, Grangemouth and the London riverside of the major ports had implemented Phase II. Most other ports were close to settlement and the militants suddenly realised that the national claim was a perfect weapon for levering up the final price of Phase II.

The nature of the claim was surprisingly complicated. While it looked like a straightforward demand for an 80 per cent increase in time rate, the unions were not asking for any increase in piece rates and, theoretically, it would only affect those parts of earnings which derived from timework – the few hourly-paid jobs, stand-by payments to pieceworkers and overtime premiums.

As Tonge realised, however, it would be difficult for employers to concede a timework increase and resist subsequent pressure on piece rates since a move in one was followed customarily by revision to the other. Moreover, the danger of spin-off to men other than the 46,000 registered dockworkers was enormous. For instance, the raising of the guarantee in 1967 was quickly reflected in demands from busmen, lorry drivers and even dustmen; but within the industry there were some 50,000 ancillary workers whose wages inevitably were linked to the dockers' and the repercussive effect on such grades as office staff was unlikely to be confined to the ports.

NAPE's greatest fear, however, was that an increase now would price Phase II out of the market. Tonge reckoned the claim, if granted, would eventually add 50 per cent to earnings and there then would be no incentive to change the port wages structures. He said: 'An increase in the national time rate at this stage would not only fail to face up to the basic issue of reforming the wages structure but would seriously imperil such reform.' and 'The paramount consideration facing the ports at this time is the programme of modernisation of the wages structure and working practices. It must not be jeopardised.'[109]

O'Leary and Jones recognised the force of these arguments but, during the month's strike notice, they were victims of their own failure to spell out the exact nature of the claim to their membership.

Four days before the strike was due to start on 14 July, Robert Carr, the Conservative's new minister for Employment, opened conciliation talks at his Department and, only then, did the unions quantify the claim into pounds, shillings and pence. These talks lasted until the the eve of the strike ultimatum, with the new government exhibiting an unusual willingness to face the stoppage, if need be. The employers and unions went to and fro from the Department. The TUC and CBI were consulted – but Carr coolly refused to give up a trip to Glyndebourne in the middle of the marathon talks.

Jones, acting like Cousins nine years before as *de facto* joint chairman of the NJC, worked out that the full claim only amounted to £2 5s a week, about 7 per cent, half deriving from the increased overtime premium and the rest from dribs and drabs on time-work calculators. On the eve of the strike, the employers at last made a reply to these terms. Hitherto, they had offered to concede a £20 guarantee and to make special arrangements for the 15 per cent of the labour force who were genuine low-earners and probably would not be covered by Phase II agreements; now they added an offer of an extra £1 a week on the modernisation payment – which could have no repercussive effects on the wage structure in ports which had not already merged this payment into the basic rate. The package was costed at 4·4 per cent on the wages bill.

Jones undertook to put the offer to a delegate conference in two days' time and appealed on television for the strike to be delayed, pending the delegates decision. He was in a very tricky position since his appeal, albeit quite constitutional, had the appearance of overriding the delegates earlier decision, and the strike was already turning out to be a test of rank-and-file strength against union leadership.

Shopfloor support for the strike was based partly on the retention of a wages structure which had manifold opportunities for exploiting its weaknesses. Elsewhere it was seen as a means of asserting the unity of dockers at a time when inter-port differences in wages and types of work made it unlikely that common ground would be found again. But the most commonly-stated aim of the militants was to harass Jones and O'Leary, particularly over the union's failure to get better definitions of dockwork.

O'Leary made no secret of his right-wing position. He told the Pearson Inquiry that his men complained of him not being militant enough. 'I confess that I must have slipped up to be in the situation I am in now. I am more to the Right of any other dock leader since

1926, yet it falls to me to lead a national strike.' But the attack on Jones was more surprising. The responsibilities of leadership seemed to have alienated him from the militant rank-and-file and, among the delegations which lobbied TGWU headquarters during the strike, a sprinkling of banners stated 'You're not alright, Jack.'

Jones' and O'Leary's first task was to brief the TGWU national committee – the 22-man lay committee which gave guidance to the larger delegate conference. Jones posed all the important issues. Were the men fighting for a national increase on a rate which had almost ceased to exist meaningfully, or were they fighting for the 7,000 dockers from small ports who would probably be excluded from Phase II? Was it worth a massive confrontation with employers when Phase II deals were on the way and was it right to create a high wage industry, only if it meant a more rapid run-down of the labour force?

He had one trump card to play – an indication that Carr would look favourably on a thorough examination of the effects of containerisation and redefinition of dockwork, if this package was accepted – and this persuaded the committee to make no recommendation as to whether the strike should take place to the 76-man delegate conference, which opened one hour later.

Jones' appeal to defer the 14 July strike-date until after this conference on 15 July, had been widely ignored and he was promptly rebuked for splitting the ranks and causing some men to believe that settlement was near. In reply, he could only wax philosophical and remind men that retreats were sometimes necessary before victory! He asked for the strike to be deferred for four weeks to give negotiators time to examine the new offer and devise appropriate tactics. O'Leary said he was thinking in terms of one-day strikes, Lindley of action in the small ports alone and Michael Byrne, the general secretary of the STGWU, of regular concerted stoppages to pressurise the employers.

But Jones' resolution was lost by 39 to 43 votes and Nicholson, of the London docks group, moved support for the original strike resolution and won by 48 to 32. At this stage London and Liverpool, who provided nearly a third of the delegates were almost solid for the strike – although they stood to gain little compared with the small ports which held the voting balance in conference. But Nicholson, who was active in the Workers' Control movement and especially in the fight to implement the Bristow report, saw the strike primarily as a means of forcing dockers into a united front, from which they could stand against the march of technology. Defeating Jones and O'Leary now was, for him, the guarantee of future accountability and militance, with the union in control.

The strike lasted until 3 August and was far from the expected trauma. Most essential cargoes were handled, like medicines or perishables; most non-Scheme ports like Felixstowe, Harwich and Shoreham joined the stoppage and thus prevented serious internal union conflict; the Government proclaimed a state of Emergency but did not use troops and the few instances of violence came from unlikely village ports, where some traffic continued.

The compromise settlement was reached by a Court of Inquiry under Lord Pearson (with Will Paynter of the mineworkers as union representative). It gave a 7 per cent award through the careful splitting of the basic rate into its calculator functions. The basic rate itself was not moved, but a £16 calculator was allowed for overtime premiums, the guarantee was fixed at £20, with overtime excluded from the qualification, and the extra £1 modernisation payment was offered 'across-the-board.'

To the *Economist*, the Pearson settlement was a hopeless and inflationary compromise, but it settled the strike and did not commit employers, engaged in Phase II, to more than an extra £1 a week – from the final recommendation – if they chose to be firm. But in many cases they did not. While Liverpool and Southampton only gave £1 more London conceded £2, which bought the co-operation of the NASD in the enclosed docks deal and enabled Phase II to start six weeks later on basic rates for fit men of £36 10s a week, with an extra £2 10s for shipworkers.

CHAPTER FIFTEEN

Conclusions

'All of us working in the port are at the mercy of these modern innovations.'
John Kiernan, chairman of the London Port Employers.

In the months following the national dock strike, most major ports concluded their Phase II agreements. Hull, which had negotiated in the wake of the London enclosed docks, introduced its deal a week ahead; Glasgow, Southampton and Bristol followed by the end of the year.

The modernisation agreements had an overriding feature in common; they all raised the minimum weekly wage far above the paltry national time rate. But they split into two camps over the choice of working hours and the retention of bonus.

The key agreements were those of Middlesbrough and London. Middlesbrough's incentive bonus, converted from piecework to simpler tonnage targets, was copied on the London riverside, and in Grangemouth, Glasgow and Bristol while the London pattern of eliminating the entire incentive element was adopted by Southampton and Hull.

Liverpool remained a maverick. The employers wanted to move cautiously and James Leggate, their chairman, at one time envisaged a six-year transition period from Phase I to Phase II. But their hand was forced by the 1967 strike and the Scamp award, which oriented the wages structure away from time-rate factors to incentives. Although the employers would have liked an extended, trial run, the nature of the Scamp guarantee (a 2s an hour bonus yield) caused difficulties. It created an automatic threshold from which the men sought to improve piecework prices and they applied continuous pressure for bonus rates to be improved above the guarantee level, especially by disputing local awards for impediments to earnings potential. The port was afflicted by numerous petty strikes and these persuaded the employers to end the award system as a primary objective, before looking at the wages structure as a whole.

The method of piecework calculation was changed by putting all men on to gang-day payments, but the first pay award of November 1969 had the specific aim of ending commodity awards, for dirty or obnoxious cargoes, and this was accompanied by raising the basic wage to £16 – virtually buying out the Scamp guarantee.

At the start of 1970, Liverpool employers were as uncertain as London's about the ultimate wage structure they wanted. The stewards had put forward a remarkable claim of £60 for a 20-hour week and, although the men regarded it as something of a giggle, it remained their ostensible negotiating position. The employers offered a £21 basic rate as a holding position, but negotiations only began in earnest after the appointment of R. F. Hunt, of British Leyland, to be the port's full-time industrial relations director. He made an offer of an up-standing weekly wage of £36 15s a week, with no bonus and dis-cretionary shiftwork, but this was summarily rejected; the talks then moved towards the retention of piecework and progressed at last.

In October 1971, a Phase II deal was introduced. It kept piecework for loading and a simpler tonnage incentive for discharging; it also retained the few remaining contingency awards. But the main innova-tion was a stringent framework for controlling the hours of work. All overtime was abolished by putting the 10,000 men on a rotating shift system, with a minimum of four-fifths of the labour force on an eight-hour day shift and up to 20 per cent on a six-hour evening shift. These carried basic wage rates of £26 and £29 a week respectively. An emergency midnight-to-dawn shift, well known in the United States as the graveyard shift, was also agreed.

The Liverpool agreement is unique in retaining piecework and thereby carries the danger that the port will not rid itself of the niggling bonus disputes which characterised the industry in the 1950s and 1960s. But there is a coherent rationale in the limitation of working hours which is designed to end, once and for all, the Mersey dockers' predilection for spinning work out into overtime to get enhanced overtime rates rather than incentive effort. It should also put paid to the surviving forms of the welt.

Liverpool also provides the fullest working coverage of any major British port, with a possible 22 out of every 24 hours when cargo can be handled. A similar hours structure has been used in Southampton with the difference that Southampton's all-night shift is restricted solely to baggage handling on the passenger trade, not general cargo-handling.

Table 9 shows the main Phase II agreements which have been concluded, together with the date of introduction and the numbers covered.

To pass definitive judgements on the success of the modernisation programme is hazardous. Most agreements have had less than one year in which to prove themselves and most apply to a wide range of undertakings within a single port agreement, so that individual companies offer widely different opinions about performance.

The overriding difficulty is to isolate the impact of labour agreements from the impact of technology, company reorganisation, commercial policy of port-users and the behaviour of port authorities. The ports expected imminent nationalisation throughout the years of the Devlin programme and, after the 1970 general election, they were then asked to stand on their own feet and to regard themselves as self-supporting and profitable enterprises – not as candidates for baling out by the state.

In a period of rapid change in labour practices, the climate of financial crisis in port operation was unfortunate. In the 1969–70 financial year, most of the major ports returned large deficits. The Mersey Docks and Harbour Board lost £3,000,000; the PLA lost £1,980,000; the 16 ports of the British Transport Docks Board lost £440,000; Bristol lost £300,000 and the Forth Ports Authority £389,000. While Middlesbrough turned in a £201,000 profit, only Manchester had a healthy margin of £1,160,000.

Labour problems played only a small part in causing such losses. The main source of trouble was the burden carried by each authority in providing facilities for the container. In the sense that containers merely replaced existing traffic, they generated no new revenue, but no port felt able to opt out of the heavy investment in new berths for fear of dying on its feet. Overall, some £300 million was spent in providing new facilities and the interest charges were crippling. In Liverpool, they were £4,000,000 and in London £4,800,000 on a capital debt of £80 million; for the BTDB, it was £5,000,000 on a debt of £109 million.

The predicament was uncannily similar to that of the London dock companies at the end of the nineteenth century, when the opening of new dock basins closer to the mouth of the Thames left obsolete and unprofitable berths upriver. There is even a parallel in the competition of the two old companies to attract custom by over-investment and the

Table 9 Devlin Phase II agreements (at major ports) in date order

Port	Number of Dockers	Date	Brief Details of Agreement
Tees and Hartlepool	600	4.8.69–26.1.70	Flat rate of £25 or £30 per week according to output levels of preceding month, plus additional payments where output targets are exceeded. Two shifts
Grangemouth	450	15.6.70	Basic wage of £30 plus bonus of approximately £8 for 40-hour week
London riverside	3,000	6.7.70	Basic wage of £28 10s for 40 hours, plus company bonuses. Optional shiftwork
Hull	2,800	14.9.70	Basic wage of £36 15s for 40 hours, with shiftwork at employers' option at a premium of £1 per shift
London enclosed docks	9,700	21.9.70	Basic wage of £36 10s for fit men for two shifts of 31¼ working hours, plus 10s per shift for ship work
(Tally clerks)	1,700	21.9.70	Basic wage of £40 10s for shifts of 32¼ working hours
Glasgow	1,300	30.11.70	Basic wage for 40 hours of £26 plus bonus designed to yield average earnings of £38 to £40, including overtime. Provision for shift work at employers' option. Three-year agreement
Southampton	2,000	30.11.70	Basic wage of £38 10s for 40 hours. Standard small evening shift, occasional third shift all night
Bristol	1,400	14.12.70	Basic rate of £26 10s, with bonus of roughly £8 plus 10s per day extra when allocated to work, with provision for night shift
Liverpool	10,000	5.10.71	Basic wage of £26 and continuation of piecework. Overtime abolished and round-the-clock cover introduced with three shifts. Maximum of 20 per cent of labour on evening shift, at £29

competition of ports today to attract containers, with scant regard to the likely needs of the market; already there is a danger of an over-population of container berths, just as there was an overpopulation of docks seventy years ago in London.

The near-collapse of the Mersey Docks and Harbour Board in 1970 was a fate which could easily have overtaken London, but for the providential sales value of the PLA's upriver land. Liverpool was not so fortunate and, although it was decided to shut down the entire south end of the docks, the sales potential of the land was negligible compared with the value of the London, St. Katharine and Surrey dock acreage on the Thames.

The fact that most ports are struggling on the edge of a financial abyss has contributed to the overall costs of port use and it has affected the commercial decisions of the ship-owner. There has also been an unquantifiable effect on the men themselves and it clearly would have been preferable to start the Devlin programme from a stable base and not with jeremiads about the likely demise of both London and Liverpool as major centres of trade.

A further constraint against the meaningful evaluation of perform-ance is the dearth of statistics. Because the docks are a service industry, where the interests of port-users differ from trade to trade and where, even within a trade, job-content may change on every occasion, port-wide statistics are confined to simple areas of comparison like the number of days lost through disputes, levels of earnings, levels of trade and the amount of underemployment. It has not proved possible to construct 'total sum' costs to compare the use of one British port with another, let alone to compare British and Continental ports. This deficiency was criticised sharply by the 1962 Rochdale report. 'We found on several occasions that information about the functioning of ports which we regarded as vital to our inquiries was not regularly produced and could not be deduced from the figures available to us; in particular we would cite the cost of passing goods through ports . . . and the comparative shipping turn-round performance of ports.'[110]

The National Ports Council has subsequently built up a large volume of data but costings still tend to be the jealously-guarded secrets of individual shipping companies and stevedores and these are seldom released, except for some readily identifiable operations like unitised or container services.

In looking at the first year of the Phase II agreement in London's

enclosed docks, it must therefore be stressed that this is the performance of one pioneering deal, affected by many teething problems which
were unique to a particular time and set of circumstances. It is not a
happy record but, within the overall picture of rapidly rising costs
and declining outputs on conventional trades, there were individual
success stories, attributable to good management and co-operation
from the men. Though hidden in port-wide statistics, they approach
most closely to the spirit of the Devlin programme.

WORKING TOGETHER IN LONDON

The aims of London's Phase II deal were set out graphically in a
letter circulated to all dockers on 21 September. It was signed by
Hovey, Shea of the TGWU, Newman of the NASD and Dick Butler of
the PLA and it serves as a poignant reminder of the optimism with
which modernisation was launched. Devlin Phase II was a long leap
forward, it stated.

'Let no one underestimate the magnitude of this change. The
situation, whereby the traditional methods of cargo handling were
being drastically and inevitably altered, demanded drastic action if the
port of London – and with it our jobs – was going to have a future.
Two-shift working and an upstanding weekly wage will provide conditions especially suitable to the development of modern, modernised
operations. The extra hours available will give us the chance to speed
up the turn-round of conventional trades, thus safeguarding the business of the port.

'You understand that conditions such as these can only be achieved
if an employer is able to utilise the services of his men much more
effectively than had been possible in the past. Now that you will get
the same basic wage every week it is the employers' special responsibility to so organise the manpower available to him that the work can
be done as quickly and as efficiently as possible. This will be in the
long-term interest of everyone in the company; provided, of course,
that this does not result in any individual being treated unreasonably.

'The course which we have set ourselves is a revolutionary one but
it has to be followed if our jobs are to be safeguarded and a future is
to be provided for our port. We are in this together. It will be up to the
employers to provide not only money for mechanisation but the kind
of first-class management which considers both the efficiency of the

job and the interest of the man doing it. It will be up to each one of you to show a sense of responsibility to ensure that throughputs are maintained and improved wherever possible, despite the removal of the piecework incentive.

'We cannot afford to fail. If we succeed, as indeed we must if all will pull together, then the rewards of this success will be forthcoming when the Agreement is reviewed in July next year.

'We ask everyone in our industry, whether he be manager or superintendent, whether he be trade union official, foreman, shop steward or registered worker, to face these great challenges in a spirit of co-operation, and to give of his best in the common good, so that we may all make certain this new agreement meets with the success it deserves.'[111]

There is a hint of desperation in this letter, as in most of the public utterances of the negotiators as Phase II came to be implemented. The agreement had no built-in controls; so much was imponderable; no one knew if outputs would be maintained. So both sides turned to exhortation and pleaded for the industry to work together, as if harmony could suddenly descend and sheer goodwill could make up for the work norms, which so few companies had begun to establish.

In the first weeks of Phase II there were immediate difficulties and delays in turn-round, but no one worried unduly since the main sources of difficulty stemmed from the ancillary trades, like road haulage and lighterage, which had not adapted to the longer hours of work which two shifts allowed.

Road hauliers, although they had had ample warning of Phase II's approach, claimed that the Government restrictions on drivers' hours prevented them sending lorries to the docks after 5 p.m., although the dockers worked until 9 p.m. The lighterage negotiations were stalled over the issue of transferring surplus labour to the docker's register and barges, essential for overside working, were only being manned on a one-shift basis.

Furthermore, shipping schedules were not fully recovered from the summer dock strike and this caused shed congestion. Then, just as Phase II was introduced, Rotterdam dockers embarked on their most serious strike in a decade, forcing more re-scheduling of vessels and diversions. Finally, there was an acknowledged shortage of fit dockers, and more particularly tally clerks, to man the two shifts and a major recruitment of 750 men was started in November, albeit three months too late.

Many of these problems should have been anticipated. As it was, they clouded the real issue of the dockers' performance. For a time, the PLA claimed that it was just a conspiracy of ill-fortune – even down to the appalling weather – which was hampering Phase II. Then, Mr Walter Lewis, the new chairman of the port employers, decided that the charade must stop. In a series of remarkably candid statements, he tore into his fellow employers for ruining Phase II.

'I blame employers because they didn't think out the situation in advance,' he said at the end of October. 'The road hauliers should have approached the Government months ago for a dispensation from the drivers' hours regulations to fit in with the new dock working. It is local management that seems completely incapable of new thinking and controlling the situation. That applies to port employers as well.'

The full extent of the crisis reached the press. *The Times* set the ball rolling by reporting that 60 ships had been diverted from London. The *Daily Mirror* devoted its first and second page to attacking management. 'This time the bosses are the fools,' its headline said. 'This newspaper has never hesitated to criticise the dock unions when they have merited criticism,' it went on, 'Or to bash Mr Dash (now retired) in his more disruptive days as a dockland agitator. But today it is the bosses who richly deserve the crack of the whip.'[112]

The *Financial Times* recorded the plight of two ships in London. The *Port St Lawrence* had docked on 13 September with 13,000 carcases of New Zealand lamb. Discharging had not started until 12 October and did not finish until 3 November, a turn-round of seven and a half weeks, instead of the one week she could have expected three years earlier. At Tilbury, the *Jalajanya* had docked with a cargo of jute on 1 November and did not finish discharging until mid-December; this performance prompted Mr W. Firminger, London chairman of the UK jute goods association to protest that 'the whole affair smacks of either rank bad management or lack of foresight, or it is an attempt by labour to wreck the new dock scheme.'

These were extreme examples, but the decline in productivity was confirmed when the PLA started to release weekly performance figures. As Figure 3 shows, 90 ships had been diverted by the end of October and the average weekly tonnage handled across the quays had dropped from a pre-Phase II average of 192,000 tons to 145,000 – about 23 per cent.

Within each dock area, performance figures varied widely. In the West India and Millwall docks, where job security was least because of impending berth closures, outputs had hardly dropped at all; in the Royals, they were consistently low and at Tilbury, exporting began well and declined, while the import curve showed a reverse trend, with a poor start but improvements in the second month, except for overside discharge into barges.

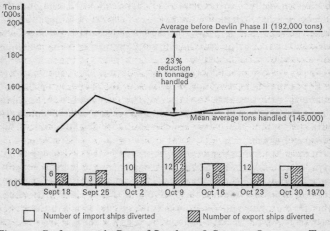

Figure 3   Performance in Port of London, 18 Sept.–30 Oct. 1970. Tons handled and ships diverted (conventional trades).

Not surprisingly, this poor start frightened the ship-owners and many trades were hurriedly shifted to other ports. Ellerman and Bucknall took 84,000 tons of South African discharging away from London to Hull and other east coast ports. West African trade was lost to Middlesbrough and a quarter of the 250,000 tons of New Zealand meat discharged in London was removed to Southampton, Avonmouth and Liverpool.

With the Australian and Far East trades being containerised, London could ill-afford to lose any of its remaining conventional cargo and the port was punished further when the India–Pakistan shipping conference and the UK–Ceylon eastbound conference placed 25 per cent surcharges on all ships using London.

However, the real chance to assess Phase II came in the summer of 1971 when wage levels were reviewed. The original agreement had stipulated that future wage increases were to be related solely to productivity factors and the unions agreed to a thorough examination of performance, although they knew their prospects were bleak.

Initially, the employers selected a three-month period of comparison between March and May 1970 and a similar period in 1971. However, the unions insisted that a seven-month period be chosen and the October to May figures for the two years showed a 26 per cent increase in wage costs per ton; the labour force had declined by one per cent from 10,315 to 10,199 men and the wage bill had gone up by 18 per cent to £12,274,447.

The most significant fact, however, was that the overall decline in throughput was only 6 per cent because the serious drop in conventional trades was matched by a doubling in container traffic and a 26 per cent increase in packaged timber at Tilbury. These figures are fully spelt out in Table 10, which was the document used at the negotiating table.

In the event, the renegotiation of Phase II in the enclosed docks in 1971 was achieved with the employers conceding an increase roughly commensurate with the higher cost-of-living and, after minor alarums, this was accepted by both the TGWU and NASD. On the riverside, where the retention of bonus had kept outputs steady but average wages rose by 20 per cent to more than £50 a week, it also proved easy to renegotiate at a modest level.

The first year of Phase II was a far cry from the aspirations of the employers and the forecasts of AIC, who had demanded productivity to *increase* by a third to keep costs stable. Not surprisingly, the ocean trades employers took pains to blame the men for the slackening off in effort and it is revealing to see how their arguments moved away from Lewis's original self-flagellation.

Commander Dermod Jewitt, who had succeeded Hovey at LOTEA, initially took the view that the men had put their hearts into making Phase II work, but after three months he identified a fresh series of problems, which put the unions and men in poor light. One was the imbalance of the labour force, with a shortage of young fit men and a

Table 10   London tonnage/manpower data

	Pre-Phase II Oct. 1969–May 1970	Phase II Oct. 1970–May 1971	
	Quantity	Quantity	Per cent change + or −
Imports (D/W tons × 1,000)			
Forest products	557	700	+26
Container traffic	317	615	+94
Conventional general cargo	2,446	1,819	−26
Total imports	3,320	3,134	−6
Exports (D/W tons × 1,000)			
Container traffic	292	598	+105
Conventional general cargo	2,067	1,596	−23
Total exports	2,359	2,194	−7
Grand total, imports and exports	5,679	5,328	−6
Number of men	10,315	10,199	−1
Wages paid	£10,388,481	£12,274,447	+18
Tons per man	550·6	522·4	−5
Wages cost per ton	£1·83	£2·30	+26

N.B. The data do not include costs attributable to: protective clothing, catering subsidies, N D L B levy, mechanical equipment, etc.

surplus of the sick and elderly. He claimed that 22 per cent of the labour force could not be turned to the arduous forms of quay and ship work and called for the compulsory severance of the 800 least fit.

He also showed that neither men nor management had come to terms with the old problem of improving the number of effective working hours, after the outside problems of haulage and lighterage industries had been solved. 'This produced a slowing down of the tempo of work and our problem now is to enthuse management and men of the *urgency* of working at full bore throughout the period of the shift,' he said.[113] It will be recalled that Hovey's research had showed that only 6·1 hours out of 9·2 attended were actually *worked* per day during Phase I, a ratio of roughly two out of three.

Jewitt's figures showed that this ratio had in fact remained constant and that only 4 hours out of each 6¼-hour shift were being worked. He broke down the delays as follows:

Late starts due to making ready, opening sheds, providing equipment etc.	30 minutes
Extension of mealbreak	15 minutes
Early finish	20 minutes
Transport delays (lighterage and road)	30 minutes
Weather	30 minutes
Equipment delays	20 minutes

It was easy to blame the men for avoidable time lost, but the unions resented it. They claimed that it was management's duty to manage and that the employers had the disciplinary powers to ensure good time-keeping. The fact that shop stewards had refused to co-operate in introducing time-study measurements was acknowledged as a fault, but Shea frequently accused the employers of reverting to an incentive mentality instead of developing better standards of line management. During the review negotiations, he cited many instances of managers trying to get good outputs by telling men to finish a job and go home. This defied the purpose of fully utilising working hours and also encouraged poor time-keeping, he maintained.

The argument that no one knew how to manage without a carrot and stick was, in large measure, justified. With Hovey's departure from London to set up the Southampton end of the Far East container trade, LOTEA fell under the control of men who made no secret of their distaste for the upstanding weekly wage. Jewitt, who came from Scruttons-Maltby, and his deputy Joe Payne, of Thames 65, had both wanted to retain incentive bonuses and another senior employer, who played a vital part in policing Phase II, was heard to say – on the day the new agreement was introduced – that he hoped London could drag other ports down to the same level of inefficiency that he was sure would come. This was hardly the example to set as the port embarked on 'a revolutionary course which could not afford to fail.'

THE DEVLIN ACHIEVEMENTS . . .

The lessons of Phase II in London translate easily into the wider context of the Devlin programme as a whole. By far the most important achievement of the London deal was to open the way to containers and, at heart, this was the *raison d'etre* of modernisation.

Curiously, the forward-looking purpose of the Devlin Inquiry was never explicit in the Committee's terms of reference. Lord Devlin was asked to make good the legacy of the past, but it was fundamentally the pressures of transport technology which directed the attention of the Government, employers and trade unions to the reform of labour relations in the 1960s. Imminent containerisation was implicit in the *timing* of the Inquiry; the industry had passed through a comparatively stable period, compared with the late 1940s and the decade of the 1950s, when it turned at last towards the reforms which had been advocated nearly 50 years before in the Shaw Report. It could have staggered along, had there not been such major technological changes in the offing. But the casual system, with attendant casual attitudes, could not have coped with the container.

Casualism could only operate, in a socially-acceptable form, under very circumscribed conditions. It demanded sufficient underemployment to keep a pool of labour; but sufficient security to give the entire labour force reasonable prospect of employment and adequate earnings.

Unit-loading and containers, with their vast manpower savings, would have destroyed this precarious balance. Containers demanded specialist teams of labour at terminal berths and, while these men would have had excellent earnings and top security, the majority in the casual pool would have become more casual, as the availability of conventional work declined. In fact, the rank-and-file struggle to stop men accepting permanency in the post-war years would have been a mild foretaste to their opposition to containerisation, had a casual system been retained.

For all the shortcomings of the Devlin programme – as implemented – in terms of cost and performance, this basic task was achieved and the co-operation of the docker in moving through a staggeringly-rapid change of his industry was won.

The second achievement, made necessary by the first, was to increase the security of the docker. Although the industry's average earnings had outstripped the national average after the Second World War, the very nature of casual employment and the enormous weekly fluctuation in earnings tied his status and his responses to the lowest expectation. Decasualisation gave permanent employment and, although Phase I transfer clauses and the existence of a Temporary Unattached Register means that one man does not necessarily work for one employer all the time, some buffer is still needed to counter fluctuations in trade. However much a few diehards mourn the halcyon days of the pool and the free call, there is no doubt that the docker is more secure now than ten years ago and the vast majority of men recognise it.

Phase II has, to a large extent, carried the security of employment into security of earnings. Only those men parked in the TUR or at small ports without Phase II agreements receive the industry's guaranteed minimum wage of £20 a week; most have minimum basic rates of £25 to £40 a week, whether they work or not, and the cost of underemployment is no longer borne by the men, but by employers.

The movement towards the upstanding weekly wage has brought Britain more in line with US and Continental ports, where incentive bonus is seldom paid; it has also enabled the docks to set standards which are pace-setters for the labour movement as a whole, in terms of sick pay and pensions, severance payments and the minimum earnings level. As a humanitarian reform, the Devlin programme has, in most essentials, paid the debt of a bitter past.

The third achievement stems from the Devlin Committee's insistence on root-and-branch overhaul of the structure of employers and unions; the industry's response, although insufficient, has been more wide-ranging than any previously attempted.

The number of employers has been vastly reduced. From roughly 1,500 undertakings in 1965, only some 450 remain in business. In table 11, the extent of the reduction can be seen. The 1965 Devlin report cited envisaged reductions for the London enclosed docks, Liverpool, Hull, Glasgow and Bristol. In Glasgow, this figure has been undercut and in Hull it has been virtually matched.

The number of effective employers, in fact, is smaller than the figures suggest. Some retain a licence in case they may need to take on men in the future. In London, for instance, there are less than 30 actually operating in the enclosed docks and in Southampton one company has 98 per cent of the labour force. On the other hand, some small companies, previously registered, have been driven outside the dock-gate and now aggravate the problems of container jurisdiction.

	Number of Employers			Jan. 1 1971[1]		Devlin
Port	Jan. 1 1962	Jan. 1 1965	Dec. 5 1967	licensed	registered	figure
London	389	318	247	210	148	16[2]
Liverpool	115	112	52	40	40	10
Hull	121	90	73	23	13	10
Bristol	77	77	30	28	28	8
Southampton	26	17	8	18	11	
Glasgow	23	14	5	4	4	6
Total	c. 1,500	1,514	734	c. 450	c. 400	

Table 11 Number of employers in scheme ports

[1] The 'licensed' column shows the total number who are entitled to employ, if they so choose. The 'registered' column shows the number who actually have a labour force.

[2] This figure refers only to the enclosed docks. Three-quarters of the registered employers in London now are wharfingers or in lighterage.

Meanwhile the TGWU has absorbed the lightermen and Scottish TGWU in mergers, thereby reducing the number of waterfront unions from five to three. Following the severe strictures of the 1965 report, it made a sustained attempt to restore its authority in Hull and Liverpool and its action in sacking the Hull dock officers was bold in the extreme. In Liverpool, it beat the challenge of the Blues, even if the cost has been the devolution of too much authority to shop stewards; and in London it succeeded in controlling the second stage of modernisation negotiations successfully within its committee structure.

This is not to say that the TGWU has solved its problems – far from it – but it has identified them and, through the shop stewards' system, it has stretched its communications down to the shopfloor. It no longer denies its own failings and, if it can live in peace with the Blues and somehow absorb the shop stewards into its institutional structure, it will be able to claim greater control of the waterfront than at any time in its history.

Finally, the sum of these achievements has changed the entire nature of labour relations. Many of the old sources of grievance, stemming from casualism, irregular work and irregular earnings, have been removed. To this extent casual attitudes have also been removed. Important areas of conflict remain, both of interest and of right, but the old complaint – that agreements signed at the negotiating table were not worth the paper they were written on – cannot be sustained.

Prior to the modernisation programme, with piecework, the all-powerful gang system and the protective practices of casualism, the bargaining power of the dockers resided at the dock-gate. If the men could overcome internal and sectional differences, their strength was easily turned against employer and union alike. By removing the bargaining power of the gang, a more coherent method of determining grievances has been established and the results can be seen in the record of disputes.

During Phase I, the dockers' customary responses changed little because the wages system was little changed and the increase in security was confined to the bottom end of the earnings scale. But, with the introduction of new payment systems and the virtual buying out of the rulebook in some agreements, dockers have given up their old constraints on managerial freedom.

Mobility within companies and flexible manning scales have been largely respected and, in London at any rate, the very concept that a wage review should not be a naked test of industrial strength but the product of a detailed analysis of port performance was revolutionary.

These changes can be seen in strike figures. One hesitates to impose any pattern on the incidence of disputes in the docks, since they have tended to fluctuate wildly from year to year without apparent connections between the peaks and troughs. Also, there are grave problems attached to the recording of dock stoppages, and these are noted in Appendix 7.

Before the war, dockland's strike record was little worse than that of many industries, with an average of 285 days lost annually for every 1,000 men insured between 1930 and 1938. But a deterioration began in the last months of the war and the incidence of strikes continued at a high overall level until the end of the Phase I period. The average rose to 3,340 days lost per 1,000 insured in the first nine years of the Scheme up to 1955, and fell to 1,021 in the nine years up to 1964.

From 1965 to 1971 inclusive, it has been 5,206. (These are artificial spans of time, but determined by the date of publishing the 1956 and 1965 Devlin reports.)

The losses in peak years are attributable mostly to single disputes which had a major impact on the statistics. For example, the zinc-oxide strike of 1948 represented three-quarters of the days lost in

Table 12   Strike figures

	DOCKS			ALL INDUSTRIES	
	Number of stoppages	*Total days lost*	*Days lost per 1,000 employed*	*Total days lost 000's*	*Days lost per 1,000 employed*
1947	77	132,470	1,687	2,433	NA
	84	312,600	c. 4,000	1,944	95
	54	441,850	c. 6,000	1,807	88
1950	41	106,000	1,440	1,389	66
	59	339,878	4,240	1,694	80
	37	12,901	160	1,792	85
	61	32,015	430	2,184	104
	117	714,569	9,540	2,457	115
1955	112	693,209	8,590	3,781	175
	107	18,756	240	2,083	95
	109	94,077	1,230	8,412	380
	68	338,785	4,840	3,462	160
	70	39,322	550	5,270	240
1960	131	245,813	3,390	3,024	135
	97	155,346	2,020	3,046	135
	80	93,949	1,296	5,798	250
	106	35,850	550	1,755	75
	150	130,637	2,210	2,277	97·5
1965	132	106,037	1,628	2,925	125
	150	108,895	1,742	2,398	100
	183	571,578	9,625	2,787	120
	281	74,439	1,316	4,690	200
	373	242,220	4,593	6,846	300
1970	374	656,100	13,986	10,970	475
1971	288	159,402	3,555	13,558	590

Source: Dept. of Employment and NDLB.

1948. The Canadian Seamen's strike accounted for 90 per cent of losses in 1949. The protests against the 1951 pay settlement accounted for two-thirds of that year's losses. The London overtime dispute of 1954, the inter-union disputes in Liverpool and Manchester next year and the London strike in support of Smithfield workers in 1958 each accounted for 85 to 90 per cent of the total. Similarly, the Decasualisation strikes and the national dock strike overwhelmed the combined total of other disputes in 1967 and 1970.

However, it can tentatively be argued that the pattern of stoppages in the post-war period conforms with the all-industry pattern for this period, with an increasing trend to use industrial action, but for shorter periods. Further, the more frequent occurrence of major blow-ups soon after the war points towards some institutional instability, with neither men nor employers recognising each other's limits within the new structure of the Scheme.

Table 13   Strikes in London and Liverpool during the Devlin years

| | LONDON | | LIVERPOOL | |
	Number of stoppages	*Days lost*	*Number of stoppages*	*Days lost*
1966	26	31,800	25	22,500
1967	32	252,126	21	252,800
1968	50	12,793	64	31,200
1969	33	43,300	97	100,300
1970	21	220,500	61	161,300
1971	10	21,400	83	50,200

[1] Excludes Birkenhead, Garston and Ellesmere Port.

Source : N DLB.

The major upheavals are more rare after the mid-1950s, but recur during the change-over period of both stages of the Devlin programme. However, the incidence of minor stoppages over pay become more common and reach their hey-day in Liverpool, after the Scamp award. Table 12 gives the strike figures for the post-war period and shows the extent to which the docks were strike-prone compared with industry as a whole, while Table 13 gives the figures for London and Liverpool alone during the Devlin period.

Statistics are at their most misleading after Decasualisation, when individual employers assumed responsibility for submitting returns to the NDLB, instead of local board managers. The change has tended to produce an over-recording of disputes – but not of days lost. No single policy is followed for recording 'political' stoppages, which is important in view of their increasing incidence (in strikes against the Labour and Conservative Industrial Relations Bills and Labour's nationalisation plan); also, the NDLB has chosen to record strikes which have a common cause but occur in more than one port as a separate stoppage per port. Thus, the national dock strike appears as more than fifty stoppages.

While the incidence of stoppages seems to reach its highest point in 1970, the peak in fact was reached the year before and, in London, in 1968. Discounting the national dock strike, London has been remarkably trouble-free in the past two years, when the Phase II deal was either in existence, operated or about to be introduced.

The reason, quite simply, was the abolition of piecework and all bonus awards and the contrast with Liverpool, where incentives remain, is remarkable. London's record would be even better if the 'political' stoppages were removed, since these account for well over half the days lost in 1971.

In conclusion, the second stage of modernisation got to the root of many former grievances and swept them away. Future disputes will therefore tend to be the issues of right, like defining dockwork, or the annual confrontations over wages. But the prevalence of bonus disputes should disappear along with the piecework system.

. . . AND THE DEVLIN FAILINGS

The Devlin Committee was only indirectly concerned with setting a price to modernisation. The main report did not mention levels of reward – it dealt with matters of principle and how they should be implemented; the industry itself was meant to decide the cost of buying out its past.

However, at a time when some argued that dockers should get no increase for being decasualised since it was their supposedly cherished dream of half a century, the Committee made clear in its subsidiary reports that a large cash inducement was needed to get modernisation off the ground. The first report of 1964 made a generous settlement of the current national wage claim and the third report of 1966 bluntly admitted that its Phase I award was a sweetener for the future.

In practice, the Devlin programme gave an enormous boost to earnings and, judged from the imperfect view of Government incomes policy, it was decidedly inflationary. We have seen how earnings jumped by nearly 30 per cent in the fifteen months after Decasualisation and Table 14 shows the extent of wage movement in the four and a quarter years of 1967–71. NDLB statistics indicate a national increase of 80 per cent, with individual port earnings ranging between 57 per cent of Southampton and 117 per cent for Glasgow.

Table 14 Earnings movement during the Devlin years

Port	1967[1]	Phase II[2]	1971[3]	Percentage increase 1967–71	1967– Ph. II
Tees/Hartlepool	£23 9 11	£38 12 0	£41·95p	74	64
Grangemouth	£23 3 11	£35 19 1	£40·85p	76	55
Hull	£21 11 8	£39 8 5	£43·74	102·5	83
London[4]	£23 7 11	£37 15 0	£40·55p	73	62
Glasgow	£19 4 4	£33 9 3	£41·77p	117	74
Southampton	£28 14 5	£34 12 5	£47·20p	57	25·5
Bristol	£22 2 6	£32 14 5	£40·57p	83	44
Liverpool	£20 13 3	—	£37·76p	83	—
National	£22 14 9	£37 18 2[5]	£40·90p	80	—

[1] Figures in this column refer to the second quarter of 1970 and do not include perms; had they been included, overall earnings would have been higher.

[2] This column refers to the last quarter before the introduction of the Phase II agreement. In cases where the national dock strike would have caused distortion, figures for the second quarter of 1970 are used.

[3] Third quarter, 1971.

[4] All dockers in London.

[5] Average for 1970 as a whole.

Source: NDLB.

But an important qualification must be made. Prior to Decasualisation, the NDLB only recorded the earnings of casual dockers and not those of permanent men whose wages were higher. Even from published Government sources, it is not possible to deduce the earnings of the whole registered labour force since the Department of Employment's minimum list heading includes ancillary staff in ports and waterways. In the early years of the Scheme, when perms were often allocated to unpopular and low-yielding bonus work, their advantage in earning was not high (see Appendix 2, General Table II), unless there was heavy underemployment among pool labour. But once perms tended to become the nucleus of specialist gangs, the disparity in earnings widened and I would estimate that all the figures in column 1 could be increased by 5 per cent to give a more accurate picture of overall earnings levels. Equally, the percentage increases must be reduced, if the base figures are raised.

Very broadly, one can estimate that the true rise in earnings was nearer 70 than 80 per cent, but the Table clearly shows that the bulk of these increases stemmed from the Phase I period although no national increases, except to fringe benefits, were conceded between the De-casualisation award and the dock strike settlement of 1970. In short, Phase I was a period of rapid wages drift.

The effects were widely felt outside the docks. In Liverpool, the Scamp award of 1967 led immediately to new claims for busmen and lorry-drivers – and the special rates won in road haulage were the genesis of the Mersey differential which drivers were seeking in the 1972 'blacking' campaign which, in turn, took the TGWU to the National Industrial Relations Court. London's Phase II agreement led to spin-off in meat haulage and the Smithfield Meat Carriers' Association conceded a guaranteed earnings level of £41 a week, one of the highest in the country for drivers.

Furthermore, in ports where piecework was converted to a higher basic wage, the earnings of ancillary staff had to be kept in line and some 50,000 were affected. The extent of this pressure was graphically described by Geoffrey Robinson, senior executive of the Tees and Hartlepool Port Authority, to Lord Pearson. So far, he said, he had persuaded his office staff that the dockers earned their wage increases through increasing productivity, but any further increases would give the game away: it would be a concession to industrial strength and his basis for negotiating with his ancillary grades would disappear.

The pace of increase in dockers' wages clearly exerted inflationary pressures in trades associated with the ports and it was keenly felt by ship-owners, in the price they paid for cargo-handling.

Stevedoring companies customarily charged on a contract price, according to the tonnage involved and special requirements of the service, but in periods of uncertainty they did not hesitate to switch to a cost-plus basis and the direct wage cost could be plussed up by nearly 100 per cent, to cover insurance, the NDLB levy, tallying and office administration.

The combination of higher direct labour costs, longer turn-rounds and higher port charges – as port authorities were forced to increase revenue from conventional trades to cover their interest debts on container investments, was severe. For many ship-owners, the cost of port use doubled in the Devlin years. One ship-owner estimated that unit labour costs in London rose by 30 per cent in the year after Decasualisation alone, from £2·81 per deadweight ton to £3·82 on loadings, while Continental costs remained a fifth cheaper over the same period, and on discharging, London costs rose by 20 per cent while Continental prices would have shown a slight decline, but for devaluation.

The year in which Phase II was introduced to London also showed large cost increases and, in the last days before the Australian trade was containerised, handling costs were estimated to have risen by 79 to 115 per cent.

This is the record at its worst and the dockers' performance can be judged in a much more favourable light if the unitised trades are included in the total sum, setting the rise in earnings against the very substantial increases in tons handled per man-year and against the increases in the cost-of-living. Figure 4 provides a crude guide to productivity and the close relationship between the movement in earnings since 1947 and the rise in tonnage is remarkable. At the time of the Shaw award, dockers moved some 300 tons per man-year and this had risen to 655 tons when the Scheme began; the average had risen to 2,580 tons by 1970.

Of course, the increase is due, almost entirely, to mechanical innovations in cargo-handling and the brute effort in the dockers' work has declined. But the increase has been made possible by the wider range of skills acquired by the men and their willingness and ability to work larger cranes, drive appliances like bogeys, forklift trucks or the giant straddle-carriers for containers.

So long as levels of wages are to be determined by market forces and without a national framework to govern differentials and relativities, or to impose common restraint, it is desirable for the unions to have front-running groups of workers whose ability to force up their own earnings helps to pull the weaker brethren along in their wake. It matters little whether the front-runners get to the fore because of the skilled nature of their work or because of their inherent industrial strength.

The point to remember about the dockers is that they were already a high-earning group when modernisation began and in the past seven years they have essentially consolidated this status, moving

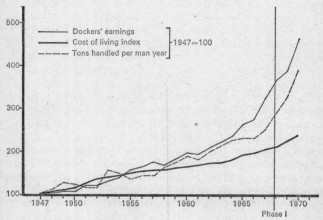

Figure 4 Productivity.

from fourth to second place in the earnings league, while their numbers have dropped from 65,000 to 42,000.

However, at a time when the Government was making a serious attempt to control the economy through an elaborate incomes policy, the movement of earnings in the docks, with its inflationary consequences, was clearly inconsistent with restraint. It was therefore surprising that the Government only intervened once to block a pay increase – the £17 London guarantee in 1967 – and shut its eyes to the fact that modernisation could not conceivably be justified as a copper-bottomed productivity deal.

The trouble was that the Government lost its nerve. Although it possessed in the Prices and Incomes Board the means of scrutinising the Phase I and some Phase II wage deals, it did not use this machinery for fear of provoking a strike. By holding up exports, a dock strike could weaken confidence in sterling and impede, perhaps fatally, Labour's attempts to convert an inherited balance of payments deficit into surplus. The seamen's strike of 1966 had halted only UK vessels, not foreign shipping, and it caused a severe run on the pound. This was stabilised temporarily by the wages freeze of July 1966 and this precedent was enough to persuade the Government that the ports should be kept open at all costs during the dockers' negotiations.

The cabinet's dilemma is understandable as its primary objective was to restore the balance of payments to a state of health. Some 85 per cent of all exports (by value) passed through the ports and a stoppage would be reflected at once in monthly trade figures. Ironically, a partial stoppage – such as the Decasualisation strikes of 1967 – could be far more damaging than a total shut-down, because exports would be strike-bound in transit sheds while incoming goods could be diverted to ports still operating. With a national dock strike, imports too would be stopped and the damage would be residual, in terms of export orders lost because of the delay.

After 1966, the Labour Government felt it could not afford further draconian measures against the working-class, but the cost of appeasement in the docks was less dramatic. The difference between efficiency and inefficiency might by 1p on a pound of meat or £10 on the price of a car and, in the long term, another upwards jolt towards wage inflation. But no blow-up.

In the event, the Government virtually exempted the docks from the criteria of incomes policy. A test came in December 1968, when the London tally clerks were going slow in pursuit of a 13 per cent wage demand. They had the power to shut down the entire ocean trade docks but the Cabinet decided this increase should be passed. The political decision to buy off the docker was instrumental in pricing the modernisation agreements and it was clear throughout the negotiations that the employers had lost the prop of Government support – even of Government neutrality – before the battle had begun.

Another major cause of wage inflation lay in the nature of the Devlin recommendations. The Committee realised that the industry's own efforts to decasualise had failed because too much was demanded too quickly: hence the phasing of modernisation into two stages.

But the difficulty of separating reform of the system of employment from reform of the wages structure was that *both* contributed inextricably to the inefficiencies of dockland. Wasteful practices were the response to the insecurity of casual hiring and to insecurity of earnings under piecework; and the removal of one form of insecurity without removal of the other was bound to lead to some form of pressure from the shopfloor.

Lord Brown was one person who saw the dangers only too clearly. He argued that the pressures would erupt on piecework prices, especially among low-earning gangs, in order to make up for continuing fluctuation in the pay packet. With the constraint of unemployment removed but the opportunity for exploiting piecework still there, he predicted that the wages structure would become even more uncontrollable. The fact that wages drift was so high in the first year after Decasualisation showed him to be right, and the conclusion is that the industry was unable to regulate the intermediary stage in the modernisation programme, before the real benefits could be brought under Phase II.

Ironically, the Devlin Committee had foreseen the problem but its solution – of enforcing work-sharing – was largely ignored. The report stated that the higher guarantee would force employers to re-distribute work among the labour force, since equal earnings would offset the cost of the guarantee. It went on to recommend positive steps towards work-sharing, through buying out the privileges of the higher-paid workers with cash sums.

Work-sharing was, in fact, a union ideal of long-standing. It was seen as a means of reducing sectional rivalry and establishing common aims for dockers; thus, Tillett insisted on a single port rate for London in 1911 and Bevin on a single national rate in 1920. In the Devlin era, a common rallying cry was to make all dockers equal and not to segregate them into first- and second-class citizens and the London liaison committee was appealing to this desire for uniformity when it advocated the abolition of permanency while casualism persisted and asked for all men to come under the allocating control of the dock labour board after Decasualisation. During Phase I negotiations, union officials echoed these demands in more realistic form by seeking assurances that an increasing number of men would not be left to draw the guarantee after Decasualisation.

Only the lighterage industry, however, moved successfully towards institutional work-sharing. In the 1957 work distribution agreement, the free call was abolished and the small fringe of men who were not attached to employers were guaranteed work for at least half the time by rota allocation.

In some ports, notably in South Wales, the men virtually abolished the free call and distributed work fairly with the help of the dock labour board manager and Southampton had moved some way towards this position. A further aspect of work-sharing concerned the final allocation at the ship's side. This was normally the prerogative of foremen, but there were numerous instances of the men taking over. In Southampton, for instance, gangs used to draw lots to determine which hatch they should work. In August 1969, some Liverpool gangs refused the foreman's allocation and re-formed the gangs as they thought fit, also picking hatches by lot. Next month, PLA shipworkers in the South West India Dock staged a token strike to improve rota allocation.

The concept of work-sharing had been recognised in the 1961 and 1965 national directives and it was fundamental to the organisation of dockwork on the Atlantic and Pacific coasts of the USA. But, in preparing for Phase I, British employers paid it no more than lip service. It was assumed that work-sharing was not a matter for port-wide negotiation but for internal organisation within a company. The result was that there was no commitment, even in principle, and the means of distributing work differed from company to company.

But work-sharing was most needed between men in employment and those parked on the temporary unattached register at £20 a week. Suddenly, during the 1972 container crisis, people realised that work-sharing could provide a transitional answer, at any rate, while the labour force was stabilised. London tally clerks got the employers to set up a holding company – like David Lloyd's B Plan of 1963 – rather than send them back to the TUR and work-sharing became the main concern of the emergency committee under Lord Aldington of the PLA, which was set up in the shadow of the pending national strike, to find ways of restoring full employment to the docks.

The Devlin programme has been much criticised for not changing or abolishing the Dock Labour Scheme. Undoubtedly, the use of Scheme discipline is unsatisfactory, the adjustment of the register is cumbersome and its original function to maintain the labour force has been taken over by employers after Decasualisation.

But there is no reason why it should be seen as an incubus and Lord Devlin's comments of 1956 are still true today: the weakness of the Scheme lies not in its nature but in attitudes towards it. It may not be a symbol of industrial partnership, but it is a part of the furniture of dockland and it would be totally impractical to remove it. Moreover, its abolition would be contrary to the increasing participation of working men in their industrial lives, unless it were replaced by equally far-reaching agreements.

Criticism of the Scheme in relation to the most pressing problem of the ports today – the need to redefine the dockers' role in the container age – is misdirected. It should really be aimed at the modernisation programme itself.

As the Devlin report realised, the underlying cause of casual attitudes was the lack of job and earnings security. But the Committee, coming as the successor to the Rochdale report and in response to external pressure on the industry, was only directed to look at labour relations outside the context of changes to the industry as a whole. It therefore could not pay sufficient regard to the *changing reasons* for job protection and failed to foresee that behaviour rooted in the insecurities of casualism could flourish just as easily in the insecurities of declining job opportunity. Jobs still have to be protected for the labour force as a whole, not because men were not taken on at the call or because their pay fluctuated between £11 and £40 a week, but because mechanisation was removing jobs altogether.

Here was the fundamental flaw. The Devlin Committee dealt with improving work on the waterfront and its very success in this narrow ambit allowed more work to leave the immediate port area. The implications of this success – and the march of technology – lay outside its ambit and were largely ignored.

No attempt was made to assess the manpower requirements of the ports within a coherent national framework, while Devlin modernisation was introduced. No attempt was made to anticipate the position of the docker – statutorily confined to work in the vicinity of the port – as jobs moved inland, or to redefine working rights in the light of container economics.

The task, of course, was daunting. Demarcation of working rights is notoriously difficult and, in the historical context of the docks, it is even harder since the registered dockworker has his job circumscribed by law and must now compete in a much wider labour market, where his legal rights must be discarded or they tether him to the water-front.

The Devlin Committee was at fault in not foreseeing this area of conflict. Quite simply, it failed to take evidence in detail from the only people who could have talked authoritatively about future labour requirements – the ship-owners. Even the ship-owners might have given a conservative guess since they were amazed by the pace of the changes they initiated.

Kiernan, of Furness Withy, could only plead that everyone in the docks industry was at the mercy of innovation and Philip Bates, the chairman of ACL, said: 'We all know everybody's gone too fast into containers; it's been too fast for all of us.' But a glance in 1965 at the kind of tonnage on order at the world's shipyards would have told its own story – and it was just such a survey, made in 1959–62, which forearmed the ILA in its US East Coast negotiations.

Once the pattern was apparent, the Government, unions and employers all shrank from the vexed issue of job rights. As we have seen, the NDLB – acting on behalf of the men – tried to extend dockers' territory through the constitutional channel of the industrial tribunal and the High Court, but was thwarted by legal interpretation of the Scheme – decisions which Tim O'Leary now calls 'lawyers' lunacy'. In setting up the Bristow Committee, port employers did no more than declare their interest with the men's and they never had the power to implement the 'dockers' corridor' without the consent of other parties affected. The Government, when it signified its approval of a major inquiry at the time of the national dock strike, at least recognised the existence of the problem, but it proved singularly reluctant to tackle it.

Within the industry's bargaining machinery, efforts were directed to alleviating the effects of contraction through voluntary severance and better pensions; but the rank-and-file are concerned not to make a graceful exit from their livelihood, but to stake a claim to the future.

With the blocking of all official channels for change, it was not surprising that the extension of dockwork became the single rallying cry for the shopfloor and that the men looked to their shop stewards for a lead. In a nine-point charter, adopted by the stewards and the TGWU officially in January 1972, a call was made for the Bristow corridor to be introduced and for all stuffing and unstuffing of containers to become registered dockwork – together with demands for retirement at 60, a 35-hour week and minimum manning scales to protect gang strengths. Then, in March, Liverpool stewards took the law into their own hands by blacking lorries whose containers had not been loaded by registered men. They insisted that all part-load containers – those with multiple consignments which would previously have been put together on the quayside – should be done by dockers and they maintained the blacking, even when ordered to desist by the National Industrial Relations Court.

Their contempt led to the TGWU almost being fined £55,000, and sparked off a wave of sympathy in other ports and, once again, initiative was taken away from the TGWU's constitutional committees into the hands of a re-born unofficial movement. For this alone, the crisis was a tragedy for dockland, since the TGWU was ham-strung by the law – at Industrial Tribunal level as well as by the NIRC – from giving the lead which could have maintained the ascendancy it established during the Devlin period.

But the failure to anticipate the depth of feeling over job rights was just as much a tragedy for its impact on modernisation agreements within the ports. No matter how successfully the Devlin reforms were translated into practice, insecurity was bound to affect attitudes at work, once efficiency was synonymous with declining job opportunity.

The outstanding need now is to make good what was left undone in the Devlin years. First, the union movement must come to a general understanding on the respective rights of dockers and other groups working with containers. Clearly, dockers have the coercive strength and the willingness to use it to win back some of the jobs they have lost – just as they won the right to work at Aintree in 1969.

But coercion is ugly when it sets worker against worker, and this is bound to happen. It has already led to TGWU shop stewards, from the general workers' trade group within the union, taking dockers to the NIRC because dockers' pickets outside Chobham Farm container groupage depot in East London (set up by a shipping consortia less than three miles from the waterfront) caused them to be laid off. Nor can coercion solve the principles of inter-group demarcations; it can only lead to numerous guerrilla actions and one-off settlements, whose variety may be the source of future conflict.

A preferable method would be to identify the proportion of traditional dockwork in operations outside the ports and for the unions to agree that dockers should have a prior right to this share. This would place the responsibility for defining workers' rights where it belongs –

within the labour movement; and the means of doing it already exists, through the transport committee of the Trades Union Congress. It would then be necessary to find a framework in which employers could negotiate on union interpretations or suggest their own. The difficulty would be to bring together undertakings as varied as warehousing, packing and road haulage; but it might be enough to create a national committee, with representatives of employers' associations and the unions, which could issue general guidelines.

The main obstacle would be the issue of the dockers' registration. It would be virtually impossible for an undertaking to register as a port employer solely for a proportion of his labour force and to conform to the conditions of the Scheme for these men. Fortunately, a simpler solution is available in the existence of the release register, which allows a docker to give up his registration when he leaves the port, but gives him priority of selection during any dock recruitment, if he seeks to return to his old calling.

With such a plan, the rigid definition of dockwork would be slowly eroded. The docker would seek work without any important prejudice to his privileges and the declining band of men on the waterfront could look more readily to the new pastures where progress has directed them.

So far, Britain's experience has been akin to that of American longshoremen on the West Coast. Where jobs are secure, the modernisation of labour practices has been successful, but as soon as it is threatened, conflicts re-emerge and the men try to extend their jurisdiction to new forms of work.

Once British dockers begin to take up new jobs, the insecurity which has stultified the Devlin reforms will be removed and fresh attempts can be made to build on the sound foundations of modernisation. Much needs to be done. Management must learn to manage better, the unions must come to terms with each other and with their shop stewards; port finances must be put on a better footing and the organisation of work, with the continuing division between ship, quay and shed labour, must be critically examined.

The cost of reform has already been high but the achievements of five years, which swept away casualism and provided a platform for greater efficiency, will be entirely wasted if the momentum of the Devlin programme is not extended to other fields of port operations and if the men are not given the prospect of a secure livelihood.

Appendices

Appendix 1   General Table I

	A Numbers employed[1]	B Percentage unemployed[1]	C Number of permanent men[1]	D Percentage of permanent men[1]	E Tonnage handled (000s)[2]	F Tons per man/ year
1913	NA	NA	NA		c. 67,000	
1921	125,000	NA	NA		c. 37,000	296
1924	118,000	27·25	NA		c. 67,000	567
1929	110,000	30·85	NA		c. 67,000	608
1931	111,000	39·8	NA		c. 52,000	466
1935	104,000	31·2	NA		c. 61,550	591
1938	100,000	26·5	NA		c. 66,970	669
1947	78,458	8·90	9,879	12·6	51,530	655
1948	78,200	14·00	c. 11,000	14·0	56,560	724
1949	75,047	10·50	c. 12,000	15·9	60,500	807
1950	75,264	9·20	12,569	16·4	59,820	796
1951	80,088	5·98	13,535	16·9	60,150	752
1952	79,798	14·83	14,274	17·89	60,265	757
1953	75,160	9·90	14,453	19·23	77,240	1,029
1954	74,937	5·88	14,966	19·97	75,146	1,005
1955	80,674	5·70	16,363	20·28	72,349	897
1956	78,722	10·22	17,004	21·60	73,673	936
1957	76,691	9·53	17,112	22·34	73,477	960
1958	74,132	11·40	16,977	22·90	81,147	1,090
1959	71,846	10·05	16,596	23·10	83,273	1,160
1960	72,550	6·42	16,382	22·58	93,658	1,290
1961	71,679	11·35	16,436	22·93	86,285	1,210
1962	66,811	10·32	15,761	23·90	88,465	1,325
1963	64,597	7·38	15,413	23·95	91,697	1,420
1964	64,083	4·89	15,323	24·00	97,103	1,515
1965	65,128	5·49	14,881	22·80	100,609	1,550
1966	62,522	7·12	15,430	24·31	96,471	1,550
1967	60,144	8·60	14,122	23·20	99,713	1,660
1968	56,563	5·91	Decasualisation		107,988	1,910
1969	52,732	7·52			112,736	2,140
1970	46,912	4·98			121,154	2,580
1971	43,647	10·53				NA

Sources

1. Ministry of Labour and NDLB. Figures in column A are the year's average, except for 1971 which is for December 31.
2. Liverpool Steamship Owner's Association.

Appendix 2 General Table II Dockers' basic rates, earnings and guarantee 1947–70

	Dockers' basic rate	Dockers' guarantee	Dockers' earnings (casual)[1]	Dockers' earnings (perms)[2]	All dockers' earnings	All industry earnings[3]	Docks industry wages bill[4]
							£ millions
1947	104s 6d	88s 0d	159s 0d	no		123s 5d	—
1948	104s 6d		159s 11d	accurate		134s 0d	29·7
1949	104s 6d		168s 11d	figures		139s 11d	30·3
1950	104s 6d		172s 10d			145s 9d	35·6
1951	104s 6d		196s 6d	204s		160s 2d	36·8
1952	123s 9d		189s 6d	202s		173s 7d	35·2
1953	123s 9d		205s 4d	210s		185s 11d	35·8
1954	132s 0d		219s 8d	217s		197s 8d	37·8
1955	132s 0d	104s 6d	249s 7d	253s		217s 5d	46·7
1956	154s 0d		259s 10d	279s		235s 4d	48·3
1957	154s 0d		276s 6d	292s		241s 6d	50·4
1958	162s 3d		273s 0d	300s		253s 2d	49·5
1959	169s 7d	132s 0d	292s 5d	321s		262s 11d	50·0
1960	169s 7d	140s 3d	317s 7d	344s 6d		282s 1d	51·1
1961	180s 7d	148s 6d	312s 10d	383s 10d		301s 4d	53·1
1962	180s 7d	156s 9d	334s 3d	406s 9d		312s 10d	52·5
1963	189s 0d		361s 4d	425s 0d		323s 1d	55·3
1964	189s 0d	180s 0d	381s 5d	452s 4d		352s 5d	59·9
1965	208s 4d		414s 10d	489s 5d		378s 2d	64·4
1966	221s 8d		440s 4d	523s 8d		405s 0d	65·0
1967	221s 8d	220s / 320s	450s 5d		460s 5d	411s 7d	63·3
1968	221s 8d				588s 6d	445s 3d	75·4
1969	221s 8d				629s 0d	496s 6d	77·4
1970	221s 8d	400s			£37·91	£28·05	78·6
1971	221s 8d				c. £41	£30·93	

1. NDLB statistics only covered casual dockers up to 1967, but perms' earnings can be deduced from employers' levy contributions to the Board. Earnings are the average for the calendar year, except for the last entry which relates to September 1967.

2. Perms' earnings relate to the fiscal year. The last figure is for April 1966–7.

3. All industry earnings for males, 21 and over. April was the base month up to 1968, thereafter October.

4. These figures exclude the cost of the Dock Labour Board levy.

Appendix 3   Registration at Ten Ports, 1931

Name of scheme (date started)	Composition	Number of employers Supporting	Not supporting
Bristol June 1916, reconstituted Feb. 1919	Joint five-a-side with independent chairman and port labour adviser jointly paid	100	—
Cardiff and Penarth Jan. 1924	Joint five-a-side	60	—
Grimsby and Immingham	Joint chairman, eight TU and nine employers	All except fish docks	—
Hull	Joint four-a-side	252	Master stevedores only partial
Liverpool July 1912	Joint twelve-a-side. Employers' Chairman	52	Contain special classes
London Feb. 1920, reconstituted Sept. 1925	Joint seven-a-side, including joint chairmen	350	A few small firms
Middlesbrough	Joint	25	4
Manchester	Operated by Ship Canal Co. in consultation with TGWU	1	—
Newport Oct. 1917, revised 1926	Joint four-a-side	21	1
Southampton 1916, revised 1925	Joint five-a-side	14	—

Source : Maclean Committee.

Number of men covered	Rules on recruitment	Remarks
2,788 plus 383 casual carters and warehousemen	Preference to sons of deceased dockers. TU membership compulsory	Difficulty of immobility over large area. Concern at age of register. Maximum demand (1929) 2,930. Minimum 533. Average 1,738 per day
1,572 practically all casual	No special arrangements	In six months up to April 1930, 50·3% worked more than half possible days. 21·3% worked less than quarter
1,896 casuals	Restricted to dockers' sons, some ex-servicemen nominees	1929 Maximum demand 1,700 Minimum demand 900
7,804 almost no permanent men	Preference to dockers' sons and ex-servicemen	—
21,500	Preference to dockers' sons and previous tally holders	Lack of facilities militates against decasualisation
37,118 permanent and casual	Preference to dockers' sons and employers' nominees	Central call stands made difficult by size of port
1,900 split into many sub-registers	Sons of dockers, although age is a stipulation for hatchway men	Regularity of employment high. Half the men are 'attached'
3,000	TU membership compulsory except for temporary registration	Maximum demand 3,087 Minimum demand 1,430
1,011	Recruitment from boy labour	Maximum demand (June 1930) 451. Average demand (June 1930) 199
2,888 casuals (not coal porters)	Employers' recommendation and physical fitness	—

Appendix 4 Labour requirement compared with men available (*a*) national, 1947–71, (*b*) London, 1947–70, (*c*) Liverpool, 1947–70.

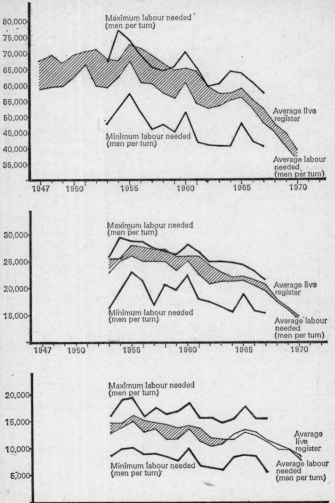

Appendix 5 The area of the Port of London recommended by the Bristow Committee, and the London docks.

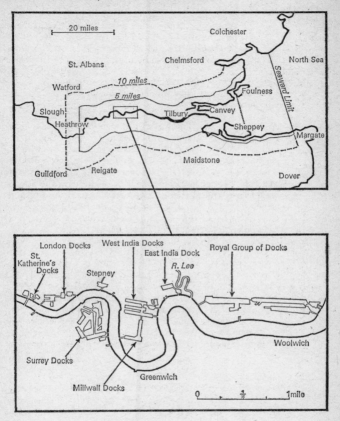

Appendix 6 Summary of Major Dock Strikes 1945–71

1945 March	Protest by 10,000 in London at the moving of the Dock Labour Corporation control inside the gate of the Royals. This grievance – dating back to the earliest days of union organisation – masked friction over discipline and overtime. 50,000 days lost.
1945 Sept.–Nov.	Six-week campaign, starting at Birkenhead and spreading south, over national pay award. Settled after Evershed inquiry. 1,100,000 days lost.
1948 May–June	*Zinc Oxide Strike.* A gang of eleven men in the Regents Canal dock, London, rejected a piecework price for discharging 100 tons of zinc oxide. Scope for dispute lay in disparity of wharfinger and short sea trade prices. After employers were upheld by inspection committees, the men were harshly disciplined – one week's suspension and three months disentitlement to attendance money and guarantee. The strike spread over this punishment (later reduced to two weeks' disentitlement). 19,000 on strike by mid-June, then 9,000 walk out in sympathy in Liverpool. 1,000 troops sent into London. 205,000 days lost.
1949 April	*Ineffective Strike.* On national instruction, the London dock labour board ordered thirty-three men who were old and ineffective to be struck off the register. (Twenty-eight belonged to the TGWU, four to NASD and one was a lighterman.) Although party to the board decision, the NASD called an official strike in protest. TGWU and WLTBU tried to keep order, but 15,000 walked out for a week. This stoppage caused the NASD to be expelled from all dock labour board representation. Of the thirty-three, one was reprieved on appeal. 49,000 days lost.
1949 May–July	*Canadian Seamen's Strike.* Dockland's most obviously political stoppage, led by Communists in support of the Canadian Seamen's Union which was fighting for survival. Starting at Avonmouth, dockers refused to work certain Canadian ships. It spread to Bristol, Liverpool and London and severely undermined the authority of the NDLB and TGWU. The Board ordered all men to return to work with the proviso that 'failure will jeopardise the very existence of the Scheme.' George Isaacs, Minister of Labour, promptly disclaimed the Board's threat. The TGWU tried to put down the revolt. 408,000 days lost.

1950 April–May	*Expulsions Strike.* The TGWU executive, after examining the conduct of eight leaders of the London Central Lock-Out Committee during the above strike, expels three from membership – Ted Dickers, Harry Constable, C. H. Saunders – and debars four others (including Jack Dash) from holding office. The new Port Workers' Defence Committee calls a strike until the three are reinstated; a maximum of 19,000 men respond; 3,000 troops sent in; London dock labour board threatens to withdraw registration from strikers on 1 May; strike folds. 103,000 days lost.
1951 Feb.–April	Protests in London, Merseyside, the Clyde and Manchester after the NJC accepts a new wage deal. In each port, different issues provided the catalysts. In Liverpool, the 'Dockers' Charter'; in London, the arrest and trial at the Old Bailey of seven of the strike committee. Their acquittal led directly to the withdrawal of the 'No-Strike' order 1305, a left-over of war-time emergency powers. 230,000 days lost.
1951 April–June	*Manchester Overtime Strike.* After two men in one gang refuse to work overtime on the *Princess Maria Pia*, 2,500 stop work for six weeks. Unofficial leadership, who kept trying to broaden the issues (free school meals for dockers' children, etc.), eventually rejected by the men. 86,000 days lost.
1954 Oct.–Nov.	*Overtime Ban Strike.* This had complex origins. The NASD in January banned all overtime on the grounds that there was no contractual obligation to work it. For many months, there was no show-down, although 38,000 cases of overtime being refused were recorded. Then employers refused to discuss any matters with the NASD until the ban was lifted; the union retaliated by calling a strike on 1 October. Two weeks later the lightermen join in officially. The port is virtually shut down and sympathy stoppages start in Southampton, Manchester, Liverpool and Hull; they last until the Evershed inquiry's interim report tries to clarify the meaning of 'working reasonable hours'. 700,000 days lost.
1955 May–July	*NASD Recognition Strikes.* The NASD had opened a branch office in Hull in August 1954 and soon moved on to Liverpool and Manchester – all supposedly TGWU territories. In October, the TUC suspended the NASD's affiliation for poaching but, next month, the Blues demanded representation on the Mersey Dock Labour Board. This was refused and, in May 1955, a strike was called until local recognition should be granted. This

lasted for six weeks in London, Liverpool, Manchester and Hull, with 18,000 to 20,000 men on strike. 650,000 days lost.

1958
May–June

The Smithfield Strike. This dispute – and a stoppage in 1957 in support of Covent Garden porters – stemmed from the close links between the London riverside and the markets. (In some cases the TGWU branches overlapped.) Smithfield drivers had agitated since March for a pay rise to accompany the raising of the speed limit from 20 to 30 m.p.h. In mid-May, 2,000 Tooley Street dockers walked out over handling 'black' meat. As produce rotted on the wharves, employers used unregistered labour to clear it and 20,000 dockers walked out. Strike settled when inquiry into Smithfield under D. T. Jack set up. 333,000 days lost and 60,000 in 1957.

1960
Sept.–Oct.

Ocean Shipowners Tally Clerks' Strike. No OSTS (who are a sub-register peculiar to London's enclosed docks) had been recruited since 1955 and there were now acute shortages. From January to August, ninety were recruited without protest; then the London board ordered the transfer of fifty dockers to the OST register. The clerks walked out claiming the recruitment was unnecessary and would not have been authorised had the OSTS had their own representative on the board. They also objected to the transfer as opposed to recruitment from the waiting list of sons and relatives. The strike by 1,500 caused 13,000 dockers to be made idle for two weeks. 210,000 days lost.

1961
April–May

Cohen's Wharf Strike. Men on the riverside and in London dock objected to the London board's decision to let D. Cohen operate from Lower Oliver's wharf, as a strawboard manufacturer, with six listed men – i.e. non-registered employees 'listed' to do occasional dockwork. They tried to get the wharf shut down until the Rochdale Inquiry was finished, but the strike collapsed with considerable acrimony within the unofficial ranks. 90,000 days lost.

1961
April

Bristol. 1,700 men walk out over piecework prices for phosphates. This was the first dock strike declared official by the TGWU since the Second World War. 12,500 days lost.

1967
Sept.–Nov.

Decasualisation Strikes. Maximum of 19,000 men involved. In Liverpool, the whole labour force struck over the pay terms accompanying permanency, seeking better piecework rates since the welt was purportedly to be abolished. In London, the pay issue was quickly dropped in favour of interpreting the continuity rule and a third of the dockers struck. 530,000 days lost.

1970
July

National Dock Strike. Official strike by all unions in support of pay claim, to increase NJC basic rate from £11 1s 8d a week to £20. Settled by Pearson award, worth 7 per cent. 496,170 days lost.

Appendix 7   Statistical Sources

There are several pitfalls for the student of dockland statistics and, in try-ing to avoid the worst, I have had to make some important interpolations or assumptions which I here set out.

Earnings. In a casual industry, compilation of wages statistics has always been difficult. Before the Dock Labour Scheme, there was no sure means of finding the level of real earnings. The Ministry of Labour collected data under a minimum list heading of docks, wharf and riverside which included twice the number of people properly understood as dockers. As research in Liverpool showed (see Table I), Government statistics thus tended to exag-gerate the level of dockers' pay in any period of above-average unemploy-ment.

Between 1947 and 1967, the National Dock Labour Board recorded the earnings of casual workers only. Initially, permanent men's earnings were little higher but, in later years, the gap widened as the perm became the nucleus of specialist gangs, trained to use mechanical equipment. My esti-mate is that the average earnings of the entire register – perms and casuals – were at least 5 per cent higher than the NDLB figures. Again, Ministry figures are no help, since they include ancillary trades.

The cost of labour to the employer, of course, was higher. Not only did he have to pay insurance, but also the Board levy as a percentage of his wages bill. Before 1967, this ranged between 12 and $22\frac{1}{2}$ per cent for casual men – depending on the degree of underemployment which the Board had to finance through the guarantee – and about $4\frac{1}{2}$ per cent usually for perms. After De-casualisation, the standard charge has been $2\frac{1}{2}$ per cent on all labour, to cover the cost of Scheme administration; but severance and pensions con-tributions are also levied and these – at the start of 1972 – stood at $7\frac{1}{2}$ and $2\frac{1}{2}$ per cent respectively.

Productivity. Registered dockers do not handle Britain's coal and oil trades and thus, for productivity tables, special assessment is needed of the cargoes actually passing through their hands. This has been done for at least fifty years by the Liverpool Steamship Owners' Association and I have used these figures. Recently, the National Ports Council has produced more sophisti-cated statistics but it still relies to a great extent on the Association's returns.

Strike statistics. In the docks, these are not easy to record or digest. As in many piecework industries, there has been a tendency to under-record be-cause the National Dock Labour Board, like the Ministry, does not catch all small stoppages in its net.

The Government only records those strikes which involve ten or more men, last more than a day or result in at least 100 man-days lost. The NDLB tries to record all stoppages, but, with hiring by the half-day under casual-ism, usually missed those which were settled within the turn.

Equally, there is no means of recording disputes which may affect output dramatically – such as when men chose to go 'day-work' (a form of go-slow) – but do not result in an actual stoppage. With employers able to replace unwilling labour with fresh men under casualism, the incidence of this form of dispute tends to get further hidden.

Another cause of recent under-recording has been the growing incidence of disputes with a non-industrial origin. The 'political' strike has a long history in the docks. In 1919, Bevin refused to allow his men to load arms to Poland, for use against the Bolsheviks, on the *Jolly George*; the Canadian Seamen's Strike was essentially political in origin. In Hull, dockers have refused to load arms to Nigeria during the Biafran war and they blacked Pilkington glass, in a vain gesture of support for sacked rank-and-file leaders at St Helens. In London, dockers stopped work briefly in support of a nurses' wage claim and, more embarrassingly, in support of Enoch Powell.

Many port employers follow the Government's example in not recording political action as a strike. They maintain that the stoppage is an unauthorised absence from work, because there is no quarrel between the company and its employees. With recent 24-hour stoppages against the Labour and Conservative Industrial Relations bills and against Labour's bill for nationalising the ports, the incidence of political strikes has increased in the past two years, but not all these man-days lost are recorded.

However, changing methods of recording disputes since Decasualisation have tended to increase the apparent number of strikes and, since the area of under-recording is constant, this has caused an up-turn in the NDLB's statistics.

From 1947 to 1967, it was the responsibility of local board managers to collect information for the NDLB and they often would record stoppages which affected a variety of undertakings as one strike, if there was a common origin. After Decasualisation, compilation of figures for the NDLB became the responsibility of individual companies with the result that stoppages with a common origin often appear in the final statistics not as one dispute, but as as many disputes as there were employers affected.

There is also a suspicion that employers are less than honest in submitting information. For instance, in the early 1960s many piecework disputes were recorded in London but, under Phase I Devlin, they suddenly disappear while Liverpool went through exactly the opposite process, from a clean sheet to meticulous detailing of trouble.

Another difficulty lies in the NDLB's decision to record strikes which occur in many ports, but with a common cause, as one stoppage per port. Prior to the national dock strike, it had no set policy in recording multi-port disputes.

Finally, there remains one further hazard for interpreters of dockland's troubles. Analysis of strikes by cause are best found in the Department of Employment's master record, but the standard government classification of strikes by cause is not well-suited to the problems of a casual industry. Second only to issues of wages, the most important source of conflict in the casual era of the docks was job protection, either through regulation of manning scales, hours of work, definition of working right or control of hiring practices. These simply do not fit neatly into any of the Standard Industrial Classifications (1968) and the difficulty of listing a dispute over hiring, when it was a twice-daily process, under 'disputes concerning employment or discharge of workers (including redundancy questions)' is self-evident.

Notes

1. Committee of Inquiry Into Shipping, Command 4337, 1970, paragraph 393. This report points out that the disparity in profits *after* tax between shipping and other industries would be less, because of lower charges against shipping companies.

2. Circular of Hovey Antwerp to its labour force, 18 September 1967.

3. *Works of John Taylor*, printed for the Spenser Society, 1869, p. 176.

4. Royal Commission on the Poor Law, 1909 Minority Report, p. 801 onwards and p. 1186 onwards.

5. Charles Booth, *Life and Labour of People in London*, Series 1, Vol. IV, 1902–3, p. 28. This essay was written by Beatrice Webb (*née* Potter) originally in 1887 and first appeared in *Nineteenth Century*, September 1887.

6. *Mayhew's London*, edited by P. Quennell, 1969, p. 568.

7. Ben Tillett, *Memories and Reflections*, 1931, p. 76.

8. B. Webb, *My Apprenticeship*, Penguin Books, 1971, p. 209.

9. Eleanor Rathbone, *Labour at the Liverpool Docks*, p. 41.

10. *Life and Labour*, Series 1, Vol. IV, p. 15.

11. Sir James Sexton, *Agitator, The Life of the Docker MP*, 1936, p. 69.

12. Sexton, *Agitator, the Life of the Docker MP*, p. 72; and Sexton's evidence to the Royal Commission on the Poor Law, Vol. VIII, 84243.

13. *The Times*, 29 August 1889.

14. Sir Joseph Broodbank, *History of the Port of London*, Vol. I, p. 259.

15. L. H. Powell, *The Shipping Federation*, p. 5.

16. *Fairplay*, 17 July 1891, pp. 123–4, and Brysson Cunningham, *Port Economics*, 1924, p. 104.

17. An invaluable account of early London organisation is found in John Lovell's *Stevedores and Dockers* in which he draws on much original material of the Stevedores' League.

18. Royal Commission on Labour, 1891, Group A, Evidence 24, 943.

19. Booth, *Life and Labour*, Series 2, Vol. III, p. 399.

20. *The Dockworker: An analysis of Conditions of Employment and Industrial Relations in the Port of Manchester 1950–51*, edited at the Department of Social Science, University of Liverpool, Liverpool University Press, 1956, pp. 66–7.

21. Committee of Inquiry into Unofficial Stoppages in the London Docks, Command 8236, 1951, paragraph 23.

22. *British Journal of Sociology*, March 1950, and Prof. Hugh Clegg, *How to Run an Incomes Policy*, 1971, p. 71.

23. Lord Francis Williams, *Ernest Bevin*, 1952, p. 36.

24. *Life and Labour*, Series I, Vol. IV, p. 32.

25. *The Dockworker*, 1956, p. 67.

26. Royal Commission on the Poor Law, Evidence, Vol. VIII, 84402, quoted in majority report, Part VI, para 276.

27. Lovell, *Stevedores and Dockers*, 1969, p. 218.

28. Rathbone, *Labour at the Liverpool Docks*, p. 41.

29. Col. R. B. Oram, *The Dockers' Tragedy*, 1970, p. 47.

30. Minutes of evidence to Roche Committee, 12 May 1919.

31. *Daily Herald*, 27 September 1913.

32. F. G. Hanham, Report of Inquiry into Casual Labour in the Merseyside Area. Quoted by the author from a Board statement, p. 18.

33. Robert Williams wrote two important books on the experiment, on which I have relied. They are *The Liverpool Docks Problem* and *First Year's Working of the Liverpool Docks Scheme*.

34. Lascelles and Bullock, *Dock Labour and Decasualisation*, 1924, p. 91.

35. Lord Mayor of Liverpool's mandate, ordering a new survey of casualism, 1929.

36. In *Agitator*, Sexton recalled his standard speech in favour of registration (p. 224 onwards). He used to tell men they were registered at birth, christening, marriage and death and they should not object to one further occasion. 'You are registered when you are christened, are you not . . . although I regret to say that the odour of sanctity does not seem to abide very long with some of you.'

37. Tillett, *History of the 1911 Transport Workers Strike*, 1912, p. ix.

38. This and following quotations are taken from the transcript of evidence to the Shaw Inquiry.

39. Report of the Shaw Inquiry, 1920, paragraph 17.

40. Bevin, speech to dockers, 16 March 1920, Royal Albert Hall.

41. The clause read: 'Cases of serious misbehaviour of failure to work should be reported to the Port Labour Committee in order that the Committee might, if after investigation they think it necessary, cancel the registration and withdraw the tally of the man complained of.'

42. Minutes of evidence to the Maclean Committee, 14 October 1930.

43. The minutes of Bevin's briefing are preserved and form a remarkable document, anticipating most dockland reforms up to the 1960s.

44. TGWU memorandum to Maclean Committee, 1931.

45. Lord Sanderson, *Ships and Sealing Wax*, p. 143.

46. It was cheaper to pay a guarantee on a monthly than on a weekly basis

and this concept dates back to 1913 at least. It recurs in national negotiations in 1946 and, in London, briefly in 1964. Occasionally, employers put forward proposals for a quarterly guarantee which would have added even less to the industry's costs.

47. Liverpool, Birkenhead, Manchester, Preston, Garston, Bromborough, Ellesmere Port, Partington, Widnes, Runcorn and Weston Point.

48. 'The casual nature of the work must go. If we are to impose obligations and to insist on continuity of effort, it cannot be done on the basis of past methods of picking up a man one moment and dropping him the next,' Bevin, House of Commons, 21 January 1941. This pledge was reiterated in 1944.

49. 1947 Scheme, Clause 8, paragraph 5a and b. These obligations were not altered in the 1967 Scheme.

50. Ken Coates and Tony Topham, *The Debate on Workers' Control*, 1970, pp. 33–4.

51. Report of Labour Party Port Transport Study Group, 1966, p. 33.

52. TGWU evidence to the Forster Inquiry, 1946.

53. Leggett Report, Command 8236, 1951, paragraph 28.

54. Report of a Committee to Inquire into the Operation of the Dock Workers (Regulation of Employment) Scheme 1947, Command 9813, 1956, paragraphs 33 and 91.

55. Ministry of Labour to NAPE, 16 January 1968.

56. House of Lords, 16 November 1954.

57. This terminology comes from Manchester but was more commonly applied, after the publication of the *Dock Worker*. In Manchester, it was found that drifters, who represented a fifth of the labour force, formed a nucleus of discontent and their behaviour had a disproportionately important effect on labour relations for the port as a whole.

58. *Portworkers' News*, Vol. I, Number 12.

59. *The Dab*, Christmas, 1963.

60. National Dock Labour Board, Annual Report, 1953.

61. The NDLB's method of including labour shortages in the maximum requirement tended to exaggerate fluctuation in a port like Liverpool, where morning shortages could be offset by nightwork.

62. Letter to *The Times*, 21 July 1970.

63. W. Lindley, evidence of NJC unions to Devlin Committee, January 1965.

64. TGWU Record, February 1951, *Chaos is their Objective*.

65. Leggett Report, Command 8236, paragraph 32. Devlin Report, Command 9813, 1956, paragraph 29 (4). Devlin Report, Command 2734, 1965, paragraph 114.

66. Set up in 1919 as a counter to subversion, the Economic League was supported heavily by London employers. It boasted a board of top industrial-

ists and, for a time, was chaired by Lord Rochdale. It sent lectures to the dock-gate as well as providing employers with a remarkably accurate account of most unofficial activities. Moral Rearmament has sometimes had a substantial foothold in the NASD.

The information service provided by the police to employers – accounts of mass meetings, etc. – was also resented by the men.

67. *Portworkers' News*, Vol. I. Number I. *Portworkers' News*, special supplement, February 1954. NASD broadsheets, 16 April, 14 May and 3 June 1955.

68. House of Lords, 25 May 1971, NDLB *v*. John Bland and others.

69. Queen's Bench, 9 July 1969, NDLB *v*. John Bland and others.

70. Court of Appeal, 6 May 1970, NDLB *v*. John Bland and others.

71. Court of Appeal, 29 July 1971, BSC *v*. NDLB and NDLB *v*. BSC.

72. Institute of Industrial Relations, University of California, *Monthly Labour Review*, October 1966, p. 1070.

73. Speech at Thurrock Technical College, 15 October 1969.

74. Sir David Burnett to Peter Shea, 12 May 1969.

75. *The Observer*, 22 November 1970.

76. CBI to employer associations, 20 January 1970.

77. Speech at Thurrock Technical College, 13 January 1970.

78. This and subsequent extracts are from the personal papers of David Lloyd.

79. The London sectors are Tilbury (number 3), Royals (4), West India and Millwall (5), Surrey (1), London (6), riverside (2, 7, 9) and downriver (8). They should not be confused with the numerical 'divisions,' which relate solely to areas of TGWU organisation.

80. TGWU circular to dock officers, 20 March 1963.

81. *Time for Decision*, Manifesto of the Labour Party, general election 1966, p. 13.

82. Devlin Report, Command 2734, 1965, paragraph 205.

83. Circular signed by T. Cronin, acting London docks secretary, autumn 1962.

84. Evidence of NASD to Devlin Inquiry, 17 February 1965.

85. Honeyman report of an Inquiry held under Paragraph 5 of the Schedule to the Dock Workers (Regulation of Employment) Act 1946, Command 36–306, 1966, paragraph 72.

86. Ministry of Labour to National Modernisation Committee, 20 March 1967. The second occasion when the Cabinet got involved in a docks wage dispute was in December 1968. Ministers then chose not to fight, but sanctioned a 13 per cent pay award to London tally clerks – highly inflationary by the standards of the day.

87. Ministry of Labour statement, 14 September 1967.

88. Devlin Report, Command 3104, 1966, paragraph 16.

89. Noelle Whiteside's unpublished PhD manuscript for Liverpool University on dock workers and Decasualisation up to 1947 has been a helpful source.

90. *Personnel Management*, December 1967.

91. The fate of rank-and-file leaders in the ILA, before the clean-up of 1953, was unamusing. In 1939, Peter Panto challenged the power of Albert Anastasia in the Brooklyn locals and was murdered. In 1945, William E. Warren headed another Brooklyn revolt and was drummed out of the union for 'non-payment of dues.' An ILA official later said Warren was free to seek work on the waterfront 'but if he falls and hurts himself, it'll be no one's fault.' Next day, Warren reported for work, fell and hurt himself. I am indebted to Daniel Bell's essay on longshoremen in *The End of Ideology* for the above material.

92. Circular to London dockers for D-Day, 1967.

93. Quotes in *The Port*, 20 May 1971.

94. Statement of 17 October 1967.

95. Jack Dash, *Good Morning, Brothers!*, 1969, p. 53 (Mayflower edition).

96. Devlin Report, Command 2734, 1965, paragraph 36.

97. O'Leary to docks delegate conference, 24 January 1966.

98. NAPE directive, 3 September 1968.

99. National Ports Council, *Transhipment in the Seventies*, p. 2.

100. Speech to TGWU Number One Docks Group Committee, 9 June 1967.

101. TGWU Number One Docks Group, 3 January 1968.

102. Sir Andrew Crichton, Memorandum of 24 January 1969.

103. Papers of John Kiernan.

104. *The Reorganisation of the Ports*, Command 3903, 1969, paragraph 15.

105. Kiernan, statement of 3 July 1969.

106. Memorandum of Kiernan to London Port Employers' Association.

107. Minutes of meeting under Conrad Heron, chief conciliation officer, at the Department of Employment, 10 July 1969.

108. With the closure of the London and St Katharine docks, the size of the Number One Docks Group was reduced from 13 to 11 men.

109. Statement of 30 June 1970, and evidence to Pearson Inquiry, 21 July 1970.

110. Report of the Committee of Inquiry into the Major Ports of Great Britain, Command 1824, September 1962; paragraph 10 and Appendix C, p. 239.

111. Joint circular to all dockers in the London enclosed docks, to accompany Phase II, 21 September 1970.

112. *Daily Mirror*, 27 October 1970.

113. LOTEA statement, 7 January 1971.

Bibliography

(Wherever possible I cite editions of books which are in print and in paperback.)

Allen, V. L., *Trade Union Leadership*, Longmans, 1957.

Bell, Daniel, *The End of Ideology*, The Free Press, N.Y., 1960.

Beveridge, William, *Unemployment, a Problem of Industry*, 1909 and 1930, Longmans, 1930.

Booth, Charles, *Life and Labour of the People in London*, Macmillan, 1902.

Broodbank, Sir Joseph, *History of the Port of London*, Daniel O'Connor, London, 1921.

Bullock, Sir Alan, *The Life and Times of Ernest Bevin*, Vols I and II, Heinemann, 1960.

Clegg, Hugh, *How to Run an Incomes Policy*, Heinemann, 1971.

Clegg, H., Fox, A. and Thompson, A. F., *A History of British Trade Unions since 1889*, Oxford, 1964.

Dash, Jack, *Good Morning, Brothers!*, Mayflower Paperback, 1970.

Evans, A. A., *Technical and Social Changes in the World's Ports*, International Labour Office, 1969.

Goldstein, Joseph, *The Government of British Trade Unions*, Allen and Unwin, 1952.

Gosling, Harry, *Up and Down Stream*, Methuen, 1927.

Hanham, F. G., *Report of Enquiry into Casual Labour in the Merseyside Area*, Liverpool, 1930.

Hobsbawm, E. J., *Labouring Men*, Weidenfeld and Nicolson (goldback edn.), 1968.

Jeffery, A. E., *The History of Scruttons*, 1971 (for private distribution).

Jensen, Vernon H., *Hiring of Dock Workers*, Harvard University Press, 1964.

Jensen, Vernon H., *Decasualisation and Modernisation of Dock Work in London*, ILR Paperback, Cornell, 1971.

Johnson, K. M. and Garnett, H. C., *The Economics of Containerisation*, Allen and Unwin, 1971.

Jones, D. Caradoc (ed.), *Social Survey of Merseyside*, Liverpool, 1934.

Lascelles, E. C. P. and Bullock, S. S., *Dock Labour and Decasualisation*, P. S. King and Son, 1924.

Liverpool University, Dept. of Social Sciences, *The Dockworker*, Liverpool, 1954.

Lovell, John, *Stevedores and Dockers*, Macmillan, 1969.

Mann, Tom, *Memoirs*, Labour Publishing Co, 1923.

Mayhew, Henry, *Mayhew's London* (ed. Peter Quennell), Spring Books, 1969.

Mess, H. A., *Casual Labour in the Docks*, London School of Economics, 1916.

Oram, Col. R. B., *Cargo Handling and the Modern Port*, Pergamon, 1965.

Oram, Col. R. B., *The Dockers' Tragedy*, Hutchinson, 1970.

Powell, L. H., *The Shipping Federation*, British Shipping Federation, 1950.

Rathbone, Eleanor, *Inquiry into the Conditions of Labour at the Liverpool Docks*, Liverpool Economic and Statistical Society, 1903-4.

Russell, Maud, *Men Along the Shore*, Brussel and Brussel, N.Y., 1966.

Sanderson, Lord, *Ships and Sealing Wax*, Heinemann, 1967.

Sexton, Sir James, *Agitator*, Faber and Faber, 1936.

Smith, H. Llewellyn (director), *New Survey of London Life and Labour*, P. S. King and Son, 1931.

Stafford, Ann, *A Match to Fire the Thames*, Hodder and Stoughton, 1961.

Tillett, Ben, *Memories and Reflections*, John Long, 1931.

Tillett, Ben, *A Brief History of the Dockers' Union*, Twentieth Century Press, 1910.

Tillett, Ben, *History of the London Transport Workers' Strike*, 1911, NTWF, 1912.

Webb, Beatrice, *My Apprenticeship*, Penguin, 1971.

Williams, Lord Francis, *Ernest Bevin*, Hutchinson, 1952.

Williams, R., *The Liverpool Docks Problem*, Liverpool Economic and Statistical Society, 1912.

Williams, R., *The First Year's Working of the Liverpool Docks Scheme*, Liverpool Economic and Statistical Society, 1914.

INQUIRIES

Material on casual labour and union organisation is plentiful, up to the First World War, and is fully listed by John Lovell in *Stevedores and Dockers*. To the laymen, however, Government inquiries remain the most accessible source of official information and they too are plentiful – to the point that the docks have been called Britain's most 'inquired-into' industry. Important reports are marked with an asterisk. The chairman's name for each inquiry is in brackets.

* Royal Commission on Labour, 1901, Command 6708, 6795, 6894, 7063, 7421.
* Royal Commission on the Port of London, 1902, Cd 1151-3.

* Royal Commission on the Poor Law, 1909, Cd 4499.
* Departmental Committee on the Checking of Piecework Wages in Dock Labour, 1908.
  Report on the Disputes affecting Transport Workers in London (Clarke), 1912, Cd 6229.
* Report concerning Transport Workers' Wages (Shaw), 1920, Cd 936–7.
* Report on Port Labour (Maclean), 1931.
  Report on Port Labour in Aberdeen and Glasgow (Irvine), 1937.

  Report into London docks Dispute, March 1945 (Ammon), 1945.
  Report on National Minimum Wage (Evershed), 1945.
* Report under Paragraph I (4) of the Schedule to the Dock Workers (Regulation of Employment) Act 1946 (Forster), 1946.
  Report on objections to draft Scheme (Cameron), 1947.
  Report into the amount of the guaranteed wage (Hetherington), 1947.
  Review of British Dock Strikes, 1949, Cd 7851.
* Report into Unofficial Stoppages in London (Leggett), 1951, Cd 8236.
  Report on the Manchester–Salford dock strike 1951, Cd 8375.
  Interim and Final report into the London docks dispute (Evershed), 1954, Cd 9302, 9310.
* Report into the Operation of the Dock Workers (Regulation of Employment) Scheme 1947 (Devlin), 1956, Cd 9813.
  Report into a dispute between employers and work people on the NJC for the Port Transport Industry (Cameron), 1958, Cd 510.
  Report into Cold Store Undertakings (Lloyd Williams), 1959.
  Report on Ocean Shipowners Tally Clerk difficulties in the Port of London (Lloyd Williams), 1960, (36–254).
  Report into (1) list of ports to be covered by 1947 Scheme and (2) the application of the Scheme to pitwood or timber handling (Lloyd Williams), 1960, (36–251).
  Report on objections to the draft Scheme amendments (Forster), 1961, (36–261).
* Report into the Major Ports of Great Britain (Rochdale), 1962, Cd 1824.
  Report on the appointment of foremen at Southampton docks (Flanders), 1964, (36–290).
* Devlin Committee
  1. Report into wage dispute of NJC, 1964, Cd 2523.
  2. Report into Decasualisation and causes of dissension, 1965, Cd 2734.
  3. Report into the Wages Structure and Level of Pay, 1966, Cd 3104.
  Report into the Bristol and Avonmouth Docks Dispute (Flanders), 1966, (36–299).
  Report into the operation of fork-lift trucks at North Shields (Clegg), 1966, Cd 3061.

* Report into the causes of NASD strike in the port of London (Wilson), 1966, Cd 3146.

Report on objections to the draft Scheme amendments (Honeyman), 1966, (36–306).

Report into the employment of coal trimmers in the ports of Blyth, etc. (Scamp), 1967, (36–318).

* Report into the locally-determined aspect of payment in Liverpool (Scamp), 1967.

Report on the reduction to 65 of dockers' compulsory retirement age (Wordie), 1968, (36–329).

(Report on the redefinition of dockwork in London (Bristow), 1969.)

* Report into Shipping (Rochdale), 1970, Cd 4337.

* Report into wage dispute of NJC for the Port Transport Industry (Pearson), 1970, Cd 4429.

Report on loading coal at Immingham (Scamp), 1970.

Index

Aberdeen, 47, 84, 85

AIC management consultants, 255, 264, 265

Aintree Containerbase, 146, 196

Alexander, Lindsay, 176, 221

Allen, E., 123

Ammon, Lord, 104, 111

Antwerp, 12, 53, 173, 239, 266

Australia, 45, 248, 299

Barrett, R., 127, 170, 205, 208, 220

Baker, C. 'Buck', 188, 198, 200

Barrett, T., 188, 202, 204

Battie, H., 244, 269-70

Benbow, J., 195, 206

Beveridge, Lord, 26-8

Bevin, E., 47, 54, 60, 64, 71-93, 127, 302

Booth, Charles, 18, 26-7, 46, 62, 64, 118

Bristol, 24, 30, 79, 101, 112, 164, 194, 213, 278, 280, 292

Bristow Committee, 148-50, 276, 305

British Transport Docks Board, 30, 241, 280

Brown, Lord, 182-5, 232, 236, 238, 302

Burns, John, 45, 48, 53

Calling-on, 18, 22-3, 106, 303
  responses to, 49, 56-7
  secondary systems, 68-9, 98

Cameron, Lord, 95, 107, 135

Cardiff, 43, 84, 194, 213

Carr, Robert, 274-5

Castle, Barbara, 108

Casualism, 10, 17-28, 106, 110, 112, 290
  effect on employers, 27-8, 33, 46, 126, 167, 260
  effect on men, 21-2, 28, 74, 76, 112, 197, 212, 293, 302

Cattell, George, 124, 153-4, 237

Clegg, Prof. H. A., 53, 173

Clyde, see Glasgow

Coastal short-sea trades, 24, 40

Communist party, 129-30, 195, 198, 203, 210

Containers, 10-12, 134-54, 235, 250, 290, 304-7

Container bans, 142, 205, 239-70

Cousins, F., 131, 158-9, 161, 192, 205

Crichton, Sir Andrew, 105, 155, 158-9, 172, 176, 181, 247, 267

Cronin, T., 193, 195

Dash, Jack, 54, 66, 109, 129, 131-2, 169, 188-9, 198, 202-4, 212, 249, 263, 268

Deakin, A., 99, 127, 129, 132

Decasualisation, 54, 59, 93, 107, 152, 156-62, 174-5

Dept. of Employment, Dept. of E. and Productivity, see Labour, Ministry of

Devlin Inquiry, 9-10, 12, 52, 59, 96, 150-1, 162, 172-80
  Lord Devlin, 93, 158, 172, 176, 181, 248

1956 report, 101, 105, 107, 130, 135, 304
1964 report, 172, 208
1965 report, 52, 110, 128, 130, 159, 165–6, 177–80, 217, 263
1966 report, 172, 181, 183
Phase I Devlin, 13, 177, 182, 189–91, 203, 221–4
Phase II Devlin, 13, 148, 236, 278–89
Devonport, Lord, 48, 76, 78
Discipline, 82, 89, 98, 103–4, 106–11, 184, 186, 203, 249
Dock, Wharf, Riverside and General Labourers Union, 45, 47, 49, 59
Docks
accidents, 117–18
amenities, 180, 263
bargaining structure, 38, 40, 42
definition of d.work/job rights, 13–14, 71, 90, 94, 124, 135–54, 209, 276, 303–7
D. and Harbours Act 1966, 67, 139–40, 183
Dockers
blue-eyed boys, etc., 113, 222, 232
D.s' Charter, 132, 169, 305
D. Workers (Regulation of Employment) Act and Order, 95, 148–9
kinship/community, 29, 50, 123
Donovan, J., 103

Ella, 39
Encounter Bay, 248
Emergency Powers Act (various), 93–4, 103, 107, 148, 277
Employers, 30–42
deficiencies of, 126–7, 228
numbers of, 32, 124, 167, 178–9, 291–2
registration/licencing, 94, 112, 181
single employer concept, 258
structures, 42, 126, 166–8, 255–63
Evershed Inquiries, 219

Fairland, 138
Felixstowe, 135, 138, 151–2, 246, 277
Fluctuation, *see* Trade or Wages
Foley, M., 117, 200, 208, 246
Ford, Sir Sidney, 173, 238
Forster, Lord, 95, 103, 136, 157
Foulness, 149
French, J., 201
Fry, Bert, 197, 200, 245

Gasworkers, 45–7, 79
General and Municipal Workers Union, 46–7, 79, 192
Gifford, J. Morris, 158
Glasgow, 33, 46, 51, 83, 85–6, 112, 164, 214, 278, 281, 292
Gosling, Harry, 48, 72
Grangemouth, 24, 138, 194, 278, 281
Greenock, 24, 51, 194
Grimsby, 24, 46–7, 84
Gunter, Ray, 12, 108, 162, 173, 181, 184–6, 203, 207, 210–11, 236

Hamburg, 33, 138, 173
Hartlepools, 47, 83, 85, 160
Harris, W., 200
Hawaiian Merchant, 138
Heaton's Transport (St Helens), 150
Hegarty, W., 177
Hetherington, Sir Hector, 95
Honeyman Inquiries, 136, 184, 203
Houghton, Joseph, 81, 83
Hovey Antwerp, 42, 125, 156
Hovey, John, 125, 221, 246, 264–72, 283, 289
Hughes, G., 269–70
Hull, 24, 30, 47, 84, 101, 112, 114, 119, 125, 147, 160, 187 (Decas. strike), 213–14, 278, 280–1, 292; *NASD organisation*, 127–8; *TGWU reform*, 193–4, 206; *Phase II*, 278, 281

Incomes policy, 184–7, 267, 300–1

Industrial Relations Act, 9, 14, 209, 298, 306

Industrial tribunals, 140–2, 247

Insurance Acts, 70, 85–6, 89, 91

International Longshoremen's Association, 143, 194

International L. and Warehouseman's Ass., 143–6

Jalajanya, 285

Jervis Bay, 270

Jewitt, Dermod, 287–9

Jones, Jack, 118, 147, 149, 188, 192, 195, 205–6, 274–7

Kerrigan, P., 205

Kiernan, John, 221, 247, 255–6, 259, 278

Labour Governments (*1945–51*), 95, 99; (*1964–70*), 12, 161–2, 300–1

Labour, Ministry of, 82, 84, 89, 109, 148–9, 154–5, 160, 238, 249, 264, 266–9

Labour Party port study group, 25, 100, 258

Labour Protection League, 44–5

Lady Jocelyn, 39

Larkin, James, 33, 192

Leggate, James, 278

Leggett inquiry, 52, 104, 130

Leith, 47, 84, 160, 194

Lewis, Walter, 271–2, 285

Liaison committees, 131, 186, 188, 199–200, 203, 220, 302

Lighterage trade, 120, 243–4, 255, 303

Lightermen, 43, 51, 119, 147, 192, 200, 270

WLTBU, 130, 292

Lindley, Bill, 127, 202, 276

Liverpool, 24, 30, 45, 47, 67, 89, 101, 115–16, 121, 128, 214, 280, 292

1912 experiment, 62, 68–71, 91, 98, 194

1961 reforms, 163, 171, 213

Phase I talks, 187–8, 215–16

Phase II talks, 278–9, 281

container blacking, 9, 14, 150, 196, 209, 298, 306

TGWU reforms, 193–6, 206

wages structure, 176, 222–3, 231, 277

Liverpool Steamship Owners Ass., 32

Lloyd, David, 155–60, 165–6, 168–9, 256

Lloyd, L., 193

Lloyd-Williams, H., 135–6, 151

London, 20, 24, 26, 62, 84, 101

1961 reforms, 156–60, 163, 213

Phase I, 185, 188–9, 216–21

Phase II, 109, 125, 216–21, 239, 272

Phase II review, 282–9

dock companies, 35, 62, 280

employers, 40, 108–9, 110, 120, 247, 249, 255, 292

enclosed docks,

L. and St Katharine's, 30, 36, 206, 282

Millwall, 36, 207, 241, 252

Royals, 131, 138, 169, 188, 189, 198, 267, 271

Surrey, 36, 157, 189, 206, 207, 282

West India, 36, 45, 188, 189

(*see also* Tilbury)

Master Stevedores Ass. (LMSA), 40, 43, 59, 206

Ocean Trade Employers (LOTÉA), 248, 257–8

Ship-Owners Dock Labour Committee, 40, 42, 156, 257

TGWU reform, 196–211

wages structure, 176, 277

Lyons, D., 198

M. and M. agreement, 59, 144, 159, 168, 201

Maclean, Sir Donald, 84, 87, 91

Macmillan, Harold, 158, 160–1

Maltby, T. F., 41–2, 223, 253, 266, 269, 289

Manchester, 50, 84, 101, 121, 128, 187, 280

Maintenance, 74, 76, 78, 86–9

Mann, Tom, 45, 47

Mayhew, Henry, 18, 21, 22, 29

Mersey Docks and Harbour Board, 30, 124, 280, 282

Middlesbrough, 84, 89, 160, 261–2, 269, 278, 280–1

Modernisation, 96, 116, 124, 248–55; *effective hours*, 252–5, 289; *outputs*, 234, 284; *shift-work*, 221, 249, 252–3, 254, 266, 279, 283; *turnround*, 32, 55, 240, 243, 250, 283, 284–5

Munday, W., 241

National Association of Port Employers, 24, 40, 42, 95, 103, 107, 124, 136, 158, 174, 175, 221, 226, 236–7, 243, 264, 271–7; *London–Liverpool rivalry*, 175–6, 229

National Amalgamated Stevedores and Dockers, 80, 102, 110, 169, 178, 205–11, 249, 266, 270

National Dock Labour Scheme, 50, 85, 88, 93–133, 157, 183–6
   NDL Board, 96–7, 115, 117, 127, 174, 267
   NDL Corporation, 94
   joint control, 69, 83, 98, 103–5, 152
   local boards, 94, 103, 109, 116

National Joint Council, 77, 78, 87, 88, 95, 118, 158; *1961 manifesto*, 159–60, 163, 167, 175, 177–8, 186; *1965 directive*, 181, 203

National Modernisation Committee, 124, 154, 178, 182, 184, 185, 201, 214, 236–7, 256

National Ports Council, 158, 174, 240, 250, 261, 282

National Transport Workers Federation, 48, 65, 72, 78, 87

National Union of Dock Labourers, 29, 33, 34, 46, 47, 68, 69, 193

National Union of Port Workers, 81

Nationalisation, 42, 100, 164, 258

Newcastle, *see* Tyne

Newman, L., 270, 283

New York, 29, 33, 34, 144, 194, 239, 250

New Zealand, 65, 124, 136, 248, 251, 285

Non-Scheme ports, 135–6, 151–3

OCL–ACT, 42, 158, 239, 246–7, 248, 260, 267, 270

O'Hare, P. J., 171

O'Leary, T., 55, 160, 168, 174, 195, 205, 229, 247, 274–7, 305

Olsen Lines, 207, 241–3, 252, 257, 259–60, 261, 266

Orita, 271

Orsett containerbase, 246–7, 267, 270

Parker, Lord Chief Justice, 141–2

Paris, 39

Paynter, Will, 238, 277

Pearson, Lord, 118, 225, 229, 275–7

Pensions, 87, 118, 119, 181, 236, 249

Permanency, 26, 27, 37, 64, 111, 113, 114, 163–6, 186, 198

Port of London Authority, 30, 34, 35, 40, 42, 62, 112, 120, 165, 240, 255–63, 280, 285

Port St Lawrence, 285

Port Talbot, 141, 194

Portsmouth, 135–6

Potter, F., 80

Powell, Enoch, 54

Rathbone, Eleanor, 26, 27, 62, 67

Registration, 68, 70, 72, 91, 93, 103, 153–4
  Anti-R. League, 83, 85
  common register, 206, 271
  control of register, 97, 112, 115–26, 135
  dormant register, 120, 121
  release register, 119
  supplementary registers, 122–3
  temporary unattached register, 98, 125, 126, 209

Rice, E., 131, 198

Riverside (London), *see* Wharves

Road haulage, 274, 284, 285, 298

Rochdale, Lord, 9, 30, 152, 158, 161, 163, 282

Roche Committee, 64, 82, 86

Roffey, T., 155–6, 165–6, 201

Roll-on/roll-off, 24, 137, 235, 246

Rotterdam, 31, 125, 152, 173, 175, 238, 239, 248, 250, 266, 284

Royal commissions (*labour*), 44; (*Port of London*), 26; (*Poor Law*), 18, 21; (*trade unions*), 173, 236

San Francisco, 138, 145

Sanderson, Lord, 88, 156, 226

Scamp, Sir Jack, 23, 173, 187, 278

Scottish TGWU, 60, 81, 84, 112, 164, 192, 292

Scottish Union of Dock Labourers, 79–81

Scruttons, 34, 40, 42, 59, 64, 223, 253, 266, 269, 271, 289

Severance, 117–22, 125, 126, 249, 264, 267, 288

Sexton, Sir James, 29, 34, 45, 46, 47, 60, 69, 71

Shaw Inquiry, 17, 54, 55, 74–9, 207, 226

Shea, P., 147, 150, 170, 186, 192, 200, 202–3, 207, 243–5, 247, 249, 283

Shipping,
  economics, 10–12, 22, 90, 115, 299
  Federation, 39, 40, 42
  ship-owners, 31, 32, 40, 124, 149, 255–9, 268, 285–7

Shop stewards, 131, 193, 195–9, 210, 262, 267, 270, 305

Shoreham, 135, 152

Smith, R., 165

Southampton, 30, 42, 51, 97, 116, 123, 160, 194, 214, 262, 267, 277, 281, 292

Southern Stevedores, 41, 42

Steer, B., 209

Stevedores (*see also* NASD), 43, 45
  Amalgamated S. Labour Protection League, 44, 59, 79

Strikes, 13, 39, 52, 101, 107, 117, 155, 160–1, 200–7, 210, 293–6, 301; (1889), 33, 35, 37, 44, 45, 53, 55, 58, 63; (1911 and 1912), 39, 44, 48, 58, 66, 76, 91; (1967), 187, 189; (1970), 58, 271–7

Sutherland, Thomas, 37, 38

Tally clerks, 51, 107, 155, 165, 185, 301

Thames Stevedoring, 41, 66, 114, 189, 289

Thompson, F., 80

Thorbjorg, 270

Thorne, Will, 44, 45

Tilbury, 24, 30, 36, 42, 73, 138, 140, 152, 189, 206, 239

Tillett, Ben, 20, 22, 23, 45–8, 71, 72, 302

Timothy, A., 113

Tonge, G. 'Bill,' 147, 158, 274

Trade: *fluctuations*, 23, 115, 151, 175; *meat*, 136, 251, 285, 298; *tea*, 139, 140, 246; *timber*, 136, 138, 140, 239, 260, 270

Trades Union Congress, 65, 128 130, 205, 275, 307

Transfers, 98, 123, 134, 155, 174, 181, 189, 216–19, 244

Transport and General Workers Union, 54, 60, 80, 83, 181, 292
  ballot, 268
  Branch structure, 149, 193, 196–8, 209–10
  breakaways, 80–2, 266–70
  internal discipline, 110, 200, 204
  national docks delegate conference, 161, 184, 205, 229, 275–6
  negotiating tactics, 168–71, 201, 235
  number one docks group, 150, 196, 197–8, 200–2, 239–48, 266
  post-Devlin reforms, 179, 192–211
  rivalry with NASD, 60, 102, 127, 130, 132, 165, 169, 198, 206

Troops, 72, 93, 107

Trotskyist groups, 127, 129, 130, 195, 203

Turner, Stanley, 245–6, 252, 265

Turner, V., 200

Tyne, 47, 83, 85, 101, 119, 135

Unemployment, 18, 20, 27, 83, 124

Union organisation, 43–61, 73, 208; *effect of Scheme*, 126–7; *hiring control and U. ticket*, 58, 112, 129, 194, 206; *weakness of*, 48, 102, 103, 132

USA, 10, 137, 142–6, 149, 173, 175, 238, 250, 307

Voluntary retirement, 119–21

Wages, 183, 189–90, 225–38, 287, 296–301
  basic rates, 20, 73, 108, 225, 228, 249, 273–7

contingency payments, 228

fluctuation, 21, 221–3, 291

guarantee, 82, 102, 157, 170, 176, 183, 185, 229, 262, 267, 273

modernisation payments, 176, 183, 277

piecework bonus, 55, 77, 108, 110, 182, 187, 222–4, 226–38, 248, 264, 269, 279, 289

Phase II, 264–71

spin-off, 274, 298

Upstanding Weekly Wage, 235–8, 265, 291

Wallis, T., 41, 189

Wasteful practices, 159, 181, 212–24, 240
  absenteeism, 85, 94, 95
  bad time-keeping, 77, 289
  ca'canny, 55, 77
  continuity rule, 95, 188–9, 212, 216–19
  manning levels, 213, 249, 252, 271
  mobility/flexibility, 183, 214, 249
  overtime, 183, 209, 214, 219
  sling loads, 214
  welt, 187, 215–16
  work-to-rule/going daywork, 108, 232–4

Webb, Beatrice, 18, 21, 26, 29, 46, 54

Wharves, 36, 40, 114, 137, 232, 270, 278, 281, 287; *Buchanans*, 246; *Hay's Wharf*, 147, 200, 258, 267; *Lower Oliver's*, 131, 158, 200; *New Fresh*, 243; *Victoria Deep*, 257, 267; *Samuel Williams*, 241, 257

Wilson, Harold, 12, 188, 210

Wilson, Sir Roy, 207

Work-sharing, 59, 181, 302–3

Workers' Control, Institute of, 100, 276